REGIME SHIFT

A volume in the series

Cornell Studies in Political Economy

Edited by Peter J. Katzenstein

REGIME SHIFT

COMPARATIVE DYNAMICS OF THE

JAPANESE POLITICAL ECONOMY

T. J. PEMPEL

Cornell University Press

Ithaca and London

First published 1998 by Cornell University Press

First printing, Cornell Paperbacks, 1998

Printed in the United States of America

Cornell University Press strives to use environmentally responsible suppliers and
materials to the fullest extent possible in the publishing of its books. Such materials
include vegetable-based, low-VOC inks and acid-free papers that are recycled,
totally chlorine-free, or partly composed of nonwood fibers.

Library of Congress Cataloging-in-Publication Data

Pempel, T. J., 1942–
Regime shift : comparative dynamics of the Japanese political
economy / T. J. Pempel.
p.   cm. — (Cornell studies in political economy)
Includes bibliographical references and index.
ISBN 0-8014-3532-3 (cloth : alk. paper). — ISBN 0-8014-8529-0 (pbk. : alk. paper)
1. Japan—Economic conditions—1945–   2. Japan—Economic policy—1945–1989.
3. Japan—Economic policy—1989–   4. Economic history—1945–
I. Title.   II. Series.
HC462.9.P413   1998
338.952—dc21   98-30185

Cloth printing   10 9 8 7 6 5 4 3 2 1
Paperback printing   10 9 8 7 6 5 4 3 2 1

For Kaela

CONTENTS

PREFACE

Changes, like nettles, are toughest to grasp when at their ripest. No matter how earthshaking or trivial any transformation may appear in hindsight, in its midst, we can be overwhelmed by their apparent randomness, magnitude, complexity, and incomprehensibility. Even in the face of undeniable newness, moreover, it is often tempting to dismiss what is new as trivial, falling back on the truism that "the more things change, the more they remain the same."

This book tries to grasp the nettlesome transformations taking place in Japanese politics and economics at the end of the twentieth century. These are complex, consequential, and certain to result in substantial alterations in Japan's political economy. Yet, they are equally unlikely to sever Japan's future completely from its past. The truly challenging questions surround the *particular* fusions of changes and continuities.

Historical sensitivity is vital to understanding Japan's present flux. To comprehend Japan's current dilemmas, we must understand why for such a long period over the postwar years, its political economy was so dramatically different from that of other democratic capitalist countries. Japanese democracy resulted in an unusual thirty-eight years of single-party conservative rule. The Japanese economy delivered growth rates roughly double those of the other capitalist countries. And Japan's conservative governance resulted not in the gaping income inequalities of other conservative capitalist countries but in a socioeconomic equality more akin to that within the social democracies. It is as shifts from these fundamental anchoring points that Japan's current changes are best understood.

By the early 1990s Japanese successes had morphed into a sudden ending of single-party rule, the collapse of the ever-expanding economic bubble, and rising social inequality. Structures and practices that had for decades allowed Japan's political economy to adjust to an unending stream of external challenges suddenly met conditions with which they could not cope. As Japanese political and economic elites struggled to deal with the tumult of the 1990s, they, and those observing them, confronted fundamental questions about the viability of Japan's well-entrenched institutions. Had these "unique" and seemingly deep-rooted institutions been no more than artificial constructs of "catch-up developmentalism," the cold war, or presumptively phenotypical "Asian values"? Were these seemingly impregnable institutions only feeble breakwaters in the face of a tsunami of globalization? Were the same forces that had McDonaldized much of the world's eating habits exerting a similarly eroding effect on the institutions and practices of Japan's political economy?

These broad questions can be best answered by situating Japan in a comparative perspective. Dynamics in other major industrialized countries provide necessary perspective on the depth and direction of changes in Japan. Narrowly country-specific efforts to make sense of each and every particular event often fail to capture broader trends. Conversely, when events are funneled though the narrow ideological filters of neoclassical economics, principal-agent games, or normative democratic theories, nuance gives way to doctrinaire arguments about pending inevitabilities. Japan has hardly been alone in confronting the apparent failure of institutions to perform as they once did; major redirections were under way in numerous other countries during the late 1980s and early 1990s. Situating the Japanese experience on a spectrum of shifts in other countries promises far greater understanding of Japan's particularities as well as an enriched appreciation of the changes occurring elsewhere.

For too long the study of comparative industrial democracies has relegated Japan to an outer ring of irrelevance, much as medieval mapmakers filled the borders beyond what they knew firsthand with pictures of dragons and other strange beasts. This book, although it is empirically weighted toward an examination of various "Japan problems," offers an argument that transcends country specificity. I have relied on important work in comparative politics and comparative political economy to provide perspective on Japan's problems and choices. I hope this perspective will both benefit those who trace the nuances of Japan's day-to-day developments and will move Japan to a more central place in the theorizing of those primarily concerned with North America and Western Europe.

This book strives more to present new interpretations than to advance hitherto unknown empirical material. I have tried to provide sufficient interpretive insight so that specialists on one or another aspect of the broader story will be tolerant of shortages of detail. At the same time, readers not steeped in Japanese social and economic history will find sufficient factual material and contour maps to appreciate the otherwise unfamiliar landscape.

Not surprisingly, completion of this book has taken far longer than I had originally expected. The protracted work in preparing it was made far less onerous by the criticisms, help, and suggestions of many generous friends and colleagues. My greatest overall debt is to Peter Katzenstein, whose blend of friendship and penetrating questions has provided me with a continuing, provocative seminar for nearly half my lifetime. More immediately, he read three drafts and provided considerable input in clarifying the overall argument. Had Peter chosen a career in horticulture, he would clearly have been a master at creating the complex symmetries of an English or a Japanese garden rather than the unstructured berry patches of the Pacific Northwest.

I also owe a considerable debt to David Asher, Gerald Curtis, Ron Dore, Sheldon Garon, Miriam Golden, Walter Hatch, Ikuo Kume, Joel Migdal, Richard Samuels, Michael Shalev, Wolfgang Streeck, Sidney Tarrow, Keiichi Tsunekawa, Kozo Yamamura, and an anonymous reader. All provided me with the kind of detailed comments and criticisms that make authors appreciative of the embarrassments from which they have been saved by the ability to scrap or redraft their original formulations.

It is impossible to acknowledge fully my broader debts. The footnotes provide only a partial template. I also gained greatly from ongoing discussions and open argumentation with David Cameron, Haru Fukui, Peter Hall, Hiwatari Nobuhiro, Inoguchi Takashi, Iokibe Makoto, Chalmers Johnson, Kabashima Ikuo, Ellis Krauss, Greg Luebbert, Muramatsu Michio, Noguchi Yukio, Ōtake Hideo, Sato Hideo, Shinkawa Toshimitsu, Sven Steinmo, Tsujinaka Yūtaka, Tsunkewa Keiichi, and Watanabe Akio.

Jack Keating, Mary Alice Pickert, and Ethan Scheiner gave me valuable research assistance. I also presented my preliminary findings at seminars at Australian National University, Columbia University, Harvard University, Kobe University, and the University of Tokyo. Comments from participants were invaluable in developing my arguments. Research support came principally from the Japan Foundation, the Japan Committee of the Social Science Research Council, and the Northeast Asia Council of the Association for Asian Studies. Visiting appointments at Kyoto University and the University of Tsukuba gave me important writing time, while the Jackson School of International Studies at the University of Washington provided me with released time to prepare the final drafts of the manuscript.

Roger Haydon of Cornell University Press deserves special thanks for his unflagging support of this project and his continued ability to suppress open laughter at the sequence of unrealistic promises for delivery of this manuscript.

Finally, I thank my wife, Kaela, who has been exceptionally patient and supportive throughout my work on this book. It is to her that this book is lovingly dedicated.

T. J. Pempel

Seattle, Washington

REGIME SHIFT

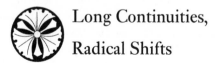 Long Continuities,
Radical Shifts

In the late 1990s the Japanese political economy was sharply different from what it had been two or three decades earlier. Thirty-eight years of electoral dominance by the Liberal Democratic Party (LDP) had ended with the party's internal fragmentation, its loss of a parliamentary majority, and the subsequent scrambling of the entire party system. In July 1993, the handsome, youthful descendent of a long-standing samurai family, Hosokawa Morihiro of the Japan New Party, cobbled together an ideologically disparate, seven-party coalition that made him Japan's first non-LDP prime minister since 1955.

Soon thereafter, the Social Democratic Party of Japan (SDPJ; previously the Japan Socialist Party, JSP), long the LDP's bête noire, and standard bearer for a radically different array of policies, ended nearly fifty years in the political wilderness as its leader, Murayama Tomiichi, became prime minister in coalition with the LDP and a small conservative party, Sakigake.

The mid to late 1990s were marked by a jumble of new parties. After twenty-five years of exceptional electoral and party stability, parties split and recombined with the speed and unpredictability of amoebae, but totally without policy or socioeconomic logic. Although the LDP reemerged as the nation's largest party and regained cabinet control following elections in 1996, it was not the same party it had been, nor did it enjoy any of its once sweeping dominance.[1] The national bureaucracy, once lauded for its internal cohesion, the quality of its decision making and personnel, and its predominance in policymaking, was scarred by an series of policy failures, revelations of self-indulgent bribe-taking and collusive information divulgence by top civil servants, the humiliating arrest of dozens of its top personnel, and a dwindling capacity to shape macroeconomic or individual corporate behavior.

Economically, the changes were equally striking. Four decades of unprecedented growth, from the early 1950s until the end of the 1980s, came to a sudden halt with the simultaneous collapse of both stock and land prices; seven years of slow-to-no growth; the massive collapse of numerous financial institutions; at least $600 billion in unrecoverable loans; an international downgrading of Japanese bonds; and a huge explosion of public debt. Numerous banks and corporations, once touted as world beaters, swam in red ink and pleaded for life preservers from the government. Others, which only twenty-five years earlier had been almost exclusively dependent on the domestic market, were heavily invested in production and marketing facilities throughout the world, remaining Japanese more in name than in personnel, production facilities, or corporate alliances. For many of these the power game in Tokyo had become but a sideshow next to the more compelling worldwide power plays in which they were involved.

For most of the postwar period, Japan had differed considerably from the other OECD countries. Politically, a single conservative party dominated Japan's electoral and governmental spheres in ways unmatched in any other industrialized democracy—two-to-one majorities over the next largest party; complete control of virtually all cabinet posts; and government influence over wide swathes of the economy.

Economically, Japan was also without parallel. National growth rates were typically double those of other OECD members; labor productivity in manufacturing was far greater; unemployment and inflation were dramatically lower; current-account surpluses increased more quickly; the currency strengthened geometrically; savings rates remained consistently higher; overseas investments and holdings exploded more dramatically; and the country demonstrated a much greater ability to adjust to international economic crises. Its successful dexterity shocked the rest of the seemingly less flexible industrialized world.

The end to high growth and predictable politics made Japan the subject of serious debates, both internally and abroad. Was its political economy actually changing at some deep and substantive level? and if so, what was the character of that change? Had global economic forces and domestic changes begun to propel the country toward some "normality" that presumably prevailed among other industrialized countries? Or was the political and economic turmoil merely a series of unpleasant and disruptive speed bumps to be followed by a return to some smoother, "essentially Japanese" system. Were the tides of change meaningful, deep, and real (*honne*), or were they merely cosmetic disguises (*tatemae*) masking some unchanging core?

Such questions form the puzzle at the start of this book: Japan, so distinctive from the other industrialized democracies for so long; and Japan in the 1990s, so different from its own recent past. The Japanese specifics, however, are particular manifestations of much more general puzzles.

First, why do political economies differ from one another? What accounts for the multiple and distinct historical trajectories followed by individual nation-states? More perplexing is the question, Why do these distinctions remain in effect for so long; why do they not all converge on some version of "best practice"?[2]

Equally perplexing is the problem of social change. For most countries last year's behavior typically offers a good predictor of next year's. Social behavior is largely "path dependent." Where one is at time t_2 will be largely a function of one's location at t_1. Where a country is now will, to some extent, always reflect where it has been in the recent past. Yet even the most "stable" countries, having followed the most consistent patterns for sustained periods of time, periodically lurch onto paths quite at odds with the one long traveled. Following such deviations, similarities to the past are less striking than are the breaks from it. Path-dependent equilibrium is periodically ruptured by radical change, making for sudden bends in the path of history.

"Punctuated equilibrium" is the term often used to characterize such mixtures of long continuities followed by dramatic shifts. Examples include the period of agricultural protectionism and Conservative rule in Britain before the repeal of the Corn Laws in 1846, followed by generations of enhanced democratization, freer trade, and Whig and Liberal rule; Germany's long period of authoritarian modernization and expansion culminating in the Third Reich, its destruction, and the subsequent German embrace of pacifism, parliamentary government, and the enhancement of personal wealth; the era of Manchu rule followed by nearly a century of chaos and civil war before the successful imposition of communism under Mao Tse-tung, and then the dramatic if tempered embrace of selective elements of capitalism after 1978; Argentina's long succession of military coups, the terrorist period of "desaparecidos," and the subsequent wave of democratization and party rule; or the long Republican predominance and unabashed pro-business policies in the United States from the great depression of the late nineteenth century until the Depression of the early 1930s—followed by the subsequent period of New Deal social welfarism that prevailed until at least the mid-1960s.

Such instances illustrate how individual countries can quite suddenly veer from a predictable path to an alternative direction. Why they make such changes is less obvious than the fact that they do. Such breaks with the past are comprehensible when they follow some unquestioned failure; they are far less understandable when the original path offered continuing rewards.

Such debates about continuity and change recur regularly in studies of the industrialized democracies.[3] Two competing interpretations are constantly at odds: those that focus on historically generated differences among countries, and those that focus on the presumed or anticipated uniformity of such countries in the face of one or another presumably homogenizing global force.

Debates over the relative predominance of domestic and international forces have gained renewed currency since 1980. The end of the cold war, the multinationalization of capital and manufacturing, diffusion of best practices, growing international trade and investment, generic globalization, privatization, deregulation, tax constraints, checks on welfare and public employment, and even the alleged "end of history"—these are but a few of the suggested forces seen as pressing for convergence among the advanced economies.

Many observers had, of course, earlier suggested that one or another "transnational" force would obliterate important differences among nation-states. In the nineteenth century it was Karl Marx, Herbert Spencer, and Henri Saint-Simon;

more recently it has been Charles Kindleberger, Clark Kerr, Raymond Vernon, and Daniel Bell.[4] Whatever the specific force identified—class conflict, technology, markets, capital flows, communication—the underlying presumption is that existing distinctions among countries will disappear and that the world will give way to greater political and economic homogenization.

Contemporary Japan is a particularly suggestive window through which to examine these interlaced problems. From the last third of the nineteenth century through its defeat in World War II, Japan followed a historical trajectory broadly consistent with Germany, Italy, Spain, Austria, and other late industrializers. Political conservatism, militarism, and (for most) external expansion were the hallmarks. But over the subsequent four to five decades, Japan pursued a different path, one dramatically at odds with its own prewar history. Moreover, that new path was characterized by a combination of politics and economics that distinguished Japan from all other industrialized democracies.

In one broad sense, of course, postwar Japan looked quite like these other countries. Electoral democracy, capitalist economies, high levels of industrial productivity, and standards of living dramatically better than those enjoyed by the bulk of the world's citizens, defined all of the twenty-odd capitalist democracies as a cluster distinct from the other 150 or so countries of the world.

Yet, even though at such a level the industrialized democracies look similar to one another and different from the remaining countries, closer scrutiny reveals important differences among them. Postwar Japan was by far the most unusual. From the 1960s into the mid-1990s, Japan had no evident "siblings" such as it had during the prewar period with Germany, Italy, or Austria.

For long periods during the years after World War II, France and Italy formed a pair, as did New Zealand and Australia; Sweden, Norway, and Denmark formed a group, as did the Benelux counties. The Anglo-American countries differed from continental European democracies. Yet Japan stood far apart from them all. It was never easily paired with any other industrialized democracy,[5] a point symbolically typified by the way in which official photographs of leaders from the G-7 invariably showed six Western leaders clustered together in a (perhaps artificial) show of equality and friendship, while Japan's various prime ministers lingered on the fringe.

Yet, by the late 1990s Japan had departed from its earlier self. The sudden shifts represented by the loss of LDP hegemony, the new electoral system, radical alterations in the party system, an overall decline in the country's economic performance, and, finally, internal structural changes in finance, employment, and manufacturing—all underscored Japan's departure from its path of the preceding forty years. This change was unmistakable, whether or not one believes that the country was becoming similar to the other democracies.

Thus postwar Japan fits into the debates about comparative capitalism and potential convergence in two significant ways. First, Japan enjoyed a long-standing period of internal consistency in its political economy; yet this was a political economy that was organized and that behaved quite differently from those of the other industrialized democracies. Second, as Japan approached the end of the twentieth century it had undergone substantial changes. In this regard, contemporary Japan offers three layers of comparison: the differences between it and other democracies, its own changes over time, and its convergence or distinctness.

The Japanese Difference

Two overriding puzzles encapsulate Japan's striking differences from the other industrialized democracies; one is political, the other economic. At the political level, the fundamental question concerns the longevity of the ruling Liberal Democratic Party (LDP). From 1948 until 1993, all but a handful of cabinet positions were held either by LDP parliamentarians or by those from predecessor parties. For nearly forty years after its genesis, the LDP maintained roughly two-to-one parliamentary majorities over the next largest party, the Japan Socialist Party (JSP). At the local and prefectural levels, conservative preeminence was even greater. Not until the 1989 elections did the party lose its majority in the upper house. In the more powerful lower house the LDP held unchallenged majorities for four additional years. The 1948–93 period gave Japan by far the longest epoch of conservative electoral continuity and dominance of any modern industrialized democracy.

Although the LDP regularly won most elections, it hardly enjoyed the unquestioned affection of the Japanese citizenry, at least if public opinion polls are an accurate guide. These show that the high point of LDP popularity was never much above 40 percent, a figure reached in 1960. A rather steady decline to a low of about 25 percent followed into the mid-1970s. From then on, citizens identifying themselves as nonpartisan outnumbered LDP supporters.[6] All democracies experience episodes of government unpopularity; however, the Japanese numbers are strikingly low, especially since the party never lost power despite its apparent lack of overwhelming popularity.

Nor did the LDP enjoy a reputation for selfless governance. Monumental scandals permeating the highest levels of politics broke at least once every five or six years—Shōwa Denko, the Black Mist, Lockheed, Recruit, and Sagawa Kyūbin, to mention only the more notorious. Japanese citizens did not simply accept these with a cynical tolerance of "politics as usual." Following each scandal, the party's popularity would plummet, the media would lead an array of public bodies in calls for an end to "money politics," reforms would be proposed, and pundits would inevitably suggest, with apparently total historical myopia, that "this may well mark the end of conservative rule."[7]

At such times, including the case of Prime Minister Sato in April 1972, Prime Minister Tanaka in September 1974, Prime Minister Ōhira at the end of 1979, or Prime Minister Miyazawa in the summer of 1993, public support plunged to percentages in the low teens or to single digits, and these prime ministers became even less popular than the party they headed.[8] In virtually any other democracy, such numbers would surely have portended a loss of power, even if only for a perfunctory period of penance in the oppositional wilderness. Yet in the elections following the first three of these surveys, the LDP won 55, 49, and 57 percent of the seats in the lower house.[9] Only in 1993 did unpopularity finally translate into the loss of electoral control over the important lower house, and this loss resulted from the LDP's internal splintering rather than from a massive voter shift to the opposition.

Such conservative continuity is puzzling because throughout the postwar years Japan has had well-institutionalized democratic political processes: a well-read and independent press, an informed electorate, open competition among an ideologically diverse array of political parties, a plethora of autonomous interest associations, and elections that, by any comparative standard, have been free, competitive, and energetically participatory. Indeed, one survey of comparative democracies done in the mid-1960s ranked Japan seventh out of twenty-three countries studied, ahead of such classic examples as the United States (sixteenth), Denmark (eleventh) and New Zealand (tenth).[10]

Surely, if Japanese democratic institutions had constituted a powerful check on government, at least once or twice during their forty years of rule the conservatives should have been thrown unceremoniously from office, however briefly. Alternatively, even if voters did not revolt, internal LDP differences should perhaps have led to internal fragmentation and some temporary ejection from power. The question thus posed is relatively straightforward but critical: why, as has happened in every other democracy on at least one and usually on far more numerous occasions during this period, did Japan's conservative rulers stay so well entrenched in power? The LDP performed like an Olympic team against a high-school junior varsity. The magnitude and duration of its dominance was without parallel.[11]

A number of other features set Japan off from the other democratic countries. The socioeconomic base of conservative rule in Japan was unparalleled in the postwar industrial world, dependent as it was on an alliance among big and small business as well as organized agriculture; meanwhile, organized labor was more systematically marginalized in national policymaking than in any other industrialized democracy. Nor did Japan's peculiar electoral system have any clear parallels. Furthermore, the government bureaucracy was, per capita, the smallest in the industrialized world, even though it exerted an unusual array of powers.[12] Japan's mixture of public policies, including economic protectionism, small government, high reliance on occupation-based social welfare programs, and its strong reliance on bilateral military ties with the United States also differentiated Japan from most other democracies. In short, Japan was politically anomalous.

The second puzzle is economic: why was Japanese capitalism so much more successful than capitalism in the other industrialized democracies? How did the country, for nearly forty years from 1952 to 1990, manage to achieve GNP and productivity increases roughly double those of the OECD average? From 1950 until the early 1970s this figure was a phenomenal 11 per cent. This undeniably amazing period is understandable in light of the severe devastation suffered by Japan's industrial capabilities during World War II, the shifts in the labor force, the subsequent freeing up of surplus demand and latent productive capabilities, and the overall expansion in world trade. Far more astonishing was the Japanese performance over the subsequent decade and a half.

Following the collapse of the Bretton Woods system of stable exchange rates in 1971 and the massive increases in world oil prices in 1973, the industrialized democracies saw their economic boom of the preceding two decades come to an end; they faced instead a hitherto unfamiliar mixture of slow growth, high inflation, budget deficits, unemployment, and stagflation. Virtually every one of these countries, regardless of ideological composition, went through sustained periods of economic anemia and an alleged "ungovernability" that saw virtually all incumbent governments forced from office.[13]

In contrast, the Japanese economy went through a short but painful adjustment and soon resumed—although at a slower rate—its dramatic outpacing of the other democracies on virtually every measure of economic success.[14] Accompanying this growth, once again roughly double the average of the other democracies, were low unemployment, low inflation, geometric increases in labor productivity, a continually strengthening currency, trade successes, high savings rates, increases in the current-account surplus, and rapid improvements in per capita income and standards of living.

Actual economic performance was only one way in which Japan operated according to a totally different calculus. The organization of Japan's firms, the links between labor and management and between banks and manufacturers, the peculiar balance between products exported and products imported, and the unusual export dependence on the U.S. market all marked Japan as operating something other than a "more successful" capitalism. Rather, Japan was practicing a categorically different species of capitalism.[15]

These two puzzles—the electoral and governmental success of conservative politicians and the economic success of Japan's businesses—are integrally related. As I will try to demonstrate, they can best be understood neither within a self-referentially "Japanese" context nor as two isolated problems of "politics" and "economics." They form a single riddle: one cannot understand the unusual character of Japanese politics during this period without understanding its economics, nor can Japan's economy be understood in isolation from its politics.

Several components of these two overarching puzzles make the apparent exceptionalism of Japan's political economy even more nuanced and complicated. One particularly perplexing question is why, following nearly forty years of uninterrupted conservative rule, Japan's social policies looked like those of no other nominally "conservative" regime. The country was marked by numerous and striking exceptions to the pro-business, anti-welfare policies associated with "traditional" conservative politics. Three such exceptions are particularly noteworthy.

First, in most countries, consistently low unemployment figures have been highly correlated with the enduring effectiveness of organized unions in the marketplace and the persistent strength of the political left in parliament.[16] Japan was almost a singular exception. Despite long-standing conservative political rule and socialist and union weakness, Japan's unemployment levels remained consistently among the lowest of the industrialized democracies. In the 1950s and early 1960s, rapid growth worldwide, cheap energy, declining transportation costs, faster communication, and a host of other factors combined to give almost all of the industrialized democracies low unemployment. Yet, by the mid-1970s unemployment rates steadily escalated, jumping even higher in the late 1970s and early 1980s, oftentimes reaching 12–15 percent or more of the working population.

Only five major countries stood as exceptions, countries which Goran Therborn argues evidenced an "institutionalized commitment to full employment."[17] One of these, conservatively ruled Switzerland, had a ready if only partial solution to the employment problem in its small country: it deported 10,000 of its foreign guest-workers, "solving" the national employment problem with a series of train tickets. The remaining three, Sweden, Norway, and Austria, were countries with long-standing, left-of-center governments, ongoing public commitments to full employment, extensive nationalized industries, and large public sectors that served as the "employer of last resort."

Conservative Japan's adherence to similarly low levels of unemployment with no major layoffs thus made it a conspicuous ideological outlier. Even in the early 1990s, following the bursting of the economic bubble, the chaos wrecked on the financial sector, declining profit margins in manufacturing, and the presence of many "troubled industries," Japan did not experience massive job losses and severe belt-tightening. Firms explicitly resisted emulating even the minor labor retrenchment measures they had pursued during previous recessions.

Nor was Japan's employment commitment fulfilled through reliance on expanded public employment. Instead, from the early 1970s into the 1990s, virtually all of the country's new jobs were generated within the private sector. Japanese unemployment remained low as a result of the maintenance or expansion of "real" and "productive" private-sector jobs, rather than by jumps in the "less productive" but more politically plastic public sector, such as took place, for example, in Austria and Sweden.[18] By the mid-1990s Japan experienced a slight increase in unemployment (and a decline in the number of jobs available for new entrants to the workforce), giving rise to worries about a national "hollowing out." Yet even then Japan's official unemployment rate never rose much above 4.2 percent, a rate that, even if it understated reality, and even if increasingly high by Japanese standards, was unquestionably several percentage points below what is happily accepted as "full employment" in the labor markets of conservative economies such as the United States, Britain, or Canada. Thus, for the bulk of the postwar period, on the key issue of employment Japan was a stark exception to the expectations usually associated with the combined image of "pro-business, anti-worker" conservatism.

A second facet of Japan's unusual policies relates to the nation's broad income equality. For most of the postwar years, Japan was extremely egalitarian.[19] In a famous study of income equality in ten major countries, Malcolm Sawyer found Japan to be the second most egalitarian country before taxes and the fourth most egalitarian after taxes.[20] For the period 1978–82, David Cameron found that of eighteen OECD countries, Japan ranked as the third most egalitarian in distributional equality, behind the Netherlands and Belgium and just ahead of Sweden. Of the countries studied, Japan was the only one of the top eleven countries that had no social democratic or labor party participation in government from 1965 to 1981.[21] Imada Takatoshi in a different longitudinal study found that Japan's Gini index registered a dramatic improvement in equality from 1963 until 1970, a slight reversal around 1975, and then a relative leveling out during the bulk of the 1980s.[22]

In addition, the gap between the income going to Japan's top 20 percent and that going to its bottom 20 percent was also low, a similar indicator of intragenerational equality. Martin Bronfenbrenner and Yasukichi Yasuba, Sidney Verba and his associates, Yutaka Kosai and Yoshitaro Ogino, and John Freeman all found similar results using different time periods.[23] Finally, as Yasusuke Murakami notes, Japan's equality was even more striking when distributions are adjusted to place greater emphasis on the income shares of the lowest brackets: in effect, Japan's poor have been relatively less poor than in most other industrialized countries—Japan simply has no semipermanent underclass of significant size, no standing army of the unemployed.[24] The growth of Japanese capitalism did not entail yachts for executives, massive corporate dividends to stockholders, and layoffs and downsizing for the workforce. Conservative politics did not generate the same economic tradeoffs as in North America or Western Europe.

Nor is Japan's "equality" a disembodied artifact of income statistics alone. In numerous other areas, such as education, infant mortality, crime, health care, caloric intake, and so forth, Japan has been strikingly egalitarian since the 1950s. Daily life in Japan is far less differentiated by class than it is in most "conservatively ruled" countries. Similarly egalitarian are figures on the distribution of capital goods such as cars, refrigerators, color televisions sets, telephones, and even computer games for children. It is little wonder that 90 percent of Japan's citizens typically identify themselves as middle class.[25]

Virtually all comparative studies of industrialized democracies demonstrate that on the question of income equality, Japan resembles social democratic Sweden or Norway more closely than more conservatively governed countries such as Canada, the United States, the United Kingdom, or Italy. The fundamental question is, Why is politically conservative Japan so socially egalitarian?[26]

A third anomaly concerns labor conflicts. Japan has been widely applauded for its allegedly harmonious labor-management relations. Indeed, Japanese writers typically cite that trait, along with "permanent employment" and "seniority based wages," as one of the three golden treasures of Japan's "unique" and "traditional" labor-management relations. Yet, in comparative terms, such harmonious relations have been relatively unusual within conservatively governed countries.

As Walter Korpi and Michael Shalev have demonstrated, labor harmony in most highly industrialized countries has come on the heels of burgeoning union strength combined with left-of-center political control over the executive branch of government. Labor's political strength transports conflicts of interest between labor and management from the factory arena to the political arena. In effect, managers who might have had strong bargaining positions at the factory level cannot exploit them to the fullest without encountering opposition from political officials who consider such settlements too "one sided." Typically, therefore, left-of-center victories and the growth of unionism lead to less industrial conflict. Public policies shift to meet labor demands and to curtail the unbridled political power of management.[27]

Unlike labor quiescence in most of Europe, Japanese labor peace was never the result of a breakthrough in the political power of labor; on the contrary, it came after a steady and stunning diminution in the power of Japanese labor and the Japanese left. From a high of about 50 percent in 1950, Japanese unionization rates fell to 23 percent by the mid-1990s. This decline is a clear exception to the pattern among OECD countries. Worldwide unionization rates increased uniformly from the 1950s into the late 1960s and early 1970s, and as Jelle Visser shows, from the early 1970s on, only three countries experienced substantial declines in unionization rates—the United States, France, and Japan.[28] The decline in Japanese unionization and militancy owes more to labor's national political weakness than to its having somehow won a series of institutional rights.

Hence, the image of Japan as unswervingly conservative must confront several empirical curiosities. In key areas such as unemployment, income distribution, and labor-management relations, the nation's political economy defies the broad policy experiences of other conservatively governed countries. Japanese conservatives followed a path that seemingly contradicts accepted images of conservatism and right-of-center government. Certainly, neither the Japanese government nor Japanese managers pursued the more draconian, class-riven policies undertaken by conservative regimes in the United States under Ronald Reagan and George Bush or in Britain under Margaret Thatcher and John Major, or even the more moderate adjustments carried out in Germany under Helmut Kohl.[29]

Many aspects of Japan would appall a committed social democrat, a libertarian, or even a moderate pluralist.[30] The point here is neither to praise nor to criticize the Japanese political economy; rather, it is to point out how anomalous many of its characteristics are for a country that has long been ruled by a nominally conservative political party. Japan's behavior hardly fits what might be expected cross-nationally. If the Japanese economy offers a different version of capitalism, Japanese politics presents a different version of conservatism.

For the study of industrialized democracies to be comparatively meaningful, such fundamental puzzles about the Japanese political economy must be confronted as more than Asian or Japanese "idiosyncrasies," the temporary but ultimately transient consequences of "late industrialization," "Confucian culture," or "conservative paternalism."[31] This demand is as salient for the single-country specialist as for the generalist devoted to a comparative understanding of political economies.

Even a static comparison of Japan's political economy with those of the other industrialized democracies presents a daunting problem. But the difficulty is further complicated by fluctuations in Japan's postwar political economy, which far surpass the simple variations found in any dynamic society. By the 1990s Japan's overall political economy had grown vastly different from what it was in the 1950s, 1960s, or 1970s. These differences too demand analysis.

Japan in Transition

During its long reign, the LDP withstood a range of internal and external crises, the likes of which had toppled dozens of governments in other industrialized democracies: sustained conflicts between business and labor during the 1950s, tumultuous public demonstrations over the U.S.-Japan Security Treaty in both the early 1950s and in 1960, the political and economic confusion engendered by the ending of the Bretton Woods financial system and Nixon's dramatic reversal of U.S. China policy, powerful citizens' protests against environmental pollution in the late 1960s and early 1970s, the two oil shocks and their consequent unleashing of worldwide inflation, massive student protests, sweeping local-level successes by the left in the mid-1970s, and a host of other problems.

Similarly, Japan's economy continually defied the basic laws of gravity. Like the daruma doll, the Japanese symbol of persistence, no matter how overwhelming the downward pressures, Japan's economy always righted itself with alacrity. To highlight only some of the most extreme external shocks that were overcome: the severely depressed conditions following World War II; the rapid reduction of tariffs and quotas, particularly following the Kennedy, Tokyo, and Uruguay Rounds of GATT negotiations; the breakdown of the Bretton Woods monetary system in 1971; the dual oil shocks of 1973 and 1979–80; the doubling of the value of the Japanese yen with tremendously negative consequences on Japanese exporters in the early 1970s and its further increase in value from the 1985 Plaza Accord into the mid-1990s; the sequence of trade-related crises in textiles, steel, autos, semiconductors, and other vital Japanese exports; the liberalization of the previously closed financial sector starting in 1980; the formation of the European Union and NAFTA with their implicitly anti-Asian trade focus; and a host of other changes in external circumstances that could well have impeded the continuation of Japanese economic successes.

Consider the first oil shock, which left most other industrialized democracies mired for several years or longer in inflation, stagnation, and their socioeconomic consequences. Even after twenty years some of these countries, including Australia, Belgium, Sweden, and France, had not fully readjusted. In Japan, however, the first oil shock created an extreme but short-lived bout of inflation. Then, after a two-year period of what Finance Minister Fukuda labeled "crazy prices," costs stabilized, unemployment remained low, and growth rates returned to levels double that of the other OECD countries.

Or consider the appreciation of the yen, which essentially tripled in value between 1971 and 1991. Without a big jump in productivity, neoclassical economic logic would have predicted a dramatic drop in Japanese exports. Instead, productivity and exports continued to expand geometrically, and Japan's trade balances with most of the world became even more favorable.

In short, rather than fumbling and flailing in the face of external political and economic adversities, Japan's political economy successfully adapted to the hostile conditions it confronted. Such adjustment and adaptation led to conservative longevity and economic success. For nearly forty years, Japan manifested an incredible "creative conservatism."[32]

Such adaptability raises a puzzle, however. And the puzzle is one that cannot be understood through any of the static models that have been offered to explain Japan, valuable as many have been for different purposes. Much has been learned about Japan through concepts such as "developmental state," "truncated pyramid," "patterned pluralism," "bureaucratic-inclusionary pluralism," "reciprocal consent," "crisis and compensation," and the like.[33] Yet such snapshots of an essentialist and unvarying Japan provide no basis for interpreting any deep and long-lasting structural changes in that country.

Japan, like any complex political economy, is always changing. But for most of the period since the 1950s, changes in Japan seemed to be far less important than the underlying continuities. Changes appeared to reinforce, rather than to challenge, the underlying structural relationships captured by static snapshots. Throughout the 1970s and 1980s, for example, most adaptations and changes worked to enhance Japan's economic competitiveness and the electoral appeal of the LDP. Flexibility was only a small part of the system of continuing conservative rule and economic success. It was the continuities that drew the greatest attention.

Yet the focus on continuity lost its power by the 1990s. If adaptation was so endemic to the system, why then did the Japanese economy fail to adapt successfully in the early 1990s? What generated the economic bubble that soon burst with such devastating consequences? Why did the ruling Liberal Democratic Party split? Why did the close and quietly maintained economic and security relationship between Japan and the United States give way to boisterous confrontations?[34] Why, in short, did the apparent capacity for positive adaptation suddenly disappear?

The answer, I believe, is that the initial adaptations were more than just the response of a flexible but unchanging system—the bamboo tree bending in the howling gale. Rather, adaptation brought about a sequence of substantive changes in key components of the Japanese political economy, and these changes in turn opened fissures that stymied further positive adaptation. In short, despite continued LDP rule, consistently high economic growth, and close ties to the United States, Japan's political economy underwent a series of sometimes dramatic alterations, particularly from the mid-1970s into the late 1980s, that fundamentally transformed key elements of the political economy and laid the groundwork for the dramatic transformations of the 1990s. Proceeding at different rates along multiple paths, these changes meant that by the late 1980s and early 1990s the Japanese political economy had strikingly diverged from what it had been in the 1950s or 1960s. Numerous parts of the once fine-tuned machine no longer meshed so smoothly.

Of course, most of these changes were path dependent. Consequently, many similarities with the past remained, making it difficult to separate continuity from change in unchallengeable ways. To many Japan watchers the changes that had taken place by the late 1990s were fundamentally irrelevant compared to the continuities. The economy, it was pointed out, still had numerous areas of strength: dozens if not hundreds of manufacturing firms with competitive product lines and established markets, a positive national trade balance, extensive foreign reserves, a talented labor pool, and experienced managers. Following an inevitable shakeout, went the argument, the Japanese economy would be back "stronger than ever." Politically, moreover, the LDP actually *was* back—in a coalition government from June 1994 until the fall of 1996 and, following the elections of October 1996, with a sufficient parliamentary plurality to form its own single-party minority government. By mid-1997 the party had even gained a majority in the lower house. In effect, many argued, not much had really changed. The bureaucracy was under sweeping attack, but the agencies had hardly thrown down their arms and surrendered. Relations with the United States were periodically quarrelsome but the security relationship and the economic connections remained fundamentally intact. In the more extreme formulations, any apparent changes were dismissed as merely "surface level" or superficial adaptations—the ever present *tatemae*—masking the far deeper continuities consistent with an inherent Japanese uniqueness—the *honne*—that would always keep Japan distinct from other countries.

A very different school of interpretation held that the changes Japan had undergone in the 1990s were making it "more normal" and that the country was slowly converging with the other industrialized nations. In response to the overwhelming forces of world markets, globalization, internationalization, and deregulation, Japan was undergoing a complex mixture of reluctant and enthusiastic dismantling of the structures and processes that had long kept it unique.[35] While the convergence was not yet complete, the argument went, Japan's trajectory would make it increasingly indistinguishable from the other capitalist democracies.

I adopt neither perspective in this book. I argue instead that the Japanese political economy did change in many fundamental ways from the 1960s to the 1990s, ways sufficiently important to constitute a "regime shift." At the same time, this shift is ongoing and as of this writing has not yet reached a new point of equilibrium with clear outlines and well-institutionalized processes; further changes are almost guaranteed. Moreover, the break with the past is far from complete; threads of continuity connect the present to the 1950s or 1960s. Japan's adaptations have been filtered through a set of nationally specific political and economic institutions sufficiently powerful to prevent Japan from simply mimicking the Western democracies.

I seek to unravel the changing character of the postwar Japanese political economy by focusing on questions in three main categories. The first comprises broad comparative queries that relate to the apparent uniqueness of Japan's political economy within the panoply of industrialized democracies: why conservative political dominance? why such a strikingly successful capitalism? and why a "conservatism" that seemed so substantively "social democratic"? The second set of questions relates to Japan's subsequent adaptations. How and why were these carried out? Why did they result in the long-term persistence of conservative politics and exceptional economic growth? The third set relates to the performance of the Japanese political economy over time. Why had Japan become so economically dismal and so politically fragmented by the mid-1990s? Why had the political economy not adjusted successfully to new circumstances, as it had earlier? What key changes made the Japanese political economy of the 1990s so different from that of the 1960s? And what direction did these changes portend? Toward what other model of political economy, if any, was Japan coverging?

The Argument in Brief and the Plan of the Book

Japan's political economy during the mid-1960s differed from other industrialized democracies in several respects, the most prominent of which were linked to the long-standing rule of the LDP and the phenomenal success of the national economy. Furthermore, Japan's "conservative" politics hardly resembled the conservatism associated with laissez-faire doctrines and high-level market competitiveness. A high level of mercantilism limited foreign direct investment, as well as the import of most manufactured products and consumer goods. At the same time, Japan produced a great number of internationally competitive exports. Japanese conservatism was also far more egalitarian. Moreover, particularly during the 1950s and 1960s, Japanese economic policy marginalized militant labor and the political left to a degree not seen in any other advanced industrial democracy during the postwar period.

As a consequence, Japanese politics abjured the extensive government expenditures associated with the Western welfare state, just as it rejected any recreation of Japan's prewar military machine or the high military expenditures of the United States and several European countries. In their place emerged a broad public consensus in support of national growth, rising living standards, and consumerism. The Japanese political economy of the 1960s was by no means static, however. Over time it made substantial adaptations to external and internal challenges: Japanese firms made extensive investments abroad; the domestic market was liberalized in important areas; the conservative political base shifted as organized labor lost much of its initial radicalism; and the LDP, moving away from its earlier dependence on agriculture and small business, began to attract substantial electoral support from urban voters, private-sector union members, and white-collar salaried employees. Increased politicization of the regulatory process, massive mismanagement of the domestic economy, corruption scandals, and political opportunism all combined in the mid-1990s to break apart the LDP, overhaul the electoral system for the lower house, and completely reorder the party system. The result was a broadscale shift in Japan's political and economic mix.

A central theme of this book is that Japan's postwar political economy must be understood in comparative historical terms. The concept of regime is critical to that understanding. The book is divided into two main parts. Part I is a comparative analysis of Japan during the 1950s and 1960s; Part II concentrates on regime adaptability and regime shifts. I examine the concept of a regime in Chapter 1. A regime is the composite of three interacting and reinforcing variables: socioeconomic coalitions, political institutions, and public policy profiles. Within most industrialized democracies since World War II, the three were mutually reinforcing, generating a stable equilibrium for long periods. Under such conditions, powerful political actors had only limited incentives to challenge the basic makeup of the regime; rather, political battles were waged over specific issues that took the ongoing regime as a given. I further explore the interaction of the three variables in four relatively stable regimes during the mid-1960s: corporatist Sweden, pluralist United States, two-party parliamentary Britain, and coalitional party–driven Italy.

In Chapters 2 and 3, I examine the unusual character of Japan during the early postwar years and show how politics and economics reinforced one another to produce an unusual and stable regime. These two chapters analyze the functioning of the Japanese political economy during the mid-1960s, the high point of conservative dominance and economic growth. Chapter 2 provides a broad-brush overview of the most critical aspects of the regime. Fused in mutually supportive ways were (1) a policy of "embedded mercantilism," (2) highly concentrated political and economic institutions, (3) and a socioeconomic coalition resting on agriculture and business. Meanwhile, organized labor was politically marginalized, despite many union gains of power within individual corporations. The overall result was a regime sustained and stabilized by a "virtuous cycle" of conservative politics and economics.

This conservative regime was an explicit historical and political creation. I lay out how and why it was created in Chapter 3. In brief, I contend that Japan was not always "unique" and that its prewar development was similar to other late industrializers such as Germany, Austria, Italy, and even to some extent France. But defeat in World War II—and the radical reformulation of political and economic institutions in all five of these countries—left Japan with substantially different traits.

In this chapter I also examine the political contingencies and choices that allowed conservative political entrepreneurs to institutionalize the regime. A variety of institutional and policy uncertainties that had long bedeviled Japanese conservatives were eliminated, and a regime was created that in time acquired at least a superficial unity, fusing conservative actors into a single bloc and institutionalizing their economic and strategic policies. This chapter makes clear how historically contingent and politically constructed the conservative Japanese regime of the 1960s really was.

In Part II the focus turns to transitions from stability. A central problem for any stable regime involves change; certain changes are ongoing and constant and serve largely to reinforce a regime's existing relationships. These typically involve incremental moves fitting the image of path dependency. Other changes, however, are far more dramatic and result in a significant reconstitution or a reequilibration of the regime's underlying character. In Chapter 4, I consider the limitations within which any democratic regime must operate and the types of ongoing changes that occur in every democratic regime, however stable. Here I provide a basis for differentiating between ad hoc adjustments and the far-reaching changes that portend a fundamental "regime shift." I identify three different levels of change. Most countries consistently undergo "first-order changes," those that involve minor shifts in public policy or in the support base of the governing coalition. Existing relationships are tinkered with in ways that essentially preclude more dramatic changes. Far more significant and comprehensive are "second-order changes." These are typically less frequent but are often critical to the maintenance of a regime. They usually involve combinations of coalitional adjustment and significant redirection of important public policies. And finally there are the comprehensive "third-order changes" involved in a "regime shift." These are alterations within all three components of an existing regime in ways that effectively terminate a regime's equilibrium and put it into transition to a new point of equilibrium. I explore how these processes work out in the Swedish, U.S., British, and Italian cases, with a chronological focus from the late 1970s into the 1990s. Then, for a variety of reasons, serious shifts moved all four countries substantially away from the regime relationships outlined in Chapter 1.

Chapters 5 and 6 return the focus to Japan. Chapter 5 compares the Japanese political economy in the late 1980s and early 1990s with that of the 1960s. This new portrait of Japan demonstrates how much had changed in the earlier regime of "embedded mercantilism" and examines the newly emerged socioeconomic and institutional arrangements.

In Chapter 6 I explain how and why Japan in the 1990s had become so different from Japan in the 1960s. I am interested in two central problems: first, the various challenges to regime stability that confronted conservatives, primarily from the early 1970s into the mid-1980s; and second, the socioeconomic and policy responses made to these challenges. I contend that Japan's conservative leaders—while remaining in place under nominally unchanged institutions—and Japan's economic institutions—while remaining highly competitive—in fact underwent a number of first- and second-order changes. Most fundamentally Japan moved from "embedded mercantilist" to "international investor." Simultaneously, the political base of the regime shifted as major players in the conservative coalition that dominated the "exporter" regime were supplemented by groups that played a critical role in the "investor" regime. Yet these adjustments took place without any major electoral realignment or political defeat of Japan's long-ruling LDP and no serious derailing of Japan's economic advance. Despite many deep changes, important components of the regime remained intact. Indeed, in many instances, adjustments that subsequently might have appeared desirable were avoided. Overall, there were few visible signs of massive change in the ruling elite or in economic performance. Yet, responses to the various challenges of the 1970s and 1980s—and the failure to meet many of them—opened up a series of structural fissures within the conservative regime. Ultimately, the failure to reconcile such internal conflicts threatened the regime's institutional foundations. The result was the splitting of the LDP, the introduction of a new electoral system, and the fragmentation and reorganization of the former party system, along with the bursting of the asset bubble, the radical overhaul of numerous economic organizations, and the anemic economic performance that characterized the 1990s.

In the concluding chapter I sum up the major lessons to be drawn about regimes and regime transformations. I then offer what seem to me the three most plausible scenarios in which the Japanese regime might reach a new equilibrium.

PART I

REGIMES—DIVERGENT
APPROACHES TO
POSTWAR STABILITY

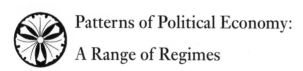 Patterns of Political Economy:
A Range of Regimes

In this chapter I discuss two broad categories of questions about regimes. The first concerns why most industrialized democracies have since 1945 gone through relatively long periods during which the fundamental character of their political economies remained largely unchanged. Day-to-day shifts and undulations were little more than surface-level turbulence above deep currents of continuity and consistency. What accounts for these continuities? The second set comprises some related questions. Why have these countries pursued such consistently divergent paths? Why have some industrialized democracies had governments that for decades provided elaborate and comprehensive public services involving more than 50 percent of the nation's GNP while others delivered dramatically less? Why did certain countries experience extended stretches of civil tranquility while their neighbors were racked by recurring disputes? Why did some nation-states have powerful proactive executive branches while others were fragmented, reactive, disjointed, or passive? Why were the economies of most nations open to foreign trade and investment while others conspicuously resisted substantial foreign penetration?

In this chapter I also lay the groundwork for a third set of problems. Here the question is, Why does a political economy that has for decades followed a relatively consistent path suddenly verge off in some strikingly new direction? I address this problem of change in Part II.

The concept of regime is central to answering all three sets of questions. After examining the concept in the abstract, I sketch the fundamental character of postwar regimes in four different countries—Sweden, the United States, Britain, and Italy. These four sketches illustrate the concepts developed earlier in the chapter and set the theoretical and comparative stage for the more detailed examination of Japan that follows in Chapters 2 and 3.

The Nature of Regimes

The term "regime" refers to a middle level of cohesion in the political economy of a nation-state. A regime is far less sweeping and comprehensive than a "political system," "constitutional order," or "economic system." At the same time, the character of a regime usually transcends several specific administrations, presidencies, cabinets, sultanates, or juntas and is more comprehensive than any time-bound economic direction such as deficit-finance, balanced budgets or loose money. "Regime" refers to the mid-level complex of legal and organizational features captured in terms such as "the New Deal," "Australian protectionism," "Gaulism," or "Scandinavian corporatism." All are mid-level consistencies that transcend individual governments but that are far more differentiated than "democracy" or "capitalism."

Before offering a more specific definition of the term, a word of justification is in order. As a phrase, "regime" often carries pejorative undertones.[1] My usage is meant to be evaluatively neutral. "Regime" does not connote likability; it refers simply to the shape, coherence, consistency, and predictability of a country's political economy over time.

A regime is composed of three essential elements: socioeconomic alliances, political-economic institutions, and a public policy profile. These three overlap and reinforce one another; they resemble the three legs of a tripod that collapses when any one is removed. They interact in complex ways, developing and responding to a discrete internal logic. In many countries the three elements are in unstable tension. Coalitions and alliances come and go; institutions are born and swiftly die; policy directions shift like the wind. Regimes thus may have little or no enduring stability; they lack equilibrium.

Within the postwar industrialized democracies, however, the pattern has been one of sustained periods of relative stability within each of the three elements along with generally equilibrated relations among the three. In essence, institutions, socioeconomic alliances, and public policy directions have been highly consistent; each has interacted with the other two in symbiotic rather than antagonistic ways. Specific socioeconomic groups have developed long-term alliances; particular alliances have exerted a preponderance of political influence.[2] Meanwhile, key political and economic institutions have remained largely unchanged, while the prevailing mixture of public policies has been internally consistent and persistent. So unified is the mixture that its properties cannot be fully appreciated by a simple summary of its parts. The cumulative result has been to reduce drastically the incentives for the most powerful actors to defect from the political and economic game; less powerful actors either support the rules or are powerless to change them.

Thus, quite typically, the prevailing public policy mix sustains and reinforces the dominant socioeconomic power base as well as a particular set of political institutions. Swedish Social Democratic governments, in carrying out specific policy programs in labor relations, housing, and social welfare, thereby bolstered the labor unions that were an essential part of its electoral constituency, while also reinforcing a host of corporatist bargaining institutions critical to Social Democratic success.[3] Margaret Thatcher's policies of selling off council (public) housing to its occupants and opposing liberal immigration policies simultaneously split her Labour Party opposition while also broadening her own socioeconomic base and recalibrating the biases of national political and economic institutions in pro-Conservative directions.[4]

Similarly, socioeconomic powers can typically be enhanced by the utilization and occasionally the reorganization of specific political and economic institutions. The Republican and Democratic Parties, for example, have long manipulated New York State electoral laws to impede independent, dissident, or third-party candidates from seriously challenging the incumbents. German bankers and bondholders have systematically seen their economic power enhanced by the strong powers and the anti-inflationary bias of the Bundesbank. French bureaucrats have benefited similarly from control over *dirigiste* economic planning. Bargaining continually reinforces the power of peak business and labor associations in various corporatist systems as well as reaffirming the broad spirit of cooperation in national economic adjustment.[5] In the Netherlands, institutionalized societal "pillars" with links to confessional political parties have generated public policies that reinforce the power of religious organizations throughout the political economy.[6]

Stable regimes thus consist of mutually reinforcing relationships among three sets of variables: the dominant socioeconomic coalition, the major political-economic institutions, and the profile of public policy. More tangibly, such regimes are characterized by the broadly consistent direction in which the country proceeds (its public policy), by the groups that empower—and are empowered by—this movement (its socioeconomic alliances), and by the regularized organizations of decision-making through which it channels and manifests such power (its political and economic institutions).

All three components are constantly reinforcing and sustaining one another through "virtuous circles" or "positive synergies."[7] Constant bolstering of its most important pivots leads in turn to greater predictability and stability.[8] Conversely, when the three clusters of variables are in disjunctive tension, a "negative synergy" ensues, creating a "downward spiral." Predictability becomes more problematic and equilibrium is undermined. Such a spiral must be corrected by internal adjustments; if these do not suffice, the regime will eventually collapse, and a new, differently ordered regime may emerge.

Stable regimes are thus characterized by what E. E. Schattschneider has labeled a prevailing "mobilization of bias."[9] They have what the French "regulation school" terms a particular "social structure of accumulation."[10] They are what Yamaguchi Yasushi means by *seiji taisei*,[11] and what Michael Shalev refers to as a political economy's gestalt.[12] Indeed, in their relatively unchallenged predominance, regimes are the political equivalent of what Thomas Kuhn means by a "prevailing paradigm."[13]

The Three Key Elements of Regimes

The industrialized democracies demonstrate a considerable range across each of the three variables.

Socioeconomic Sectors

Underpinning any regime is a specific set of relationships among important socioeconomic sectors. Along what lines and how deeply do a society's fissures run? How plural is a society? How homogeneous? Which sectors are well organized and which are not? What groups ally with one another, against whom, around what issues, and on how permanent a basis? Ultimately, who is "us" and who is "them"?

The possible lines of societal division are many, but within contemporary advanced democracies two rather different, although sometimes overlapping, dimensions have been of particular salience. One line revolves around religion, language, ethnicity, and race—elements often thought of as reflecting "emotions," "primordial sentiments," or "segmental cleavages."[14] A second line of cleavage revolves around the more tangible interests embedded in economics and material welfare.

That a nation's political and economic trajectory is heavily influenced by such long-term historical alliances is well established. In one of the earliest and most widely cited examples, Alexander Gerschenkron demonstrated the historical salience for German authoritarianism of the coalition between "Iron and Rye," that is, Prussian industrialists and Junker landlords.[15] In a similar vein, both Barrington Moore and Dietrich Rueschemeyer, Evelyne Stephens, and John Stephens have offered broad analyses of the ways in which similar socioeconomic coalitions—in interaction with state forces—have led to widely different types of regimes.[16] Ronald Rogowski, relying on a parsimonious three-sector model, offers a persuasive argument for the historical importance of the relative positions of land, labor, and capital and the alliances they forge.[17] Ruth Collier and David Collier show how labor's inclusion or exclusion from such alliances shaped the political evolution of eight Latin American countries.[18] In examining Europe during the wars, Gregory Luebbert shows how such social alliances were the key element in the evolution of four major types of political economy—liberalism, corporatism, fascism, and authoritarianism.[19]

Soon after World War II, labor and business within most major democracies had largely reconciled their most extreme differences and collaborated in the advance of industrial productivity. Meanwhile, in Rogowski's words, "even while providing generous death benefits, [they] presided over domestic agriculture's demise."[20] In several countries such as Italy and to some extent France, this simple picture was complicated by an internally divided labor movement, only part of which was cooperative with business, while labor-business arrangements were tempered by a powerful agricultural sector. Elsewhere, in land-rich countries such as the United States, Australia, New Zealand, and Canada, agriculture remained economically powerful because of its strength in world markets. The result was a number of agribusiness alliances. But even here some form of business-labor accord was simultaneously in place.

While such economic cleavages are vital, noneconomic forces—linguistic, ethnic, racial, and religious differences—have been critical in shaping politics in many democracies, despite a general waning in their contemporary salience. Language differences in Belgium and Switzerland, religious differences in Germany, the Netherlands, and the United States, and cultural and linguistic divisions in Finland are all salient in structuring political cleavages. Thus the seven-member Swiss Federal Council is based on proportional representation of the three largest language groups; the Belgian constitution dictates that cabinets be made up of roughly equal numbers of Dutch-speaking and French-speaking ministers; and the Maori are entitled to a quota of special seats in the New Zealand parliament.

When cultural or emotional divisions overlap with economic divisions, socioeconomic tensions can grow exponentially. The religious division between Catholics and Protestants in Northern Ireland thus heightens the sharp differences in economic opportunities and status between the two groups. Many French-speaking Canadians believe themselves victims not only of economic but also of cultural discrimination by the English-speaking majority. Nonwhites, particularly recent immigrants, in England, France, and Israel, not to mention the United States, occupy disproportionately large numbers of the economy's lowest paying and lowest status jobs and are subject to disproportionately high ethnic and social discrimination.

Less deep but increasingly important in many countries are such noneconomic identifications as "environmentalist," "feminist," "civil libertarian," "post-materialist" and the like. These too provide many citizens with valuable, though issue-specific, politically relevant self-identifications.

The long-term structure and direction of any country's political economy is heavily influenced by such socioeconomic divisions and cohesions. Yet such alliances do not form in an institutional vacuum. Alternative institutional arrangements may promote particular socioeconomic friendships or hostilities.

Institutions

Institutions are slow to be established, difficult to change, and powerful shaping forces of any regime.[21] In the words of James March and Johan Olsen, institutions are organizational mechanisms that remain "relatively invariant in the face of turnover of individuals and relatively resilient to the idiosyncratic preferences and expectations of individuals."[22] At least three types of institutions weigh heavily in shaping any regime: governmental institutions, economic institutions, and those that connect government, economy, and society—for example, electoral systems, interest associations, party systems, and economic policy networks.

Governmental institutions are typically established by constitutional fiat, enshrined by long years of tradition, and difficult to alter for short-term political advantage. Specific government bodies—the civil service, courts, parliaments, cabinets, the military, the police—and the delimitation of powers among them profoundly shape a nation's political economy.[23]

A diversity of political and governmental institutions can be found among the industrialized democracies. Some are federal; far more are not. A limited number are presidential; far more are parliamentary. In a few democratic regimes, the judicial system and the courts enjoy high levels of autonomy; elsewhere, the legal system is under far tighter control. Moreover, a major distinguishing feature among democratic regimes is the extent to which individual state agencies have the tools to develop and pursue agendas in isolation from, or even in opposition to, powerful social groups.

One important differentiating feature in industrialized democracies is whether a regime's institutional mixture concentrates or disperses power and authority. Are institutions centripetal or centrifugal? Do they pull toward a common center or gravitate around multiple access points? Are institutions designed to reflect (or create) unified and clear-cut national action or to reflect (and reinforce) internal social and economic diversities?[24]

At one extreme, countries such as the United States, Switzerland, or Belgium have highly differentiated governmental institutions. The United States is perhaps the most fragmented, with its deeply entrenched system of "checks and balances" consciously engineered to *prevent* the emergence of any single center of power. A well-institutionalized territorial federalism further disperses governmental power in the United States, Switzerland, and elsewhere.

At the opposite pole are the centralized parliamentary systems found, for example, in Britain, New Zealand, or Sweden. In the first two, no single written constitution delimits the powers of parliament, leaving that body legally, if not practically, capable of passing virtually any law. As one commentator wrote of New Zealand, "The central principle of the Constitution is that there are no effective legal limitations on what parliament may enact by the ordinary legislative process."[25] Similarly, one pundit has succinctly categorized Britain as an "elective dictatorship."[26]

In between such extremes are the more common mixed systems, such as the federal systems of Australia, Germany, or Canada, all of which remain more cohesive than the United States or Switzerland; or generally centralized systems such as those of the Netherlands or Denmark, which are more diffused than Britain or New Zealand. This wide range makes it clear that democracy may take a variety of institutional forms; no particular system best exemplifies it.

Just as democratic institutions have many faces, so too does capitalism. Differently structured firms, banking systems, trade associations, informal business networks, and the like generate individual "social systems of production" that differentiate one version of capitalism from another.[27] The size, scope, autonomy, and integration of individual firms and sectors also differ widely. So does the extent to which firms and sectors are horizontally and vertically integrated. Different countries vary widely in government's powers over financial systems and asset allocation, in the financial, insurance, and pension systems that prevail in major corporations, and in the manner in which individual firms and the national economy fuse with the broader international economy. Enormous diversity—complex mixes of firms, loose strategic alliances, formally established business groups, combines, networks, conglomerates, enterprise groups—pervades the economic landscape.[28]

Moreover, a number of economies are dominated by nominally "national" firms that are in fact truly multinational in their production, marketing, operations, and finance. The result is a vastly different "national" economy from countries in which most firms draw their resources, employees, capital, and markets preponderantly from within the national borders.

As with governmental institutions, a critical difference lies in the cohesiveness or dispersion of a nation's economic structures. Is the economy marked by highly individualistic, market-driven agendas with little central coordination and restriction? Or is there extensive concentration and coordination that transcends short-term market orientations? Such concentration varies considerably. The top five French and German business enterprises, for example, have sales equivalent to 12 percent of their respective national GNPs. The same figure for the United States and for Japan is a much smaller 7 percent.[29]

States are also quite diverse in their interaction with markets.[30] OECD member states oversee different mixtures of public and private ownership, varying forms of revenue collection, singular mixtures of state intervention into market economics, different labor market policies, and a multitude of institutional arrangements to deal with economic growth, the monetary supply, inflation, research and development, unemployment, national budgets, foreign direct investment, protection of infant industries and agriculture, and corporate investment.

A central distinction in this diversity is the extent to which institutional arrangements separate the political and economic spheres or bring them into fusion and cooperation. A few countries, most notably the United States and Britain, have long sought to institutionalize the ideological tradition of laissez-faire by restricting the regulatory capacity of government agencies. More often, in countries like France, Japan, and to some extent Germany, government-business ties are regular, intimate, reciprocal, and embedded.

Finally, one last set of intermediary institutions is critical: interest associations, political parties, party systems, and electoral systems. These provide vital linkages between the socioeconomic character and cleavages of a country and the institutions of governance. Here again the range is wide. At one extreme, social groups are free to form, raise monies, and engage in their chosen activities without government authorization, oversight, and control. At another, the viability of such groups rests on the status, funding, and oversight accorded them by some government agency. At one pole lie the pluralist regimes described by Philippe Schmitter as having a large number of "multiple, voluntary, competitive, nonhierarchically ordered and self-determined" socioeconomic interests; at another, those corporatist systems in which a far more limited number of interests are organized into "singular, compulsory, noncompetitive, hierarchically ordered and functionally differentiated categories . . . recognized or licensed by the state."[31]

The range and representativeness of different party and electoral systems is no less wide. The weight and scope of individual ballots, the threshold for parliamentary representation, the number and programmatic orientation of major parties, the direct versus indirect choice of government, the electorate's capacity to express opinions through referenda, and a host of other features all vary widely. With such variations come differing levels of voter control, coalitional possibilities, and public policies.

Yet, with all of the focus given to elections within democracies, it is well to recall the admonition of Stein Rokkan: "votes count; resources decide."[32] Even under systems with powerful electoral controls, citizen votes are but one of many socioeconomic resources that influence political and economic outcomes. The shape of any regime and the holders of governmental office will reflect voter power only to a limited extent. Other resources, partially independent of electoral politics, will have profound effects on a regime's character. These resources are demonstrated most clearly in the third key element of any regime, its public policy profile or paradigm.

Public Policy Paradigms

Control over all or key pieces of a nation's public policies has historically been a central goal of political competition. In a democracy it is a driving force behind electoral campaigns, although the campaigns themselves may mask overall policy objectives. Control over authoritative governmental agencies and their decisions allows groups to advance their own interests, the interests of their supporters, and— if one credits them with elements of altruism—their notions of the national interest. Public policies, in this sense, are a political system's classic "outputs."

Simultaneously, however, "policy shapes politics." Numerous policies hold the potential to legitimate or strengthen old social groups, create new ones, and bolster or fragment alliances. New interests emerge not from the ether of society but from explicit political institutionalization or enhanced empowerment through public policy shifts. Theda Skocpol has demonstrated how certain interest groups form and gain political salience primarily *after* public policies are formed. In the United States, for example, veterans groups arose following the introduction of pension programs for Civil War veterans that gave vets spoils over which to organize.[33] Bo Rothstein has shown how unionization rates in Sweden shot up once unions gained control, through public policies oriented around the Ghent system, over unemployment funds.[34] Control over the social policies affecting successive waves of immigrants bolstered the power of the Israeli Histadrut. Gøsta Esping-Andersen's examination of the Scandinavian democracies demonstrates how the introduction of particular social policies was critical to long-term political dominance by the Swedish Social Democrats, whereas in Denmark the failure to pursue similar policies led to the much earlier demise of social democracy.[35] Francis Castles came to similar conclusions about the links between policy paradigms and regime stability in Scandinavia.[36]

Similarly, specific public policies can fuse social groups that might otherwise have been irreconcilable. Protectionist trade policies and expanded military budgets for naval construction allowed Bismarck to forge the nationalist Prussian coalition of "Iron and Rye," noted above. Richard Nixon linked policies on the Vietnam War with those opposed to affirmative action, thereby splitting off "hard hat Democrats" and fragmenting a previously "solid Democratic South."

In short, public policies play a critical role in the constitution of any regime. A compatible mixture of public policies can glue socioeconomic coalitions and political institutions together. With time these policies become so commonly accepted that they define the regime itself.[37] "Free markets" thus operate as an unquestioned starting point for economic politics in certain regimes; elsewhere the starting point is "protection of the currency," "prevention of inflation," "catch-up economic growth," "inherent rights of citizenship," "codeterminism," or "gender equality."

When policies come to rest on such unquestioned assumptions, they function, as Max Weber suggested, as "switchmen, determin[ing] the tracks along which action has been pushed by the dynamic of interest."[38] These tracks in turn become part of the gestalt through which policymakers communicate. They are influential precisely because they are taken for granted and move beyond regular scrutiny.[39] They acquire a status beyond compromise, becoming instead what Durkheim calls "social facts" and what Gramsci labeled "hegemonic projects," that is, broad and coherent thrusts or biases in a nation-state's policy behavior that gain the status of hallowed truths and unchallenged assumptions by subsequent generations of policymakers and citizens.[40]

Such broad and largely unchallenged thrusts to public policy paradigms can be found in the broad agendas of trade protectionism and social welfare in Australia, codetermination and vocational training in Germany, social democracy in Norway or Sweden, defense of the pound sterling in Britain until 1967, or socially funded adjustments to economic transformations in Austria. Japan, as we will see in the next chapter, pursued a similarly defining public policy paradigm that I label "embedded mercantilism."

The unchallenged biases around such mixes of public policies serve as broad and well-institutionalized channellers of a nation's conduct. As Schattschneider puts it, "He who determines what politics is about runs the country, because the definition of the alternatives is the choice of conflicts, and the choice of conflicts allocates power."[41]

Public policies thus serve a twofold function in any regime. In the short run, they serve as tangible manifestations of the regime's power configuration, an ongoing calculus of the concrete rewards of gaining and holding power. In the longer run, however, they reinforce and solidify institutional arrangements and coalitional alliances guaranteeing systemic and semipermanent rewards. To cite Peter Hall, "The consequences of policy can gradually alter the societal organization of a nation, just as the shape of policy is in the first instance heavily influenced by that organization."[42]

Policies are the gold rings on the carousel of politics. Grabbing the ring wins a free ride; grabbing a handful of rings, lots of free rides.

Four Types of Regimes

All three variables are thus wide ranging. Theoretically, therefore, they could generate an almost infinite number of regime possibilities. In historical actuality, the combinations have been limited; patterns and clusterings prevail. This section explores four different types of regimes that achieved high degrees of stability for first three to four decades of the postwar period.

The four differ substantially from one another and provide divergent regime prototypes. They also provide a diverse set of comparative templates against which to measure the Japanese regime. The first is small, ethnically homogeneous Sweden with a dominant socioeconomic alliance in which organized labor held a key position. Postwar Sweden was also marked by a powerful set of corporatist economic arrangements that generated the public policy profile that has become prototypical of social democracy and the strong welfare state; this profile resembles those of other Scandinavian countries and, in some instances, of Austria as well.

As a second case, the United States is distinguished by its high level of institutional and social pluralism. Fragmented political and economic institutions, a minimalist and privatized approach to social welfare, and religious and ethnic divisions that crosscut economic divisions generated social alliances in the United States that were far more temporary, less class specific, and more ad hoc than in most other democracies. Yet the two-party electoral system frequently led to certain longstanding and structured exceptions. Particularly predominant, and prevailing for much of the postwar period, was the regime typically labeled the New Deal.

The third case, Britain, represents a strong parliamentary system that has neither Sweden's corporatism nor (especially by the 1960s and 1970s) its ethnic homogeneity. At the same time, the British experience resembled that of New Zealand and to a lesser extent Australia and Canada. Historically, class-based socioeconomic cleavages were played out in Britain through a two-party politics similar to that of the United States. Yet through most of the postwar period Britain pursued a public policy mixture far more supportive of an extensive social welfare state than anything developed in the United States. The dominant regime in Britain during the postwar period is one most often labeled "collectivism."

Finally, Italy presents a case that in many respects closely parallels Japan. Striking about Italy is the long-term dominance of the conservative Christian Democratic Party and a socioeconomic alliance structure that fused agriculture and business, both quite similar to Japan. In addition, Italy like Japan was marked by strong left-right cleavages especially in foreign policy and a public policy profile that for most of the postwar period enjoyed relatively high economic growth and a junior partnership with the United States. Yet the Italian regime under Christian Democracy had far weaker political and economic institutions than any of the other countries under examination; Italy's underlying socioeconomic alliance was far more suffused with religion than anywhere else except perhaps the United States, and the Italian public policy profile was far more pocked with patrimonialism and pork than most of the other regimes. In this regard it resembled the Fourth French Republic or Weimar Germany. It was a regime best characterized as *partitocrazia*.

The brief sketches that follow are designed to do two things. First, they provide a schematic overview of several prototypical ways in which capitalism and democracy assumed discrete patterns in the first three to four decades after the end of World War II. As such, they provide a panoply of alternative "capitalist democracies." They highlight how the three key variables interacted in different countries to maintain substantially different but equally stable regimes. Second, they provide a set of comparative cases for a detailed examination of the Japanese regime in the next two chapters.

Corporatist Sweden: Left-of-Center Hegemony and the Social Welfare State

Under corporatism, the political economy's key decision-making units are socio-economic blocs organized around different economic functions and highly cohesive internally. Their leaders are able to make commitments for the bloc as a whole, confident that these will be honored by their followers.[43] Bargaining among these blocs is ongoing and regularized in a constant search for commonly acceptable arrangements. The process continually recreates a spirit of cross-class and cross-interest cooperation.[44]

From the late 1930s into the 1970s, Sweden was a prototypical example of corporatism. The country was characterized by a small number of distinct and hierarchically structured interest associations, most fundamentally those of business and labor, but with most other important societal interests organized similarly. These organized interests gained regular access to policymaking through systematic participation in the numerous official investigative commissions (*utredning*) charged with the investigation of policy reform initiatives, as well as through representation on the boards of the state agencies charged with implementing those policies.[45] These arrangements privileged the representatives of such groups within a complex and mutually interdependent policy network.

The importance of interest associations and corporatism in Sweden during this period was reflected in the relatively limited role of parliament, which Hugh Heclo and Henrik Madsen argue, was expected to do little to oversee administration or to advance policy proposals. Instead, parliament largely affirmed or denied policy recommendations initiated elsewhere, typically in the commissions.[46]

Nonetheless, political parties were important organs for political contestation. From the 1930s into the early 1990s, Sweden's party system was impressively consistent in the number of parties, their relative bases of socioeconomic and policy appeal, and in their proportionate shares of the popular vote. With a rather high 5 percent threshold for parliamentary representation, new parties found it next to impossible to mount successful challenges to the prevailing monopolies on voter loyalties to the established parties.

Sweden's social democratic regime rested on the famous Red-Green alliance. In the early 1930s this alliance fused organized labor and agriculture against a more divided business and white-collar sector. As Esping-Andersen has noted, the beginnings of the alliance were not particularly auspicious. Lacking a clear majority when it took office in 1932, the Social Democratic Party (SAP) found its initial Keynesian employment programs vetoed by the nonsocialist parties in 1933.[47] But the party was able to draw on the nineteenth-century legacy of a common struggle for democracy between workers and farmers and on declines in world trade that drove both sectors to cooperation. It was thus able to put together a package of programs and institutions that held the coalition together for two decades. Workers got public-sector jobs and unemployment protection; farmers got subsidies and tariff protection for their crops.[48]

The Red-Green coalition allowed the Social Democratic Party and organized labor to bargain with Swedish business from a position of electoral and parliamentary strength. With a parliamentary majority in place, the new regime could effectively threaten business with the possibility of state action should marketplace negotiations fall too far short of labor's goals. The business community backed off from its earlier posture of militant opposition to labor that had predominated in the 1920s. Instead, recognizing the potential benefits of cooperative labor-management relations, it entered into the famous agreement between labor and business reached in 1938 in Saltsjöbaden, an agreement that laid the groundwork for five decades of cooperative and quiescent labor-management relations.[49] The alliance also helped to foster the incredible growth of trade unionism in Sweden, to the point where 68 percent of the national workforce was unionized as early as 1970.[50]

Initially on the basis of this alliance with agriculture, and then subsequently in a reconfigured alliance between blue- and white-collar workers, the SAP became the most successful social democratic party in the world, enjoying forty-four years of single-party rule from 1932 to 1976.

As a result of the governmental and economic power of the left, Sweden's public policy profile consistently pursued the development and institutionalization of an extensive social welfare state undergirded by the provision of universal, comprehensive, and institutionalized benefits. Simultaneously, Sweden's social democracy remained highly accommodative of big business and private capital. In contrast to far less nominally socialist countries such as Britain, Italy, and France, nationalization in Sweden was low; as of the late 1970s, 87 percent of business remained under private ownership. Effective corporate taxes were also minimal, and numerous schemes were designed to push profits into investment rather than into corporate dividends. Government provided extensive corporate funding for research and development. Moreover, plant-level autonomy by management remained high despite strong unions—a notable contrast to Britain and an important similarity to Japan.

Nor did social democracy impede the pragmatic encouragement of oligopoly and monopoly. Industry in Sweden was big and concentrated, approximately 40 percent more concentrated than in the large industrialized democracies.[51] Capital was similarly concentrated, with only 2 percent of the nation's stockholders owning more than two-thirds of the stock as of the mid-1970s.[52] Until as late as 1984, Swedish capital markets were almost completely insulated from foreign takeover, further encouraging Swedish business and finance to cooperate with the social democratic regime in a national economic project designed to enhance the international competitiveness of Sweden's niche market exports.[53]

A key to this competitiveness abroad was Sweden's corporatist bargaining at home. Business-labor cooperation was high; strike rates were among the lowest in the industrialized world; and Sweden's policy profile included the country's famed "wage solidarity." Relatively egalitarian and nationwide agreements on wage increases kept a squeeze on Sweden's least efficient and internationally uncompetitive firms while providing an implicit subsidy for the country's more productive and efficient firms through lower-than-market wages. Swedish firms were thus encouraged to modernize plants, invest in research and development, rationalize production, and strive for ever higher levels of efficiency and larger shares of world markets.

Finally, state policies of job retraining, economic assistance, and relocation allowances eased the personal adjustment of workers displaced by firms not faring well in the marketplace; those firms that adjusted quickly to market conditions reaped hefty profits with little confiscatory taxation from the state. Those that did not were forced to reorganize, but their workforces were given state-sponsored benefits and incentives to allow them to relocate or retool their skills.

The mixture of social welfare plus extensive job programs and economic assistance to business generated government spending that was usually the highest in the industrialized world as a percentage of GNP. During 1968, for example, that figure was 42.8 percent, and in 1976 it was 51.7 percent—11 and 14 percent above the OECD average.[54] Between 1960 and 1975, public employment in Sweden more than doubled.

The positive and reinforcing nature of the social democratic regime initially came under challenge in the 1976 election. Sweden was confronted, as were all the major industrial democracies, with oil-shock-driven economic inflation in 1973–74. The SAP's own policies had been foundering as wage costs spiraled, public-sector employment mounted, tax rates rose, and divisions appeared within the workforce over a wage solidarity package that seemed to reward "unproductive" and numerically increasing public-sector workers at the expense of more "productive" workers in the private sector. While the Social Democrats managed to maintain full employment far better than almost any other industrial country,[55] economic tensions were clearly emerging within the ranks of their own supporters, as the union movement faced what Peter Swenson has analyzed as the trilemma among fair wage differentials, higher wages, and full employment.[56]

Furthermore, the issues of nuclear power and collective wage earner investment funds confounded the previous social democratic internal unity. As a result they were replaced electorally by the so-called bourgeois coalition. As an intriguing demonstration of the inherent stability of the "Swedish Way," however, during the six years that this coalition remained in power, the preexisting institutions and policy agenda remained largely hegemonic. Little was done to dismantle the well-established social welfare state or its policies. Indeed, the nonsocialist governments actually increased state subsidies for declining industries—hardly the expected behavior of an allegedly market-oriented government. In turn, most of the public policies put in place under the social democratic regime were retained by the bourgeois government, suggesting that no serious regime shift had taken place despite the change of government.

In an ironic twist, when the Social Democrats returned to power in 1982, they kick-started the economy with a 16 percent devaluation of the kroner, giving a major boost to Swedish exports. The government also reduced subsidies to lame duck industries such as textiles and shut down Sweden's no longer efficient shipyards in Malmo and Uddevalla, as well as the public mine at Kiruna.[57]

The corporatist regime thus remained largely stable even following the 1976 electoral shifts. The bourgeois coalition kept social welfare intact; the returning Social Democrats provided a big boost for business and the economy. Overall, Sweden's regime mixed strong left-of-center political control with corporatist bargaining between business and labor to create a dynamic national economy and an extensive social welfare system. It generated a regime marked by positive-sum relationships that were good for business, good for labor, and not at all bad for the Social Democrats.

The United States: Socioeconomic Pluralism and the New Deal Regime

The predominant regime in the United States during the same period was almost a polar opposite of Sweden's. It was also unlike most of the regimes in continental Europe or Japan. Socially and institutionally the United States was the prototype of pluralism. An extensive system of national governmental checks and balances combined with federalism made U.S. politics resistant to quick, coherent, and comprehensive decisions. Nor has the United States ever embraced corporatism in a serious way.[58] Few of its multiple interest organizations combine into meaningful peak associations; few if any business or labor associations have the power to bind members to peak-level decisions.

Instead, national politics has been marked by multiple, entrenched, and often contradictory pockets of functionally specific power.[59] This power is most commonly manifested as "iron triangles" uniting one or more interest groups, congressional committees, and executive offices in semipermanent but periodically shifting alliances forged around day-to-day legislative, court, and executive actions.

Meanwhile, states, cities, and neighborhoods enjoy comparatively high degrees of funding and policy autonomy. Social welfare in Alabama or Arkansas differs widely from that in Minnesota or Michigan. Labor market policies in Philadelphia, Tucson, or Tallahassee are similarly disparate. Within the single city of New York, different sanitation, snow removal, and educational services are found in the Bronx and Staten Island.

Two "catch-all" political parties have long had a duopoloy over national American elections. Not since the 55th Congress (1897–99) has a third party held more than 10 percent of the seats in the Congress, and between 1939 and 1996 third-party representation has never topped 1 percent. Either a Democrat or a Republican has won the presidency ever since the election of Franklin Pierce in 1852, and in the thirty-four elections between 1864 and 1996 there have been only six contests in which a third party or an independent has won the electoral votes of even a single state.[60]

At the same time an plethora of interest associations and ethnic and religious affiliations strip the United States of the social bloc cohesion and the tight fusion between parties and socioeconomic blocs found in Sweden or any other corporatist country. Classes in the United States are also far less cohesive than in Britain, New Zealand, or Australia—three English-speaking countries where two-party politics also prevails.[61] Socioeconomic allegiances find economic interests entangled with ethnic, religious, and other cultural affinities.

Electorally, parties and individual candidates mobilize the support of multiple small groups and individual citizens rather than relying on preexisting interest associations. Logically enough, in contrast to most other industrialized democracies, the capacity of American parties to control the actions of either their parliamentarians or their voters is limited. While frequently allied with one or another of the two major parties, many sectoral interests and interest groups periodically shift their allegiances or, more commonly, burrow their way into close accord with bureaucratic agencies and congressional committees, forming functional alliances that guarantee them a continuing influence independent of the outcomes of party or electoral politics. As Thomas Risse-Kapen formulates it, "Constant building and rebuilding of coalitions among societal actors and political elites is fairly common. . . . The openness of the political system provides the society with comparatively easy access to the decision-making process."[62]

When one party controls the executive branch while another controls the legislative, the executive may have difficulty setting and maintaining a single public policy direction. The coalitional bases for individual legislators frequently differ from those for the executive—even within the same political party—leading to governments with internally competing socioeconomic constituencies and complex policymaking networks. Yet a fluid electorate—one not tightly organized into mutually exclusive blocs—has made it possible for many chief executives to forge new electoral coalitions from disparate elements by invoking ever changing issues.

Similarly, the executive often finds it difficult to exert leadership over the national bureaucracy. As James Wilson notes, there are two kinds of government executives in the United States: "Political executives are appointed by the president . . . in order to satisfy the elected official's political needs; career executives are appointed from within an agency (or brought in from a comparable agency elsewhere) because it is required by law or because there are no overriding political needs that must be served."[63]

In such a "government of strangers," actual bureaucratic power lies less in sabotage or disobedience than in the simple capacity to withhold enactment of programmatic goals set elsewhere.[64] As a consequence, the political loyalty of individual agencies in the quest for politically defined "regime goals" is highly variable. It is correspondingly difficult for either the president or the legislature to define and pursue a public policy nexus with great consistency and internal coherence.

Nonetheless, within this inchoate set of institutions and socioeconomics, a relatively cohesive regime known as the New Deal prevailed over the national political economy from the 1930s into the late 1960s or early 1970s. In the United States the world depression of the late 1920s and early 1930s gave rise to numerous social movements posing disparate challenges to the long-standing Republican-dominated "system of 1896." As Thomas Ferguson has put it, "Taking office at the moment of the greatest financial collapse of the nation's history, President Franklin D. Roosevelt initiated a dazzling burst of government actions designed to square the circle that was baffling governments elsewhere: how to enact major social reforms while preserving both democracy and capitalism."[65]

The New Deal brought together an electoral coalition of organized labor, urban ethnics, and southern whites mobilized through minimally coordinated city- and statewide Democratic Party machines. But the New Deal coalition also put together an economic bloc of capital-intensive industries, investment banks, and internationally oriented commercial banks.[66] The New Deal thus not only mobilized the power of the traditional lower and working classes, it fused these groups and their voting power with the economic muscle of the most important and internationally competitive segments of the business and financial communities. These latter split off from the previously united—and definitely Republican—business sector, leaving the Republicans in the 1940s and 1950s aligned with domestically oriented, small-scale segments of the American business community.

The principal appeal of the Democratic Party to these segments of finance and business involved the "break with orthodoxy," the replacement of neoclassical economics with Keynesian demand stimulus and an internationalist thrust to the conceptualization of "markets."[67] The economically less orthodox segments of the business and financial community were tolerant of the New Deal's state-directed efforts to expand the size of the unionized workforce through the Wagner Act and to lay the foundations for a conspicuously limited expansion of social services. The New Deal thus emerged as an institutionally strong executive supported by a powerful bloc of internationally oriented capital-intensive firms willing to provide generous labor policies for their workers. Workers, in conjunction with other members of the lower classes, provided the voting power behind a policy regime based on "multinational liberalism."[68]

After the defeat of Germany and Japan, FDR's national coalition came under challenge as the Republicans were riven by tensions between midwestern isolationists and eastern internationalists and the Democrats divided into three ideological factions. But the cold war, the creation of a permanent and expanding military establishment, and a generous politics of pork barrel sustained the existing regime—albeit with minor readjustments in policy direction and support base.

From the 1950s into the early 1970s, meanwhile, workers and businesses joined in a "labor-capital accord."[69] Market driven, nonstatist, and not party enforced, the accord involved a set of tacit private-sector agreements in highly oligopolized, mass manufacturing industries such as steel, autos, petrochemicals, electrical machinery, and transportation. A series of long-term labor contracts ensured workplace tranquility in exchange for job security, union rights, and regularized pay raises. Unlike wage solidarity in Sweden, however, wage hikes in the United States provided little incentive for management to increase productivity, whether through labor-saving devices or technologically sophisticated manufacturing processes. Instead the huge size of the American market, combined with limited competition from foreign-manufactured goods both in the domestic market and abroad, allowed such oligopolistic manufacturers to pass on rising U.S. labor costs to a consuming public politically and economically unmotivated to protest. This broad stability in the nation's political economy changed only when highly competitive foreign products began to penetrate the U.S. and world markets and expanded the choices available to American and international consumers.

Meanwhile, in foreign policy, the regime was organized around an alliance of procapitalist or at least nominally anticommunist countries. In addition, the United States adopted the role of international economic hegemon, creating and sustaining the Bretton Woods monetary system and the GATT trading system. As a testament to the internal political unity of the regime, both parties (and most major interests) agreed that "politics stops at the water's edge."

For most of the period from the 1930s into the 1970s, the fiscal policies of the New Deal regime rested on the sequential and largely unintegrated development of public programs for specifically targeted social groups. The culmination of this process came with Lyndon Johnson's Great Society, a set of social programs whose costs, when combined with the Vietnam War effort (both without raising taxes) and with the oil shock and the breakdown of the Bretton Woods system in the early 1970s, led to the massive inflation that ultimately undermined the economic base of the coalition.

Britain: Party-Driven Collectivism

Several shared features—language, cultural heritage, a legacy of political democracy, the single-member district system, two-party politics—account for the frequently drawn comparisons between the United States and Britain. Early industrial development in both countries, powerful financial institutions, and a deeply entrenched philosophy of laissez-faire add to the temptation to see Britain and the United States as trans-Atlantic mirror images. Yet in Britain the postwar political settlement and the consequent regime differed fundamentally from that in the United States. From an institutional perspective, the most important difference is that political parties and parliament have been far more coherent and politically powerful institutions in Britain than they have been in the United States or, for that matter, in most other countries. Parties, governing through parliament, have set the broad framework for the postwar British regime.

A party-based cabinet in Britain automatically enjoys far more political clout than does any American executive by virtue of its ability to enforce party discipline in parliament. A U.S. president may be highly persuasive in lobbying Congress or the bureaucracy, but, as Richard Neustadt and others have argued, "the power of the president is the power to persuade." A British prime minister has the power to command. Or as Sven Steinmo has put it, "Britain allows governments to act on their electoral platforms no matter how ill-conceived or antagonistic to the opposition's interests."[70]

Organized interests in Britain have also long enjoyed considerably more cohesion than their American counterparts. In Britain, with its two-class, two-party system, the most significant interests were traditionally organized business and organized labor. Indeed, Samuel Beer has gone so far as to suggest that these interest associations had become so powerful in Britain that the country was in danger of falling prey to the U.S. problem of "pluralistic stagnation."[71] Yet, unlike the institutional pluralism of the U.S., which so easily spawns its "iron triangles," interests anxious to exert influence in Britain must gain and maintain it through the party system.

For most of the postwar period, Britain's two main parties drew the bulk of their support from competing social blocs. The Labour Party was organized largely around craft unions, which represented about 45 percent of the workforce from the mid-1960s into the mid-1970s. The unionized workforce was organized into the peak association of the Trade Unions Congress (TUC), representing more than 90 percent of all union members. Business was generally far more organizationally diffuse. Some 150 national employers groups belong to the peak Confederation of British Industries, but the CBI was formed only in 1965. Individually and collectively, however, business has gravitated naturally to the Conservative Party. Because commercial agriculture in Britain was virtually eliminated by the end of the nineteenth century, an unmediated and uncompromised interaction between business and labor has dominated British politics.

From the end of World War II until the Thatcher Revolution of 1979, the Labour and Conservative Parties, despite different class bases, broadly agreed about the desirable shape of the British regime. During World War II, Britain's national government included representatives of both major parties. When the war ended Labour won a decisive victory and began a major shift in the country's policy profile that included substantial nationalization of industry and expanded welfare services. By 1960, these nationalized industries accounted for about 18 percent of total fixed investment, produced about 10 percent of the national income, and employed some 8 percent of the national workforce.[72] When the Conservatives returned to power they and Labour gravitated toward the regime that Beer has characterized as "collectivist politics." Mutual acceptance of the nationalized sector and big government was bolstered by a consensus on the egalitarian underpinnings of the welfare state and political regulation of the market designed to ensure national economic growth with low unemployment.

Unlike Sweden but like the United States, Britain's collectivism never took the form of corporatist bargaining among economic interests. The closest approximation, the National Economic Development Council (NECD), was always on the margins of real economic decision making and never gained serious support from labor. Far greater economic power in Britain rested with the Treasury and the City.

Government economic management under the Treasury and the Bank of England consisted largely of a mixture of fiscal and monetary tinkerings designed to respond to market fluctuations. Regardless of which party held control of parliament, economic policy was largely reactive; rarely was it able to generate any collective national economic growth agenda. Each party tilted fiscal or monetary policies toward its constituent base, with considerable freedom left to the ad hoc operation of markets, individual firms, and the power of finance.

Within this system, the power of the City of London was overpowering. The City has been the world's most significant financial and credit center. Its economic and market resources have rarely been hampered by serious electoral constraints; politicians have typically been more worried about keeping the City happy than the reverse. Of particular concern during the period of collectivist politics was the vigorous effort exerted by the City and Treasury to protect the value of the pound sterling.

In Britain—as in the United States and France but not in most other postwar democracies—the policy profile was interlaced with the residues of empire. Comparatively high military spending, the British Commonwealth, the maintenance of foreign bases, and a major campaign to protect the value of the pound sterling from devaluation all reflected this thrust. Bilateral ties with the United States, enshrined as part of a "special relationship," complemented Britain's involvement in NATO.

The cumulative picture of Britain is thus one of a postwar regime that was broadly cohesive in its overall policy profile. That profile preserved a large place for a variety of residual welfare programs that made for relatively costly governance. But unlike Sweden and far more like the United States, Britain lacked any cohesive governmental economic policy beyond the standard Keynesian reliance on fiscal and monetary policies. Rather, a powerful financial sector drove Britain's economy while much of manufacturing and industry languished, eventually leading to the *Economist's* famous declaration that Britain was the "sick man of Europe."

Italy: Regime without Governance

Postwar Italy has been marked by fragmented political institutions, sharp socioeconomic divisions between business and labor, and a public policy profile that long put patronage and pork ahead of national economic growth. The institutions most responsible for shaping the regime have been the political parties. Presidential weakness combined with parliamentary and cabinet fragmentation have resulted in a regime without governance.[73] That regime, despite numerous feints and twists, remained essentially intact from the late 1940s into the early 1990s.

Italy's fascist legacy left many of its postwar constitution makers committed to a government with limited decision-making powers rather than one of command and control. For most of the postwar period the Italian parliament was a two-house behemoth of roughly 950 members, the two houses having equivalent powers but no coordinating committees to resolve differences. From the end of World War II until 1993, the electoral system was based on proportional representation with a low threshold for party representation, resulting typically in a dozen or more parties being seated in parliament.

Cabinets were highly fragmented multiparty creations "of short duration and of little consequence."[74] They were unwieldy and unstable coalitions reflecting the varying electoral fortunes of the system's numerous political parties. Parties consequently had what Gianfranco Pasquino has called an "excessive and suffocating presence" throughout Italian society. Italy was a regime of *partitocrazia*.[75]

In the early postwar years the legacy of the U.S. occupation and the cold war also shaped the regime. Italian conservatives benefited tremendously, both politically and economically, from U.S. anticommunism. The result was a stymieing of the rising left and a highly controversial foreign policy that tied the country to the United States through its military bases and NATO membership.

The broad ideological spectrum of Italian parties included an initially pro-Soviet Communist Party (PCI) and a more moderate Socialist Party (PSI) on the left, the center-right Christian Democracy (DC) and the Liberals (PLI) in the middle, and neofascist remnants on the extreme right. The DC and the PCI, the two poles of the party system, each typically drew between 25 and 35 percent of the vote in most postwar elections. From 1946 until the early 1990s, the DC was the consistently anchoring element in all cabinets, while the PCI was invariably the largest parliamentary opposition party. DC–led coalitions sought to prevent a linkage between the communists and the third largest party, the socialists.

The DC rested on a socioeconomic alliance of the rural south, small business, professionals, state workers, and big business (although segments of business were also close to the PLI). In the initial postwar years, the DC also had a heavily confessional support base as a result of its historical ties to the Catholic Church. Small businesses were proportionally more numerous than in almost any other major country (except Japan), and as late as 1967 nearly one-quarter of the Italian labor force was employed in agriculture.[76] Finally, Italian labor was highly fragmented. The DC enjoyed the support of a large segment of organized labor—unions in Italy's noncommunist labor confederation, the CISL. In contrast, the PCI drew its support heavily from the blue-collar workforce, whom it long claimed to represent, while at the same time receiving substantial middle-class support.

DC dominance rested on what Sidney Tarrow has labeled its "soft hegemony"— the party's willingness to avoid stark confrontations between business and labor and between confessional Catholicism and tolerance. This combined with a readiness to share patronage, if not power, with the other political parties, including during the 1970s with the PCI.[77] The result was a relatively inclusive but flaccid regime.

State resources were mobilized by the DC to perpetuate its own dominance. The Italian regime provided a host of social welfare services, typically clientelistic and directed to male heads of household, that put Italy in the moderate middle of the industrialized democracies. But far more salient to DC dominance was patronage. The longer the DC was in control, the more patronage expanded, leaving Italy with a "big state," but one marked by corruption, waste, and clientelism, and incapable of developing a coherent national economic agenda.

More than one-half of the civil service positions in Italy were exempt from competitive examinations. The country also had over a thousand parastatals including such huge operations as the ENI (Ente Nazionale Idrocarburi) in energy resources and IRI (Instituto per la Ricostruzione Industriale) in heavy industry. Nationalization of industry was more widespread in Italy than in any other industrialized democracy. State owned enterprises accounted for 38 percent of the workforce and 45 percent of the sales in industry and services in the 1980s, making the Italian state a major stakeholder in the national economy.[78] Almost all state-owned enterprises carried extensive patronage responsibilities.[79]

Despite the absence of clear government economic policies, Italy enjoyed extensive economic growth in the early postwar years. The GNP doubled between 1950 and 1962, and during most of the 1960s its rate of growth was about 4 percent, the highest in Europe except for West Germany. The monument of prosperity had feet of clay, however,[80] and between 1970 and 1975 GNP growth per capita dropped from 5.2 percent to 1.6 percent, the biggest slump of the major industrialized democracies.[81] There were subsequent positive bumps in the Italian economy, most typically the result of dynamism in the small-scale, family-owned private firms that dominate the national economy. Indeed, in 1975 the major business association, Confindustria, and the unions reached a "producer's alliance" that tied wages in the export-oriented industrial sector to moderate price increases in the national economy.[82] This also separated economic policies for the private sector from the pork-laden policies in the public.

Italian politics in practice accommodated or even encouraged local and regional differentiation economically.[83] At the same time, however, most efforts to generate national economic reforms failed, and the regime was unable to sustain and institutionalize positive performances after the mid-1960s, when it became difficult to speak meaningfully of a national economic agenda.

Many of Italy's economic problems can be traced to politics and patronage. Hence, when growth slowed, no government program or private initiative was generally capable of restarting the engine. Instead, the state treasury served as a piggy bank for political payoffs.

The politics of economic chaos owed a great deal to business-labor fragmentation and confrontation, which in turn arose from the militancy of the CGIL, the union federation tied to the PCI. On the other hand, the major federation of private business, Confindustria, initially fought to keep down wages, even as public-sector employers worked closely with unions to enhance wages and ensure a steady and reliable supply of skilled labor. On the whole, Italy has been marked by high levels of labor-management discord, almost invariably the highest among the OECD countries.[84]

Party political interests also account for the lack of agricultural modernization. Italian food exports were 7 percent of total exports while food constituted 20 percent of Italian imports.[85] Italy pays huge sums to the European Agricultural Fund but has gotten little in return. Changes in the social security system and regional development programs might have led to greater agricultural productivity, but these have been resisted by the DC due to clientelistic battles within the party.

Italian government agencies were not structured for economic action either. Thus, three different ministries long shared economic responsibilities: the Finance Ministry, charged primarily with collecting revenues; the Treasury, responsible for debt management and spending; and the Budget and Planning Ministry, coordinator of the other two. And meanwhile, the collection of information used by the first two agencies was entrusted to private companies under the control of IRI.[86] Governmental tax collection capabilities were systematically weak, with perhaps one-half of the annual budget deficit traceable to uncollected taxes. Yet, DC ties to the nation's major tax evaders—small shopkeepers, self-employed professionals, and businesses—removed any incentive for a crackdown. Italy's "submerged" economy was huge and would have increased the GNP by between 18 and 25 percent if it had been included in official figures.[87]

Meanwhile, the Bank of Italy was, at least until the "divorce" of 1981, far more responsive to party demands than to monetary and industrial needs. Consequently, Italian monetary policies were often loose and the economy highly inflationary; deficit finance dominated budgeting from the mid-1960s onward. In the early 1980s, the height of the Reagan deficits, for example, Italy, with a total GDP of about one-sixth that of the United States, had a deficit equal to one-half that of the United States. Debt service reached about 10 percent of GNP at its worst levels. But by following the path of deficit finance, a variety of coalitional governments, particularly the five-party government led by Benito Craxi, pushed up private disposable income for the whole decade of the 1980s.[88]

In sum, the early postwar Italian regime differed strikingly from the other three countries examined. It was by far the most highly "politicized," not only in terms of the penetration of the entire system by political parties and their patronage networks, but also in the extent to which other organs of governance showed little capability of operating independently of party politics. The result economically was a regime periodically demonstrating high economic competitiveness within selective areas at the micro level but by extensive bloat and high debt at the macro level.

These four sketches demonstrate the extent to which each regime was marked by a different mixture of institutions, coalitions, and policy profiles. In each country the mix remained internally consistent for long periods during the early postwar years. Each of the three elements of the regime depended on and reinforced the others.

These cases are a prelude to the next two chapters on Japan in two ways. First, they provide a set of empirical reference points by which to compare and highlight important elements of the Japanese conservative regime. Second, they highlight, despite their differences, the many ways in which the Japanese case starkly diverged from the experiences of most other capitalist democracies. As Chapters 2 and 3 will make clear, Japan's early postwar regime shared various individual characteristics with the four regimes presented here, but more notable overall is the extent to which the Japanese mixture mirrored none of them.

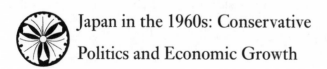

CHAPTER TWO

Japan in the 1960s: Conservative Politics and Economic Growth

The mid–1960s were the golden age of Japan's conservative regime. The Liberal Democratic Party (LDP) was dominating elections and public policy, the economy was expanding at white hot speed, and problems of foreign policy were either absent or casually ignored. The regime's components were meshing with a silky smoothness that gave the nation's political economy an aura of effortless achievement. In the process, Japan was growing more and more distinct from the other industrialized democracies.

This chapter addresses three central questions: What were the key traits of the conservative regime during this glorious period? What allowed the regime's various elements to interact with such fluidity and mutual reinforcement? and How did the conservative regime in Japan differ from those in the other industrialized democracies?

The Well-Oiled Conservative Regime

Japan's conservative regime was unusual in four important ways. First, its economic institutions were dramatically different from those of the other capitalist democracies, and its economic performance was vastly superior. Second, its politics were marked by the industrial world's longest—and least compromised—dominance by a single political party. Third, despite long-term rule by nominal conservatives, Japan's political economy showed far greater egalitarianism than did conservative regimes elsewhere. Fourth, Japanese foreign and security policies were bilaterally tied to those of the United States, setting the U.S.-Japan relationship apart from the more interwoven and multilateral alliances that linked the United States to most other democracies. Simultaneously, Japanese foreign policy confronted no serious international crises that might have undercut its smooth and purposeful domestic predisposition.

To appreciate the complicated mosaic of Japan's early postwar regime, we might examine a few of its component pieces at a single point in time. Most appropriate is 1964–65, when key aspects of the conservative regime were in full relief and the regime was functioning at its smoothest.

Begin with the Olympics. Perhaps no single event in the postwar period was more symbolic of Japan's transformation from prewar authoritarianism, international isolation, and early postwar economic devastation than Tokyo's hosting of the 1964 Summer Games. The International Olympics Committee had awarded the 1940 Games to Tokyo but then revoked the invitation following Japan's 1937 invasion of China. Regaining the venue was thus demonstrable evidence of Japan's postwar transformation and its international acceptance. Few Japanese could oppose the Olympics and the spirit of national unity and optimism it embodied.

Japanese filmmaker Ichikawa Kon's *Tokyo Olympiad* provides a stunning metaphorical linkage of the Olympics, Japanese economic growth, and national pride. The film opens with shots of men clearing land and tearing down the old Tokyo to begin construction of the new athletic facilities. Mount Fuji provides the backdrop for single runners carrying the Olympic torch across the country. The final torchbearer, Sakai Yoshinori, runs up the stadium steps, breathing hard, his heart pounding, and lights the Olympic flame. Produced using 164 cameramen with 1,031 cameras at a cost of over $1 million, the film resonates with echoes of Japan's nationwide economic cooperation and success over the preceding decades.[1]

Some five thousand athletes gathered in Tokyo in 1964, the first time that an Asian nation had hosted the Games. Over 3.5 million Japanese citizens applied for the sixty thousand tickets available for the opening ceremonies. National pride peaked as the Japanese women's volleyball team, an exceptionally well-disciplined—some would suggest robotic—team, captured the gold medal. For many Japanese, the team's success symbolized how the country had impressed itself on the world.

The Games themselves climaxed the more comprehensive development sweeping through the entire economy. For example, in January 1964 the Building Standards Law was revised to eliminate the thirty-one-meter height restriction on Tokyo buildings; subsequent construction of the Hotel New Otani and the Kasumigaseki Building began the age of Japanese skyscrapers. On October 1, the Japan National Railroad opened the Hikari Shinkansen (bullet train) for passenger traffic between Tokyo and Osaka.[2] Capable of speeds in excess of two hundred kilometers per hour, well beyond anything in the world at the time, the new train chopped travel time between Japan's two largest cities to three hours.[3] The first section of the Tokyo Metropolitan Expressway also opened in 1964. Along with the bullet train it provided a political justification for obtaining land, hiring contractors, speeding up work schedules, and mobilizing the citizenry for a national interest project.[4]

Mirroring these triumphs, Japan's GNP in 1964 surpassed that of Italy and the United Kingdom and drew close to that of West Germany, putting Japan on track to become the third largest economy in the world, behind only the United States and the USSR. Essential to this catch-up was export success, and 1964 also marked the last year in a twenty-year string of unfavorable balance of payments for Japan. As world trade tripled between 1955 and 1970,[5] Japanese products garnered ever larger shares, leading eventually to massive national surpluses.[6]

In 1964, numerous Japanese firms including Matsushita Electric, Sony, Hayakawa Electric, Toyota Motors, Sanyo Electric, and Nissan Motors registered between ten- and twentyfold increases in sales and profits over the preceding decade. (In contrast, Ford Motor Company, even in its most flourishing ten-year period during the 1920s, did not achieve such spectacular advances.)[7] For the most part, success in the automobile industry and the electrical and electronics industries was based on firm-driven innovations, quality production, and exceptional international competitiveness.

In 1964 Toyota's "just-in-time" plant at Motomachi and the Nissan plant at Oppama began producing the country's first truly internationally competitive automobiles. Symbolically, national bicycle and motorcycle production leveled off; production of three-wheeled vehicles fell to one-third of what it had been in 1963, and the number of automobiles exceeded 500,000 units for the first time. (In 1967 the figure was up to 1.4 million; in 1968 it topped 2 million.)[8] As late as 1960, Japanese-based firms had only 1 percent of the world market in automobiles; by 1970 this share had rocketed to 20 percent.[9] By 1972, Japanese firms were producing 4 million units per year, over one-quarter destined for export.[10]

In contrast to such privately engineered successes in automobiles, government industrial policy figured heavily in the computer industry. For example, Fujitsu—in conjunction with NEC and Oki and in coordination with a government project directed by the Ministry of International Trade and Industry (MITI)—produced the FACOM 230–250, Japan's first joint government–private-sector machine. Also in 1964, MITI began another computer project involving the nation's six largest producers and aimed at developing specialized integrated circuits.[11] The HITAC 5020 was installed at Tokyo University as the nation's largest mainframe computer,[12] and Japanese computer manufacturers' share of the national market leaped from 29.7 percent in 1963 to 42.8 percent in 1964, up from less than 7 percent only five years earlier. In 1965, this trajectory of indigenous control went to over 52 percent, distinguishing Japan as the only industrialized nation in which IBM did not hold a majority stake in the national computer market.[13] There, the government's role in developing the computer industry was constant and critical.[14]

Government efforts to restructure many Japanese industrial sectors fell largely to MITI. That agency's efforts also peaked in 1964, with the introduction of the Special Measures Law for the Promotion of Designated Industries.[15] As the brainchild of MITI's Sahashi Shigeru, the law's aim was to enhance the agency's capacity to reorganize "designated" industries, such as had been done in computers. From the MITI-Sahashi perspective, Japan's economy continued to be dominated by an excess of protected enterprises, too many small factories, and too little capacity to generate true international competitiveness. Private-sector collaboration under

MITI's leadership was deemed essential to modernize sectors critical to the long-term enhancement of the national economy. Without such coordinated modernization, MITI argued, Japan as a nation would remain highly vulnerable to the depredations of international competition.[16]

The LDP and the Ikeda governments had approved the bill for submission. Critics, meanwhile, castigated the proposal as little more than another effort to enhance the already oligopolistic character of Japanese firms, making them even more subject to bureaucratic oversight and correspondingly less responsive to consumer interests and international competition. The battle over this proposed law, which eventually resulted in its quiet demise in mid-1964, was a microcosmic reflection of the broader regime orientation toward industrial policy and sectoral reorganization; it was also one of the high points of Japanese bureaucratic efforts to oversee the national economy.

Japanese consumers were both catalysts and beneficiaries of the nation's rapid rise in productivity. In the mid-1950s hardly any Japanese owned electric vacuums, washing machines, refrigerators, or television sets; by 1964, 27 percent had vacuums, 61 percent had washers, 38 percent had refrigerators, and nearly 90 percent had televisions. Similar jumps occurred in transistor radios, cameras, radios, and sewing machines.[17]

Marking Japan's new level of manufacturing and financial sophistication, the country joined the OECD and advanced to Article 8 status in the International Monetary Fund (IMF) during 1964, effectively ensuring its acceptance as a full-fledged member of the community of industrialized democracies. Japan's new stature was recognized as well by the fact that the general meeting of the IMF and the World Bank, with some 1800 representatives from 102 nations, was held at the Hotel Okura in Tokyo during the fall of 1964. Japanese Prime Minister Ikeda gave the keynote address just as his plan to "Double the National Income in Ten Years" was at its midpoint and well ahead of its scheduled 9 percent per annum growth rate. Ikeda proudly noted that postwar Japan had achieved in twenty years what had been impossible for prewar Japan to achieve in eighty.

Overall, as Table 1 demonstrates, the 1960s were, statistically, phenomenal years. The rates of economic growth, investment, and labor and manufacturing productivity were all at their high points during this period.

At the same time, the conservative political regime involved more than simply "economic success," "picking winners," and "increased competition." It also sought to improve conditions in those sectors that such an economic whirlwind might otherwise leave behind. For example, in agriculture—one of Japan's least competitive sectors but also one of the conservative regime's primary sources of support—1964 saw LDP backbenchers force through a substantial 14 percent increase in the price paid by the government to rice growers. This price increase, the largest ever in a single year, demonstrated the ability of farmers to extract high prices for their inefficiently produced goods.[18]

The year 1964 was also marked by the highest number of textile bankruptcies in the postwar era.[19] The government responded with a textile bill under which the

Table 1. Selected economic indicators for Japan

	1945–50	1950–55	1955–60	1960–65	1965–70	1970–75	1975–80
Growth rate	9.4	10.9	8.7	9.7	12.2	5.1	5.6
Investment rate	8.3	10.8	8.7	18.5	18.5	17.8	14.7
Relative price	0.89	1.37	1.45	1.25	1.02	0.98	0.86
Labor productivity growth	9.4	10.9	8.7	9.7	12.2	5.1	5.6
Increase in manufacturing productivity	—	12.0	9.6	7.9	12.3	2.0	7.0

Source: Yutaka Kosai, *The Era of High-Speed Growth: Notes on the Postwar Japanese Economic System* (Tokyo: University of Tokyo, 1986), pp. 5, 7.

Japan Development Bank offered ¥1 billion to textile firms so they could reduce "excess capacity." In addition, the Agency for Small and Medium Sized Industries was directed to help such firms with low interest loans. Over the next two years, the government provided subsidies totaling ¥6.3 billion (U.S. $17.3 million).[20]

Agriculture and textiles were not alone. The coal industry was in serious decline.[21] Steel minimills had several more years before serious troubles set in, but they too were showing signs of declining competitiveness. In short, although segments of the Japanese political economy during 1964 were growing rapidly and becoming more competitive internationally, declining and uncompetitive industries were posing serious problems. The government responded with cartelized reorganization and subsidization.[22]

The tremendous expansion of the economy, the improving lifestyles of citizens, and the generous compensation for those not favored by "the market" combined to fracture opposition to LDP rule. As recently as 1960, the opposition parties and their allies had mobilized huge segments of the population, bringing the capital to a standstill for two months and nearly toppling the Kishi government. But the previously united opposition quickly fractured as dissident groups in the labor movement split from the then dominant federation, Sōhyō, and eventually formed Dōmei—a more moderate, largely private-sector federation. In addition, 1964 saw the formation of the IMF-JC (International Metal Workers' Federation—Japan Committee), an economically oriented federation that was to become a voice for depoliticized unionist activities in subsequent decades. When Tekkō Rōren (Federation of Steel Workers' Unions) joined IMF-JC two years later, the organizational and strategic division between public-sector and private-sector unions was essentially complete; Sōhyō and its largely public-sector affiliates pursued a radical class and political agenda while Dōmei, the IMF-JC, and their private-sector affiliates opted for more moderate economic unionism.

In parallel, union membership, which had been as high as 50 percent of the workforce in 1950, had fallen to 33 percent in 1964; from there it continued to drop steadily over the next three decades.[23] Yet, in 1964, strikes, days lost to labor disputes, and total numbers of workers involved in strikes were all at historic highs.[24] Relations between business and labor remained brittle and fractious, hardly foretelling the "labor-management harmony" that subsequently captured so much international attention.

Opposition to the LDP was further diluted by the formation in November 1964 of the Clean Government Party (CGP—Kōmeitō). Heavily dependent on the support of Sōka Gakkai, the religious movement, it represented a second "party of the center" along with the Democratic Socialist Party (DSP), which had formed in 1960. These two small, centrist parties marked the beginning of the end of the two-party competition that had prevailed since 1955.[25]

Two other emblematic political events from 1964 warrant mention: first, the unprecedented third election of Ikeda Hayato as the LDP's party president in July, and then less than six months later his retirement and replacement by Sato Eisaku. Both men had been long-term bureaucrats before entering electoral politics. Both were also singularly committed to, and deeply associated with, a political economy of high growth, close ties to the United States, and a minimal tolerance for the ideological confrontations that had earlier divided Japanese society. Indeed, 1964 also saw an end to the Commission on the Constitution, which had for a decade been considering the highly charged issue of constitutional revision. The combined twelve years of executive control by Ikeda and Sato was the background for what Yamaguchi has labeled the "Golden Age of LDP Politics."[26]

The LDP benefited at the polls from the economy's stellar performance, its own internal leadership coherence, the fragmentation of its political opponents, and the compensation for those slow to adjust economically. Intriguingly, a 1963 public security report recognized the key role played by national economic success in the electoral turnaround of the early 1960s, noting that economic growth had defused the political appeals of the Japanese left and given rise to a more pervasive ideology of GNP-ism.[27] A mere three years after the 1960 toppling of the Kishi government, the LDP won 55 percent of the vote in the lower house elections and over 60 percent of the parliamentary seats, while the main opposition party, the JSP, drew only 29 percent of the vote.[28] In the upper house, the conservatives held 142 of 250 seats (56.8 percent) compared to only 66 seats (26.4 percent) for the JSP.[29] No other political party in the industrialized world commanded such a dominant electoral position.

Turning finally to international affairs, 1964 was also the year in which China first tested nuclear weapons and entered the five-nation "nuclear club." Although China was Japan's major geopolitical counterweight in Asia, and the White House concluded that China's testing would lead Japan to respond by "going nuclear," in fact the Japanese government's commitment to a low military posture remained unshaken. The country continued to trust its defense to the U.S.-Japan Security Treaty, the American nuclear umbrella, U.S. troops on Japanese soil, and a powerful U.S. Seventh Fleet. In 1964, Japan's national defense expenditures were only 1.2 percent of GNP; three years later they fell below the 1 percent mark where they remained for another twenty years. Overt shifts in the Asian power balance were either not perceived as such by Japan's leaders or not deemed sufficiently threatening to alter the country's commitment to low military expenditures and its focus on economic growth.

This policy balance was captured in one 1964 issue of the prestigious journal *Chūō Kōron*. An article entitled "Japan as a Maritime Nation," by Kyoto University professor Kosaka Masataka, touted the wisdom of Japan's low military budgets and the national focus on economic advances: "From a strictly military point of view, Japan's 'neomercantilist' diplomacy has been adequate for two reasons: First, the development of nuclear weapons has greatly lessened the ethical justification, as well as the effectiveness, of military power. Second, since Japan has been fully protected by the U.S. Seventh Fleet, in terms of defense her own rearmament would have been superfluous. From a political point of view, Yoshida's 'neomercantilism' has harmonized with Japan's postwar democratization."[30]

Congruent with this viewpoint, the U.S. Department of State, in conjunction with Japanese Ambassador Edwin O. Reischauer, sent to the White House a secret policy paper on the future of Japan. Urging continued top-level U.S. support for Japanese economic goals, the report recommended a "firm Executive Branch resistance of American industry demands for curtailment of Japanese imports."[31] America's anticommunism became the justification for keeping the American market open to support Japan's export drive.

At best, such snapshots capture only freeze-frames of highly complex interactions. What happens outside the frame, or before or after the picture is taken, may well be vital to understanding the events depicted. Any attempt to capture Japan's political economy by summarizing a dozen or so events at any single point in time is obviously selective and impressionistic. By adding dynamics and change, however, snapshots can turn into something like a video that highlights and contextualizes key aspects of the regime.

I noted in Chapter 1 that a regime has three critical components: a public policy profile, political and economic institutions, and a socioeconomic coalitional base. Focusing on the mid-1960s, I shall now examine each element in detail and emphasize how it differed from its counterparts in other industrialized democracies. Because public policies are typically the most visible and malleable elements of any regime, they provide a fruitful starting point.

The Public Policies of Embedded Mercantilism

The conservative regime's policy profile, particularly in regard to economics, was simultaneously the glue holding the conservative regime together and the lubricant smoothing interactions among its components. Otherwise fractious groups with diverse and competing agendas became fused into a singular "conservative" bloc through the benefits each received. The result was the continuing agglutination of the socioeconomic alliance undergirding the conservative regime and the insulation of prevailing institutional arrangements from serious political challenges.

Underlying Japanese policies was a pervasive economic nationalism that had dominated elite thinking since the arrival of Perry's Black Ships in 1854. Yet, for the first time since the Meiji Restoration, Japan could pursue its economic agenda without being involved in, or preparing for, war. Japan's postwar economic nationalism was decoupled from past links to high levels of military spending. Postwar policy involved a mercantilistic, rather than a militaristic, economic nationalism; the samurai surrendered to the salaryman.[32] It is a complex that can best be characterized as "embedded mercantilism."

Mercantilism seeks to advance the macroeconomic interests of a nation-state through catch-up policies involving the protection and nurturance of domestic industries. Japan's mercantilism stood in stark contrast to the more internationally pervasive doctrines of laissez-faire and economic liberalism, which promoted easy market entry, price competition, and the short-term economic choices of individuals. Because Japan's protectionism was intended to develop export industries, however, its mercantilism differed from standard import substitution policies such as were pervasive in much of Latin America, which focused primarily on domestic autarky. Finally, Japan's mercantilism departed from continental European economic policies, which invariably included strong elements of social welfare benefits and individual citizen protection.

Japan's policies were straightforward: macroeconomic success through ever more internationally competitive Japanese firms in high-value-added industries. Achieving that goal required two broad transformations. First, the economy had to be converted from its heavy reliance on agriculture and small industry to one that was more capital intensive and that produced ever more technically sophisticated products, particularly in manufactured goods. Vital to this effort were improvements in the national economic infrastructure, including port and road facilities, industrial water supplies, rail networks, electricity generation facilities, and the like, along with human infrastructural improvements such as higher levels of education, improved health, and better workplace training.

Second, production and organization methods within Japanese firms had to be upgraded to make them more internationally competitive. Doing so required investment capital, new production technologies, fewer bottlenecks among suppliers, producers, and distributors as well as a host of microeconomic firm- or sector-specific improvements. Positive results at this level required a fusion of macroeconomic government policies and changes in the microeconomic behavior and organization of individual firms.

Official governmental policies designed to achieve these goals were sweeping, complex, and interrelated. For analytic purposes, however, it is possible to think of Japan's mercantilism as a fabric woven from three main threads.

First, domestic markets were almost completely sealed off from foreign competitive imports in such areas as agriculture, basic materials, and the sophisticated manufacturing industries in which Japan sought to gain international competitiveness. Most of the Japanese market was thus restricted to competition among products made within Japanese-owned plants. In addition, the Japanese capital market remained under domestic control, which prevented easy foreign takeovers of Japanese firms and allowed broad domestic control over savings, monetary policy, and national capital utilization.

Second, mercantilism enhanced the international competitiveness of numerous firms and products. With key sectors buffered from outside competition, the government pursued an aggressive industrial policy, which in conjunction with private-sector actions reshaped many of Japan's manufacturing industries. Yet while the Japanese market was heavily insulated from unwanted external penetration, the country hardly pursued autarky; improved sales were sought not just in the domestic market but worldwide. Walled-off domestic markets were intended to generate export strength, not just to prevent foreign competition.

The third thread involved strict limitations on domestic government expenditures. In addition to encouraging household savings and limiting individual consumer purchases, the government kept the tax burden low, pursued tight fiscal policies and held down expenditures for social welfare and defense. The national civil service also remained small.[33]

Although these policies all appear to be congruent with "economic common sense," despite their departure from neoclassical economic theory, one additional component was economically at odds with the logic of mercantilist growth: the government provided, for obvious political reasons, generous side payments to many politically important but economically inefficient sectors of the economy and regions of the country, thereby creating a broadly egalitarian thrust to Japan's economic transformation that left the country with far fewer personal and regional inequalities than all but the most committed social democracies.

Each thread blended with the others when woven into the fabric of the conservative regime's overall public policy profile. For analytic purposes, however, each can be examined in relative isolation.

Insulation of the Domestic Market

At the end of World War II, productivity in the United States was approximately three times what it had been during the prewar years. The nation's GNP was fully six times greater than that of the second-ranking economy, Great Britain (by the mid-1990s it was less than twice as great). American corporations emerged from the war untouched by bombings and invasion, leaving them with an international competitiveness vastly greater than most of their overseas competitors. This comparative imbalance allowed numerous American firms to expand their foreign operations and to gain important market shares throughout the world. In the 1950s and 1960s, U.S. products and U.S. capital dominated world markets to an extent reached neither before nor since.

Yet, in contrast to most Western European and Latin American countries, Japan remained virtually unpenetrated by U.S. (and other) foreign capital. Even though Japanese firms were in dire need of capital and technology, most were wary of surrendering managerial control to foreigners. Unlike many of their European coun-

terparts, Japanese business and political leaders had long been suspicious of significant foreign penetration of the core of the Japanese economy. As David Landes observes in his comparative study of Japanese and European industrialization in the
nineteenth century: "In Japan, industrial growth was unmistakably the answer to
the menace of foreign domination. In Europe, there was strong dissent on this point
right into the twentieth century."[34]

How quickly foreign dominance could be gained over an entire sector had been
made clear by the ease with which Western firms penetrated the Japanese oil refining industry during the U.S. occupation as well as by the unbalanced treatment
forced on Japan through both aviation and fisheries treaties.

Economic barbed wire was consequently erected around Japan, preventing penetration of the domestic economy by foreign firms, their products, and their capital. Only a few narrow gates were left open for essential imports such as the raw materials and the machine tools needed for domestic manufacturing. Equally insulated
were the nation's capital markets; transactions by potential investors and borrowers
were confined within the nation's borders; foreign money was essentially kept out,
Japanese money kept in.

Critical to the maintenance of these barriers was the Foreign Exchange and
Control Law (FECL) and the Foreign Investment Law (FIL) which imposed a
strict quota system over the allocation of foreign currency used for imports. The
FECL was also based on a "negative principle" whereby all foreign exchange
transactions were effectively prohibited, except for those explicitly allowed by the
government. As James Horne phrases it, "The operation of the law, and the cabinet orders, ministerial ordinances and notices which set out the details in practice,
reflected the belief of government that it, and not the market, was the best judge
of how to maximize the benefits that could be derived from available foreign exchange."[35]

In practice, only a handful of foreign-owned subsidiaries were approved in Japan
during the 1950s and early 1960s. Accordingly, during the 1950s Japan was a less
popular host for U.S. foreign investment than any other industrialized country, as
well as such less appealing markets as Columbia, Peru, and the Philippines.[36]

Balance of payments considerations provided the initial rationale for these restrictions. Subsequently, other concerns were introduced; for example, investment
was allowed only if it did not unduly challenge small-sized enterprises, seriously
disturb industrial order, or severely impede the advancement of Japanese technology.[37] A series of liberalizations took place in 1963 when Japan was preparing to join
the OECD; others followed in July 1967, March 1969, September 1970, and August 1971. But the burden of proof continued to fall on potential investors, who had
to convince Japanese officials—invariably dubious—that the proposed investment
would not be detrimental. Into the early 1970s, with few major exceptions, Japan
was a country almost devoid of significant foreign direct investment.[38] As late as
1970, despite being the largest foreign noncommunist market, Japan still ranked
eleventh among recipients of U.S. foreign direct investment, well behind many European countries as well as behind Venezuela, Brazil, and Mexico.[39]

Tariffs and quotas played an initial role in limiting imports. Tariff rates rose with technological sophistication, from virtually zero on raw materials to over 60 percent on finished items such as automobiles. In addition, during the 1960s Japan retained import restrictions on some four hundred product categories. Only in 1962 did the government replace its short list of items which *could* be imported by a list of items which were explicitly prohibited. Until 1960, some 84 percent of Japan's total imports were subject to one form of restriction or another. In 1964, when Japan achieved Article 8 status in IMF, many of these overt measures of protection were discarded.[40] But a number of provisional tariffs were introduced, and overt export promotion policies were replaced by newer and more subtle policies such as extra depreciation for exports and overseas market development reserves.

The limits on foreign direct investment meant also that intracompany trade contributed little to foreign imports. Extensive restrictions on the import of most manufacturing goods and the high degree of manufactured exports from Japan left the country with one of the most skewed import-export balances in the industrial world.[41]

Until 1968, all technologies brought into the country were also governmentally screened, leaving Japan as the only OECD nation with such restrictions at that date. Until as late as 1974 restrictions were maintained on numerous technology imports. Furthermore, the government typically insisted that no single domestic company be allowed to enter into monopoly use agreements with holders of foreign technologies.[42] Foreign investment rights were typically surrendered only when the new technology was shared by several Japanese companies and only when it would increase exports from Japan.

Protection of Japan's manufacturing sector was complemented by national insulation from world capital markets. Because Japanese firms and citizens were essentially prohibited from investing abroad and foreign capital was controlled through the FECL, the nation's capital markets were buffered from fluctuations in worldwide interest rates and capital movements. Moreover, capital restrictions hindered foreign takeovers through stock accumulation or direct buyout.

Nor did Japanese capital flow outward. Thus, from 1951 until 1971, total Japanese direct foreign investment totaled just over $4 billion, with nearly 60 percent of that total coming between 1969 and 1971.[43] Through fiscal 1972, nearly three-quarters of Japan's limited overseas investments were in nonmanufacturing sectors. In effect, Japanese firms were not terribly active as overseas investors, and such investment as did occur was primarily for the acquisition of raw materials linked to the export of manufactured goods from the home islands.

Insulation from foreign capital markets also permitted the Ministry of Finance to maintain a low value for the Japanese yen. From 1949 until the breakdown of the Bretton Woods system in 1971, the yen was kept closely pegged to a rate of 360 yen to the U.S. dollar. As Japan's economy grew in strength and its balance of payments became increasingly positive, the yen become ever more undervalued. While this obviously undercut the comparative purchasing power of the Japanese consumer (and of Japanese importers as well), it provided an additional barrier to foreign imports. The ¥360 exchange rate made foreign goods extremely costly in Japan.

Capital market insulation also limited the options available to Japanese savers. For individuals, the most logical place to deposit their savings was the postal savings system. The system's interest rates, exceptionally low by international standards, were set by the government, making for negative, if tax-free, real rates to savers. Since Japanese personal savings rates, for a host of reasons, were among the highest in the world, vast sums thus became available to the government and the banking system for subsequent lending to corporations at exceptionally low rates.[44] Japan's economic growth thus rested heavily on a massive transfer of funds from Japanese households to Japanese corporations.

The sweeping restrictions on foreign competition served several purposes. The home markets of Japanese firms were insulated against direct competition from foreign firms enjoying much more sophisticated levels of production, particularly in areas such as steel, automobiles, cameras, and consumer electronics. Meanwhile, with little choice but to "buy Japanese," domestic consumer purchases provided in-country stimulation for numerous domestic producers. Given the large size of the Japanese domestic market, with its 110 to 120 million citizens, the "hothouse" strategy of nurturing domestic firms by home market protection worked exceedingly well for many Japanese manufacturers and for the national economy as a whole. Relatively secure home bases enabled many Japanese firms to develop market positions abroad, secure about their home flanks in ways that many European firms never were.

In effect, long after the war, Japan had a home "market" that was closed off from most signficant foreign competition. Somewhat like a minor league in sports, Japan was kept insulated from foreign competition until such time as the local players had demonstrated sufficient capability to move up to the more competitive major leagues, the international market. Hosting little foreign investment, purchasing relatively few foreign manufactured and consumer goods, and with a capital market effectively shut off from foreign monetary movements, Japan was less like the other advanced industrial democracies and far more like many of the developing economies of the world.

Moreover, unlike countries where there was a substantial cadre of self-interested business leaders who could profit economically by markets open to foreign direct investment, for the most part, Japan had few powerful compradors willing to cast their economic and political fortunes with foreigners at the risk of alienating the domestically oriented Japanese elite. A compelling economic nationalism and the homogeneity of Japan's political and economic elite worked as a strong counterbalance to any potential short-term interest particular firms might have had in greater foreign investment or manufacturing imports.[45]

Industrial Policy, Economic Concentration, and Export Promotion

From behind this protective barbed wire an extensive domestic industrial reordering was carried out through industrial policy, economic concentration, and export promotion. When the war ended, Japan had an exceptionally limited domestic base for production and international competition. Industrial restructuring and export promotion were logical choices. Japan's economic bureaucrats and business leaders rejected the philosophy of laissez-faire, "free trade," or "open markets" prevalent in Britain or the United States. To them, as Charles Kindleberger has suggested more generally, these concepts conveyed little more than protection for the economically powerful and the established exporter: "the headstart is regarded as a divine right, and [protection] to let a foreign industry gather strength to meet import competition as an offense against morality."[46] Rather than accepting the inevitable "comparative advantages" described in Riccardian economic theory—advantages that would have directed Japan toward production based on its extensive supply of cheap labor—Japanese economic bureaucrats sought to use activist policies as a means of generating "competitive advantages" for Japanese firms.[47] To carry out this transformation, a bevy of policies were put into place.

A series of economic plans issued by the Economic Planning Agency provided broad guidelines within which national industrial policies were shaped. Actual industrial reorganization was carried out primarily by MITI through sector-by-sector restructuring. In the earliest stages, the targeted industries involved such basics as steel, electric power, coal, shipbuilding, and chemicals as well as such quality exports as binoculars, simple electronic equipment, and motorcycles. Gradually, as technology and production processes improved and domestic markets developed, resources and attention were redirected toward more complicated manufacturing processes for automobiles, heavy machinery, and more complicated consumer electronics.

More concentrated oligopolistic structures were one result. During the 1960s, more than five hundred major and minor mergers occurred each year; by the end of the 1960s and the beginning of the 1970s this figure was over a thousand annually.[48] In 1960, 93 percent of Japan's companies had been capitalized at less than ¥500,000; by 1974 this figure had dropped to 76 percent, while the number of corporations capitalized at over ¥1 billion had more than quadrupled. Industrial concentration continued steadily. By 1974 five corporations or fewer controlled 90 percent or more of the markets in the steel, beer, nylon, acrylic, aluminum ore, automobile, and pane glass industries.[49] The capstone of MITI's "merger mania" took place in 1968 with a huge merger in the steel industry. New Nippon Steel, built out of the fusion of Yawata and Fuji Steel, became the world's second largest producer with 36 percent of domestic market share.[50]

While many mergers took place at MITI's initiative, not all of its consolidation efforts were successful, including attempts to bring about greater cohesion in automobiles and electronics. MITI's power, real as it no doubt was, had its limits. Mergers involved more than simple government fiat. Congruence with business and financial goals was critical to most MITI successes; government and business were engaged in a process involving what Richard Samuels has labeled "reciprocal consent."[51]

Governmental control over scarce capital was one of its major tools for reorganization. Targeted use of this capital was critical. Thus the Ministry of Finance, starting in late 1957, began a policy subsequently known as "window guidance," under which individual banks, through linkages to the Bank of Japan and the ministry, were "encouraged" to lend to specific firms or types of firms. While basic monetary policy remained tight, specific exceptions were made for designated industries. Between 1963 and 1967, equity financing provided only 6.2 percent of the new capital for nonfinancial corporations, compared to 57.3 percent from public or private loans and 30.5 percent in trade credits.[52]

Financial assistance to targeted firms came in the form of low-interest loans, aid in securing loans from private banks, accelerated depreciation, and tax-free reserves. Moreover, through the FECL, MITI used selective allocations of scarce raw materials and scarce foreign exchange credits to further its industrial targeting goals. MITI also assisted favored firms in acquiring overseas technology, duty-free equipment, tax subsidies, and sweeping exemptions from the country's ever weakening antimonopoly laws. A good deal of the authority to carry out these policies rested on formal legal provisions, but a not insignificant amount grew out of the less formal power associated with "administrative guidance."[53]

The successes that resulted for Japanese manufacturing are widely known. Japan moved from producing approximately one-tenth of the world's ships in 1950 to one-half in 1972. Technological improvements in steel production were so rapid as to preclude foreign steel from entering Japanese markets, allowing Japanese steel producers to more than double their output between 1953 and 1959, almost double it again by 1962, and to become the world's third largest manufacturer by 1964. Petroleum and coal products, also government targeted, expanded at the rate of 17.9 percent per year between 1953 and 1971. Chemicals expanded at nearly 15 percent per year during the same period.

Massive spillovers occurred to sectors not subject to explicit government targeting. As late as the 1950s, Japan had virtually no meaningful automobile production capability; by 1972 it was producing 4 million units per year, of which nearly one-half were destined for export. As late as the mid-1960s, Japan's companies were barely coming to grips with the simplest of computer chips; by the end of the 1970s they controlled about 40 percent of the world market in 16K RAM chips. Although the specifics differ, the picture is similar in 35 mm cameras, home electronics equipment, watches, calculators, small trucks, machine tools, and dozens of other products.

A great deal of this success came from the economies of scale achieved by reorganization and oligopolization advanced by MITI and carried out by individual firms. Improved production processes, personnel practices, technology developments, and the like were also essential to the overall success. Indeed, several of Japan's most successful industries (e.g., 35 mm cameras, household appliances, and consumer electronics), as well as several of its individually most successful firms (Sony, Matsushita, and Honda), were not the targets of explicit government assistance. All the same, government actions in a host of industries, particularly those that provided important forward or backward linkages, contributed unmistakably to the overall improvement of the national economy.[54] Perhaps most important was the pervasively pro-business climate generated by government policies, conducive to a firm's risk taking and expansion whether or not it was a direct recipient of government largess.

Two central points are clear. First, Japanese policies were not designed in accord with any sacrosanct abstraction called "the market," nor were they designed to advance "consumer interests." Government officials took their central task to be the shaping of the economy in ways they deemed beneficial to the national interest, and this was measured largely in macrostatistics rather than in enhanced consumer choices or lower prices. Second, in manipulating market forces, the formal and informal tools in the governmental tool kit were plentiful. The result, as I have argued elsewhere, was that the Japanese government became the doorman determining what came into and went out of Japan.[55]

Government protection to specific firms or industries typically creates at least two problems. First, as most neoclassical economists are quick to point out, protection and guaranteed domestic markets reduce the pressures on sheltered firms to modernize equipment, engage in extensive research and development, improve product quality, pursue most effective production methods, and continue technological upgrading. Why improve efficiency and consumer responsiveness when there are few incentives to do so? Second, when governments seek to create "national champions" at home, these champions are often absolved of the need to achieve competitiveness beyond the nation's borders. Instead, the political temptation is strong to make such firms the high-paying employers of last resort for inept cronies. Politicians mandate prices so as to benefit end users of the national champion's products. Producers who dominate domestic sales can revert to high prices and poor quality, making them dubious competitors in the international marketplace. In short, a host of inefficiencies are built in.

Japanese industrial policies avoided both problems. When specific industrial sectors were restructured, several manufacturers were aided simultaneously. Government policy encouraged individual firms to pursue the most sophisticated technologies, internationally best practices, high research and development, and continual upgrading of facilities.

Competition among major firms thus remained vigorous if compartmentalized and domesticated. Although they rarely competed on price, firms still had strong economic incentives to pursue continual innovation, improved products, better service, and a host of other characteristics. In turn, this made many of them highly competitive internationally. Moreover, firms competing internationally had every incentive to become as sophisticated and as cost- and quality-conscious as possible. Cooperation and coordination were made compatible with competition.[56]

Because Japan in the late 1980s and early 1990s was widely seen as a "trading state,"[57] it is well to remember that in 1960 Japanese exports accounted for only about 3 percent of the world's total exports (imports were only a slightly higher 4 percent). In 1965, imports and exports combined represented less than 10 percent of Japan's total GNP.[58] Nevertheless, a major goal of governmental cartelization and industrial policies was the promotion of Japanese exports. Thus, under the Export and Import Trading Act of August 1952, the Japanese government explicitly permitted exporters to enter cartel agreements on price, quality, design, or other matters connected to the export of their products. During the same year, the Export Income Deduction System allowed companies to take a straight tax deduction for a portion of their net income from export sales.[59] A host of export incentives were also offered: special tax deductions, exemption from anti-cartel provisions, preferential access to scarce credit, lower borrowing rates, more rapid depreciation on equipment, customs exemptions for specified imported machinery, special tax status for firms with substantial increases in exports, tax deferments, and in some cases overt subsidization.

In addition to such firm-specific measures, the government established the Japan External Trade Organization (JETRO) as a quasi-official export promotion body to aid overseas market research activities, as well as trade centers and advertisements for Japanese products. Also funded from the national budget was the Japan Plant Export Association, designed to foster the export of heavy machinery and entire factories by performing international consultation services. At least another ten research centers, promotion projects, and export associations were governmentally funded during the late 1960s and early 1970s.[60] All provided generic export assistance to any Japanese firm seeking to its help.

Japan's wartime reparations also stimulated development of overseas markets. Reparations payments to several Southeast Asian countries began in the early 1950s. Typically involving export credits, tied loans, plant exports, and long-term investment projects that relied on Japanese capital, these opened markets for Japanese firms as well as providing tremendous opportunities for personal profit by many Japanese business and political leaders.[61] The reparations experience subsequently became the model for Japan's broader efforts at "foreign aid" to the region. Until 1972 Japanese aid was typically tied to the purchase of Japanese goods. Untied Development Assistance Committee (DAC) aid from the Japanese government remained exceptionally low by comparative standards.

In addition to Southeast Asia, Japan's other major export market was the United States. Here, U.S. governmental policies were at least as critical as Japanese policies in the development of markets for Japanese companies. Emerging from World War II as the major economic and strategic hegemon of the Western world, and committed to an economic system based on open markets and economic linkages, plus a system of alliances designed to "contain communism," the U.S. government welcomed Japanese imports on both economic and political grounds. U.S. governmental policy for at least the first thirty years following the war remained focused primarily on the strategic and military aspects of the bilateral relationship, demanding little in the way of economic reciprocity through the opening of Japan's markets to U.S. products.

This combination of economically dominant trade links to Southeast Asia and politically constructed trade links to the United States left Japanese exports headed in two directions—south and west to Asia, or across the Pacific to North America. During the mid-1960s, approximately 30 percent of Japan's exports went to Southeast Asia and another 27–28 percent went to the United States. In contrast, Europe took only about 10 percent, Africa 7–8 percent, and Latin America about 5 percent. With the exception of Canada, no other industrialized democracy had such a heavy reliance on so few markets.

Balanced Budgets and Small Government

Tight fiscal policy and small government were the third key element of the conservative Japanese regime's overall policy profile. From the end of the occupation until 1965, Japan pursued exceptional fiscal austerity, often generating overbalanced budgets.[62] Such austerity meant an exceptionally low utilization of public-sector bonds, which limited private competition for scarce funds. Since private firms dominated the market for scarce capital, their overall capital costs were lowered. Tight fiscal policy also permitted the government to hold down the overall tax burden. Indeed, in many years, the budget was sufficiently overbalanced to allow for tax cuts, an exceptionally popular political measure in any nation.

Japanese budgetary politics is a well-told tale. Every year, the Ministry of Finance would issue guidelines that set upper limits on requests from individual governmental agencies. Initially, these limits were rather generous; they were constricted over time. Consequently, individual ministries, despite their most ardent desires to begin new programs, could do so if and only if they could submit a budgetary proposal that did not exceed ministry guidelines. This normally meant that each agency continually had to revise its priorities, scrapping or reducing its less favored programs to allow for new or expanded activities somewhere else. The zero sum game of agency-to-agency competition in budgeting was thus reduced.

The two largest budget items for most industrialized democracies during the postwar years were defense and social welfare. Japanese budgets kept both items contrastingly small, typically the lowest of any major industrialized country. From the 1950s to the early 1970s, the United States devoted between 7 and 9 percent of its GNP to military expenditures, and most of the major Western European countries were spending at least 4–5 percent. In contrast, from 1956 on, as a matter of policy, Japan's military budget rarely consumed more than 1–1.3 percent of that country's GNP.[63]

Not that the choice of a civilian orientation was completely autonomous. Demilitarization policies under the U.S. occupation had completely dismantled Japan's war machine, while pacifist sentiments had been institutionalized in Article 9 of the Constitution. Serious disagreements about this policy arose at various times within conservative political ranks (these are detailed elsewhere). But during the mid-1960s significant increases for military expenditures had no effective support within the conservative camp. As a proportion of the total budget, military expenditures fell sharply. In 1950, they accounted for 19.8 percent of the government's general expenditures; by 1960 this was down to 10 percent, and by 1970 it was just over 7 percent. As a percent of GNP, military expenditures fell from 1.8 percent in 1955 to 0.79 percent between 1955 and 1970. Low expenditures for defense in turn meant more money and talent for the civilian sector, lower government expenditures, and a reduced demand for scarce capital.

The contribution of low military expenditures to Japan's national growth has been estimated by Hugh Patrick and Henry Rosovsky. They conclude that if Japan had spent as much as 6 or 7 percent of GNP on defense, the national growth rate would have dropped by as much as two percentage points annually. In this sense low spending translated to a 30 percent increase in the total economy during the period 1954–74.[64] Without question, 30 percent slower growth would have made for a substantially less prosperous, and undoubtedly politically quite different, Japan.

The Japanese governmental budget was sparing in social welfare as well—quite a different pattern from the one emerging in Europe. Unlike Japan's low military expenditures, which were markedly inconsistent with prewar practices, low expenditures for social welfare measures represented a historical continuity. The Japanese government had long avoided sweeping and costly nationwide programs in health care, retirement benefits, or other social welfare measures. Instead, occupation-based systems were supplemented by a thinly woven, publicly funded "safety net" that offered low levels of benefits for those who would otherwise be ineligible for occupation-linked benefits.

The Employees Pension System (EPS) and the National Pension System (NPS) were established in 1954 and 1959 respectively. These were paralleled by the National Health Insurance (NHI) and Employee Health Insurance (EHI) programs. The two "employees" programs (EPS and EHI) were linked to job status; the "national" programs (NPS and NHI) provided government safety nets. Unlike most Western European systems, neither health care nor retirement benefits were treated as "rights of citizenship."[65] Essentially, the public programs remained small and residual; they provided low benefits and, in the case of the pensions system, required a long period of contributions to gain eligibility.

Public welfare expenditure in Japan during the early 1960s thus accounted for only 7 percent of GDP, while the comparable figure was 17 percent in France, 16.5 percent in Germany, 13.6 percent in Italy and Sweden, 12.6 percent in the United Kingdom, and 10.3 percent in the United States. Income maintenance expenditure also showed no substantial change throughout the 1960s. Japan spent 2.1 percent of GDP for such programs in 1962 and 2.8 percent in 1972, only a third of the OECD average.[66]

Retirement pensions for the noncontributing elderly were minuscule even into the early 1970s.[67] Only about 3.4 million Japanese were eligible for benefits as recently as the early 1970s. As Japan moved into the 1970s, it was clearly the industrial democracies' most conspicuous "welfare laggard."

At the same time, despite the absence of a European-style welfare state, Japanese citizens had universal access to reasonably good health care. The elderly were typically cared for by families. Labor market policies were designed to provide neither unemployment checks nor public relief jobs.[68] Instead, a proactive labor-market policy fusing government and business activities put in place a market-oriented nexus of job training policies. These in turn helped sustain relatively full employment and, more important, avoided measures that might otherwise have resulted in a permanent or semipermanent underclass of unemployed. Thus, despite limited public-sector welfare spending, Japan's national unemployment rate remained among the lowest in the industrialized democracies while its infant mortality rate dropped and the life expectancy of its citizens rose to among the highest in the industrialized world.

Finally, keeping government small entailed freezing or shrinking the number of government officials. Few countries have demonstrated any sustained ability to reduce the size of their civil services. A series of administrative reforms starting in the early 1950s made Japan an exception. Bureaucratic reform combined outside political initiative with a great deal of latitude for individual ministries and agencies in the specifics of their restructuring. Curbing bureaucratic sprawl aided conservative efforts to maintain low-cost government. It also bolstered the overall competitiveness, efficiency, and esprit of the agencies and personnel still in place.

Thus, in two critical areas, military expenditures and social welfare, the conservative regime's spending policies were exceptionally low by comparison to the other industrialized democracies, but they fit into the much broader national pattern of balanced budgets and minimalist government. Government size was kept down, furthering inexpensive government. Low-cost government in turn meant more and cheaper capital for private (typically manufacturing) interests. Once the economy began to grow at double-digit rates, government revenues increased automatically, allowing expanded government activities along with frequent, and politically popular, tax cuts.

Side Payments

These first three elements of Japan's policy profile are consistent with "pro-growth" efforts. They also help to explain Japan's tremendous economic performance. Yet, equally integral to the conservative regime's economic policy profile were policies that had a political rather than an economic rationale. These involved side payments to the country's less economically advanced sectors: rice farmers, the small-business sector, geographical regions lacking high-growth industries, and, increasingly, industries in decline.

In the mid-1960s agriculture played a minuscule role in Japan's total economy. At the time of the Meiji Restoration, approximately 80 percent of Japan's employed population was involved in farming. As late as 1908 agriculture contributed just under 30 percent of Japan's total net domestic product. Immediately after the Second World War, farming still engaged over 50 percent of the population,[69] and in 1953 it accounted for some 17.5 percent of the net domestic product.[70] By the mid-1960s these figures had dropped to about 15 percent of the population and 8 percent of the NDP.[71] Furthermore, between 1960 and 1965, the farm population was falling by about 5 percent per year.[72]

By this time, Japanese farms were highly efficient in productivity per acre but hardly economical in total returns. In the mid-1960s, Denmark, France, and West Germany all had farm outputs *per unit of land* that were only 21–31 percent of Japan's, yet their output *per laborer* was from three to four times higher.[73] Japanese farming had become intensive horticulture on Lilliputian plots.

The vote from farmers and their families nevertheless remained vastly more important to the electoral fortunes of many individual LDP parliamentarians than any contribution they might make to the national economy. Meanwhile, the Ministry of Agriculture had its Food Agency, an extensive food control system with twenty thousand employees; crop prices were a critical component of the Ministry's budget and activities. Hence strong political and bureaucratic pressures continued for government programs to subsidize rice farmers.

Under the food control system put in place during and immediately after the war, there was effectively no private market for rice sales. Instead the government bought all the rice produced within the country at one price and then resold it to consumers at a different price. Originally the two prices were relatively close. By the 1960s, however, the gap had widened considerably, providing an extensive subsidy program for rice farmers.

As Michael Donnelly has noted, one of the unique features of this program was that government policy sought to remunerate family labor in farming at levels "substantially equivalent to average wage rates in manufacturing."[74] If rice farmers could not increase their efficiency through labor-saving devices, the government would compensate them by buying their rice at high prices. And because the setting of the price of rice took place outside the normal budgetary process, rice subsidies were not subjected to the same tight Ministry of Finance controls as the annual budget. Producer prices doubled between 1960 and 1967, leaving official deficits linked to the program of rice prices at record highs.[75]

Similarly, the rapid growth and technological modernization of Japan's larger businesses in the mid-1960s still left the Japanese economy "teeming with small-scale family enterprises, more so than any other advanced industrial country."[76] From then to now, Japan's has been simultaneously an economy of a few giants striding above numerous pygmies, the latter often linked to the former through extensive subcontracting arrangements.

Not surprisingly, such small businesses were also the object of compensatory policies, again because of their electoral clout. Generally speaking, most such businesses relied heavily on low wages and labor-intensive operations. Higher wages in the country's rapidly expanding larger firms put great pressure on the smaller ones to modernize or to raise wages. The governmental response was essentially twofold: policies to help smaller firms upgrade and modernize, and policies to sequester these firms from "excessive" market competition.

Many measures to encourage modernization came from the Basic Law for the Modernization of Small and Medium Sized Enterprises, enacted in July 1963, which set standards for product design, quality control, plant modernization, and product specialization and rationalization for these smaller firms. The government offered special subsidies, tax exemptions, and preferential financing from a special corporation set up to aid smaller firms in reaching these goals. In the early to mid-1960s some twenty industries were so designated; by 1966 the number had expanded to sixty-eight, and by 1974 it was up to 118, covering some 70 percent of the sales volume of smaller and medium-sized firms.[77]

Simultaneously, a sequence of measures protected slower moving firms from economic disaster. Most typically these occurred in sectors unamenable to easy modernization, for example, traditional commerce, retailing, services, and some manufacturing. Of particular note was the Small and Medium Enterprise Law of 1957, which allowed "business unions" aimed at preventing "excessive competition" and infiltration by larger firms.[78] Meanwhile the Large-Scale Store Law, originally passed in 1956 and revised in 1973, gave smaller firms, acting through their local Chambers of Commerce, the de facto right to prevent larger stores from competing against them in their local markets.

Also benefiting both sectors was the government's laxity toward farmers and smaller businesses on matters of environmental pollution, labor standards laws, tax collection, and zoning. In effect, an implicit bargain was struck between conservative politicians and the two sectors: "support us and we won't tax you."[79] Although it was not until much later that the phrase gained popularity, Japan had a "nine-six-three" tax system: wage earners paid 90 percent of the taxes they owed, small business 60 percent, and agriculture only 30 percent.

Regional policy was a third area in which political rationality trumped economic rationality. Japan's most successful firms were disproportionately concentrated in a relatively narrow industrial belt that ran along the Pacific Coast between Tokyo and Osaka. The country therefore developed several programs targeting specific regions for industrial development. In 1962 fifteen "new industrial cities," largely outside the Pacific coastal belt, were identified for special development funds; in 1964 six "special areas for industrial consolidation" were added. The result was a transfer of capital from Japan's major cities to its most underpopulated and industrially disadvantaged areas.

Conservative politicians also used the public works budget and various regional development schemes to transfer huge sums to their home districts, further distributing public pork. During the mid-1960s public works expenditures accounted for between 15 and 19 percent of the national budget—roughly twice as much as other major industrial countries.

Thus while Japan's economy modernized at warp speed in many sectors, other sectors and regions were actively protected, thereby warding off the worst consequences of rapid growth. Normally, rapid growth widens gaps in income and wealth; in Japan, politically driven policies of compensation reduced such gaps. Such compensation policies served as exceptionally powerful income levelers.

Two things are especially striking about the public policy profile of Japan during this time. First, policies typically dovetailed rather than operating at cross-purposes. Protection from outside competition complemented industrial policy and export-led growth; low-cost government allowed the concentration of scarce public re-sources on targeted industrial sectors; capital insulation gave government a power-ful weapon in industrial restructuring; the undervalued yen aided exports, and so on. The cumulative consequence was an ever deeper embedding of the entire na-tion in the complex of mercantilist policies.

Second, this policy profile had, unsurprisingly, a political rather than simply an economic logic. Political supporters of the conservative regime who did not benefit directly from the high-growth policies were amply rewarded from the public cof-fers. As a consequence, so long as exports brought high growth, economics and politics reinforced each other: there was little political incentive for government to dismantle protectionist barricades or for economic sectors to view their political in-terests as dramatically at odds.

Mercantilism and protectionist catch-up were widely accepted by most Japanese institutions and socioeconomic sectors. Erstwhile domestic critics of various fea-tures of the Japanese economy rarely challenged its broader mercantilist thrust. Unlike so many other industrialized democracies, therefore, Japanese elections were never seriously fought over issues of open versus closed markets; exporters and importers rarely clashed over macroeconomics; and powerful government agencies were uniformly tolerant of the nation's economic thrust. Japan's embed-ded mercantilism thus stood as a stark exception to the "embedded liberalism" that John Ruggie correctly argues permeated the OECD countries as a whole.[80]

The Socioeconomic Underpinnings
of Embedded Mercantilism

Critical to the character of any regime is its underlying socioeconomic base. How do the major segments of the economy ally with or oppose one another? Japan's un-derlying socioeconomic alliance structure during the 1960s was unique among the postwar democracies, resting as it did on a coalition among three key sectors—big business, smaller businesses, and agriculture—in support of the prevailing conser-vative regime, while organized labor was systematically excluded from government and formed the principal socioeconomic support base for the main opposition to the conservative regime.

As I noted in Chapter 1, soon after World War II labor and business within most major democracies had largely reconciled their most extreme differences. For coun-tries such as Italy and to some extent France, this simple picture was complicated by a divided labor movement, only part of which was cooperative with business, and by the enduring socioeconomic power of small farmers. In land-rich countries such as the United States, Australia, New Zealand, and Canada, agriculture re-mained economically powerful because of its strength in world markets, but even there some form of business-labor accord was in place.

In Japan, no such business-labor alliance emerged; rather, business and agricul-ture forged an antilabor alliance that relied, not on open domestic markets, but on the embedded mercantilist policies described above. The next chapter examines the process whereby this unlikely alliance was constructed. At this point, it suffices to say, the policies generated under embedded mercantilism both were aided by the alliance and served to keep that alliance intact.

Although portraits of Japan as socially homogeneous are overdrawn, cleavages in race, ethnicity, language, immigration, or religion were far less critical in Japanese politics than they were in many other industrialized countries. Instead, Japan's politics during the early postwar years pitted self-styled "conservatives," with their relatively fixed socioeconomic alliances, against self-styled "progressives" and their own support base. Even though there were several parties in the opposition, as late as 1976 they buried their differences on major issues in the interests of opposition unity. Their confrontations played out primarily over two issues. First, there was the standard business-labor division that had critically shaped the political economies of Western Europe, North America, and Australasia from the beginnings of the Industrial Revolution well into the 1950s and 1960s. Overlapping this split, second, were the deep divisions over defense and security that prevailed in many democracies during the cold war. Divisions on these two big issues set the dominant and opposition coalitions into stark relief, untempered by significant cross-cutting cleavages that might have muted the differences. Japanese politics during the early postwar years was a game of high stakes poker with no wild cards. Winners would shape the country to redound to their long-term benefit, and losers would go home in their ragged ideological underwear.

The gap between the two camps was particularly wide on security matters, to which the Japanese left devoted much of its energy. Hindsight makes clear that the JSP's dominant concern—judged by their actual efforts rather than their policy statements—was security, not the economy. Successful mobilization of large numbers of Japanese citizens during the 1960 protests against revisions of the U.S.-Japan Security Treaty, along with the radicalism of the party's grassroots cadres, enhanced that focus. Unionization, economic distribution, social welfare, and environmental problems were downplayed as issues to which the left was willing to commit time and energy. Into the late 1980s, the JSP continued to support a "dictatorship of the proletariat," even as national economic policies virtually eliminated all who might qualify as proletarians and as private-sector unions focused on factory-level efforts to capture the economic benefits of high growth for their members.

The benefits of embedded mercantilism to the alliance's participants were undeniable. For example, by the end of 1960 Japan's net fixed capital stock was ¥14,353 billion (in 1965 yen); by the end of 1971 it had grown 327 percent to ¥46,880 billion.[81] Moreover, because government restrictions limited competition from technologically and managerially sophisticated, capital-rich overseas firms, Japanese products dominated the expanding domestic market, securing for Japanese manufacturers a solid home base from which to expand their markets internationally.

In a similar vein, the export-driven economic success, the protective fortress for agriculture and small businesses, and the continued stream of direct subsidies, tax incentives, pork barrel projects, land use policies, and side payments all fostered the continued collaboration of these two key sectors. Moreover, small-business owners also benefited from direct assistance programs as well as from a politically driven laxity in the enforcement of labor, environmental, and tax laws.[82] As late as the early 1970s, agricultural expenditures as a proportion of total government spending were typically four times greater in Japan than in France, Britain, the United States, or West Germany.[83] Incomes for farm families remained as high as those in urban and manufacturing areas while regional income disparities were also kept low. Farm subsidies were so extensive that "rice farmers and agricultural cooperatives had become political wards of the state."[84] Continued high growth was essential to maintaining such costly economic inefficiency.

As Chapters 5 and 6 will show, continued high growth and the consequent socioeconomic transformations ultimately confounded the bipolar simplicity of the socioeconomic clarity that prevailed in the mid-1960s. High growth in Japan, as in so many other countries, worked to defang erstwhile radicals, particularly because growth led to tangible and broadscale improvements for most citizens. In Japan, unlike many other countries, a rising tide *did* lift most boats. An expanding middle class, largely working in the service sectors, began to blur the once clear lines between business and labor. In the mid-1960s, however, the alliance structures of the two major camps were cleanly drawn, and the gap between them was wide.

To understand how Japan's socioeconomic cleavages were structured, we must turn to the final component of the conservative regime, the institutional arrangements that undergirded the regime of embedded mercantilism.

The Institutional Framework of Embedded Mercantilism

An interlaced network of political and economic structures held the socioeconomic alliance together and helped to shape the public policy profile. At the national governmental level, two institutions were especially relevant: the Liberal Democratic Party (LDP) and the national bureaucracy. The entire state apparatus remained under relatively unchecked LDP control for some thirty-eight years. Meanwhile, state bureaucratic powers, although less arbitrary and absolute than during the prewar period, remained formidable.

Meanwhile, interests and sectors tied to the LDP and to bureaucratic agencies had regular and steady access to power; anticonservative interests or nonaligned citizens found it correspondingly difficult to organize and to operate. As a result, conservatives could mobilize governmental power with singular cohesion in the interests of whatever agenda they set.

From its formation in 1955 the LDP was a vote-gathering wonder. The party typically captured 55–60 percent of the seats in both houses of the parliament and dominated most prefectural and local legislatures and executive branches by even greater margins. Conservative control over the country's executive and legislative institutions was virtually absolute. Concomitantly, conservatives held control of such key state organs as the police, the military, the tax offices, government-owned media, communications, and a vast array of public-sector corporations. Virtually all aspects of social life requiring governmental registration, permission, or licensing were thus under conservative control.

The vast majority of these tasks were administered by a well-entrenched state bureaucracy with extensive powers and a strong predisposition toward the active pursuit of the national interest. Particularly during the 1950s and 1960s, when so many other arenas of public life had seen their elites completely discredited, the national civil service attracted a large pool of Japan's "best and brightest."

Senior career officials were the product of a long trial by educational fire, most typically culminating in four years at the University of Tokyo's Faculty of Law.[85] Competitive exams for senior civil service positions were intense; during the 1960s, twenty thousand or more applicants competed annually for roughly fifteen hundred positions.[86]

Individual agencies had sweeping powers to affect specific sectors of society, in large measure due to their extensive licensing and regulatory powers. For much of the postwar period, despite slight reductions over time, some ten thousand regulations by various Japanese government agencies were in effect.[87] Moreover, in Japan, it is extremely difficult for interest associations to form and to function *without explicit approval from one or another government agency.* Strict qualifications on size of staff, financial resources, office space, memberships, and tax-deductible contributions limit the number of Japan's truly autonomous, critical, and free-floating interest associations.[88]

As noted above, the national bureaucracy played an active role in the care, nurturing, and structuring of the economy. Two agencies were particularly active and powerful in this arena. Japan's Ministry of Finance (MOF) had sweeping de jure and de facto responsibility over monetary, fiscal, and taxing activities, powers normally divided among several agencies in most countries. In one U.S.-Japan comparison, for example, the authors observed:

> The MOF combines the functions of the U.S. Treasury, Office of Management and Budget, Internal Revenue Service, Securities and Exchange Commission, Commodities Futures Trading Commission, Office of the Comptroller of the Currencies, activities of the Justice Department and Federal Trade Commission related to the financial system, state banking and insurance regulators, supervisory functions of the Federal Reserve, Federal Deposit Insurance Corporation, Federal Savings and Loan Insurance Corporation, Federal Home Loan Bank Board, National Credit Union Administration, and state credit union regulatory agencies.[89]

The United States is clearly more governmentally decentralized than Japan and provides a less-than-ideal comparative standard. Still, MOF carries out multiple tasks that in Germany and continental Europe are also divided among several bodies. Not surprisingly, Japan's Finance Ministry has been dubbed "the world's most powerful bureaucratic institution."[90]

Unusually valuable to MOF was its control over the Fiscal Investment and Loan Program (FILP, or Zaisei Tōyūshi Keikaku), often referred to as "Japan's second budget." The monies in the FILP come from the extensive national postal savings system (administered by the Ministry of Posts and Telecommunications) and from various special accounts such as welfare insurance and national pensions. Japan's postal savings system is the largest financial institution in the world; during the mid-1960s FILP monies alone constituted somewhat over 5 percent of Japan's total GNP.

During the early 1950s the FILP supplied 21 percent of the total funds used for heavy and export industries and 37.2 percent for the four basic industries of electric power, shipping, coal, and iron and steel.[91] In addition to financing such critical industries at a time of major reorganization, the FILP was a key contributor of public capital for toll roads, ports, airports, irrigation facilities, subways, railways, public housing, and other critical infrastructures.

If MOF had preponderant control of Japan's money, MITI exerted its greatest powers over industry. It had the authority to allocate foreign exchange, raw materials, and overseas technologies to companies as well as to shape industrial reorganization. Like all agencies, MITI had both formal authority and powers of "administrative guidance."[92] It also had oversight responsibilities for twenty-two *tokushū hōjin*, or special legal entities—quasi-public corporations with extensive authority in specific sectors of the economy, such as shipbuilding, automobiles, petroleum, and specific types of firms. This was eight more corporations than the next largest ministry and two to five times more than most other agencies.[93] MITI also exercised extensive control over various industrial trade and export associations,[94] as well as the legalized bicycle and motorcycle racing associations, profits from which were used to promote various industries.

Thus, when the conservative regime was functioning at its most fluid, both MOF and MITI had at their organizational disposal an array of tools with which to shape the nation's financial and industrial sectors.[95] Other government agencies enjoyed less sweeping powers, but, overall, Japan's bureaucracy had considerable influence and jurisdiction, particularly with regard to the national economy.

Japan's parliamentary-cabinet system was thus structured to allow virtually unlimited powers to any elected majority. With the LDP holding majorities in both houses, controlling cabinet positions, and almost always voting as a bloc, there were no formal impediments to the exercise of collective conservative will. The cabinet also had strict control over the court system, whose top judges were appointed by the LDP. Once agreement was reached within conservative ranks, subsequent executive-bureaucratic dominance was comprehensive. Government bills dominated the parliamentary agenda; amendments were rare; nongovernment bills had limited chance of success. Once the bureaucracy drafted its legislation, LDP solidarity voted it through parliament.

Although governmental institutions were united in support of a proactive agenda, private business and agriculture provided a vital underpinning for economic action.

At least five business structures demand attention: the individual firm, trading companies, the financial system, the *keiretsu*, and peak business organizations. Also critical were Japanese agriculture and its organizational structures. What is striking about all of them is their high degree of sectoral integration and their tight linkages with the conservative political world, both political and bureaucratic.

Business Structures

The basic economic building block of Japanese capitalism was the individual company. Despite the popularity of such stereotypes, there is no "typical Japanese firm." In the mid-1960s, for example, the large firms that dominated the business headlines were capitalized at more than ¥1 billion, employed more than a thousand workers each, and together accounted for roughly one-quarter of the nation's productivity. Yet these firms constituted only 1 percent of Japan's firms. In contrast, firms with fewer than three hundred employees accounted for nearly one-half of total manufacturing shipments, 44.1 percent of wholesale and 79.6 percent of retail turnover, and 38.6 percent of total exports.[96]

Firms also varied palpably in the range of their activities, from the small and relatively inefficient mom-and-pop groceries, sake shops, and cosmetics outlets to the medium-sized cement, paper, or machine-tool producers with their higher levels of productivity, to the complex auto manufacturing or shipbuilding operations that were among the most productive in the world.

While far from identical, Japan's largest and most competitive producers of goods or services had several features in common. One of the more important was the workforce. Clichés like "permanent employment" miss the realities of how the workforce in most Japanese firms was typically organized. Most large firms (though rarely smaller and medium-sized firms) had a core workforce, almost exclusively male, the bulk of whose members were hired soon after completing their formal education. Most stayed with the firm until "retirement" in their mid-fifties. Salaries were composed of three main elements: a base amount; add-ons for family size, commuting distance, children's educational expenditures, and the like; and a biannual bonus. Permanent workers could also avail themselves of a wide variety of company services including vacation spas, health care facilities, and in some cases even marriage counselors.

The bonus typically involved payment of two, three, or even four or five months' salary biannually. This provided delayed, if involuntary, savings for workers as well as a cheap mechanism for capital hoarding by firms. Formally negotiated between management and labor, the bonus also provided management with a mechanism to link labor costs to company profitability.

The core workforce was often "white collarized": blue-collar workers enjoyed long-term employment, company-related skill development, and wages linked to company profits.[97] This contrasted sharply with countries where blue-collar workers were among the first fired or laid off in the event of a company's short-term financial setbacks. Core workers in Japan rarely faced layoffs; in periods of financial stress their bonuses might be reduced, the oldest workers might be "tapped on the shoulder" and encouraged to take early retirement, or workers might be reassigned to new jobs. For most large firms, these workers were treated as a long-term invest-ment rather than a short-term cost of production. Although it constituted probably no more than 30 percent of all workers, this core group formed the basis for most observations about "permanent employment" in Japan.

Conditions for this protected core, however, did not apply to the rest of the (typi-cally nonunionized) workforce made up of part-time and temporary workers—often predominantly female—nor did it apply to subcontractors. Their wages were dramatically lower and their job security varied from short-term to nonexistent.

A visual image of the contrast between these two types of worker is presented in Robert Wood's description of the "silver helmets" and the "yellow helmets," two groups of workers at Nippon Kimitsu Steel. The former were permanent employ-ees with the consequent salary, benefits, and prestige; the latter, with no such guar-antees, lower wages, and the dirtiest jobs, were subcontract workers.[98] And outside the gates of Kimitsu were the "grandfather subcontractors," small companies that typically employed between ten and ninety-nine workers, in a "grime-covered cor-rugated metal and cement building with amenities limited to perhaps a Ping-Pong table in a grubby recreation room."[99] Of Kimitsu's twenty-six thousand workers, just over one in four wore the privileged silver helmet.

Company practices designed to retain the "core" workforce and to enlist worker support for new management practices and technologies had been adopted by Japan's largest firms as early as the late 1950s, particularly in shipbuilding, chemi-cals, and heavy industries. In addition, as demand for manual labor and machine operators decreased and automation and managerial oversight functions increased, so did the firms' emphasis on intrafirm retraining programs, supervisory selection based on technical knowledge and leadership, and personnel management by line workers. Work-group leaders who might well be union members were enlisted in the tasks of supervision, information transfer, and personnel maintenance. Joint consultation between labor and management at the plant level, as opposed to ex-plicit collective bargaining, was a major outcome. One survey by the Japan Produc-tivity Center showed that by the early 1970s, 80 percent of the sixteen hundred major companies listed on the Tokyo Stock Exchange had established some form of permanent system of joint consultation at the enterprise level.[100] Only if such con-sultations did not successfully resolve issues did unions push for them to become part of collective bargaining. The consequence was an increasing overlap between the interests of managers and the core workforce.

Three central features of this picture deserve underscoring. First, both financ-ing and personnel practices provided strong incentives for the firm's leadership to take the long-term view in business strategizing. And this was certainly easier when politics was almost guaranteed to be under conservative control. Second, management had a variety of ways to contain labor costs short of laying off core workforce members. Third, the employment of semipermanent core workers and the development of plant-level joint consultation allowed management to wean core workers away from the agendas of their more radicalized and politicized national union federations.

The second important business structure was the trading company, another unusual and instrumental economic organization with only a few counterparts elsewhere.[101] Japan has some six thousand trading companies, but only about forty are truly world players. The ten major ones in the 1960s had sales and personnel figures comparable to other companies in Fortune's International 500. The most prominent include Mitsubishi Trading, Mitsui Bussan, C. Itoh, Marubeni, and Nissho Iwai. Beyond the brokering function implied by the term "trading company," these organizations provide an array of comprehensive services including research and development; location of markets, components, and raw materials (particularly overseas); third-party trade; major overseas construction; resource development; planning and development; and joint ventures. During the 1960s, the top ten companies handled between 50 and 60 percent of all of Japan's trade, as well as 20 percent of domestic wholesale business. The total value of their operations was typically twice the national budget and 30 percent of GNP.[102] Moreover, trading companies played a key role in advancing trade credits to firms involved in the export of goods, generally providing about one-third of the capital used by nonfinancial corporations.[103]

The third and fourth key structures—the financial system and the *keiretsu*—are interlinked. Most of Japan's larger firms, including the major trading companies and virtually all commercial banks, have been members of broader industrial groupings known as *keiretsu*. Several trace their origins and nomenclatures to the prewar *zaibatsu* holding companies, the three most prominent being Mitsui, Mitsubishi, and Sumitomo; three others—Fuyo, Sanwa, and Daiichi Kangyo Bank—are bank-centered groups developed primarily after the war.

Keiretsu structures are complicated. Although analysts have grouped them differently,[104] two structures of *keiretsu* can be readily distinguished. In one, the links are horizontal; in the other, vertical.

Horizontal *keiretsu* typically have from twenty to forty or more firms of relatively similarly size that operate in different functional areas or markets. At the hub is the group's main bank and, normally, a trust company, an insurance company, and a trading company, all of which provide diverse financial services for the companies.[105] Such *keiretsu* links are like a wheel: financial institutions form the hub, while other firms, around the rim, have spoke-like connections to the hub as well as links to one another.

The main horizontal *keiretsu* accounted for a substantial portion of the total economic activity in Japan during the high point of conservatism, as they continue to do today. Although they represent only 0.1 percent of Japan's total companies, the top six have consistently accounted for roughly one-quarter of the national GNP during the postwar period. Furthermore, they account for roughly three-quarters of the value of all shares on the Tokyo Stock Exchange.[106]

The main bank has been critical to the financing of the *keiretsu* as well as to the overall financing of business operations throughout Japan. After the end of the war until the early 1980s, Japanese firms raised needed capital, not through the equity or bond markets, but through rolled-over loans from these main banks and other financial institutions. Predictable repayment of loans plus interest provided substantial and regular profits to the financing body. Simultaneously, since corporate dividends were taxed while capital gains were not, borrowing from banks freed the individual firm from the short-term need to produce dividends for coupon-clipping stockholders. This symbiotic relationship meant that financial institutions had a steady supply of high-quality customers, ensuring a steady steam of borrowing and interest payments, while the nonfinancial borrowers were ensured regular and low-cost access to scarce capital.

Japanese capital institutions have been highly concentrated. Whereas the United States has over 14,000 commercial banks, Japan has 158. The United States has over 1,550 insurance companies, while Japan has 24. In contrast to the 1,775 property and casualty companies in the United States, Japan has only 23. Four securities companies account for over 60 percent of all stock trades.[107]

While the horizontal *keiretsu* involve ties among putative equals, the vertical *keiretsu* involve connections from the large firms at the top of a pyramid down through as many as five layers of ever smaller and more specialized subcontractors, distributors, and capital-dependent firms.[108] In just one instance, "a single large automaker typically deals with as many as 170 primary subcontractors, which in turn consign parts manufacturing to 4,700 secondary subcontractors. The secondary concerns enlist the help of 31,600 tertiary subcontractors even further removed from the parent automaker."[109]

These smaller firms constituted a far larger portion of the total national economy than did similar firms in other industrialized democracies. In the mid-1960s, for example, only 2.4 percent of Japan's manufacturing establishments had more than a hundred employees, accounting for 38.4 percent of total Japanese employment. By way of contrast, the figures were generally much higher in France (2.7 and 59.6 percent), Germany (3.4 and 66.4 percent), the United Kingdom (16.8 and 81.3 percent), and the United States (10.9 and 76.7 percent). Only Italy with 1.1 and 45.5 percent bore any similarity to the Japanese pattern. Furthermore, wage differentials among smaller and larger Japanese firms within the same industrial sectors showed significantly wider gaps than in other industrialized countries.[110]

Ultimately, power was concentrated at the top of the hierarchy. Contractors typically divided orders among several subcontractors to gain multiple alternative sources for needed parts while keeping relatively small inventories and thus holding down fixed costs. They could shift contracts among subcontractors as rewards or punishments for past loyalties, current pricing problems, quality performances, or personal whim. Still, most contractor-subcontractor relationships rested less on simple, short-term bidding and market pricing than on fixed, well-established linkages established over time—connections that Ronald Dore aptly calls "relational contracting."[111] The vertical *keiretsu* often provided vital connections for smaller firms, whose fortunes were structurally fused with those of the larger high-value-added firms and sectors of the economy. Parent firms often assisted subcontractors technically, financially, and managerially. Such assistance not only bound the smaller firms to the larger but also allowed them to upgrade their practices and technologies, increase their productivity, and meet changing marketing and techno- logical needs. Many of Japan's smaller firms thus fulfilled what Michael Piore and Charles Sabel have called a "tradition of permanent innovation and organizational plasticity."[112] These interdependent relations reduced the competitive gap between Japan's larger and smaller firms, since export success by large firms typically meant contracts, jobs, and profits to those lower down in the pyramid. The result was a tightening of the bonds between large and small business and within the conserva- tive socioeconomic alliance.

Finally, individual industries and *keiretsu* in Japan, as elsewhere, pursued com- mon goals through trade associations, sectoral groups, and of course lobbying bod- ies. These form the final important facet of Japanese business organization and structure. In Japan there are some 14,000 business organizations, or 11.1 per 100,000 citizens, whereas in the United States there are slightly fewer total organi- zations in a country with twice the population—5.1 per 100,000 citizens.[113] More than six hundred product-specific trade associations exist in industries such as chemicals, steel, textiles, electronics, heavy machinery, shipbuilding, and insur- ance. Dominated for the most part by their larger members, these associations gather a wide range of data and provide technical information and market develop- ment strategies for their members. At various times they have served as enforcers of cartel agreements, spokesmen for the collective interests of individual sectors to both the media and the government, consolidators of members' opinions on mat- ters of government policy, and conduits between government officials and firm members.[114]

Several national associations of businesses serve almost exclusively political functions. Roughly one hundred of the major trade associations and about 750 of the largest public and private corporations in Japan are organized into the Federa- tion of Economic Organizations (FEO, or Keidanren), which maintains a substan- tial permanent staff and lobbying apparatus in Tokyo enjoying regular contacts with both elected officials and bureaucrats on all manner of business and economic policies.[115] Three other national federations address different aspects of the busi- ness community's national political concerns. The Japan Committee for Economic Development (JCED) has a membership of roughly fifteen hundred top business leaders. The Japan Federation of Employers' Associations (JFEA) is essentially the business community's antilabor arm. Finally, the Japan Chamber of Commerce (Nissho) is perhaps the most broadly representative business association in both the size and geographical scope of its membership.

In all of these ways, Japanese business groups were generally well organized, highly integrated, and structured to enhance long-term productivity while keeping labor costs low and adding to the international competitiveness of Japanese prod- ucts. Large and small firms, as well as firms with divergent interests, were often linked together through the *keiretsu* system. Banking and manufacturing were also fused, principally through mutually beneficial capital transactions. In these numerous ways Japanese businesses became solid supporters and beneficiaries of the conservative regime.

Agriculture

Japanese agriculture was even more internally cohesive than Japanese business. One of the most important organized economic interests in the conservative regime was Nōkyō, an acronym for the National Association of Agricultural Cooperatives. A vast and comprehensive organization, Nōkyō has national, prefectural, and some ten thousand local organizations whose members include 99 percent of the farm families in the country. At the village level, cooperatives provide purchasing, marketing, and credit facilities, crop spraying, and equipment. They run banks, insurance companies, and small credit bureaus, as well as driving schools and mail-order bride services. Total sales from Nōkyō-affiliated businesses rank them second only to Toyota, and include a major trading company, Japan's seventh-largest bank (Nōrin Chūkin) and the world's largest insurance company (Kyōsairen). From an electoral point of view, the cooperatives were also important as a tool for voter mobilization, almost exclusively for conservative politicians.[116]

In addition to their "pressure group" tactics, including pressing for higher government support prices and against agricultural liberalization, the agricultural cooperatives performed a wide range of semigovernmental tasks for the Ministry of Agriculture, Forestry, and Fisheries. They were long essential to the government's food purchase program under the Food Control Agency, handling 94 percent of all rice marketed each year.[117] The government meanwhile provided regular fees to Nōkyō for the storage and delivery of agricultural goods. As Donnelly notes, "The cooperative system is fundamentally a creature of the government and retains political rights to 'functional representation' in national policymaking. The relationship between the nation's most significant farm group and state officials is one of reciprocal influence since government ministries rely heavily on the cooperatives as an administrative mechanism and political means to organize the rural sector behind national policy."[118]

Not all economic interest groups were so extensively woven into the fabric of the conservative regime. The agricultural cooperatives were hardly unique, however. Various associations of doctors, dentists, and other professionals, along with such noneconomic groups as veterans' and educational groups, shared many of the same traits.[119]

The Conservative Regime's Internal and External Relations

Considerable attention has been devoted to assessing the relative power of bureaucrats and politicians, on the one hand, and of bureaucrats and businessmen on the other. The implication is that these groups remained internally cohesive while involved in zero-sum games with one another.[120] Nothing more distorts the realities of Japan's conservative regime during the mid-1960s, particularly with regard to its policy of embedded mercantilism.

Without a doubt, even when the conservative regime was at its most harmonious, conservative politicians, career bureaucrats, and businesspeople frequently operated from different motivations, career orientations, personal skills, and organizational loyalties. The politician's electoral vulnerability and the civil servant's career security have distinct consequences. The civil servant can claim a "national" perspective while the politician can retort that he is closer to "the people." Business leaders must "meet a payroll"; civil servants and politicians do not.

Such differences were not irrelevant to political conflicts. But far more pervasive were the extensive ways in which all three spheres mutually supported and depended on one another, particularly as regards the broad agenda of an embedded mercantilist economy. Moreover, when conflicts did emerge within conservative ranks, these were far more likely to follow functional and structural lines than clearly defined political, bureaucratic, or business lines. This was particularly true during conservative dominance in the 1960s.

Politicians have formal control over civil servants and top civil service promotions are subject to cabinet (and hence political) oversight.[121] On the other hand, only two political appointees, the minister and the vice-minister, oversee most government agencies; these have rotated in and out of office almost annually. The result is thus a limit on day-to-day political oversight of the civil service. Moreover, investigations of public problems are typically initiated and carried out within the bureaucracy rather than in the parliament, and such investigative committees are disproportionately staffed by bureaucrats and former bureaucrats. Parliamentarians have small staffs and are rarely in a position to challenge bureaucratic expertise. Furthermore, the civil service has virtually no paths for horizontal entry, limiting the utility of patronage as a tool for politicians.

Elected officials have often forced changes in proposals offered by one or more agencies in the civil service, particularly when these have gone against electorally favored constituent groups.[122] At other times, civil servants have shown remarkable ability to frustrate the efforts of elected officials to whom they are nominally responsible.[123] As in most countries, top civil servants in Japan are invariably "political bureaucrats."[124] Rarely can they ignore "political realities." Nor can politicians ride roughshod over the frequently better informed civil service.

Further adding to the mutuality of the relationship, many retired bureaucrats actually became politicians. From the late 1950s through the early 1970s Japan's prime ministers were all former bureaucrats. Kishi, Ikeda, and Sato reigned from 1957 until 1972; also powerful within the party at the time were Shiina Etsusaburō, Fukuda Takeo, and Ōhira Masayoshi. And within the cabinet, ex-bureaucrats occupied no less than 45 percent, and often as much as 55 percent, of the cabinet positions from the first Kishi to the third Sato cabinets.[125] Approximately one-quarter of the LDP's members were also former civil servants.[126] The result during the period was a blurring of the line between elected officials and career civil servants.

Meanwhile, even though many individual conservative politicians gained some degree of specialized policy expertise, almost all depended heavily on the civil service for information, policy know-how, initiative, and the day-to-day running of the government. Most politicians, in Japan as elsewhere, are more focused on maintaining their electoral viability than on governance per se. It is primarily when bureaucratic actions threaten electoral viability that politicians and bureaucrats clash.

There have been undoubted conflicts between governmental agencies and the business world on many specifics of regulation, allocation of government funds, business cooperation with government plans, and the like. But far more striking is the extent to which these two components of the conservative regime complemented one another's activities and cooperated in pursuit of the regime's key goals of high growth and marginalization of the opposition.

One important means by which these interests were fused was the well-known *amakudari*, whereby senior civil servants would typically retire in their mid-fifties and would gain subsequent employment in private corporations or in the trade associations of those firms. During the late 1960s, 40 retirees from the Ministry of Finance, 26 from International Trade and Industry, 21 from Transportation, and 17 from Construction would annually make such moves. Even larger numbers joined the managerial ranks of various public corporations while still others entered local governments (as well as those smaller numbers noted above who sought national elective office as members of the LDP).[127]

In addition, business-bureaucratic ties were bolstered by the mutual sharing of information and the joint development of policy positions. Japanese firms were required by law to supply far more detailed information to government agencies than was true in most other countries. Moreover, an extensive network of about 250 formal advisory committees and discussion groups, and three or four times as many informal ones, regularly brought together extensive cadres of businessmen, bureaucrats, academics, and journalists to prepare policy proposals. Most large corporations, likewise, would detail one or more of their senior managers to spend two to three hours daily at the government agency responsible for overseeing the firm's activities, providing an ongoing exchange of information.

In finance, the extremely limited amount of negotiable debt, the limited private capital market, and the power of the Bank of Japan (BOJ) to increase or decrease the money supply made the latter the single tap through which virtually the entire Japanese monetary and credit supply had to flow. In the mid-1960s, the BOJ was less a "lender of last resort" than virtually the sole lender. Borrowing from the BOJ was a privilege, not a right, which made even Japan's largest and presumably most independent banks deeply sensitive to BOJ and MOF policy preferences.

The high debt-equity ratio of Japanese corporations meant that slight changes in BOJ monetary policies could rapidly shift priorities and incentives for numerous actors within the Japanese economy as cash was pushed through the city banks or withheld from specific sectors or firms. Modest alterations in the discount rate that might take months to be felt in other countries had an almost instant effect in Japan.

The Japanese government, from the MOF through the BOJ and the city banks, thus had the capacity to exert tremendous leverage over Japan's many debt-ridden corporations. But such actions demanded government-business collaboration.

The broadly cooperative relations between business and the bureaucracy can be traced back to a common set of economic goals and a politics based far more on consensus building and cooperation than on formally outlined legal powers coupled with extensive punishments for the noncompliant. For the Japanese bureaucracy to lead in the economic arena, it had to forge a consensus, not issue a command. In the bureaucratic oversight of the economy, John Haley argues, "few adversarial issues arose, and those that did could be resolved cooperatively. For this reason, the inadequacy of formal legal sanctions seldom posed a problem. Most governmental actions were designed as benefits and therefore the question of how to compel compliance rarely surfaced."[128]

Consequently, it was always the individual firm that remained the key decision-making unit in the Japanese economy—no matter how responsive the firm was to government economic policies during the 1950 and 1960s, no matter how much it benefited from integration into financial and manufacturing networks, and no matter how much its destiny was shaped by broader macroeconomic policies beyond its control. Ultimately, national economic successes and failures reflected the sum total of the successes and failures of myriad individual firms. As Fritz Scharpf puts it, "Since market economies are by definition highly decentralized, the goals of government economic policy cannot be directly realized by government action. They are produced by the innumerable microeconomic decisions of producers and consumers, employers and workers, capital owners and investors. All of them are generally assumed to pursue their own microeconomic goals, and they are not directly concerned with the impact of their choices on the overall performance of the economy."[129]

Business simultaneously maintained close connections to the LDP primarily through financial backing of the party, its factions, and its individual members. While most large firms did not get directly into the process of voter mobilization, many smaller businesses and professional associations did so.

If a number of broad linkages brought business leaders, bureaucrats, and conservative politicians together, the structural separation of parliament, the LDP, and various executive agencies was often a source of conflict within the conservative regime. But such structural divisions fell almost exclusively along common functional lines. "The Japanese bureaucracy," for example, is in fact a jumble of agencies, ministries, bureaus, divisions and sections, line agencies, and quasi-public corporations. Each has its own jurisdictional sphere; each acquires political resources through interactions with other bureaucratic and private entities, and each is staffed by individuals whose motivations are conditioned in large part by discrete structures of rewards and tenure.

Similarly, parliamentary committees and committees within the Policy Affairs Research Council of the LDP were similarly organized along functional lines, making it hard to talk about any real policymaking role for the LDP as a whole. Individual politicians and civil servants with compatible functional interests and responsibilities typically interacted with one another on an ongoing basis.[130] Intraconservative conflicts consequently fell most often along functional or sectoral lines—finance versus education, foreign affairs versus regional development, telecommunications versus international trade and industry, and so forth. Mixtures of politicians, bureaucrats, and interest associations were aligned on either of the two (or more) sides of most economic issues; rarely did these generate clear-cut divisions between the two types of careerists or between a unified business community on one side and a governmental community on the other.[131]

There is no denying the divisions, conflicts, and disagreements that have occurred within the top ranks of the conservative regime even when it was most harmonious. This is to be expected in any high-stakes political situation. But such skirmishes must be balanced against the broad agreement between the business sector and the executive and legislative branches.[132] In stark contrast, groups and individuals outside the conservative circle were the regime's constant critics, although their influence was typically marginal.

At its height, the conservative regime's coherence was enhanced by the lack of countervailing powers from nonconservative or independent interest associations. Rarely were members of the conservative camp seriously tempted to break ranks and ally themselves with members of the opposition. Far more frequently, actual or potential opponents were drawn into the ambit of the conservative regime, for, except in the rarest of exceptions, it was only by cooperation with conservatives that they could ensure the achievement of even a small portion of their goals. As noted, interest groups in Japan require official recognition. But few groups, once recognized, sought to maximize their political leverage by distancing themselves from either the government or the LDP. Instead, the long-standing conservative dominance compelled most associations—with the notable exception of labor unions, student associations, and peace groups—to enter into some form of regularized alignment with the conservative party or with a government agency. The most typical pattern would be for a newly formed group to forge links with the LDP and then, as it gained political acceptance, to build ever stronger ties with the bureaucratic agency most immediately responsible for its particular sphere of activities.[133]

These ties to a specific authorizing bureaucratic agency were developed and maintained through corporatist arrangements. Japanese interest groups have typically functioned within well-institutionalized and interdependent networks of cooperation with one or more specific government agencies.[134] These ties were established through a variety of means: legal statutes that empowered particular interest groups to perform a range of quasi-governmental administrative tasks and provided them with government financing, the creation of public corporations and extradepartmental groups (*gaikaku dantai*) that fused official and quasi-official tasks, and regularized contacts through advisory committees, official surveys, postbureaucratic jobs (*amakudari*), and the like.[135]

If most interest groups were largely ineffective as counters to the conservative regime, the media has only rarely been an independent voice of criticism. The press clubs' narrow membership, their consensual nature, and their tendency to report uncritically the views of the particular government agency or politician they cover have made independent and critical journalistic judgments of government actions from the establishment press rather rare. Television news, long dominated by NHK—the government-run public broadcaster—long tended to follow a pre-dictable pattern: Japan faces problem X; government agency Y is in charge of deal-ing with X; advisory committee Z, under agency Y's aegis, has been assigned to ex-amine X; the committee has just issued this report: new legislation is pending; problem X is resolved. In short, the media covered events largely as a stimulus-response model: problems were stimuli to which the government responded. The citizen, meanwhile, should be comforted by the knowledge that "appropriate au-thorities" were coping.[136]

Labor was the socioeconomic sector most excluded from the ties forged by the conservative parties, the national bureaucratic agencies, big finance, big industry, and the smaller and medium sized firms. During the 1960s, when labor was playing substantial and even commanding roles in the political economies of other democ-racies, Japanese unions were marginalized at the level of national politics, and at the plant level were integrated largely under management's agenda.

At the national level, labor was marked by diffusion rather than cohesion. Union membership was not especially high by the mid-1960s; roughly 35–38 percent of the workforce was unionized (well below the Swedish level of over 90 percent and Britain's roughly 50 percent, but comparable to West Germany's 37 percent and well ahead of the United States with only 25 percent). Hence, 60 percent or more of Japan's labor force was nonunionized. Furthermore, nearly 40 percent of the 12,500 unions in Japan lacked any affiliation with a national federation. Only six unions had memberships of over 100,000; over 2.1 million of Japan's 12 million union members were in organizations with fewer than 300 members.

Labor's voice was further dissipated by competition among the major federa-tions for union affiliation. The largest of these, Sōhyō, represented only one-third of the nation's union members, and the bulk of its affiliates were from public-sector unions. The next largest federation, Dōmei, represented only about 15 percent of the unionized workforce, and it was made up largely of private-sector workers. Moreover, three political parties—the JSP, DSP, and JCP—all claimed to be the genuine political representative of labor. A substantial portion of the total number of parliamentarians from these three parties have been active or retired labor unionists.[137]

It was these labor federations, and the political parties of the left, that most ac-tively articulated a political voice for Japanese labor. Aiding this effort at unity was a tactic known as *shuntō* (spring offensive), an annual ritual of wage bargaining. Furthermore, the political parties of the left sought to identify themselves with "the interests of the working class." Yet, as Ōtake has argued in regard to the JSP—but as was more widely true of the JSP, JCP, and Sōhyō—these groups placed the bulk of their political attention on matters of defense, security, and criticisms of American bases and landing rights in Japan, as well as what they perceived as a growing Japanese militarism. All were far less quick to articulate pragmatic economic policies challenging those of the conservative regime.[138]

Meanwhile, as early as the mid-1960s, individual unions were gradually being integrated into conformity with managerial objectives at the level of the individual firm. If management deemed an individual enterprise union too radical, it would frequently encourage and endorse a so-called "second union," staffed by more moderate workers. Management would then use this second union to isolate and sidestep the more radical union. Radicalism gave way to what Dore has referred to as "amiable social contacts" between the new unions and management.[139]

Most important, Japanese unions were almost exclusively formed along enterprise, rather than craft or industrial, lines. Hence, in the private sector at least, labor's interests could easily be treated by management, and be seen by workers, as congruent with those of the firm. Horizontal linkages among workers as a class carried less weight than did vertical links among "Asahi employees" or "Seibu Railway workers." Bread-and-butter unionism, rather than class consciousness or national politics, became private-sector labor's dominant orientation. For a much longer period, public-sector unions remained far more politicized, but even more economically marginalized.

In these ways, then, Japanese labor developed along a unique historical trajectory. Individual unions were structured in ways that maximized close identification with firm interests, while at the national level no political party with substantial backing from organized labor managed to gain even the slightest foothold in the executive branch of government (except for the essentially irrelevant six months when the socialists held power under the U.S. occupation in 1947–48, and when policy control rested with the Americans not with the Japanese). Consequently, organized labor could be, and usually was, highly marginalized in the formation of national economic policies.

Most challenges and criticism of the conservatives were consequently left to diminutive opposition parties at the outermost boundaries of the politically acceptable. Rarely were opposition groups effective day-to-day players in the give and take of policy resolution.[140] Citizens and unrecognized interest groups were relegated to positions even further out on the periphery.

Neither from within the regime nor from without were serious challenges posed to the broad policy outlines of embedded mercantilism. Instead, virtually all important segments of Japanese society and all major political institutions either supported the policy or remained neutral; opponents were ineffective in changing it. The result was Japan's singular political economy.

The portrait of Japan in the mid-1960s is of a country pursuing an economic policy mixture of embedded mercantilism, a policy dependent on a closed market at home and on extensive barriers to the import of both manufactured and consumer products as well as to most foreign direct investment. It also depended greatly on a strong governmental bureaucracy actively attempting to catalyze growth in the private sector through a host of oligopolistic and export-oriented policies.

The political bases of these policies at home were clear. Interlinked policies permitted key elements in Japan's conservative coalition to engage in mutually profitable back-scratching. Most businesses, but especially large businesses, benefited tremendously from economic policies during this time; they in turn were often closely linked to smaller contractors and distributors, while both groups rewarded conservative politicians with financial contributions. Agriculture and smaller businesses benefited from state subsidies and protection from foreign competition. The tradeoffs meant extensive electoral support for the LDP. With powers derived from an extensive tool kit of laws, regulations, and ordinances, most governmental agencies also profited from such policies, even if it meant being formally under the supervision of politicians from the LDP. The regulatory powers of agencies were reinforced while their budgets grew. Bureaucrats who worked closely with conservative politicians, private business, and financial firms could look forward to promotion within their agencies and to profitable and rewarding jobs upon retirement. And ultimately, the LDP benefited from high levels of electoral support at home, support from the United States in most international matters, and from the talented policymaking efforts of its national bureaucracy.

In numerous ways, then, the conservative regime in Japan was quite unlike that of any of the other industrialized democracies. Certainly, it bore few similarities to Swedish corporatism, U.S.-style pluralism, or two-party British politics, despite the ways in which bits and pieces of the Japanese political economy may have resonated with elements in one or the other. Certain similarities to Italy are somewhat more striking, but Italian labor was stronger, conservative electoral dominance was far less pervasive, parastatals and patronage were far more sweeping, and Italy's overall economic success paled in comparison to that of Japan.

From the standpoint of the 1990s, the Japanese conservative successes of the mid-1960s to mid-1980s seemed foreordained, as did the rather unusual character of the Japanese regime. However, this was not the case in the 1950s, when Japanese politics and economics were far more fluid and open to alternatives. To appreciate the difficulties inherent in creating the conservative regime, it is essential to revisit that period and reexamine the chaos and confusion that prevailed prior to the conservative hegemony.

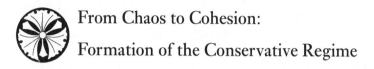

CHAPTER THREE

From Chaos to Cohesion:
Formation of the Conservative Regime

During the mid-1960s, when the conservative regime was functioning at its smoothest, Japan's combination of conservative political dominance and economic strength seemed an inseparable composite of logic and inevitability. The interlocking spiral of continuous electoral and economic successes make it difficult to imagine the Japanese political economy operating in ways fundamentally different from that described in the previous chapter.

At its height, the regime interacted with a fluidity that was indeed overly determined, mutually reinforcing, and relatively unproblematic. The Liberal Democratic Party fostered a persistently positive climate for economic growth; continued economic success reinforced the LDP's electoral hammerlock over the Japanese voting public.[1] In the phrase of Kozo Yamamura, the links between politics and economics were a "marriage made in heaven."[2]

Logical or inevitable as the relationship appeared with hindsight, the smooth-flowing regime of the mid-1960s was far from historically inevitable. Nor was Japan's postwar political conservatism and rapid economic growth simply a logical resumption of the country's "interrupted" prewar economic or cultural trajectory. The postwar Japanese regime was far too different, politically and economically, and the first ten to fifteen years after the war were far too pregnant with alternative possibilities to treat Japan's subsequent conservative regime as either endemic or inevitable. Rather, Japan's postwar miracle machine was new, politically constructed, and historically contingent.

The overarching questions for this chapter concern how the various pieces of Japan's postwar regime came together. How did Japan develop such centralized institutions in its political economy? How did it create an electoral politics with such limited control over national policy formation? How did conservatives weave together such an unusual socioeconomic coalition, fusing big and small business with agriculture? And in a related vein, why were Japanese labor and the left so weak. Why were they incapable of forging the kind of Red-Green coalition that had emerged in many parts of Northern Europe, or at least providing some partial penetration of government as had occurred in Italy or the United States? And finally, how did the mixture of policies that prevailed by the 1960s—most especially high growth and low social welfare—get implanted?

It is well to begin with unrealized possibilities.[3] The early postwar years gave little clue that Japan, in either its eventual economic prowess or its consistent conservative governance, would emerge with the regime that prevailed in the 1960s. Far more plausible seemed to be a trajectory propelling Japan—like Austria, Germany, France, and Italy, the other ex-authoritarian reorganizers—toward multiparty competition, a moderate-to-strong political left, and economic performances that, even under the most optimistic projections, would have been far less spectacular than those actually achieved. Under such circumstances, Japan's history during the next forty years would have closely resembled the postwar political and economic histories of the other reconstituted democracies—alternating governments, ever expanding bureaucracies, bigger government programs (particularly in social welfare), greater labor and citizen checks on business, more open economies, and generally slower rates of economic growth and world market penetration.

To appreciate why such a path was not taken, and why the one followed became increasingly probable, it is necessary to examine the shaping of the Japanese political economy during and immediately after the U.S. occupation. That record makes it clear that the early political actions by the American military set Japan initially on a course that was neither a continuation of the old prewar regime nor one that would inexorably evolve into the regime that predominated in the 1960s. Far more likely was a political economy with strong doses of labor power and social democracy. Only the explicit redirection of initial occupation policies laid the foundation for the conservative regime that came to function so fluidly during the 1960s.

Destruction of the Ancien Régime and Openings for the Left

In all aspects of the country's politics and economics, the first ten to fifteen years following Japan's loss in World War II were characterized by massive change, false starts, uncertainty, turmoil, and conflict. Loss of the war, occupation by an alien military force, and the dramatic overhaul of the prewar constitutional order made this an era of prolonged uncertainty. The internal coherence and predictability of both the prewar and wartime political economies had been erased; no similar verities took their place.

When the war ended, as has been well documented, Japan was economically prostrate, politically paralyzed, and internationally isolated. Eight years of mobilization for total war, following an even longer period of partial mobilization, had severely undermined the civilian economy. Months of saturation bombing had destroyed roughly one-quarter of the nation's housing and an even higher proportion of its industrial buildings and plants. Fully three years after surrender, Japan's economic output stood at only one-third its prewar (1932–36) level. Military defeat stripped away the vast territorial empire that for the preceding fifty years had been so painstakingly accumulated and so economically beneficial to the home islands. The physical destruction was valued at approximately twice the national income for the fiscal year 1948–49. Poverty and inflation haunted Japan's economy for the next several years. During 1945–46, for example, the adult Japanese lived for nearly a year on rations averaging 1,050 calories per day, about one-third the amount required for physical health. During these first postwar years, Japanese teenagers lost an entire year of physical development.

The nation's political and economic leadership meanwhile was publicly discredited and further decimated by an extensive purge by the American occupation. All authority ultimately rested with the occupation, which was initially committed to a comprehensive overhaul of the existing political economy, thereby constricting the options open to any Japanese leader attempting to act as either a political or economic entrepreneur.

Moreover, Japan, like the other defeated powers, was internationally isolated and lacked a coherent strategy for coping with the nation's new circumstances. The country, which had consistently relied on some mixture of a single-country alliance or "protective" multinational treaty arrangements, was completely shut out of international institutions and devoid of any alliance partner for the first time since the Triple Intervention (1894–95).

Three features of the seven-year occupation (1945–52) were highly instrumental in shaping the regime that eventually emerged. First, the old prewar order was replaced with a new constitutional system that enshrined popular sovereignty, electoral democracy, and parliamentary government. Second, numerous changes favored or restricted specific socioeconomic groups, which in turn constrained future socioeconomic coalitional possibilities, institutional arrangements, and public policy choices. Third, Japanese foreign, military, and security policies were, by the end of the occupation, intricately and bilaterally fused with those of the United States. The Americans thus uprooted the old regime and planted many of the seeds from which the new regime would eventually flower.

American actions were initially aimed at eradicating key vestiges of the prewar order. A host of preexisting institutions and socioeconomic groups were subjected to massive overhaul. By 1947–48, however, in the face of a whole series of domestic and international changes, the American orientation shifted. By the third year of the occupation, what is generally known as the "reverse course" was under way; American actions no longer aimed at eradicating the prewar order and turned instead toward creating a pro-Western, conservative, procapitalist order designed to serve American cold war interests and turn Japan into America's foremost strategic ally in Asia.

Before this shift, however, the American presence established democratic political institutions and bolstered labor and the left, moving Japan toward a left-of-center political economy analogous to those found in many European social democracies. Only later did the Americans shift toward conservative policies.

To appreciate the possibility that postwar Japan might have been far less conservative, it is well to recall the most important aspects of prewar Japan. The prewar constitutional order, and the political regime that emerged under it, were explicitly nondemocratic and antilabor. They rested on a classic conservative alliance of state, rural landlords, and nascent business conglomerates. The early Meiji state, modeled on Bismarckian Prussia, sought to overcome Japan's comparatively late industrialization and weak international position. Sovereignty rested in the person of the emperor, and national civil servants were explicitly his authoritarian underlings; cabinets were appointed by the emperor and had no responsibility to parliament or the electorate; extensive political privileges were guaranteed to the military; a powerful Ministry of Home Affairs circumscribed the autonomy of local authorities; universal male suffrage was introduced only in 1925; parliament and political parties were limited in their power to shape economic or political decisions; numerous official and unofficial institutions such as the Privy Council and the genro circumscribed parliamentary and cabinet powers while providing behind-the-scenes influence; duties of citizens were extensive, their rights few. In short, while the Meiji Constitution could well be applauded as the first constitution outside the West and for having the potential for greater democratization, it still created a highly centralized system only minimally constrained by elections, parties, and popular priorities.

Undergirding this system was an alliance of four major sociopolitical groups: the military, the nobility, big business (particularly the major *zaibatsu*), and rural landlords. These sectors—with only minimal input from political parties and the electoral process—essentially shaped the prewar order. Japan thus had a classic conservative-authoritarian regime based on alliances between a centralized state, rural landlords, oligopolistic businesses, and an expansionist military that was viscerally hostile to political democracy and explicitly opposed to any significant increase in the economic or political power of organized labor and the political left.[4] It was a political economy that, with admitted variations, was akin to those that prevailed in prewar Germany, Austria, Italy, and, to a much lesser extent, Vichy France.

Structural Change and Continuity

Numerous elements of this system were targeted for reform. For our purposes, the key changes were those that institutionalized the role of parliament and political parties and that reshaped socioeconomic power. At the same time, certain elements of the prewar regime, especially the extensive centralization of political institutions and the powers of the national bureaucracy, were hardly altered.

The very premise of Japanese politics shifted from imperial sovereignty to electoral democracy. The emperor became a "symbol of the State and of the unity of the people" while sovereignty was vested in the citizenry with a freely elected parliament as "the highest organ of state power." In addition, the economic system was targeted for a wholesale restructuring of monopolies and holding companies and the legalization of independent labor unions with guaranteed rights.

Monumental as such changes were, the occupation left in place the prewar structures of centralization and governmental cohesion. The new institutional arrangements built in few political checks and balances or compomise-enhancing structures. The unified parliamentary system remained. Moreover, by instituting no provisions for direct citizen initiative or referenda, and by giving no major attention to the easy creation of independent nongovernmental organizations, the occupation failed to institute important components of direct democracy, further insulating Japan's subsequent governments from citizen influence.[5]

Centralization of national governmental power was further bolstered by the occupation's failure to carry out any major modification of powers of the prewar civil service. The Ministries of the Navy, the Army, and Home Affairs were dismantled.[6] Several other ministries were reorganized and a few agencies such as the National Personnel Authority and the Fair Trade Commission were created. Yet, little was done to alter the character, social background, or training of civil servants; administrative discretion and broad regulatory powers remained sweeping; the power of elected officials over administrators was nominal and rarely relevant in day-to-day activities; and the impact of the purge removed few bureaucrats from agencies other than the police and other agencies within the Home Ministry.[7] As a result, the broad policy role exercised by the national civil service remained largely intact.[8] Indeed, a centralized and electorally uncompromised Japanese civil service provided an ideal structure through which to implement American policies. The politics of the occupation were marked by cross-national bureaucratic alliances between competing groups of Japanese and American officials and a massive 84 percent expansion in the sheer number of Japanese bureaucrats.[9]

That the Japanese bureaucracy was a major player in subsequent conservative regimes traces in part to the failure of the occupation to reshape it. But as we shall see in greater detail below, Japanese bureaucrats also benefited from the occupation's elimination, restructuring, and deep purge of many of the bureaucracy's prewar competitors, most notably the purge of Japan's prewar military leaders and politicians and from the eventual elimination of the landlord class. Potential contenders for power, many of whom had checked bureaucratic powers under the Meiji system, were suddenly gone, leaving the civil service as one of the few relatively untouched carryovers from the prewar system. The civil servants thus had a virtual monopoly on governmental expertise, representing as they did almost all of Japan's remaining "political grownups." The Japanese civil service thus retained enormous leverage to resist, bypass, or distort occupation policies as well as to set the stage for post-occupation policies.

If the overall retention of a centralized national governmental system with a strong and rather independent civil service seems in some way self-evident, consider the alternatives. In many areas the occupation largely emulated American structures and practices. This was true of the restructuring of the education system; the regulation of banking, insurance companies, and brokerages; or the constitutional provisions that paralleled and extended the U.S. Bill of Rights. Any such replication of American governmental institutions would have created a Japanese institutional matrix that reflected the early federalist ideology of frustrating, rather than empowering, centralized authority. Yet no such bias drove the occupation's political reordering.

Nor did Japan get a combination presidency plus parliament such as prevails under the French Fifth Republic, nor a German, Australian, or Canadian federalism. Instead, Japanese political institutions remained oriented toward the concentration of national executive power. Indeed, by disempowering or eliminating such prewar executive bodies as the Imperial House, the Privy Council, and the military ministries, governmental centralization became even more streamlined and concentrated. Retention of the emperor further bolstered Japan's political concentration.[10]

In summary, then, one major change and one major continuity emerged from the occupation. The change centered on the creation of a strong parliamentary democracy and the introduction of electoral and party politics and popularly elected governments. Any postwar regime would require sufficiently strong electoral underpinnings to remain in power. The continuity was a centralized and bureaucratically powerful national government. Once majoritarian cabinets came into power, the machinery was in place for relatively uncontested decision making.

Socioeconomic Shifts

Under the U.S. occupation several socioeconomic pillars of the prewar regime were swept away; others were drastically altered. The result was a comprehensive reconfiguration of political and economic alignments. Certain powerful groups reemerged with only minor modification; these typically became bedrock components of postwar conservatism. However, the old order lost several key socioeconomic components.

The military and the nobility were the most unalterably changed. With surrender and the liquidation of Japan's overseas empire, explicit civilianization began. Some six million demobilized military personnel and repatriated civilians were returned to the four main islands. The nation's military academies were closed; history textbooks were sanitized to deglamorize Japan's military legacy; veterans groups were disbanded. The nation's military machinery was destroyed, and its officers were excluded from all political activity. Article 9 of the Constitution (the so-called no war clause) further circumscribed the potential for any reacquisition of power by the military.[11] Similarly, the Japanese police, including the powerful Kempeitai, were decentralized.

Meanwhile, the prewar nobility—both the aristocracy of blood who held important posts in the Imperial Household and House of Peers and the new modern peerage of imperial appointment—was also eradicated. The previously appointed House of Peers was replaced by an elected House of Councilors.

Rural landlords were also essentially eliminated as a socioeconomic force. One of the ironies of the U.S. occupation is that land reform is rather widely touted as among its greatest social achievements; however, the Japanese government actually initiated the reforms. Once the occupation committed itself to land reform, however, it was carried out vigorously. Moreover, subsequent inflation quickly made the government's compensation payments to landlords virtually worthless, turning the program into a de facto confiscation. Thus, like the military, landlords disappeared from Japan's political landscape as a powerful socioeconomic class.

A fourth major bloc of the prewar regime, namely big business, proved vastly more complicated. Initial U.S. policy favored the rapid breakup of what were seen as monopolies linked to the Japanese war machine and undergirding prewar expansion.[12] In keeping with pervasive New Deal sentiments, American policy sought to punish the economically powerful and to pursue "economic democracy" over "growth." Not surprisingly, the breaking up of many Japanese businesses was hardly opposed by their U.S. competitors.

A succession of related missions on Japanese economic democratization, led respectively by Edwin Pauley and Corwin Edwards, pursued these themes during late 1945 and early 1946. Their combined recommendations called for the radical dismantling of the prewar *zaibatsu* down to the operating level. Pauley was particularly committed to the premise that Japan should relinquish its role as the most industrialized country in Asia: "We must always remember," he contended, "that in comparison with the peoples she has overrun, Japan has the last priority."[13]

Preliminary offers by some of Japan's major companies to reorganize voluntarily were dismissed as insufficient. The occupation instead called for reorganization from above. A December 1945 directive demanded that some 336 corporations be dissolved. An antimonopoly law was passed in April 1947 and a deconcentration law in December of the same year. The latter ordered the breakup of companies deemed to have "excessive concentrations of economic power."

Japanese efforts at self-reform were skeptically dismissed at the highest levels of government. For example, Dean Atcheson commented in a memo to President Truman: "The big business people are among the more obvious sign repainters. . . . as their chief interest is in the making of money they are inclined toward such reforms as will tend to stabilize the situation and get things back to some kind of business 'normalcy.' "[14] The Americans, clearly, initially identified financial and manufacturing concentration with the wartime regime and considered it incompatible with a new regime predicated on economic democratization. Along with the military forces, the nobility, and the landlord class, Japan's big businesses would have to be scraped.

Generic attacks on broad sectors were supplemented by the War Crimes Trials and a sweeping political purge of individual prewar leaders. Some 167,000 military officials were at the core of the 210,000 members of the prewar elite who were prohibited from holding official positions. Furthermore, between 1,800 and 3,200 business executives from some 278 corporations were subjected to the personnel purge.[15] Politicians, journalists, interest group leaders, and others from the ancien régime were similarly restricted. The purge thus provided what John Dower has referred to as "SCAP's winnowing hand."[16]

American efforts at a political gravity shift bore fruit in the election of April 1946—the first election following Japan's defeat and the last under the Meiji Constitution.[17] Some 363 political parties officially campaigned, as many as 181 running only a single candidate. Some 119 nonaligned independents were elected. Over 80 percent of those successful were first-time Diet members. Only 38 of the 456 parliamentarians were holdovers from the wartime parliament.[18] Virtually the entire prewar party elite was replaced by a new cadre of political leaders. The electoral shakeup by the Americans yielded a dramatic transformation in the socioeconomic composition of the Japanese political leadership.

Liason with the Left

The powerful attack against the old regime was bolstered by the simultaneous empowerment of the political left. Almost immediately upon their arrival in Japan, the U.S. occupation forces began fostering trade and industrial unions. The commander of Allied occupation, General Douglas MacArthur, personally informed Prime Minister Shidehara on October 11, 1945, that he expected "the encouragement of unionization of labor—that it may be clothed with such dignity as will permit it an influential voice in safeguarding the working man from exploitation and abuse and raise his living standard to a higher level."[19]

Communist and socialist labor organizers were freed from prison or welcomed back from exile; legal barriers against union formation were eliminated; bargaining rights and minimum labor standards were spelled out. An explosion in the number of unions and union members followed.

By mid-1946, some 12,000 unions with a membership of 3.7 million had sprung up. By 1948–49 these figures had grown to 34,000 unions with about 7 million members. In 1949 Japan's unionization rate reached a high point of about 50 percent of the workforce, well above that of the United States, Britain, Sweden, or most European democracies at the time. Certain sectors saw particularly high union penetration: 89 percent of transport and communication workers, 82 percent of mine workers, 72 percent of those in finance, and 67 percent of employees in the electric, gas, and waterworks industries.[20]

For a time, it appeared that Japan had the potential to develop a substantial left-of-center political economy. To most on Japan's left, America's early embrace promised a powerful cross-national alliance that would obliterate the past and replace it with a radically altered and far more populist and social democratic order, of which labor and the left would be both the primary architects and the principal beneficiaries. In the 1947–49 period, that prospect was hardly unrealistic.

To the chagrin of many Americans, Japanese unions showed little interest in modeling themselves on the largely nonpolitical, bread-and-butter, Gomperesque unions predominant in the United States. Instead, they styled themselves after European (or Soviet) unions whose activity was closely tied to electoral politics. Aiming at a fundamental reordering of the nation's political and economic system, Japanese unions forged ties to both the Japan Socialist Party (JSP) and the Japan

Communist Party (JCP).[21] Work actions at the plant level went well beyond the typical American strike. In "production control measures" workers took over plants, ejected management, and ran the operations themselves.[22] Free rail transportation was provided by strikers on the Japan National Railways. Hunger strikes, sit-downs, and slowdowns were rampant. Public demonstrations and political parades accompanied many such actions.[23]

Labor's growing power led an important segment of the Japanese business community, centered principally within the Japan Committee for Economic Development (JCED, or Keizai Dōyūkai) to call for a "revised capitalism" that, as Hideo Ōtake has argued, would embrace some form of neocorporatist cooperation with labor. Confronting the very real possibility that capitalism as it had been known in prewar Japan might be facing a fundamental overhaul, these younger executives initially proposed a series of changes in managerial control at the plant level that would have dramatically expanded and legitimated labor's role. These businessmen hoped such a plan would induce the more radical unions to adopt more moderate and less political goals.[24]

During these earliest years of the occupation, union organizers worked actively to fuel alliances with the rural sector and small merchants. The Japan Farmers' Union (Nihon Nōmin Kumiai, or Nichinō) was formed by prewar socialists in October 1945. By January 1946 some 60,000 members were enrolled; by February 1947 the membership was up to 1.2 million; by early 1949 it was over 2 million and represented more than one out of five farm households.[25]

Ties to small business were most especially sought after the JSP won the largest number of seats in the 1947 election and formed Japan's first socialist-led cabinet. The JSP also participated in the coalition cabinet which followed. The Ministry of Labor was created, giving labor its first official governmental representation. Moreover, the Katayama cabinet provided aid to small firms while the Ashida government sponsored the Law on Cooperative Unions for Small and Medium Enterprises (1948), aimed at increasing the economic bargaining power of small firms. The law also created the Small and Medium Enterprises Bureau, giving smaller enterprises direct governmental representation within the national bureaucracy for the first time in Japanese history.

Unquestionably, the early coalitional base of the JSP extended well beyond the blue-collar workforce. In the July 1948 election the party drew its largest occupational support not from labor but from farmers (37 percent); industrial workers made up only 21 percent of the JSP's support; indeed, even salaried workers contributed a more significant support bloc (27 percent) than did industrial workers. This high farm support was nearly equal to that drawn by the conservative Democratic Liberal Party (41 percent) and not far behind the Democratic Party (50 percent).[26] Indeed, 50 percent of the Socialists elected to the lower house came from sixty-nine of Japan's most rural constituencies, and thirty-nine of them were officers of farmers' unions.[27] In December 1948 the left wing of the Japan Socialist Party even formed the Labor Farmer Party (Rōnō-tō). Meanwhile, national opinion polls taken during October 1949 showed backing for Yoshida's Liberals among farmers and fishermen to be lagging more than 10 percent behind Liberal support levels nationally.[28]

The vote share garnered by the combined political left continued to rise from just about one-quarter in 1949 to just over 40 percent in 1960.[29] It was not at all improbable to imagine the emergence of some variant of a Red–Green coalition such as had developed in Denmark, Norway, and Sweden in the 1930s or some other arrangement that would empower the Japanese left.

These early efforts to forge a farmer-labor alliance, with some ties to the small-business sector, never bore fruit. Socialist appeal in the rural areas began to wane as early as the 1949 election after farmers became particularly upset by the food requisitioning policies of the Katayama government. The causes were many: JSP-JCP divisions, internal JSP feuding, the eventual socialist schism, organized labor's growing control of the JSP, land reform's defusing of rural economic discontents, and the nurturing of the agricultural cooperatives by conservatives. Perhaps the most important of these was the division between the JSP and the JCP—both of which were anxious to organize unlanded tenant farmers—over the ambiguous class position of landholding farmers. The JSP, which modeled itself on the British Labour Party,[30] was never comfortable with the inclusion of such clearly non-blue-collar members, and it gradually abandoned its broader alliance building efforts.[31] Subsequently, the JSP concentrated its rural appeals on lower taxes and higher rice prices, goals hardly at odds with those of many rurally based conservative politicians and divergent from its earlier efforts at mobilization through rural unions. After the first few years, the communists were even less successful in the rural areas. The JSP's inability to gain governmental power after 1948 and its difficulty in forging alliances beyond the blue-collar workforce became mutually reinforcing weaknesses of the Japanese left. But the failure also traced to problems within the union movement itself.

As I noted in Chapter 2, at least three factors worked to keep the unions from gaining a powerful national political presence. First, no single national federation was ever capable of articulating a unified voice for labor or representing a clear majority of union members. Japanese national federations never acquired anything like the organizational comprehensiveness of, say, Swedish, German, British, or Israeli peak labor associations. Second, individual unions were organized around the enterprise rather than around crafts or industries, both of which were far more conducive to the development of a common class identification among workers. Horizontal class consciousness, so critical to the success of much of the European labor movement, was consequently undercut in Japan. Their enterprise structure left most Japanese unions highly vulnerable to pro-management, production-oriented, and class-divisive appeals, particularly in the private sector. Third, a relatively small proportion of the total Japanese workforce was employed in the large firms that have typically been the easiest to unionize. In the 1950s (and on to the 1980s), nearly one-half of Japanese workers had jobs in establishments with fewer than 50 workers, a figure slightly higher than Italy (44.4 percent) and considerably more than the United States (15.2 percent) or the United Kingdom (15.9 percent), with most of

Western European countries falling in the 16–40 percent range.[32] Indeed, between 70 and 75 percent of Japan's manufacturing sector, and between 80 and 85 percent of all sectors excluding agriculture and finance, work in smaller firms generally employing fewer than three hundred workers.[33] As studies of labor organizational patterns have shown, such firms were typically the most difficult to unionize.[34]

Despite various failings by the Japanese left, however, the Japanese union movement continued to gain strength for several years. Labor-management relations remained bitter and confrontational. In both the public and private sectors, strikes were frequent, long, and violent.[35] It took a deliberate and powerful counterthrust by conservatives—both Japanese and American—to redirect the leftist momentum. Radical shifts in American policies, combined with amazing regenerative powers among Japan's conservatives, combined to curtail the Japanese left and forge the basis for the regime that eventually dominated.

Conservative Counterthrust:
Implanting the Conservative Regime

Japan's conservatives were hardly passive in the face of the threats to their power. Even before the war had ended, business and political leaders were meeting in private and public arenas to strategize about post-surrender Japan. Early U.S. policy directions so heavily undercut many of Japan's conservative mainstays and so empowered the political left, however, that for the first months after Japan's defeat conservatives were restricted largely to rear-guard and defensive skirmishes.

Had the American orientation not changed, it is doubtful that Japan's conservatives could have acquired anything like the power and autonomy they eventually came to command. Sparked by a host of changes in both U.S. domestic politics and international relations as well as changes within Japan, the American reorientation bolstered Japan's right and weakened its left.

Within the United States, the most prominent causes for policy change included the consolidation of the Truman administration, Republican congressional victories in 1946, the outbreak of McCarthyism, and a growing U.S. public and business climate hostile to what was increasingly criticized as the "socialist experiment" in Japan. Bureaucratic battles between the Pentagon, the State Department, the White House, and various U.S. interest groups further heightened the pressures for more pro-conservative policies. The Government Section, the most ardent advocate of sweeping reforms, began to lose influence within the Byzantine corridors of the occupation headquarters.

Internationally, all of the presumptions upon which initial U.S. policies had been predicated were undercut by massive shifts in the postwar power balance. Most dramatically, the wartime alliance between the Soviet Union and the West gave way to postwar ideological and territorial struggles. Subsequent consolidation of the communist revolution in China left the United States without its anticipated geopolitical ally in Asia, namely, the nationalist government of Chiang Kai-shek.

Communist successes in Greece and Turkey, the subsequent articulation of the Truman Doctrine, Winston Churchill's "Iron Curtain" speech, and George Kennan's "Mr. X" article in *Foreign Affairs* all coalesced into a new U.S. and Western orientation of anticommunism and hostility toward the Soviet Union, its allies, satellites, and potential friends. In short, by the end of the 1940s the international context of U.S. policy toward Japan had altered completely from what it had been when the U.S. forces landed at Atsugi in August 1945.

Finally, conditions in Japan also contributed to American shifts. High levels of poverty and inflation and the consequent costs to the American taxpayer of food and other aid led many American policymakers to challenge the merits of punitive policies toward Japanese big business and the conservative political elite. The radicalism of Japan's emergent left added to the fear of an anticapitalist and presumably anti-American regime taking control in Japan. Moreover, Yoshida Shigeru, whom MacArthur initially dismissed as "monumentally lazy and politically inept,"[36] eventually developed a warm personal rapport with his fellow conservative, allowing both men to focus on their overlapping political agendas.

By the midpoint of the occupation, the initial American goals of democratization and demilitarization had given way to economic recovery and the weaving of Japan into the fabric of the U.S. alliance system. When the occupation ended, American policies had been fundamentally "reversed" and conservatives were gaining power. It took an additional several years following the occupation, however, before one could reasonably talk of a new and stable conservative regime being in place.

Three key elements went into the development of this new regime: the major elements of the subsequent social coalition were strengthened and brought together; the electoral basis for conservative predominance was established; and policies were created to hold the coalition together and provide an economic underpinning for conservative election successes.

Social Coalition Building

During the first years after the war, as I noted earlier, core socioeconomic elements of the prewar order were either eliminated or severely restricted. Landlords, the nobility, and the military had all been effectively eliminated as political and economic forces. Business proved to be far more resilient and emerged from the occupation much stronger and indeed as a vital element in the conservative pantheon.

Initial American economic policy had demanded the breakup of Japan's monopolies and large financial groupings. Yet Japan's conservatives were hardly prepared to see their country become an "Asian Nebraska."[37] Certainly Japanese business leaders proved to be far more resilient than the military, landlords, or nobility. They refused to allow the occupation and its society shapers to sculpt them into uncomfortable, contorted forms. Rather, big business reshaped itself into a central player in the conservative regime. It did so in three ways. First, it survived an attempted American breakup, remained oligopolistic, and even grew more powerful economically through the *keiretsu* system. Second, it blunted labor's national political and plant-level economic power. Third, it deepened its ties with the political world, including both conservative politicians and government bureaucrats.

Japanese business's opposition to massive reorganization merged with American rethinking about the role of economic concentration during the "reverse course." Numerous Japanese conglomerates that were "too big to fail" were reestablished or created anew. Essentially, the deconcentration program was abandoned by 1949. The antimonopoly law was also amended in that year and was finally gutted in 1953.

Cartelization then continued. Almost immediately after the end of the occupation, the Trade Association Law was amended to encourage cartels. The Export Transactions Law exempted from antitrust proscription certain cooperative export arrangements among competitors.[38] And between 1953 and 1961, some twenty statutes permitted cartel formation in nearly every industry in the Japanese economy.[39]

Meanwhile, revisions in the Antimonopoly Law permitted manufacturing corporations to hold the shares of competitive firms. Financial institutions were allowed to hold up to 10 percent of the shares of other firms, thereby increasing ties between banks and producers. Interlocking directorates were legalized, and the scope of cartels was widened. The *zaibatsu* in particular were quick to reconsolidate their many fragments into replicas of their prewar organizational families. The result was the formation of the various horizontal and vertical *keiretsu* described in Chapter 2: sweeping oligopolistic networks of suppliers, distributors, manufacturing partners, and financial institutions. The collective economic power of these conglomerates made it essential to include them in any major policy decisions.

As the Americans began to roll back their original assault against Japanese big business, they simultaneously began a wholesale attack on labor activities. While earlier signs could be found of shifts in U.S. policy, the most dramatic demarcation came with MacArthur's direct intervention to ban a proposed general strike scheduled for February 1, 1947.[40] Subsequently, a cabinet ordinance in 1948 reversed the legalization of strikes by public sector unions; the Basic Labor Law was rewritten to make it less like America's prolabor Wagner Act and more like its antilabor replacement, the Taft-Hartley Act; communist activities were prohibited; war criminal charges were dropped against various prewar Japanese leaders; some ten thousand others were de-purged; a "Red Purge" banned some eleven thousand labor leftists from more than twenty industries; and the size of the public service was cutback in early 1949 as a result of the restrictive economic measures collectively known as the Dodge Line.[41]

Japan's conservative politicians aided the attack on labor. In January 1947 Yoshida denounced the union leaders as "lawless elements" (*futei no yakara*), a term widely used during the prewar repression of labor unions.[42] As Sheldon Garon has noted, "American and Japanese authorities began to sound more and more alike in their defense of 'democracy' and 'sound' unions against Communism."[43] At about this time George Atcheson made his famous statement that "the time has come when [conservative] Japanese aims have become virtually identical with Allied aims."[44]

Japanese business also lent its weight to curtailing labor's power. The Japan Federation of Employers' Association (JFEA, or Nikkeiren) was created explicitly to represent business interests in labor-management relations. Never ambiguous about its goals, JFEA publicly referred to itself as "Fighting Nikkeiren" and sought to roll back the initial powers garnered by labor unions. Nikkeiren waged a campaign to renegotiate early postwar collective bargaining agreements, to limit the scope of union activities, and to reassert managerial authority.

Conservative business leaders also mounted a systematic campaign to fragment and depoliticize the union movement at the plant level. Highly effective in this regard was the fostering of "second unions" that would renounce existing radical leaders and form more moderate unions willing to work within management-defined boundaries. Typically, violent confrontations between the first and second unions would take place—the latter protected by management, armed police, and often hired thugs—until the more radical union leadership had been deposed by management through "personnel curtailment" or else had become so marginalized that it posed no real threat to managerial autonomy.[45] These activities continued throughout the 1950s, culminating in the strongly antiunion activities of Nikkeiren and the Kishi government, the most notable battle of which resulted in the decisive defeat of the Sōhyō-backed coal miners' union, Tanrō, in July 1960 at Mitsubishi's Miike coal mine.

Japan's largest firms were also quick to organize for political influence. Indeed, on September 3, 1945, the day after surrender documents were signed, financial and business leaders met at the home of Nakajima Chikuhei, minister of commerce and industry, to discuss reestablishing the nation's business structures, strengthening and unifying the business world, and ensuring big business's continued preponderance within the national economy.[46] The organizational outgrowth was the Federation of Economic Organizations (FEO, Keidanren), formally inaugurated on August 16, 1946, and made up of the 100 or so largest trade and industrial organizations and the 750 or so largest individual firms.

In all of these ways, Japan's larger businesses overcame many of their otherwise important differences on such matters as firm size, location, and market, exporting versus importing, manufacturing versus finance and services, banking versus insurance and brokering, and the like. Trading associations, sectoral cartels, the *keiretsu*, and such peak associations as the FEO all helped to blur such differences and provide a cohesive political and economic voice for big business.

Finally, business deepened its ties to the national bureaucracy. Virtually every single sector of business falls under the administrative jurisdiction of a single government ministry. As a result, close ties were quickly reestablished between specific industries and their corresponding bureaucratic sectors. The banking and financial sectors, insurance, and brokerage firms all were linked with the Ministry of Finance. The Ministry of International Trade and Industry and the various manufacturing industries became closely tied. Physicians and the pharmaceuticals industry gravitated naturally to the Ministry of Health and Welfare. The communications industry was linked to the Ministry of Posts and Telecommunications, while construction firms developed close ties to the Construction Ministry and the Local Autonomy Agency. Fusing such linkages, as already noted, were the licensing powers of the various ministries and the institution of *amakudari*, through which retiring bureaucrats would "descend from heaven" to take high-level, high-paying jobs in firms within areas they once were charged with regulating.

Even as some segments of business pursued strategies that would guarantee them power in any postwar regime, smaller businesses were far more politically problematic. As was noted in Chapter 2, small enterprises have long constituted a far larger portion of the workforce in Japan than in any other country with a comparable level of industrialization. Some 99.7 percent of Japan's firms are defined by law as "small and medium-sized firms."[47] In the mid-1950s these employed 82.9 percent of the total workforce, and accounted for 68.3 percent of total national output.[48] Moreover, the 1950s and 1960s marked the period of greatest growth in these businesses, their numbers actually rising faster than GNP. Furthermore, the self-employed numbered about 16 percent of the workforce at this time. As a consequence this entire aggregation presented a voting, financial, and productivity force that could be ignored by politicians only at their peril.

As a sector, small business was never as cohesively organized for political or economic actions as were the farmers or larger businesses. Their economic interests and needs were inevitably less cohesive, divided as this sector always is into many diverse operations. Most small firms found common interest with one another principally when they faced some common outside threat—such as competition from much larger firms moving into a shared geographical market, or changes in government policy that would have systematically detrimental effects on their diverse enterprises. In fact, some fifty thousand organizations exist to serve smaller businesses. As Ishizaka Taizo, chairman of the Federation of Economic Organizations, once said, it is just as hard to organize medium and small enterprises as it is to make imported rice stick together in a ball.[49] Moreover, as noted above, the efforts of the JSP, particularly during the Katayama and Ashida governments, to improve links between the left and small business threatened to bring much of small business not into the conservative camp but into the opposition.

Even though eventually these smaller firms became a keystone in the conservative's electoral coalition, politicians were divided over how much policy attention to give to them. Thus, the Yoshida Liberals with their big-business orientation and their deflationary macroeconomic policies were relatively contemptuous of the small firms' inefficiency and lack of modernity. Even more problematic for linking small businesses to the conservative camp was the Yoshida government's acceptance and implementation of the economic austerity of the Dodge Line in 1949. This macroeconomic retrenchment program left its sharpest marks on smaller firms.

For many conservative backbenchers, however, including Nakasone Yasuhiro, who eventually became prime minister in 1983, any focus on business that ignored the smaller firms, as the Yoshida government appeared to be doing, was politically irrational. Recognizing the voter potential of Japan's sizable small-business sector, and in conjunction with the All Japan Small and Medium Sized Industries Council (Zenchūkyō), they convinced Yoshida to reverse some of the more extreme measures.[50] An Advisory Committee for the Promotion of Small and Medium-Sized Enterprises (Chūshōkigyō Shinko Shingikai) was also established in the lower house of parliament.

In addition, many conservative politicians pressed to allow small businesses to forge protective cartels, similar to those allowed for larger firms. The legal basis for such action grew out of the Provisional Law on the Stabilization of Specified Medium and Small Sized Industries of 1952. These cartels were authorized to coordinate production, marketing, and investment in specified industries under particular conditions. This law became permanent in 1953.

At about the same time, the Japan Political League of Small and Medium Sized Enterprises was created to provide an organizational forum for small businessmen and simultaneously to press for legislation that would "strengthen the unity of small and medium-sized enterprises." Its leader, Ayukawa Gisuke, in fact pressed for legislation that would make membership in the league nearly unconditional and compulsory.[51] This body proved to be an early organizational vehicle for small business, and in support of its legislative proposals the organization periodically mobilized upward of three hundred thousand businessmen for rallies outside the parliament.[52] The Law for the Organization of Small and Medium-Sized Enterprises, passed in 1957, provided tremendous organizational assistance to that sector.[53]

Even more organizationally significant, in 1961 the conservatives created the General Federation of Small and Medium Enterprise Organizations (Sōrengō), a national body designed to provide support for the government, the LDP, and the promotion of antisocialist economic systems.[54]

Thus, by the early 1960s, despite the diversity of the sector and all the ensuing organizational problems, a number of measures had built economic and institutional bridges between the small-business sector and the LDP. With only minor challenges, these remained in effect well into the 1980s, shoring up the small-business sector as an essential electoral support base of the conservative coalition. And simultaneously, larger firms were building similar linkages through subcontracting and distribution arrangements that began to knit together the economic fortunes of small and large firms.

In contrast to the organization diffusion of small businesses, the Japanese farm sector had long been highly corporatized. The rural sector remained politically and even economically vital. As late as 1950 nearly one-half of Japan's labor force (48.3 percent) was employed in the primary sector, the bulk in agriculture. Agriculture also accounted for over one-quarter of the nation's total net domestic product.[55] Like small business, farming could be ignored only by the most politically myopic.

The cooperative movement proved organizationally critical to fusing the agricultural sector with the conservative camp. Between early 1948 and the end of the year, the number of cooperatives jumped from just below 900 to nearly 29,000.[56] Eventually, Japanese cooperatives gained control of the properties, tasks, and employees of the prewar Nōgyōkai.[57] The National Association of Agricultural Cooperatives, popularly known by its Japanese acronym, Nōkyō, is "an incredibly complex, loosely knit, and unwieldy organization,"[58] composed of some seven thousand local cooperatives and enrolling nearly 100 percent of Japan's farm families. Although nominally voluntary, the agricultural cooperatives were so comprehensive in their services, ranging from the allocation of credit, production materials, and technology to the actual purchase and sale of crops, that it became virtually impossible for most farm families not to join. Moreover, the cooperatives were the recipients of a wide array of subsidies and loans from the government, enhancing their economic power over farm families and rural areas more generally while simultaneously fusing agricultural ties to government.

These organizations and the farmers they represented did not automatically fall into line behind conservative politicians. As noted, the political left was initially active in attempting to gain rural support. Increasingly critical to forging ties between the farm sector and conservative politicians were local links formed through the Nōkyō and the various personal support groups (kōenkai) of individual conservative politicians, who in turn used their parliamentary positions to function as pro-farm lobbyists. The agricultural cooperatives eventually became one of the most critical bastions of conservative electoral strength. Robert Scalapino and Junnosuke Masumi claim that during the early 1960s they were "undoubtedly the most vital affiliation for the conservatives at the mass level."[59] Still, it was not until 1960 that rural votes for conservatives began to outstrip conservative support in other areas and become the bulwark of conservative electoral strength.

These three sectors by no means define the universe of socioeconomic interests and associations underpinning the conservative regime. Muramatsu Michio, Ito Mitsutoshi, and Tsujinaka Yutaka, for example, identify some 252 major interest associations in Japan as of the late 1970s. Of these just below one-half (48.8 percent) were formed between 1946 and 1955.[60] Tsujinaka, taking a much broader perspective in later work, finds over ten thousand private organizations in Japan as of 1960, covering a host of professional, economic, agricultural, labor, scientific, administrative, and other associations.[61] Conservatives in politics and the bureaucracy were active in reaching out to the bulk of these other interests, and the vast majority of these groups developed extensive organizational and personal contacts with conservative politicians, particularly as the LDP's hold on power continued over time. Still, none had anything like the combination of economic and electoral power of the three sectors noted above. Others were certainly not in a position to *shape* the character of the dominant socioeconomic coalition in Japan; at best a few of them, such as the Japan Medical Association, were in a position to tip the balance on specific policy questions related to their own spheres of influence. As such they were, at best, shakers, not makers, of conservative coalitional possibilities.

The cumulative coalitional picture that emerges from the above sketch is clear. Key elements of the eventual conservative regime, most notably farmers, big business, and small business, all became well organized from the grass roots to the national level. This was in direct contrast to the major social bloc behind the opposition, organized labor, which was far more fragmented at both the plant and national levels. Consequently, early efforts by the Japanese left to formulate a Red-Green, or worker-farmer, alliance proved exceptionally difficult. More to the immediate point, the socioeconomic base for the conservative regime became far more substantial and cohesive than the socioeconomic base of any plausible opposition.

Creating Electoral Possibilities

One of the foremost structural and institutional problems that Japan's conservatives had to confront was the transformation of Japan into an electoral democracy. As was noted above, elections and party politics, while not completely insignificant in the formation of prewar governments, were never more than one relatively minor, often inconvenient, element in the process. Of forty-four prewar cabinets, at most seventeen could be said to have been headed by party leaders.[62] Government and the economy were thus well insulated from regularized electoral supervision. The postwar constitutional democracy, however, required that any future conservative control would need victories at the polls.

Two electoral components were particularly important: the electoral system itself and the creation of a political party able to accommodate the diversity of conservative interests and still win electoral majorities. Each was the product of conscious political calculation and engineering.

Selecting the Electoral System

Japan's new constitution provided for universal male and female suffrage, parliamentary democracy, and free elections. Yet it specified nothing about the critical question of which electoral system would be utilized. The system in use from 1925 until the end of the war involved an unusual mixture of multimember districts and single ballots. The system had worked to the advantage of prewar conservatives and was one to which they ultimately sought to return.

From the start of the occupation, conservative Japanese officials had been anxious to hold elections so as to forestall unilateral occupation initiatives; the Americans were equally desirous for an election to delineate a clean break from the prewar system, to select new leadership, to mark the change toward democracy, and to permit rapid parliamentary ratification of the new constitution.[63] In the rush toward the 1946 election, a system was used that was completely different from anything tried in Japan (or possibly the world) before. Somewhat paralleling Japan's 1900 system, it involved relatively large electoral districts (two to fourteen representatives apiece) in which each voter cast from one to three ballots depending on the number of members to be returned from the district.

Combined with the massive political purge of prewar politicians, this new system resulted in the total transformation in the nation's political leadership noted above. The prewar conservative parties that had reorganized themselves to contest this first election had been decimated by SCAP's purge. Some 83 percent of the incumbent representatives were weeded out at the time they declared their candidacy for office.[64] Others were purged following the election. Thus, the reformed Minseitō Party initially fielded 274 candidates; of these only 10 escaped the purge. The former Seiyūkai sought to run 43 candidates, of whom 33 were disqualified. Similarly, 21 of the Cooperative Party's 23 candidates were banned by the purge; of the remaining two, one was defeated and the other left the party. Massive party reorganization and electoral chaos ensued for conservative party members. Among the other surprises were the election of five members from the Japan Communist Party along with ninety-two members of the Japan Socialist Party. None of this boded well for the long-term fortunes of Japan's conservatives.

The proliferation of political parties, the success of the left, and the total alteration in parliamentary personnel led Japan's conservatives to press for a return to the prewar single-ballot, multimember district system. SCAP's Government Section was unalterably opposed; nonetheless, MacArthur and Major General Courtney Whitney left the decision to Yoshida. In a so-called forced vote (*kyōkō saiketsu*) in parliament, the election law was revised back to a slightly modified version of the 1925 system.[65] The Public Office Election Law of 1950 retained these changes, and from then until 1996 the medium-sized, multimember, single-ballot system remained in place for the lower house elections.

A number of pro-conservative biases were built into the system. First, there was heavy rural gerrymandering. Second, a premium was placed on local, as opposed to national, voter mobilization. Any party anxious to win a parliamentary majority had to elect roughly two candidates per district. With each citizen having only one vote, well-organized, grassroots campaigns by local notables enjoyed an advantage over less well-organized candidates touting national policy proposals. In the early postwar years, conservatives were particularly well-suited to take advantage of such localized politics.

A third advantage for conservatives was that voters could vote *against incumbents* without necessarily voting for an *opposition party* candidate. The system eliminated voting choices that would be zero-sum as between parties. One could vote against conservative candidate A by voting for conservative candidate B. As a result, a (large) party could be constantly regenerated over time without ever losing power.

Finally, the system stimulated a fragmented opposition by fostering minor parties. Many seats required only 12–15 percent of the total district vote. Hence candidates or political parties with thin but committed slices of support had little incentive to combine with other parties or candidates by compromising their policy or ideological positions; instead they could retain their own idiosyncrasies, mobilize their small bands of committed supporters, and gain parliamentary representation. Thus, the electoral system made it possible for the DSP to split off from the JSP following the 1960 election and to continue holding its seats in parliament. Subsequently, the system bolstered the several small niche parties that blossomed during the 1960s and 1970s.

The revision in the electoral system proved devastating to the rising left and a corresponding boon to the Yoshida forces. News reports estimated that the re-establishment of the single-ballot, multimember system cost the Socialist Party at least fifty seats in 1947.[66] Riding the crest of SCAP's "reverse course," Yoshida's Liberals went on to win a decisive victory in the 1949 election, in part due to the biases of the new electoral system, gaining an absolute majority in the lower house with 56.7 percent of the seats.[67] Added to the totals for the Democratic Party, the combined conservatives gained some 63 percent of the vote and 74.5 percent of the seats, an 11 percent premium of seats over votes. For only the fifth time in Japan's sixty-year parliamentary history, a single party had won a clear majority. The victory set a pattern of conservative domination of the electoral process that remained unchallenged over the ensuing decades.

Conservative parties continued to benefit from the system with a seat bonus of anywhere from 2 percent to over 11 percent more than its percentage of the vote.[68] The Socialists meanwhile began an almost inexorable decline, offset by only minor upticks.[69] In short, the new electoral system proved a singular boon to the electoral fortunes of Japan's conservatives in their earliest years, and then subsequently throughout their long reign.

Formation of the Liberal Democratic Party

No single event was more symbolic of the increased conservative cohesion than the creation of the Liberal Democratic Party. Following the unification of the Liberals and Democrats on November 15, 1955, Japan's conservatives had a single and eminently successful electoral vehicle through which to contest elections.

Before that fusion, Japan's political conservatives found it difficult to dovetail. In 1952 Japan had three major conservative political parties, the Progressive Party, the mainstream Liberal Party, and the anti-Yoshida Liberals centered on Hatoyama Ichiro. Except for their general hostility toward the left, the three shared little.

Issues related to rearmament, constitutional revision, ties to the United States and China, economic structure, and labor-management relations produced deep divisions among the conservatives. Woven into these divisions were clusters of politicians with divergent socioeconomic orientations (toward agriculture, small business, big business) and divergent agendas on regional autonomy, educational policies, the position of the Emperor, and economic ties to various parts of Japan's prewar empire.

Personalities were divisive as well. At the time of the purge, Yoshida had been explicitly selected by Hatoyama Ichiro to "hold his place" in the party. When Hatoyama returned to public life, Yoshida refused to surrender what he now viewed as his party. A long-standing division between followers of these two powerful and commanding individuals resulted. This division was furthered by the fact that retired bureaucrats provided many of Yoshida's most significant recruits for the Liberal Party whereas Hatoyama's followers were predominantly long-term politicos.

As evidence of their importance, former bureaucrats accounted for 17 percent of the successful Liberal Party candidates in the 1947 election for the lower house; by the 1953 election this figure had risen to 25 percent. Bureaucratic representation in the upper house was even higher; in the 1953 House of Councilors election, 40.7 percent of the conservatives elected were former bureaucrats; and in the next election (1956) this figure rose to nearly 48 percent. Former bureaucrats dominated the cabinet positions in these early governments, taking nearly half of the positions in the first Yoshida cabinet and 45 percent of them in the second Yoshida cabinet.[70]

Although this division between "pure politicians" and "ex-bureaucrats" divided conservative politicians, the ex-bureaucrats were an important bridge to the administrative world. Yoshida's civil service recruits were well positioned to gain critical policy information from their former agencies, and many were instrumental in mobilizing these agencies' support for conservative policies.

The fusion of the left and right wings of the socialist movement on October 13, 1955, was a major incentive for conservative politicians to overcome their own divisions. With the Socialists holding about one-third of the parliamentary seats, they had sufficient momentum to become the largest single party and perhaps gain a clear majority. The threat to conservative interests—constitutional, economic, security, ideological, and electoral—was clear. Consequently, as Masumi has suggested, "There was probably no alternative to a merger of the conservative parties if the government were to be defended from the advancing Socialist party. The conservative camp had lost the capacity to maintain two conservative parties."[71]

It was big-business leaders who led the merger. Various financial scandals involving business contributions to the conservative parties had left businesses reluctant to continue behind-the-scenes contributions to competing parties and politicians. Individual business leaders were similarly reluctant to pick sides when approached for contributions. Far more appealing was a merger, with regularized business donations as the guaranteed carrot. A safe funding body to supply "all" of the business world's contributions was created, the Economic Reconstruction Council (Keizai Saiken Kondankai) under the leadership of Keidanren Vice-Chairman Uemura Kōgorō.

As the *Asahi Shimbun* commented at the time, "Perhaps the people of the business world could help in purifying the political world by . . . pooling contributions. Put the contributions into a blender to remove their coloring, so to speak, consolidate them, and use them to implement policies for reconstructing the Japanese economy."[72] There is strong suspicion that the U.S. government also provided support for the merger, including funds for the new LDP. (U.S. documents on the matter have been blocked from declassification—most probably for this very reason.)

The electoral system further facilitated the merger. Individual conservative parliamentarians with their specific local roots did not have to surrender their seats for the parties to merge. Nor did they have to decide which specific conservative candidate would compete in a particular district. Rather, two, three, or four candidates from the merging parties could continue to be elected from their original districts with no major adjustments, something that would have been impossible under a single-member district system or even under a list system of proportional representation. And of course such a locally based electoral system made it easier for individual conservative candidates to obfuscate or reinterpret the policy positions of the newly formed party. The reformulated electoral system was consequently ideal for a conservative party with multiple competing individuals holding divergent views on important matters of policy.

Despite such advantages, few conservative politicians believed that the diverse and fissiparous conservative tendencies could remain quiescent under the single LDP umbrella. Miki Bukichi, for example, suggested at its formation that the party was likely to last ten years at most.[73]

Indeed, the Japanese left and organized labor showed strength and long-term potential from the early years of the U.S. occupation into at least the late 1960s. Radicalization was widespread among important segments of the Japanese population; electoral support for the JSP rose rapidly, particularly among salaried workers, the highly educated, women, and youth.[74] Meanwhile, Japanese labor unions engaged in sustained and frequently violent strikes that offered no basis for anticipating some form of "business-labor harmony."

Electoral demographics appeared to favor labor and the progressives, since the conservative's base was composed of rapidly dwindling social groups. Indeed, Ishida Hirose, an important member of the LDP and a Labor Minister in the Ikeda cabinet, in an extremely influential article offered a series of projections showing how electorally ominous socioeconomic conditions were for the conservatives. If current demographic trends continued without shifts in the voting orientations of major blocs, Ishida warned, the LDP would be ousted from power by 1968.[75]

Nevertheless, when the LDP was formed, it enjoyed a two-to-one majority over the Socialists, a ratio that lasted into the 1990s (the LDP's margin vis-à-vis the *combined* opposition parties did diminish substantially in the late 1970s). Until its split in 1993, no party ever won more seats in a lower house election; only in the 1989 election for the upper house (under which only one half of the house is elected at a time) did the party actually lose its first national election. Conservative electoral predominance remained virtually uncontestable for thirty-eight years.

Such control over governmental institutions also allowed the fused conservatives to bypass the JSP on numerous policy matters, thereby increasing internal coherence within the LDP itself. Ongoing struggles with a common enemy began to take precedence over internal disputes. In addition, the numerical superiority of the LDP allowed conservatives to determine the broad public policy directions the country would pursue over the succeeding decades.

Clearly, the major political trick was to keep the party intact and prevent either implosion or fragmentation. Dominance of government office and of the agenda for public policymaking provided the undeniable incentive for strange bedfellows to curl up together. Over time, a regular shuffling of cabinet and party positions, along with the perquisites of office, made membership in the Liberal Democratic Party the only viable career choice for those aspiring to positions of power.

Toward Policy Unity: An Economics to Fuse Politics

The creation of the conservative regime's institutional and coalitional base pre-dated the establishment of any cohesive policy paradigm that could keep the regime intact. Yet, some of the broad outlines of such a policy package were in place by the end of the occupation, including broad conservative agreement on capitalism and private ownership, as well as a defense and security posture that allowed U.S. bases to remain in Japan under bilateral security arrangements.[76] Furthermore, two im-portant dimensions of economic policy had been implanted during the occupation that were to remain long-standing components of conservative policies: a heavy dose of government-led economic planning and a commitment to fiscal austerity, a weak yen, and small government.

As early as March 1946 a group formed under Okita Saburo to plan Japan's post-war economy. It began with three assumptions: the Japanese political economy should be both peaceful and demilitarized; it would be far more egalitarian than the prewar economy; and Japan would participate fully in the international economic framework being shaped at Bretton Woods.[77] Ironically, however, it was the al-legedly market-oriented Americans who reintroduced economic planning to Japan. As American policy shifted from radical deconcentration to making Japan "the workshop of Asia," the Americans generated a series of centralized economic plans and promoted fusion among economic bureaucrats, top business leaders, and con-servative politicians. The first Economic Council, created in August 1950 by SCAP's Economic Stabilization Board (ESB) in conjunction with MITI, was heav-ily staffed by officials of the Federation of Economic Organizations on an industry-by-industry basis, a pattern that informed Japanese governmental economic plan-ning for several decades. The president of the FEO chaired a subcommittee on mining and manufacturing; the president of a leading trading firm headed the for-eign trade subcommittee; and a director of the National Shipowners Association was in charge of the subcommittee on transportation.[78] Subsequent proposals to develop a national industrial policy involved similarly close links between business leaders and the ESB, MITI, and MOF. The goal was to draft a broad outline of eco-nomic policy that would normalize Japan's export trade, increase economic self-sufficiency, and accelerate domestic capital accumulation.[79]

This pattern of close coordination in planning among senior bureaucrats from MITI, MOF, and the ESB with conservative party leaders and business leaders was carried out through meetings and exchanges, the submission of proposals, and for-mal exchanges in numerous advisory committees. The plans that emerged laid the foundation for subsequent Japanese policies of high-speed growth.

A second broad thrust to policy came in the form of fiscal austerity, an overval-ued yen, and small government. Once the Americans decided to allow a revitaliza-tion of Japanese industry, initial efforts were based on a priority production system (*keisha seisan hōshiki*) that targeted strategic industries such as coal, steel, and chem-icals. Substantial government subsidies were appropriated for those industries, necessitating an expansionist fiscal policy, deficit spending, and demand expansion, all of which threatened to generate high inflation. To reduce the inflationary impact, economic authorities in the occupation put strong limits on the withdrawal of personal savings and set a policy of tight wage restrictions.[80] And to limit the importation of foreign goods, multiple exchange rates and direct government control of all foreign trade were introduced.

Nonetheless, aid from the United States remained extremely high; Japanese governmental subsidies were rampant; and the exchange rate for Japanese yen was set on a product-specific basis ranging in 1948 from 180 to 800 yen per dollar.[81] It was against such a chaotic economic background that the major directions were set for tight fiscal policy, small government, and a fixed exchange rate. Joseph Dodge, president of the Bank of Detroit, was sent to Japan to restructure the Japanese currency and fiscal systems.

Dodge's policies began in fiscal year 1949 and were known collectively as the Dodge Line. Fiercely deflationary, they increased taxes not simply to balance the budget but to create surpluses to repay portions of the national debt and constrain inflation. In addition, larger enterprises in key industries were assisted by the government; small firms were excluded from help; a fixed exchange rate of 360 yen to the dollar was set; and a massive cutback was made in the size of the governmental workforce.

The Dodge Line brought about an end to rationing and price control. At the same time, the program represented what Maeda Yasuyuki has labeled "rationalization through unemployment" (kubikiri gōrika). The public sector saw 100,000 workers fired from the national railways while the Post Office and Nippon Telegraph and Telephone dropped about 220,000. Bankruptcies and the end of the black market led to further unemployment and to the elimination of important sponges for surplus labor. As a consequence of the Dodge Line's harshness, public sector union strength was depleted, the labor market tightened, and the winter of 1949 proved to be the harshest since the end of the war. Left-right controversies reached a fever pitch. Meanwhile, the economic recession did not end until the outbreak of the Korean War, which provided a demand stimulus to the Japanese economy.

Throughout this period, economic issues largely remained in the background. Policy debates focused on the constitution and its possible revision, numerous foreign policy issues, Japanese rearmament, U.S. nuclear testing and U.S. bases, the educational system and the replacement of elected with appointed school board members, the public sector's right to strike, the introduction of the Law to Prevent Subversive Activities, and a other noneconomic issues. Economics per se was rarely up for policy debate.

Left-right skirmishes reached a climax during the prime ministry of Kishi Nobusuke (1957–60). Kishi took office on February 25, 1957, openly proclaiming that he would seek a showdown (taiketsu) with the JSP and Sōhyō.[82] Soon after, he provoked confrontations on a host of ideologically sensitive issues. Various members of the National Railway Workers Union, including its chairman, were fired. A government ordinance withdrew union rights for certain categories of civil servants and prohibited automatic withholding of union fees. An "efficiency rating system" weakened the militant Japan Teachers Union. A temporary law preventing coal miners and electric power workers from striking was made permanent. Another bill strengthened and centralized the police.[83] A massive six-month strike at the Miike coal mine pitted the nation's business and labor organizations against one another. The result was the formation of a "second union" and what Miriam Golden has labeled a "heroic defeat" for the radical miners' union, Tanrō.[84]

Finally, in what proved to be his most dramatic confrontation with the left, Kishi oversaw the revision of the security treaty that Japan and the United States had adopted at the ending of the occupation in 1952. The content of the revised treaty and the way it was pushed through parliament generated the most vicious and sustained clashes between left and right in Japan during the postwar period. Its passage catalyzed months of public protest, massive street demonstrations and the death of one protester, public petitions by hundreds of thousands of Japanese, fistfights, boycotts, police clearings in parliament, the cancellation of a proposed visit by President Eisenhower, and the eventual resignation of the Kishi cabinet.

During the period, Kawakami Jōtarō, an elderly JSP leader, was stabbed. A month later so was Kishi, and on October 12, 1960, JSP chairman Asanuma Isamu was assassinated by a right-wing youth on live television. Early in 1961, a plot to murder the editor of the intellectual journal *Chūō Kōron* ended with the death of the editor's wife and maid.[85] The period was unquestionably one of vitriolic confrontation between the competing progressive and conservative forces.

Although in many respects, the Kishi period dealt a set of stunning defeats to the left, it also exacerbated divisions among the conservatives.[86] Party members remained divided on security policy, the possibilities for constitutional amendment, and economic policy. Three major clusters formed. Yoshida and followers like Ikeda, Sato, Fukuda—and to a lesser extent Hirokawa Kōzen—were antimilitary. Yoshida in particular strongly resisted U.S. demands for an expansion of Japan's Self-Defense Forces, and he was similarly reluctant to see any revisions in the postwar constitution. The group favored close alignment with the United States, despite the consequent loss of access to the China market and the loss of whatever international prestige might have come from a stronger military presence. Finally, this group was strongly supportive of the Dodge Line, its disinflationary budget, and sharp cutbacks in government spending. They were also generally committed to focusing national political attention away from ideologically charged issues and onto economic policies and growth. Consequently, they favored big business, disinflation, and the development of export markets, and they advocated a small but activist government bureaucracy.

In contrast, Hatoyama and his followers, including Miki Bukichi, Ōno Bamboku, Kōno Ichirō, and Ishibashi Tanzan, formed a second cluster. They favored positive rearmament, including a constitution rewritten to eliminate Article 9, a troop buildup, and a government spending policy to develop the arms industry. While hardly anti-American—indeed, Hatoyama's willingness to rearm made him John Foster Dulles's preferred candidate for the prime ministership—Hatoyama and his followers remained far more skeptical than Yoshida's group of the benefits of unquestioned alignment with the United States, the continuation of American bases in Japan, the loss of the China market, and continued hostility toward the Soviets.[87] On economic policy, the group, led particularly by Ishibashi, favored aggressive Keynesian stimulation of the economy and aid to smaller (and more electorally salient) businesses through protectionism and government subsidies. They sought a larger and more activist state and highly politicized economic policies.

The third group gravitated around remnants of the Democratic Party (formerly the Progressive Party). Miki Takeo, Ashida Hitoshi, and Kitamura Takutarō were among its major personalities. Strongly critical of the peace treaty with the United States, they pressed for Japanese rearmament and favored an Asian tilt in the party's foreign policy. They were by far the most left of center on economic policies, calling for various corrections to "abuses of capitalism" through expansion of economic planning and closer ties to unions.[88]

By the late 1950s and early 1960s, the most clear-cut division on economic and electoral issues was between the so-called Yoshida line, which favored an export-led (but market-driven) economic direction versus a line that put a greater emphasis on domestic development through central planning. The first group was generally interested in giving priority to economics; the second was willing to see other ideologically charged issues play a continued and vibrant role in national policy.

The first group, Yoshida's heirs, wanted a Japanese version of economic liberalism, albeit with a heavy dose of mercantilism; the second group was much closer to statism and social democracy. The first was externally focused, "bureaucratically rational," and largely apolitical; the second, preoccupied largely with the domestic economy, was less concerned with some abstractly defined "national interest" and more attentive to the domestic political consequences of economic policies.[89] The Yoshida group's limited political sensitivity to potential economic losers was clear in Finance Minister Ikeda's statements that "poor people should eat millet" and that it could not be helped if his proposed economic policies might result in a rash of bankruptcies and possibly suicides among small business people.[90]

Ironically, then, it was Ikeda who, later as prime minister, developed the economic policies that came to unite conservative party members. His policies managed to do at least three things. First, they put an end to the most serious left-right confrontation over ideologically charged issues like security and constitutional revision. Second, they provided a sufficient mixture of markets and planning to keep both big and small business happy. And finally, they laid out a policy direction that, if successfully implemented, could serve the interests of both the business community and election-sensitive politicians.

Ikeda became prime minister in 1960. He immediately moved toward "low posture politics" and a "politics of productivity."[91] This pattern formed the core of Japan's successful merger of economics and politics, bonded together the disparate elements in the conservative coalition, and provided the long-term policy profile under which the conservative regime sustained its stability and dominance.

Convinced that under Kishi and his predecessors the conservatives had dissi-pated far too much political capital on "ideological" issues such as defense and se-curity, foreign relations, constitutional revision, the police, and educational re-structuring, Ikeda promised to separate politics from economics. The conservatives could win on ideological issues only at a high political and economic cost since these issues provided marvelous opportunities for the opposition to mobilize and also di-verted government attention from economic improvement. As a consequence, Ikeda opted for what Meredith Woo-Cumings has aptly called a "Brumairian com-pact." "Just as the bourgeoisie of Louis-Bonaparte's France, prostrate before the rifle butt, traded its political rights for the right to make money, so did Japan."[92]

By deflecting attention to rapid economic transformation, Ikeda could deprive the opposition of its most biting issues. The opposition's greatest successes had come from tapping into the deep reservoir of skepticism about the prewar political order and the fear (real or imagined) that conservatives were endeavoring to recre-ate it. But the left had done little to distinguish itself through well-articulated eco-nomic proposals. The conservatives, in contrast, had begun to benefit from the na-tional economic growth spurt that began with the Korean War boom in 1950 and was, by Ikeda's time, nearly a decade old.

Ikeda's most successful gambit came in the implicit promise to double the na-tional income in ten years. This came against a backdrop of external demands for greater liberalization of the Japanese economy. When Japan had joined GATT in August 1955 the rate of its import liberalization as calculated by the Brussels Cus-toms Schedule was a mere 16 percent; as of 1961 it stood at only 26 percent. The Japanese government promised to liberalize to the 80 percent level within three years.

Yet economic divisions and uncertainties were widespread among different ele-ments of the conservative camp. Big business, small business, and agriculture were fearful of the possible impacts of trade liberalization. Different government min-istries were presenting conflicting demands. The LDP was similarly split; indi-vidual politicians' concerns about their electoral fortunes deepened the party's di-visions.

MITI, in conjunction with many ex-bureaucrats within the LDP and with some support from big business, favored a reorganization of selective industries for high growth. In contrast, many LDP members, particularly those with rural con-stituents, favored local infrastructural development policies in conjunction with the Ministry of Construction and the Local Autonomy Agency. The Japanese left and the labor movement meanwhile had been pressing for increased housing construc-tion and tax relief, welfare policies, and health insurance. On the latter two issues at least, they were joined in their demands by bureaucrats in the Ministry of Health and Welfare, and eventually by some LDP politicians anxious to co-opt the issues for their electoral appeal to small businesses and farmers.[93]

It was within this maelstrom that Ikeda made his proposal to double the national income in ten years. As Itō Daiichi has argued, Ikeda's proposal was "almost the only policy in whose formation the government party played an active—if limited—role. At least insofar as economic policy is concerned there was nothing else either before or after in the ten-year period [1955–65] in which the government party played such an active role."[94] Even though Ikeda gave the policy its political voice, much of the proposal had in fact grown out of plans put forth from civil servants within the Economic Planning Agency and the Ministry of Finance. Drawing the idea for the plan from an earlier slogan put forward by Prime Minister Hatoyama, Ikeda drew on his background as a former official of the Ministry of Finance to convince the initially dubious bureaucrats in that agency to support the plan, despite their earlier hesitation on economic grounds.[95]

Skeptics saw Ikeda's proposal as a political ploy to give him and the LDP credit for the rising wave of modernization and technological innovation already under way. Others criticized it for failing to give adequate consideration to the negative consequences of high growth for the environment and urban crowding. Neither captures the vital role the plan played in catalyzing national energy and mobilizing national effort toward sustained high growth, much as President Kennedy crystallized American energies by promising to put a man on the moon in ten years, or as German Finance Minister Ehrhard concentrated German economic efforts, or as the Rehn-Meidner Plan for "wage solidarity" in Sweden focused the goals of business and labor on higher productivity and higher wages within the social welfare state.

Essentially, Ikeda's plan targeted an average annual growth rate of 7.2 percent with a 9.0 percent goal for the first three years. The plan included rationalization of heavy industry, increases in social overhead capital, improvements in social security, and substantial budget increases for education and science and technology research. Linked to income doubling was a Comprehensive National Development Plan, a regional development plan targeting some thirteen new industrial cities and six "special areas for industrial facilities development" for massive government assistance in the development of industrial infrastructure. Finally, the plan called for a large shift of labor out of agriculture and small business and into large-scale manufacturing.

The plan thus served a welter of important political functions. An expanded labor market, cartelization, and rapid growth appealed to big business. MITI was happy with industrial targeting. Regional development was a boon to the areas affected as well as to local politicians, who quickly claimed credit for the influx of development funds in their districts. Equally happy were the Construction Ministry, the Local Autonomy Agency, and the national construction industry. Sufficient adjustment incentives made it clear that small and medium-sized industries and agriculture would not be left behind in the promised economic boom. And finally, by linking the plan to various social welfare measures, albeit measures quite distinct from those in the European social democracies, the plan co-opted a big issue from the left and increased the electoral appeal of the LDP.

As Ikuo Kume has suggested, the policy allowed Japanese citizens to realize that they were living in a growing economy with "income doubling" tied to popular improvement.[96] Miyazawa Kiichi, cabinet secretary-general, recollected that "it was

Ikeda's wisdom to sell 'income doubling' as a political agenda, not just as an economic prediction." Itō Masaya, an advisor to Ikeda declared, "I found that it is important in politics to convince people of some good future. . . . The experience of selling the 'income doubling plan' taught me this."[97]

This "policy with no losers"[98] thus brought together a number of potentially conflictual interests under a common ideological banner. Export-oriented liberals and domestically oriented planners were fused. The LDP, the MOF, the MITI, and the Economic Planning Agency were brought into close alliance on policy formation and policy goals.[99] Furthermore, to the extent that government planning included a heavy reliance on market forces and export-led growth, the new entrepreneurs in the business community were also more tightly woven into the fabric of the conservative regime.[100] In Ōtake's phrase, "Market dynamics remained active despite government leadership and state intervention."[101]

The focus on growth also had particular appeal to Japanese citizens. While Japanese consumers continued to bear a disproportionate share of the burden of Japan's producer-oriented economy, rapid growth finally began to legitimize individual consumption. It signaled an end to the period of sacrifice that had prevailed for over twenty years: No longer were Japanese citizens expected to suffer for some "greater good." Rapid economic growth and a doubling of the national income quickly translated into the right to pursue a doubling of one's own personal income. Indeed, the rapid growth during the next decade and beyond gave the vast majority of Japanese high expectations for their economic future: next year is virtually guaranteed to be better than last year; my children will unquestionably live better than I; the future holds greater promise than the past. It is difficult to imagine anything better for a politician and a political party's fortune than such a wave of popular optimism.[102]

In this chapter I had two major tasks. The first was to show how Japanese politics could have moved in several different directions in the postwar chaos and uncertainty. The early years after the war radically altered Japan's socioeconomic structures. Powerful prewar groups were either eliminated or drastically curtailed. Meanwhile, organized labor, given a major boost by the Americans, expanded extremely quickly, so that by 1950 Japanese unionization rates were substantially greater than in most Western European countries. Moreover, the Japanese left sought to link blue-collar unions with Japan's large farming population and to small businesses. Had this effort succeeded, Japan could well have taken on a political color similar to Scandinavia's Red-Green coalitions, West Germany's Social Democratic government in the 1960s, or Italy's conservative preeminence tempered by a much stronger and more heavily institutionalized political left. Japan might even have evolved in ways similar to corporatist Austria. In fact, of course, Japan moved toward the single-party, conservative hegemony which prevailed for thirty-eight years, the regime described in detail in Chapter 2.

The second purpose of this chapter was to show how the conservative regime gained its initial shape through an explicit political process with three dimensions.

First, a particular social coalition was forged. Second, Japan's conservatives benefited from the particular electoral system for the lower house of parliament that was reintroduced under the occupation. They also were aided by the creation of a single electoral vehicle for conservatism, namely the formation of the Liberal Democratic Party from two parties that had been erstwhile competitors and at times harsh enemies. Third, a set of public policies, particularly economic policies begun under Prime Minister Ikeda, gave direction and cohesion to the conservative socioeconomic support base.

The concentration of political and eventually public energy on the rapid expansion of Japanese national economic growth defused many of the opposition's previously most powerful issues while bringing the hitherto diverse conservatives into relative harmony. Ikeda's policies mobilized increasingly large segments of the national public around the common goal of economic betterment. The result was the combination of long-term conservative governmental rule and continued high economic growth.

PART II

REGIME SHIFTS—ADJUSTMENT,
COLLAPSE, AND
RECONSTRUCTION

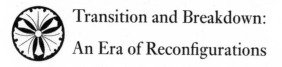

Transition and Breakdown:
An Era of Reconfigurations

This chapter and the two that follow examine regime transformations. All three question why and how stable regimes move away from equilibrium. More concretely, they explore why countries move through various incremental changes, minor adjustments, and tinkerings during time periods 1, 2, and 3 only to lurch dramatically in different directions at time period 4 or 5. What accounts for these infrequent but acute shifts in a nation's political economy?

Chapter 1 noted that although many regimes are highly unstable and in constant flux, postwar industrialized democracies have been characterized by institutional stability, consistent socioeconomic cleavages, and relatively constant public policy profiles. This was certainly the case for the four countries examined in that chapter and for Japan as portrayed in Chapter 2. This is not to deny the dynamism of these regimes. Even the most stable regime undergoes constant changes, yet most of these do not challenge the regime's stability. Like a sailboat tacking in the wind, the ship of state keeps heading in the same direction. Periodically, however, more comprehensive shifts occur in even the most stable regimes. These are marked by new coalitional arrangements, altered institutional configurations, or shifts in the underlying policy profile. Less frequently, all three alter fundamentally, and a comprehensive reconfigurationation of the regime occurs. These different degrees of change are not easily distinguished. Moments of revolutionary transformations are rare. More frequent are the minor corrections that shade into broader shifts that in turn blur into more comprehensive transformations.

In the first part of this chapter I examine three major catalysts for change within previously stable industrialized democracies. In the second, I provide an analytic basis for differentiating the changes that occur within stable regimes. These range from simple readjustments to comprehensive breakdowns and reconfigurations.

Finally, I return to the four countries discussed in Chapter 1, analyzing the substantial changes they all went through between the late 1970s and the early 1990s.

Challenges to Regime Stability

Absent a force strong enough to deflect it, any equilibrated regime will, by the very definition of equilibrium, continue unchanged. Yet change is constant in even stable industrialized democracies. Typically most confront a host of potential threats, three of which deserve special note: the socioeconomic problem, the electoral or democratic problem, and problems generated by a regime's interactions with the larger world. Each can potentially alter the incentives of a regime's political and economic actors. The results can range from minor and ad hoc intraregime adjustments to a newly configured regime.

Socioeconomic challenges result from a variety of ongoing changes. As a nation's economy expands and changes, so do the relative strengths of its industrial and socioeconomic sectors. Ever more complicated manufacturing processes replace simpler ones; the demand for highly skilled labor rises while that for less skilled labor declines; simple farms give way to complex agribusinesses; services become more critical; financial instruments and industrial alliances become ever more complicated. Economic growth also typically leads to higher levels of national education, a larger middle class, smaller families, and an aging population. Immigration and emigration can also reconfigure the population. In short, economic dynamism engenders demographic changes that in turn require constant adjustments in national political arrangements.

Any regime with a particular equilibrium is continually confronted by the changing incentives and balances of power among its supporters. Compromises, tradeoffs, and changing rewards constantly readjust the regime's support base.

All democratic regimes face a second challenge: they all require a minimum public acquiescence through the electoral process. However circumscribed the links between elections and power, the ballot box affords the voting public periodic opportunities to influence the character of governmental officeholders.

Voting and elections clearly have limited power over officials. Consider how political parties and electoral systems constrain coalitions among social groups. Voters must always choose from broad packages of policies put together by competing parties, the specific composition of which they are usually powerless to influence. Moreover, to partake in government, parties compromise with one another and with interest groups, again a process over which voters have little or no control.[1] In an electoral democracy, nonetheless, officials anxious to stay in power must periodically demonstrate that they enjoy at least the passive tolerance, if not the active support, of a significant segment of the populace. And as voters' preferences change, a regime's political leaders must ultimately respond.

One of the most frequently analyzed underpinnings of any regime is its electoral coalition—the regular or shifting delivery of votes from specific economic, occupa-

tional, regional, ethnic, class, linguistic, religious, age, or gender blocs. These align-ments help to determine a regime's biases, and major socioeconomic realignments are typically associated with "critical" elections.[2]

Yet such electoral support is only one facet of the broader socioeconomic alliance structure that underpins any democratic regime. Landholders, intellectuals, labor, the military, religious organizations, urban dwellers, or even organized crime are but a few of the groups whose support may be absolutely essential to a particular regime. Equally valuable is at least the passive acquiescence of segments of the financial and industrial communities. Critical, too, may be non-national actors, whether these be governments, international organizations, or private multina-tional corporations. Such groups and sectors provide essential socioeconomic sup-port—moral, financial, or physical—to any regime. As Stein Rokkan reminded us in Chapter 1, "votes count; resources decide." A democratic regime must maintain a socioeconomic coalitional base that transcends the electoral support it mobilizes every few years.

Most often, there will be a heavy overlap between the electoral and nonelectoral segments of a regime's socioeconomic base. Still, tensions arise between actions de-signed to appease voters and those required to meet the demands of nonvoters—which points to one of the major nonelectoral constraints on democratic govern-ments, namely, the need to sustain the national economy and provide domestic and international security. Meeting such demands, while not necessarily at odds with electoral popularity, requires support well beyond that needed to win votes and gain office.

Any modern democracy rests heavily on the confidence of those who control capital. Whether through passive support for market forces and corporate hierar-chy, through active economic intervention favoring specific sectors or corporations, or through mixtures of both, any capitalist democracy depends on regularized sup-port from those who control the bulk of the nation's economic assets.[3]

Despite differences, all countries seek to provide a mixture of capitalism, private profit, market economics, and corporate independence capable of ensuring that "business confidence" will not be eroded and that capital will not flee beyond the national borders (and the albeit tenuous control of state office holders).[4] Business confidence and electoral politics are often explicitly linked, a point that is cynically captured in an exchange between Huey Long, one of America's premier politicians, and his state's "business community." Long allegedly called a meeting of Louisiana business leaders to discuss his reelection prospects. "Those of you who come in with me now," he said softly, "will get big pieces of pie. Those who come in with me later will get smaller pieces of pie. Those who don't come in at all will get—*Good Government*."[5]

Public policies in the interests of nonelectoral supporters are critical. Consider the demands of the financial sector and the bond market for stable monetary policy and consistent interest rates—and their frequent conflict with electoral strategies.[6] No less critical are the demands of military planners or foreign-policy experts for increased arms budgets, satellite surveillance, alliance structures, or trade pacts with unpopular foreign governments, not to mention the dispatch of troops abroad. The maintenance of electorally unpopular alliances or foreign-trade pacts, inflation control measures, taxes, unpopular military installations, costly arms build-ups, intrusive police officers or foreign soldiers, and apparent compromises of national sovereignty are but a few examples of how the maintenance of economic health and security often require compromises with citizen popularity.

Measures aimed at retaining the confidence of business and ensuring external protection often conflict with electoral popularity. Many who contribute to the regime in nonelectoral ways are skeptical of the politician's responsiveness to "mere electoral numbers" and seek to reduce the electorate's power and influence over public policy. They prefer a government that is "efficient" (albeit with an efficiency biased in their favor). Conversely, voters and voting blocs rail against "special interests" interfering with mass opinion and the "national will." Such conflicts are a constant challenge to any regime.

A third important challenge to regime stability arises from the interaction between the domestic political economy and the international system. In the nineteenth century many governments were able to separate domestic politics from international pressures. Each nation-state was like a separate billiard ball ricocheting off others. Increasingly throughout the twentieth century, by contrast, international influences have become more penetrating; rarely do they take the simple form of government-to-government interactions. The leaders in any democratic regime must be sensitive to how domestic actions affect the nation-state's international posture and, at the same time, how the regime's international behavior will influence the strengths and resources of key domestic actors.[7]

International economic and security coordination among the advanced democracies have increased particularly since the breakdown of Bretton Woods in 1971 and the two world oil shocks of 1973 and 1978. In various forums such as the G-3 and the G-7, NATO, GATT, the IMF, the World Bank, the World Trade Organization, NAFTA, APEC, the European Union, and other regional and transregional organizations, the major industrialized democracies (often collaborating with less-industrialized partners) have sought to coordinate their economic and security policies. Not uncommonly, such actions have constrained the domestic political options available to the contracting parties.

Today, multinational corporations, financial institutions, insurance firms, and asset traders seek transnational market access, for which they need allies both in government offices and domestic markets. Meanwhile, international organizations collect data, press for common labor practices and rights for women and children, monitor civil liberties, and inspect hospitals, schools, and factories. Similarly, social movements and nongovernmental organizations concerned with particular environmental, ethnic, gender, ideological, religious, and other goals forge alliances that transcend national boundaries.[8]

The results can be complex. At times, outside pressures may generate enhanced domestic support. At least as frequently, they may threaten political leaders, their policy profiles, and their socioeconomic support. Non-national actors may even forge cross-border alliances that bypass domestic institutions.[9] In short, the areas of political economy that can be analyzed in purely domestic terms are shrinking, and no industrialized regime can safely ignore forces beyond its geographical borders.[10]

All three challenges—changing voter preferences and new socioeconomic arrangements, conflict between electoral demands and economic and security requirements, and competition between domestic and international pressures—have the potential to destabilize a regime. Yet, as the next section will demonstrate, adjustment to such challenges can range widely.

Between Adjustment and Breakdown

Political actors are constantly calculating the advantages and disadvantages of alternative alliances, strategies, policies, institutions, and tactics. Whenever a previously stable situation seems shaky, political calculations begin anew: how best to maintain, enhance, or minimize the damage to my interests?

Within stable democracies, the most common challenges rarely generate calculations that lead to radical overhaul of core institutions, coalitions, or policies. Ongoing relationships are sufficiently stable so that powerful leaders can respond adeptly and flexibly to challenges and changes—much as the automatic pilot makes a series of nuanced adjustments that keep an airplane on course, avoid major turbulence, and respond to circumstances that might, if unattended, lead to a crash. The more flexible a regime's key actors are at making such adjustments, the more intact, healthy, and stable the regime will be.

Perfect anticipation is, quite obviously, impossible; and crises present challenges that even if they were predictable would still necessitate substantial change. When anticipation is poor or pressures are overpowering, more drastic changes are inevitable. At the extreme, the result is a massive lurch—a regime shift—that is followed eventually by the establishment of a new regime around some new homeostasis.

Changes within a regime can thus be scaled along a spectrum. At one extreme lies unchanging continuity and perfect equilibrium; at the other, complete collapse and overhaul. Falling in between are adjustments ranging from trivial to substantive. Minor changes are the most frequent, but these do little to alter the regime's fundamentals: personalities come and go; new policies are adopted and old ones modified; bureaus are added or subtracted, and so forth. To the extent such changes are superficial, the regime's underlying coalitional arrangements, institutions, and public policy direction remain largely intact. At the other pole are challenges that infrequently generate substantial redirections: an altered socioeconomic coalition gains power, and a new public policy profile results; new institutional arrangements undermine the power bases of old coalitional supporters; public policy changes spill over into new institutional arrangements. Determining what kinds of changes constitute within-regime shifts and which are so substantial as to constitute a completely new regime is by no means self-evident.[11]

For analytic purposes, three distinct orders of magnitude can be differentiated. The simplest level are *first-order changes*, confined primarily to only one of the three major segments of any regime. Such changes are by far the most common. They rarely generate comprehensive realignments in the regime; instead, they can be categorized as intraregime adjustments.

Changes in the direction of an important public policy, or a significant recalibration of the mixture of public policies, are perhaps the most common first-order changes. President Nixon's 1971 decision to alter America's long-closed relations with China, Switzerland's decision to expel migrant workers in the late 1970s, Finland's decision to enter the European Union in 1995, and Britain's decision to devalue sterling in 1967 are all examples of policy shifts with high salience and widespread impact. But they were made with no serious reordering of the regimes' socioeconomic coalitions or institutional bases.

Much the same can be said of certain limited socioeconomic alterations. Ruling parties frequently attract small new electoral constituencies and lose others. Coalitions are periodically readjusted; new partners are added and old ones ousted or replaced. Many smaller European governments go through such processes regularly; rarely are these accompanied by massive shifts in public policy or in the nation's political or economic institutions. Such shifts too can be considered first-order or intraregime changes. The same is true of many institutional changes. New government bureaus or agencies are added constantly; firms enter into new alliances. Neither normally generates any fundamental recalibration of the regime.

Rather more substantial are what might be thought of as *second-order changes*. Characterized by interrelated and recursive shifts in two of the three variables, such changes have far greater impact. As an example, consider the shifts that took place in Sweden in 1957–59 when substantial pension reform was combined with an alteration in the socioeconomic coalition—from a Red-Green base linking labor and agriculture to a Red-White base forged around blue- and white-collar labor. Yet, substantial as the changes were in the Social Democratic regime, they led to no alteration in the underlying corporatist institutions nor to the country's basic commitment to a social welfare state.

Likewise, when the 1964 Civil Rights Bill was signed, President Johnson confessed privately that he had just signed a bill that would "kill the Democratic Party in the South." History proved him correct. Over the following three decades a systematic shift took place in the socioeconomic coalitions behind the Republican and Democratic Parties at the national and local levels. Still, these shifts had only a marginal impact, if any, on the underlying political and economic institutions of the American regime. Not until perhaps the Reagan presidency, with its sweeping institutional changes, could one speak of a comprehensive shift in the American regime.

Finally, *third-order changes* are situations in which major changes take place along all three dimensions—institutions, coalitions, and public policies. When these occur it is possible to talk of a comprehensive "regime shift."

In this sense, the three key variables of any regime are like tectonic plates. Each has its own integral shape and its own pattern of movement. To understand regime changes—from subtle adjustments to complete overhauls—what is critical is how they connect to one another, the degree of friction that develops among them, and the extent to which that friction is dissipated short of an earthquake. For varying periods of time the plates may remain motionless or shift slightly. Sometimes the direction in which they shift reduces the friction between them, and the effect is a period of relatively smooth plate adjustment. At other times, even a small movement increases the friction between plates. In one case, accommodation of ongoing and subtle changes keeps the preexisting regime intact, while in the other, stability presages serious adjustment and, at the extreme, complete transformation and movement toward a new regime.

Within this metaphor of shifting tectonic plates, day-to-day regime adjustments resemble the usually unnoticeable adjustments that constantly occur within and between the plates—at best minor blips on the seismograph. In contrast, a regime shift is more like a substantial earthquake with a strength capable of rupturing roads and toppling buildings—altering substantial pieces of the political landscape.

This process becomes clearer when one examines the regime adjustments, breakdowns, and transformations that took place within the four industrial democracies examined in Chapter 1. All four had been highly stable during the early decades following World War II. But at varying points between the late 1970s and the end of the 1980s, they all underwent relatively comprehensive changes. The causes of the shifts were myriad and varied from one regime to the next. In a few cases, major transitions involved striking breaks from the past even though no clear-cut and stable replacement regime emerged. In all cases, however, the alterations involved at least several first- and second-order changes. Where a regime shift unmistakably occurred, it was only when these changes were substantial enough to force a third-order reconfiguration.

Corporatist Sweden: Breakdown of the Blocs

From the 1930s into the early 1980s, a highly stable regime prevailed in Sweden. Major social blocs with entrenched relationships to political parties remained unchanged; corporatist relationships were well institutionalized and broadly accepted. Yet by the mid-1990s Sweden had undergone a substantial shift from its previously dominant social democratic regime; corporatist bargaining broke down and its institutional support structure was substantially eroded. Changes were rampant, although in 1998 it was still unclear precisely what shape any new regime would take.

The regime change was not the result of simple electoral politics. From 1976, when the Social Democrats lost at the polls, until their return to power six years later, there were few challenges to the ongoing policy profile, to the party system and the policy agenda, or to the corporatist arrangements that largely set the national economic agenda. Yet over the next decade, a series of underlying internal tensions within the dominant socioeconomic coalition were exacerbated largely as a result of declining Swedish export competitiveness. These tensions centered mainly on the long-standing policy of "wage solidarity."

Wage solidarity had been a key to the positive-sum mixture of Swedish labor policy and growth policy. As international economic competition intensified, however, manufactured products became subject to much higher standards for quality and cost in the international marketplace. Largely as a result of the pro-market adaptation processes built into wage solidarity, Sweden's industries had remained exceptionally adept at meeting this challenge. Productivity in large Swedish firms was high by any standard; for example, Sweden led the world in the per capita use of robotics for manufacturing. Problems arose, however, with the social democratic commitment to the use of the public sector to provide "jobs for everyone who wants to work." Expanding workforces drove down productivity in the public sector to dismally low levels, even as wage solidarity ensured that public-sector workers received consistent wage hikes proportional to those in the most profitable private-sector industries. Increasingly stark economic differentials led many businesses and many labor unions to press for wage flexibility over wage solidarity.

Workers in successful private-sector firms were able to command high salaries through autonomous bargaining and wage hikes outside the formal corporatist networks and the policy of wage solidarity. In contrast, public-sector workers enjoyed substantially less bargaining power. Yet wage solidarity inexorably linked the salary increases of the two groups. This both compressed wages and caused them to drift upward in the most competitive sectors of the economy.[12] This wage drift, along with slower growth, lowered the international competitiveness of many Swedish exports. Meanwhile rising tax burdens exacerbated tensions within the union movement.

Thus, despite the continuity of Social Democratic Party rule and the absence of any drastic revision in public policies, the internal tensions between two segments of the labor movement militated against any easy internal solution to the leftist dilemma. On the surface, regime arrangements looked terribly similar to those put into place in the late 1950s. Yet the regime faced an internal crisis that required drastic alteration, either in the public policy nexus on which it rested or on a serendipitous and long-term improvement in world economic conditions.

The tension was finally resolved by a breakdown in centralized wage bargaining that grew out of the class interests of both labor and management. In 1983 some Swedish employers, most conspicuously the Association of Engineering Employers (VF), joined with segments of the labor movement, most notably the Metalworkers' Union, to defect from peak level corporatist bargaining arrangements. Over the next several years, VF was joined by the broader Employers' Association (SAF) in its demand that peak bargaining be scrapped, and in the early 1990s "wage bargaining seesawed between peak-level and industry-level negotiations."[13]

A regime breakdown occurred in the early 1990s. It coincided with the creation of the anti-left government that took office in 1991 and with Sweden's decision to enter the European Union, but it also incorporated changes in labor-management bargaining.

In contrast to the earlier bourgeois coalition which held office from 1976–82, the new government was seriously committed to altering Swedish economic and social policies and policymaking structures. Public spending was reduced, final government expenditures were lowered, and public-sector employment was curtailed.[14] Tax reforms and financial market deregulation were also undertaken. Equally important was an "employer offensive" mounted by the Swedish Employers Association (SAF). In 1991 SAF withdrew its representatives from the boards of various state agencies, pulled out of corporatist arrangements completely, and dissolved the peak-business bargaining machinery. Wage negotiations became much more decentralized. This alleviated some of the nation's wage compression; it also ended wage solidarity and the national-level bargaining structures so critical to the prior regime.[15]

Meanwhile, Sweden's entry into the European Union put even greater market pressures on domestic actors to end wage compression and to tighten the link between labor compensation and international product competitiveness. By entering the union, Sweden opened the doors to possible flight by Swedish capital and manufacturing. Labor-cost adjustment and product competitiveness became even more essential. So did fiscal rectitude, and a budget deficit that stood as high as 10.4 percent was squeezed down to about 2 percent in accord with European Union standards, with an even broader commitment to seek a 2 percent budget surplus.

Although this fundamental reshaping of the Swedish political economy dismantled many elements of the previous social democratic system, the restructurings were, as Jonas Pontusson demonstrates, heavily bipartisan.[16] Also important for our purposes, the shifts in Sweden were characterized primarily by the fragmentation of important socioeconomic blocs within the corporatist system rather than by simple shifts in electorate preferences. The once unified union movement split in response to altered international economic conditions. Similarly, Swedish employers divided in accord with their respective international competitiveness and need for skilled workers. Internationally sheltered sectors of the economy involving both business and labor were pitted against the internationally unsheltered sectors. Ultimately, the entire mechanism of corporatism as a defining trait of the Swedish political economy came apart.

As one important indicator, the national commitment to exceptionally low unemployment rates withered. Unemployment had averaged between 1.6 percent in 1965–67 and 2.5 percent in 1980–82. It began to move upward at the end of the 1980s. Interestingly, however, although the Social Democratic Party regained power in 1994, it made no major effort to roll back the new gospel of fiscal rigor and low inflation. By the summer of 1996 unemployment had rocketed to 9.0 percent, and this number did not include many employees on training programs or special state-funded work.[17]

It is worth underscoring that in the Swedish case—in contrast to regime shifts in the United States and Britain—important changes were largely independent of the Swedish electoral cycle and occurred without party system realignments. Moreover, although some welfare benefits were rolled back, the system's underlying funding or principles were not attacked. Swedish social welfare was modulated but not dramatically overhauled. Here too Sweden stood in stark contrast with the Reaganesque and Thatcherite experiences.

The United States

Institutional and social fragmentation in the United States combined with a network of iron triangles exerting power over small segments of public policy make it much harder to identify comprehensive regime adjustments with great clarity. Rarely have regime changes in the United States involved the clearly defined splintering of groups or the coalitional realignments found in Sweden. At the onset of the Reagan administration and continuing for the next fifteen years, however, major changes took place in the socioeconomic coalition, the public policy profile, and the institutional arrangements that had dominated U.S. national politics since the Roosevelt administration.

The unraveling of America's New Deal regime had two principal causes. First, broad economic challenges arose from the difficulties of continuing America's role as both strategic and economic hegemon. This tension became particularly acute with the high inflation arising from the Johnson administration's refusal to raise taxes, cut back the Great Society, or curtail the Vietnam War. But the problems continued as many American-based industries faced increased competition from foreign products, particularly in manufactured goods.

Socioeconomic realignments were the second major cause of the New Deal's demise. These began with the Civil Rights Act of 1964 and the Voting Rights Act of 1965, both of which led to a growth in the number of black voters. But the realignments were also linked to the war and the fragmentation it caused within the Democratic Party. A coalition arose within the party that consisted primarily of opponents of the war but included other elements as well: middle-class liberals upset with the local politics of urban machines and with the "corruption" of close ties among industry, Congress, and executive agencies; blacks and other ethnic minorities catalyzed by the civil rights movement and seeking to extend their gains at both the local and national levels; and members of the women's movement seeking enhanced political influence.

The irony of this New Politics movement within the Democratic Party was that its success in capturing the party's agenda in 1968 led the party to adopt positions that kept it out of the presidency for all but four of the subsequent twenty-two years while undermining its strength throughout the previously "solid" South.[18] Significant parts of the socioeconomic coalition behind the New Deal regime essentially fled the Democrats as new social groups gained national power. Not until the Reagan administration, however, was the old regime replaced with something as substantial, integrated, and potentially long lasting.

The Democratic Party had a well-entrenched position in the Congress as a consequence of its strength in numerous localities, its long-term willingness to enter into politically valuable (if economically irrational) logrolling arrangements,[19] and the incredible advantages that incumbency provided for individual congressmen and senators. The labor movement, historically weak and constantly declining, remained a key component of Democratic strength, skirting any direct confrontation with the cross-racial tensions that divided the American workforce and thereby avoiding racial issues within the party.[20] But labor was constantly at odds with many of the party's new constituents. Despite its secular decline, organized labor continued to maintain a strong voice in the national Democratic Party by exploiting historical loyalties, mobilizing its political action committees, and providing large numbers of electoral workers and cash (particularly in the crucial Democratic Party primaries).

Meanwhile, important links between Democrats and manufacturing interests rested on particularistic amendments to the tax code that had created special benefits for corporations located in the congressional districts of privileged congressional members.[21] This domestic orientation fit with the party's union base, as American labor confronted job losses in the face of rising foreign competition in domestic markets and the movement of American-based manufacturing abroad. Yet such particularism in favor of declining industries began to undercut the economic basis for the old capital-labor accords. Earlier institutional ties with the internationalized sectors of the American economy withered as the Democrats increasingly allied themselves with the least internationally competitive segments of American manufacturing and systematically advocated ad hoc protectionist policies.

. Thus, like many political parties, the Democrats remained true to the policy preferences of their loyal cadres, eschewing efforts to expand their electoral support in a quest for the presidency. Mired in organizational sclerosis, the party watched its once indomitable base deteriorate, both in the solid (white) South, as black suffrage expanded and white voters deserted, and nationwide, as party supporters shifted allegiances for both economic and cultural reasons.[22]

Indeed, repudiating the party's nineteenth-century alliance with the Western farm sector, the Democrats increasingly became, at the national level, a fringe party centered around protection of the old industrial cities, their unionized workforces, and (frequently economically marginal) racial minorities, plus the residues of the middle-class liberal reformers left over from the New Politics movement of the late 1960s. Benefits from the national treasury were dolled out to such constituents on geographical, racial, or class lines. Apparently content to yield the presidency if it could hold on to Congress and the powers of congressional committee chairmen, the party abjured socioeconomic or policy changes that might advance its executive opportunities.

As the Democrats foundered, the Republican Party, which had appeared to be a rock-ribbed and anachronistic political dinosaur under the control of "right-wing kooks" when it nominated Barry Goldwater in 1964, had by the early 1980s forged a dominant new national coalition with a compelling policy agenda. Critical to its success was the "southern strategy" used by Richard Nixon in his 1972 reelection effort. If the Democratic Party was going to buy support through public programs and appeals to black Americans, the Republicans would counter by going after the votes of those who would be paying the bills for such programs. By utilizing a series of wedge issues on such non-economic matters as welfare mothers, abortion, homosexuality, "family values," and race, the Republicans whittled away at previously solid Democratic support.[23] Particularly in the West and the South, the party fused impregnable coalitions centered on export-oriented and high-technology industries along with tax cuts, promises of smaller government, and conservative social policies.

This new coalition gained executive power with Presidents Reagan and Bush, and the two administrations set about the creation of an internally coherent policy nexus that rested on a smaller state, lower taxes, a conservative social agenda, along with the promise that, in foreign affairs, America would "stand tall again." This last was backed by vastly higher military expenditures, invasions of Grenada and Panama, and eventually war against Iraq.

The socioeconomic shift was characterized by the development of a "stealth coalition" that straddled traditional socioeconomic categories. For example, American business, while normally pro-Republican, was divided. Mass production and other "rust belt" industries were far more supportive of the Democrats than the high-tech, service-oriented financial and entrepreneurial industries and the internationally oriented multinationals that by the early 1980s had moved solidly into the Republican camp. Other constituencies, such as the religious right, small shopkeepers, and blue-collar patriots, were drawn to the Republican camp through traditional ties and rewards of a psychological and cultural rather than an economic nature.

A major target of the new regime was organized labor, long a stalwart in the Democratic Party. Reagan's first confrontation with a powerful union demonstrated this vividly; one of his earliest presidential acts was to fire eleven thousand striking PATCO (Professional Air Traffic Controllers' Organization) members and replace them with military and nonunionized civilian personnel. As this pattern continued, the power of labor, which had been dwindling steadily over the preceding twenty years, shrunk dramatically during the twelve years of Republican presidents.

With the Democrats still strong in Congress and the Republicans generally in control of the White House, no national economic strategy emerged with any clarity during most of the 1980s. The Republicans pursued both tax cuts and dramatic reductions in governmental spending for programs they believed were of political benefit to Democratic constituents. Democrats in Congress fought rearguard actions to protect their favorite programs. Under the ever popular rhetoric of laissez-faire and market competition, America moved toward economics by tragicomedy: broad cutbacks in funding for long-standing government programs offset by radical jumps in military spending. The result was sweeping tax cuts and extensive deficit financing that combined to unravel the New Deal social coalition as well as to gut key components of the Washington bureaucracy.

Throughout the 1980s, major American corporations engaged in leveraged buy-outs and "asset reallocations." Corporate assets not generating high short-term profits were sold off regardless of the long-term corporate or national economic consequences. Thus, efforts at national coordination of semiconductor research through Semitech failed quickly for lack of corporate-government coordination, while America's major steel producer, USX Corporation, the former U.S. Steel, was pressed by its major stockholder to get out of the steel business in an effort to allow USX to "enhance shareholder value."[24] National economic policy ceased to focus on the possible implications of these changes for long-term job security, local economies, the declining value of the dollar, increased deficits, or national competitiveness in steel and related manufacturing industries.

Ironically, the antigovernmental Reagan-Bush presidencies resulted in the massive expansion of public expenditures. Electorally popular tax cuts and an expansion of military spending, favored by the Republicans, were not matched by dramatic cuts in popular entitlement programs, largely favored by Democrats. As Alessandro Pizzorno put it in a non-U.S. context, "pluralistic mechanisms bring about an unlimited possibility for the redefinition of interest and for the access of collectively shared private needs to a 'public forum' without being capable, by themselves, of defining a 'common good,'" or, in general, goals that every section of society should accept as its own."[25]

This lack of coordinated policy reinforces the point about the fragmented character of recent political regimes in the United States. At its inception the New Deal coalition was a regime composed of relatively clear blocs and social sectors with a relatively clear policy agenda; as it unraveled in the late 1960s and early 1970s it became a fragmented and frayed replication of interest group liberalism. The Democratic Party and its allies simply enjoyed pride of place at the governmental trough. The new regime that began to crystallize most forcefully under Reagan completely shifted the axis of political debate. This point was made most dramatically by the stunning Republican congressional victories in the 1994 elections. Continuing to draw electoral support around social issues such as race, homosexuality, and opposition to welfare, as well as from promises of tax relief for the "middle class" predicated on shrinking or eliminating numerous government agencies, the Republican victory provided one more nail in the coffin for the New Deal and advanced the fortunes of the anti-welfare, privatist regime that was taking its place.

The Clinton presidency, at least as much as the Republican congressional victories, provided an undeniable indicator of the extent to which a regime shift had occurred in the United States. Explicitly distancing himself from the policy profile that had been the heart of the New Deal regime as well as the historic support base of the Democratic Party, Clinton embraced large segments of the Republican economic agenda and sought to appeal to many of its middle-class constituents. Nowhere was this clearer than in his 1996 acceptance of the Republican Party's welfare proposals. These completely undercut the national programs that had evolved since the 1930s, eliminated social welfare entitlements, and surrendered control over such programs to the states. The targeting of "welfare mothers" and both legal and illegal immigrants meant the explicit marginalization of once important supporters of the New Deal regime: the urban poor, recent immigrants, and ethnic minorities.

These shifts opened dramatically wider gaps between America's rich and poor. From 1982 into the mid-1990s, the top quarter of income earners—and especially the top 5 percent—saw vast increases in their total share of wealth and income while the bottom 20 percent suffered dramatic reductions. America was moving quickly toward a more bifurcated society based on education, job skills, residence, and ethnicity.

Meanwhile, although American trade protectionism remained alive on a sectoral and regional basis, the broad thrust of foreign economic policy embraced internationalism and regional trade arrangements such as NAFTA and APEC. America's new economic internationalism was driven by industries such as computer software and networking, telecommunications, finance, brokerages, medical technologies, and the like rather than by more traditional industries such as automobiles, steel, and machine tools. In addition, government trade policy began to focus more on opening foreign markets than on protecting domestic ones. Essentially, foreign economic policy had shifted back to a favoring of high-tech, export-oriented, multinational firms over smaller, more local, or less internationally competitive segments of business. Domestic manufacturing fared particularly poorly.

Thus the major coalitional, policy, and institutional blocs were in place for a new regime that could be headed by either political party. Given the highly pluralistic nature of American institutions and the diversity of its socioeconomic groups, there is no automatic connection between any single party and the development or maintenance of a particular regime. The Democratic Party's general acceptance of many Republican-initiated changes suggests that the new regime in the United States could easily be endorsed or led by either party or by an alliance of both; it is not likely to be seriously reversed.

Britain: The Conservative Revolution

Pundits have highlighted the parallels between the conservative revolutions that occurred on both sides of the Atlantic during the 1980s. Margaret Thatcher came to power just before Ronald Reagan. Both rode into office at the head of revitalized conservative movements. Both were committed to undoing what they perceived to be the social and economic evils of the preceding regimes. Both eagerly confronted (and defeated) powerful union movements. Both carried out significant privatizations, attacks on social welfare, and a return to "market principles" that gave priority to monetarism, widened income gaps, and increased unemployment. Ronald Reagan's Grenada was matched by Thatcher's Falklands. Strikingly similar in so many ways, the two regimes were stark breaks with those in place.[26]

Thatcher's reign rejected the bipartisan collectivism embraced by her predecessors and advanced a completely different agenda. Given the party-based character of regimes in Britain, the first task of Thatcher's Conservative Party was to win election. Doing this required attracting a substantial proportion of lower-middle-class and working-class voters, the aptly identified "working-class Tories." Labour under James Callaghan had certainly done plenty to drive many of the party's core voters away. Labour's incomes policies failed and the British economy foundered, leaving England, in the *Economist*'s famous phrase, as the "sick man of Europe."

Two particular segments of Thatcher's electoral strategy were particularly effective in undercutting Labour's class appeal and fragmenting its traditional support base. One of her most popular proposals was an attack on council (public) housing. Government expenditures for such housing, she declared, simply "brought the 'serfdom' of social democracy that much closer."[27] She promised to end subsidization and to sell off council housing at half price to current residents. This blatant appeal to the home-owning aspirations of many lower-class voters was especially effective in the Midlands, New Towns, and other suburban areas.[28]

Thatcher's second major appeal was along lines of race and ethnicity, issues that divided labor in Britain much as they did in the United States. The British case was exacerbated by the large influx of migrants from Britain's former colonies in the West Indies, South Asia, and Africa during the 1950s and 1960s. Conservative policy officially favored racial harmony but also insisted that prevailing levels of migration were too high. Numerical quotas, the party contended, had to be set for foreign immigrants. Thatcher, with little effort at subtlety, defended Conservative policies in a January 1978 interview, contending that "people are really rather afraid that this country might be rather swamped by people with a different culture." Her public opinion rating soared after the remark, and she continued to defend quotas throughout the election.[29] The result was a siphoning off of many traditional Labour Party supporters.

Privatization of housing and promises to check foreign migration were important components of a strategy aimed at dividing Labour's traditional support base. Thatcher's explicit economic policies were similarly clear: tax cuts, privatization, a reduction in the size of the public-sector deficit, an end to incomes policy, and overall reductions in public-sector spending. The campaign proved successful and produced the largest swing between Labour and the Conservatives since 1945 (6.4 percent), with Conservatives winning the largest plurality of seats over the primary opposition (7 percent) since that same year.

In office, Thatcher implemented the bulk of her agenda, demolishing the "social contract" that had prevailed under both Labour and Conservative governments since the end of the war. Although slower to take on the unions than Reagan, she eventually repudiated the well-entrenched commitment of both parties to full employment.[30] Her government institutionalized its antilabor policies with the Employment Acts of 1980 and 1982 and the Trade Union Act of 1984. Several major strikes were broken in showcase defeats, including that of the Iron and Steel Trades Confederation in 1980 and the National Union of Mineworkers in 1984–85.

Strict monetary policies drove the new conservative agenda, thereby moving the government dramatically away from prior Keynesian policies. Unlike Reagan, Thatcher chose to forego tax cuts so as to lower the public-sector deficit. But like him, she and her government cut back on a variety of government activities and privatized a host of once nationalized industries from British Aerospace and Britoil to Jaguar and British Telecom. Privatization held down inflation while simultaneously raising revenue, thereby avoiding the need for new taxes to support the government's macroeconomic goals. Privatization also served to make first-time shareholders (and presumably Conservative supporters) out of many British citizens. Finally, the regulatory framework was loosened for the private sector, as were conditions governing foreign direct investment, boosting private business and encouraging an influx of foreign capital.

In all of these ways Thatcher and the Conservatives created a new basis for the British political economy. The new regime was markedly less consensual than the collectivist regime it replaced. Drawing heavily from the suburban middle and lower-middle classes, the Conservative Party created a substantially broader segment of electoral support. Its ideology and new policy programs provided substantial benefits to Conservative supporters, shifted political and economic burdens to the party's opponents, and undercut the power of organized labor.

At the same time, while the new conservative regime attacked big government and chipped away at public programs for primary education, national health, unemployment insurance, or public pensions, it did little (at least initially) to undermine these more popular parts of the welfare state.[31] Social spending actually increased in real terms in the first ten years of the Thatcher government. And at the same time, although never matching Reagan's "military Keynesian" expansions of the American defense budget, the Conservatives did increase Britain's spending for defense and crime. The new regime gained further institutionalization under John Major, who broadened the thrust of Thatcherite policies by further reductions in unemployment programs and proposals to privatize pensions, among other things.

The new conservative agenda achieved mixed results. In the early Thatcher years, Britain's economic growth was far slower than that of the European Community or the United States. But from the mid-1980s to 1997 its growth was on a par. Inflation fell slightly more quickly and unemployment was nominally lower than in the rest of Europe (although this reflects the British definition of who is unemployed).

Most notable have been the social effects of the new regime. As Peter Hall points out, the costs of austerity fell most heavily on the unemployed and the lower-income groups, widening "the disjuncture in material well-being between the affluent and the poor, between those in work and those without it, and between those with considerable power in the labor market by virtue of wealth or skills and those without such power."[32] By the mid-1990s, income for the poor had either fallen or remained flat while that for the rich was up 62 percent.[33] In Peter Jenkins's phrase, Britain had become a nation of "the haves, the have nots, and the have lots."[34]

Moreover, by the mid-1990s the differentiated regional effects of the new regime were becoming increasingly clear. London was at the heart of a successful banking industry and had seen an explosion in distribution centers, light industry, foreign acquisitions, corporate financial services, and investment banks. That the London business day overlaps partially with those of New York, Singapore, Tokyo, and Shanghai enhanced the City's capacity to become a reinvigorated global contender. Indeed, financial services, which had accounted for 13 percent of GNP in 1984, had risen to 20 percent by 1997.[35] Moreover, London was home to internationally successful pharmaceuticals, music, and tourism industries. But the country was also pockmarked by blighted industrial cities such as Manchester and Liverpool; large areas of Wales and Scotland had also been left behind in the Conservative revolution. Meanwhile many smaller cities lost well-paying factory jobs and only partially benefited from the foreign investment that brought new, lower paying jobs in telemarketing and simple assembly.

After her third victory in 1987, Thatcher promised the Conservative Party conference an "irreversible shift" in British governance. The complete remaking of the Labour Party and the successful campaign by Tony Blair and his "New Labour" in the spring of 1997 proved her correct. Blair led a comprehensive overhaul of Labour during its last years out of power. Organized labor had fallen from about eleven million members when Thatcher took office to about seven million in 1997. The Labour Party further weakened its ties to unions when it rejected Clause 4 of the Labour constitution, which had pledged the party to an equitable distribution to workers and the common ownership of the means of production. Blair even declared in the normally conservative *Daily Telegraph* that he admired Margaret Thatcher's revolution and most of its principles, a stance that would have been unthinkable for any Labour Party leader fifteen years earlier. Blair took the lead in "reinventing the left" by rejecting most forms of nationalization and campaigning to continue the broad thrust of Thatcherite economics, including a promise of no increases over Tory plans for public spending for at least two years and no tax hikes for at least five. Labour's overwhelming victory in May 1997 reflected public frustration with internal Tory divisions, sex and petty corruption scandals, and other problems. But far more significantly, it testified to the ideological distance that Labour had traveled. Blair and Labour swept into power with no big new ideas for policy transformation or socioeconomic alternatives and no promises to roll back Thatcherism. Instead they won by a generic embrace of the new British regime.

Thus by the late 1990s, Britain's movement to a new regime, like that in the United States, seemed relatively complete. What is most important to stress in the British case is the important role played by the party system in channeling the transformation. In this, Britain is distinctive from the United States and rather unlike corporatist Sweden, where so much regime transformation occurred outside party politics. Because party government has been so institutionally central to Britain, political leaders have been less vulnerable to ad hoc group pressures than their American counterparts; iron triangles have been less prevalent. Consequently, parties are also far more capable of implementing their campaign promises even when these involve sweeping changes in the nation's public policy orientation.

The decision-making power that redounds to the cabinet with a parliamentary majority also means that the party in power in Britain is far less vulnerable to forced compromises in its policy agenda than its U.S. or Swedish counterparts.[36] In short, the institutional context of British politics, most notably the strong role of parties, played a definitive shaping role in Britain's regime transformations. Nowhere, however, was the role of parties more critical than in Italy.

Italy: The Demise of One-Party Dominance

As Chapter 1 made clear, it was political parties and Christian Democracy (DC) dominance that defined and shaped the postwar Italian regime. With a broad array of political parties, the duration of Italian governments and coalitions was measured in months and weeks rather than years. But underlying the frequent governmental turnovers was the prevailing consistency of the party system and the regime as a whole. The composition of particular governments had little effect on the system as an organic entity.

The Italian regime continued throughout the series of major shocks in the late 1960s and early 1970s that had catalyzed sweeping changes in many other countries. First came the Hot Autumn of 1969, a wave of strikes by students and workers. This was followed by the monetary and oil shock crises of 1971, 1973, and 1979 that affected the entire industrialized world. Despite their profoundly negative consequences on the macroeconomy, Italy's political system survived these shocks with few deep changes.[37]

Indeed, within the private sector, economic dynamism reemerged as early as the late 1980s. Italy outperformed most of its politically more stable neighbors in terms of export and GNP growth, labor productivity, firm profitability, investment in new machinery, and accumulation of personal savings.[38] This dynamism, however, argues Richard Locke, occurred primarily in spite of, rather than because of, the character of the political system. Flexible production and firm creativity within numerous local economies allowed many of Italy's small private-sector manufacturers to work together with their local unions to enhance productivity and regional and international competitiveness. Such political connections as firms had were largely local, leaving them unfettered by the worst aspects of national clientelism and patronage.

The entire Italian system, based on pockets of economic success combined with pervasive corruption and national economic mismanagement, changed radically between the late 1980s and the mid-1990s largely as a result of four major forces: the fall of communism, corruption, macroeconomics, and regionalism. The advent of Mikhail Gorbachev in 1986 and his efforts to move the Soviet Union toward glasnost and perestroika demolished many assumptions underlying politics in Italy, just as they did elsewhere. While Italian conservatives assumed that the collapse of communism in 1989 would redound to their benefit, the PCI in 1991 renounced its faith in Leninism, reconstituted itself as the Democratic Party of the Left (PDS), and benefited from revelations about anticommunist and pro-DC efforts by the United States in the period immediately after World War II. Meanwhile, a hard-line minority objected and took the label Communist Refoundation. The creation of the PDS without the communists' more extreme segment, as well as the fall of communism in East Europe and the USSR, removed a major bulwark behind DC support. The business community in particular no longer had to "hold its nose and vote DC" since the threat of communism had largely evaporated.[39]

Then came a more immediate catalyst for the massive regime overhaul, namely, the revelations of corruption throughout the system. Given the extensive permeation of factional politics, patronage, vote trading, and pork throughout the system, corruption was long understood to be endemic. A firestorm of protests against corruption emerged, however, once the business community began to revolt at the unceasing demand for payoffs. The match that lit the anticorruption fires came when a single Milano businessman refused in February 1992 to pay a bribe to a local politician and made his refusal, and the broader problems of payoffs, into a public issue. Accusations and revelations spread, and criminal investigations were subsequently begun on hundreds of business leaders, politicians, and bureaucrats, all accused of taking bribes, and many shown to have close links to organized crime. Large segments of the political and economic elite were eventually implicated, including the finance director of the Fiat group and the leader of the Ferruzzi group, about one-quarter of the parliament, the heads of most major political parties, several cabinet ministers, and at least two former prime ministers.

Lurking beneath the surface were the economic problems generated by the patronage-ridden policy profile of the DC-led governments. Italy's public sector was profligate: welfare pensions went to young and old alike; the national bureaucracy hired thousands of no-show workers; and the parastatals ran up enormous debts. IRI, for example, had 420,000 employees in 1993 and an accumulated debt of around $40 billion. At the start of the 1970s, Italian public debt had equaled about 40 percent of GNP, roughly in line with the rest of Europe; by 1992 it had risen to 108 percent. In May 1993 Moody's downgraded Italian debt for the third time in two years.[40]

A dim awareness of the gravity of the debt problem began to form in the late 1980s, largely as a result of the strict criteria to be imposed on all European governments seeking to comply with the 1991 Maastricht Treaty. If Italy was to qualify for inclusion in the common currency arrangements, the spendthrift economic policies followed under *partitocrazia* would have to end. The Bank of Italy began to exercise tighter foreign exchange and monetary discipline. A sequence of governments stepped up taxation and tightened long-accepted loopholes and lax enforcement. In four years, the ratio of total government receipts to GNP rose from 39.4 percent to 43.8 percent. Public expenditure continued to grow, however, and the debt-to-GNP ratio went over 100 percent in 1990.[41] In short, by the early 1990s there was a heightened awareness of a national economic problem, but little agreement on a solution.

Not at all marginal to corruption and the economic problems was the regional division between the industrial north and the laconic south, and the eventual rise in the north of a new regional subculture.[42] Some industrial development had begun in the south during the 1960s, involving IRI-led projects in steel and chemicals, but these foundered following the two oil shocks and the rise in raw materials prices. Increasingly, public works and regional development assistance—linked to *partitocrazia*, patronage, and the Mafia—began to transfer ever more substantial amounts of wealth from the north to the south. In protest, the Northern League was formed in the early 1990s; it quickly gained substantial electoral strength on its promise to increase Italian fiscal federalism or actually to secede from Italy. Most tangibly the League signaled the extent to which disaffected northerners had lost patience with the old regime and its corruption and economic inefficiencies.

These forces came together in a massive voter rejection of the old regime. Voter power, however, was manifested less through new mobilization or shifts in party loyalties than through a conscious rejection of the entire set of rules by which the parties had stayed in power. Critical to the rebellion was the referendum movement. Constitutionally guaranteed and with enabling legislation passed in 1970, the referendum had become a mechanism that allowed otherwise circumscribed cabinets to appeal to citizens over the heads of parliament, as was done quite frequently under Socialist prime minister Craxi. But a citizen-led and media-supported "referendum movement" managed initially in June 1991 and subsequently in April 1993 to win huge popular majorities (generally 80–90 percent) that, despite the strong resistance of almost all the established parties, transformed the electoral system, ended preference voting and state financing of political parties, abolished several government agencies, and greatly enhanced the number of majoritarian constituencies.[43]

After the referenda, Italy swore in its first twentieth-century nonparty premier, Carlo Azeglio Ciampi. A former governor of the Bank of Italy, he moved to contain inflation, regulate wages, privatize some state agencies, reform the pension system, dismantle some of the special legislation for the south, and meet the overall targets for convergence on the Maastricht standards. Of more immediate political import was Ciampi's restructuring of the electoral system in accord with the April 1993 referenda and the calling of elections under the new system.

In August 1993 proportional representation was replaced by a system under which 75 percent of the members of both houses of parliament would be selected by majoritarian systems. The remaining 25 percent would be elected through proportional representation, but with a 4 percent threshold. Also allowed was the French practice of *desistement*, by which a party could withdraw its candidate and defer to another party in a specific district. The combined effect was to lower the number of candidates per district, encourage cooperation among parties, and move Italy toward a two-bloc electoral division.

On August 5, 1993, *L'Unita*'s headline read, "The Second Republic is Under Way." The vote was a sweeping public indictment of *partitocrazia*. Electoral reforms and attacks on *Tangentopoli* (literally Bribe City, but referring to the extensive corruption) began to gain momentum.[44] As Carol Mershon and Gianfranco Pasquino described the situation in 1993, "a *regime* transition is under way that is reshaping both the formal rules and procedures directing political life and the actual behavior that long bent and subverted those rules."[45]

The March 1994 electoral results devastated the old party system. The Socialists almost disappeared; the DC was reduced to minor party status, and a clear victory was handed to mostly new center-right and far-right parties. Approximately two-thirds of the senators and deputies had not been in parliament before the election.[46] By the middle of 1997, the entire party system had decomposed. Instead of power sharing (at least over patronage) among all major parties, a more confrontational system arose, one that potentially would sharpen the lines between government and opposition and create a politics of *alternanza*, or alternation. By 1997 two main electoral blocs could be identified, the then-governing Olive Tree Alliance on the center-left and the Polo on the right.

In the wake of the post-1993 changes, substantial alterations were made in the nation's economic policy profile. A "tax for Europe" was introduced to bring the deficit down to the Maastricht criterion of 3 percent of GNP. Harsh budgets in 1996 and 1997 squeezed inflation to an annualized rate of about 2 percent.[47] The *scala mobile*, or nationwide cost-of-living escalator, was abolished as a result of two agreements between Confindustria and the unions, thereby moving toward a system of neocorporatist wage settlements.[48] Although growth was slow, by early 1997 Italy was running the largest budget surpluses in Europe (excluding interest payments). The welfare system, particularly its corruption-ridden pensions segment, was scheduled for overhaul as well. Of course, such reforms involved a massive redistribution of wealth from pensioners, recipients of social services, and general taxpayers to the holders of government debt—generally the middle class and the elderly in the richer north.[49]

The Italian regime shift is still very much in process. It is not at all clear that the two-bloc system of party alternation will endure. Nor are there any guarantees that past economic problems will be corrected. But it is quite clear that the earlier party system has been totally shattered, political institutions have been revamped, and a fundamental overhaul of the economy has begun. Whatever the shape of the new regime, it will be unlike the old.

This chapter offers three broad conclusions. First, the political economies of capitalist democracies adjust differently to the mix of external pressures and internal tensions depending on their points of departure. Just as Japan managed to form a relatively discreet political economy in the early postwar years (analyzed in Chapters 2 and 3), so did Sweden, the United States, Britain, and Italy. All five countries evolved different mixtures of political institutions, socioeconomic cleavages and coalitions, and public policy profiles. These distinct starting points led to different types of regime adjustments in Sweden, the United States, Britain, and Italy during the 1980s and 1990s. The institutional frameworks of each country—corporatism, pluralism, party-alternating parliamentarism, and single-party-dominant *partitocrazia*—shaped the way each adjusted.

First- and sometimes second-order adjustments took place in all four to varying degrees. The United States made many small adjustments in the New Deal regime but no major break until the Reagan revolution. Britain made even fewer small shifts from collectivism until Thatcher's sharp break. As for Sweden, despite changes in the nation's governing party, not until one of the major corporatist blocs split internally did the country really experience major shifts in its regime. Meanwhile Italy's *partitocrazia*, constantly in flux electorally, rested on a base of corruption and economic inefficiency that defined and stabilized the regime until wholesale voter and media attacks overturned the entire system.

Second, the processes of the actual regime shifts were strikingly different. Under Swedish corporatism, for example, a clearly defined and dramatic shift took place as the result of alterations in a limited number of major socioeconomic blocs and consequent redirections of public policies. The changes in the 1980s and 1990s were the result of actual splits within these socioeconomic blocs that effectively ended corporatist bargaining. In Britain, major shifts in institutions and policies arose as the consequence of important socioeconomic transformations. In Britain, a mixture of changes in institutions, policies, and socioeconomics took place primarily through the electoral process. Relatively minor changes in voting support patterns from Labour to Conservative enabled a sweeping and comprehensive regime shift. The institutional power of British parliamentary majorities allowed for dramatic transformations in policy directions and governmental institutions once the Conservatives set about making them. And to the extent that these became institutionalized, they shifted the entire axis of party difference to a more right-of-center fulcrum. The soft hegemony of Christian Democracy and *partitocrazia* in Italy, meanwhile, was highly effective in limiting most adjustments to first- and occasionally second-order changes for more than forty years. This buffered the regime against comprehensive transformation for much of the postwar period. But when such tinkerings could no longer pacify business, media, judicial, and popular frustrations, a quick and complete restructuring of the party system and the economy ensued. Like the changes in Britain, those in the United States were driven primarily by electoral politics. But American institutional fragmentation made the process far more complicated than the capturing of a simple parliamentary majority. Socioeconomic and party changes occurred at different tempos regionally, institutionally, and in separate policy arenas. New Republican majorities first appeared in presidential elections, and only later did they gain control of the Congress and the judiciary.

Third, despite the sweeping domestic and international forces that all these countries have faced, each country has adjusted differently and reached a different point of equilibrium. Domestic political and economic arrangements have obviously been catalyzed by vastly enhanced international capital movements, changing world labor markets, transnational production processes, increasing political and economic regionalization, and the like. Yet adjustments to such changes, as well as the processes through which they occurred, were deeply rooted in national regime differences. Although the left has done generally less well in the new regimes than it had earlier, this was not true of Italy; and the Swedish left, though weaker, remained the largest force in government. Moreover, changes that were seemingly common to all four regimes—and that might have suggested the work of "globalization"—still left all four regimes looking remarkably different from one another.

These same conclusions will also be seen in Japan. As the next two chapters will show, Japan's long conservative dominance rested on substantial first-and second-order alterations throughout the 1970s and 1980s. These kept essential elements of the regime stable and in place. Yet by the early to mid-1990s the conservative regime of the 1960s was being replaced by something radically different. Even in the late 1990s, however, Japan resembled none of the four regimes examined above.

CHAPTER FIVE

Japan in the 1990s:
Fragmented Politics and Economic Turmoil

Japan in the mid-1960s was a country characterized by rapid economic development, rising standards of living, a close military and economic relationship with the United States, an exuberant summer Olympics, and a conservative electoral dominance in a sharply bifurcated left-right spectrum. The mid-1990s contrasted fundamentally. The stability of the old regime had been substantially undermined, and although no new equilibrium had been established, a new regime of undetermined shape was forcing its way onstage.

Japan's transformation was manifested in many ways. First, enduring institutions of conservative political dominance had been reconfigured. The previously stable party system had been completely deconstructed and the once sharp left-right division between government and opposition had disappeared. Parties broke apart and combined with total disregard for policy or ideological differences. Of the parties that existed in the 1960s, only the LDP and the JCP remaining nominally intact, and the former had undergone substantial internal fragmentation and lost its dominance in July 1993. The electoral system, once a vital underpinning of conservative electoral success, was also new. The once vaunted Japanese bureaucracy plodded through a range of problems mired in red-tape-laden ineptitude, popular mistrust, the sweeping reorganization of various agencies, the loss of numerous powers, and the promise of even further change.

Second, Japan's seemingly endless string of economic achievements ended with the puncturing of an economic bubble. The simultaneous collapse of both stock and real estate prices ushered in eight years of limp growth,[1] a staggeringly expanded national debt, a systemwide financial crisis, and a destabilized yen that strengthened from 120 to 80 yen per dollar between 1993 and 1995, only to be pierced by a massive intervention in September 1995 that sent it tumbling back toward 145 yen by mid-1998.

Meanwhile, the warm, fraternal, and dependent relationship with the United States, solidified by their common cold war opposition to the USSR, China, and communism, had given way to technonationalist competition in a host of economic sectors. Moreover, Japan's long-standing policy of avoiding activist diplomacy and use of its troops abroad had changed in a strategically insignificant but ideologically monumental way when Japan agreed in 1991 to allow Japanese military personnel to participate in UN peacekeeping operations overseas.[2] Then, during the Taiwan Straits crisis of 1996, Japan deployed a Naval Self-Defense Forces cutter as part of a show of force against China. And finally, with only the most minimal domestic debate, Japan redrew the lines of its security arrangements with the United States to expand Japanese military commitments.

Finally, from a socioeconomic standpoint the 1990s were strikingly different from the 1960s. Organized labor, the unquestioned source of support for parties of the left in the 1960s, continued to decline in membership, abandoned its class rhetoric, and had been incorporated into a plant-level economic unionism that reduced its role as an ideological partisan. Internal divisions arose, meanwhile, among once stalwart conservative support groups. Farmers became politically divided in the face of a threatened liberalization of agricultural imports. The business community meanwhile showed signs of internal divisions between, on the one hand, internationally competitive firms and sectors anxious to reduce the burden of bureaucratic regulation and taxation and, on the other, less competitive firms and sectors anxious to retain those bureaucratic regulations and tax benefits that provided them with extensive public subsidization and protection from foreign competition.

As this chapter will show, by the late 1990s Japan's old conservative regime had undergone such fundamental changes as to warrant the designation "regime shift." This is not to deny a number of real and important continuities. To cite only the most vivid, Japan still enjoyed "conservative" governance. Party reorganization was not the result of massive voter mobilization; it did not sweep out an old political elite and replace it with new personalities. Indeed, as of mid-1998 a reconstituted LDP enjoyed a slim majority in the Lower House and controlled all cabinet positions. Meanwhile, the national bureaucracy retained considerable power, particularly in regard to the regulation of both economy and society. In Steven Vogel's terminology, Japan had undergone "reregulation" but not "deregulation."[3] And despite many shifts in economic policy, numerous Japanese firms were highly profitable, Japanese foreign reserves were the highest in the world, and Japan's home markets remained among the most closed in the industrial world.

To many, such continuities were by far the most important *honne*, or realities, about Japan in the 1990s; such changes as appeared were little more than superficial *tatemae*. Determining when changes are "real" or "superficial" is obviously a matter of the standards one sets. In the case of Japan, for many observers, "real economic change" hinges on the extent to which the country undergoes privatization, deregulation, and greater sensitivity to international market forces. Political change is similarly "meaningful" only if the country moves toward two-party competition, less dominance by filthy lucre, higher minded policy debates, and a greater degree of party and citizen control over haughty bureaucrats and corrupt politicians. Finally, "real change in security policy" would require policies that emerge from a more nationally conscious and self-confident Japan—a Japan that had strengthened its military capabilities and displayed increased military and diplomatic activism in Asia and the world.

Such formulations misstate and oversimplify the problem of change, posing standards for a "truly changed" Japan that are implausibly out of touch with Japanese realities. Social changes rarely result in transformations as dramatic as those of the frog who, upon being kissed by the princess, turns instantly into a handsome prince. Few important socioeconomic changes ever completely sever links to the past, as the regime shifts in Sweden, the United States, Britain, and Italy make clear.[4] Social transformations are still path dependent, even when those paths involve sharp turns. To expect otherwise ignores the more nuanced ways in which alterations in any political economy occur. Change in Japan typically has been a matter of two steps forward and one step back. Vestiges of the past are interwoven with foreshaddowings of the future. As the analysis below will show, substantial and ongoing changes in Japan are putting into place a new regime whose eventual equilibrium will be quite distant from that which prevailed in the 1960s.

I begin with a sketch of prominent events of the early to mid-1990s. These events and those of the 1960s (discussed at the start of Chapter 2) epitomize what I believe are two fundamentally different regimes. I then examine the three key regime components—public policy profile, socioeconomic coalitions, and political and economic institutions. Although some features of all three retain significant elements from the regime outlined in Chapter 2, the more compelling picture is one of change and transformation. I conclude with several observations on the continuing tensions whose eventual resolution will shape whatever stability emerges from the present uncertainty.

The 1990s: Conservatism's Anni Horribili

If 1964 was something of an annus mirabilis for Japanese conservatism, then the 1990s represented a succession of anni horribili. Following a massive stock and land price collapse that began with the first day of the decade, the next five years saw the Japanese economy growing at a sluggish 1.9 percent per year; the last two years saw growth below 1 percent; and by the end of 1997 GDP was actually falling, with economists predicting growth at or below 2 percent for 1998. Manufacturing productivity for most of this period remained below the index level of 1990; only in 1997 did it begin to show a return to growth.[5] Japan's stock market languished 58 percent below its record high on December 31, 1989. Corporate bankruptcies exploded. Included were a number of huge firms, once thought "too big to fail," such as Yamaichi Securities, Hokkaido Takushoku Bank, and Nissan Mutual Life Insurance. The result was to drive the value of total bankruptcies in 1995 to nearly double their previous high. Public-sector debt was close to 100 percent of GNP and greater than in virtually any other industrialized country; when private-sector debt is included, the figure soared to over 200 percent of GNP. The 1990s marked the longest period of economic sluggishness in Japan's postwar history and mired the country at or near the bottom of the industrialized democracies, the opposite pole from that which it had occupied during the 1960s.

Developments in the 1960s portended enhanced international competitiveness for Japanese firms in cutting-edge industries. Developments in the 1990s suggested just the opposite. In a few industries, such as automobiles and consumer electronics, Japanese firms continued to lead their international competitors; for example, in 1997 Toyota introduced a mixed electric-gasoline engine car vastly ahead of any of its competitors, and Honda introduced a zero-emissions model. New carbon-fiber technologies, digital telecommunications, cell phone standards, ground-wave digital television, and even point-of-sale retailing from companies as diverse as Toray Industries, NTT Mobile Communications, Matsushita Electric, and Ito-Yokado led the world. But the competitiveness of Japanese industry more broadly was suffering. For example, the World Economic Forum in 1997 ranked Japan only fourteenth in international competitiveness, a dramatic contrast to its glory days as recently as 1990, when it stood in first place.[6] Japan lagged in key industries: cable access was among the lowest in the industrialized world; personal computer use was only one-third the per capita rate of the United States and lagged behind countries such as South Korea and Singapore; only 10 percent of Japanese used computers at work, and of these only 13 percent were connected to networks. Japan also had lower internet traffic per capita than almost all OECD members, as well as Israel, Hong Kong, and Taiwan.[7] Japanese firms lagged significantly behind European and American firms in mobile telecommunications, while in finance the once dominant Big Four brokerages saw their share of domestic equity sales fall to 25.8 percent in August 1997, putting them below the 32.4 percent share held by the Tokyo Stock Exchange's twenty-one biggest foreign brokerages.[8] Establishment clients like Nippon Telephone and Telegraph allowed their European bond issues to be underwritten by Merrill Lynch and Morgan Stanley without any Japanese brokerage participation. Even the Tokyo government was regularly using foreign syndicates to underwrite its municipal bonds.

Overall, the character of the Japanese economy had become less closely tied to the performance of exclusively Japanese-owned firms operating in, and dominating, the domestic market. Instead, many nominally "Japanese" firms had become truly multinational, moving beyond a pattern of export from behind the protected Japanese market, into overseas production, financing, research and development, and technological alliances. As a result, their successes and failures became decoupled from the tight bureaucratic controls of the 1960s. Elsewhere, the result was global partnerships between Japanese-owned and American- or European-owned firms—alliances such as Mazda and Ford, Toshiba, Motorola and Seimens, Hitachi and Texas Instruments, Mitsubishi and Daimler-Benz. In still others, it involved substantial outsourcing of production by once exclusively "Japanese" firms like

Honda, Sony, Toyota, Canon, and Hitachi. And in still other instances, it has meant the penetration of core Japanese domestic industries such as insurance, finance, brokering, and telecommunications by non-Japanese firms such as Merrill Lynch, American International Group, World Com, Dresdner Bank, Jardine Fleming Holdings, and the like. The sacrosanct boundaries that had marked the Japanese economy in the 1960s had become vastly more permeable by the 1990s. Moreover, the competitive pace within Japan was frequently being set by foreign-owned firms, such as Microsoft with Windows 95, Citicorp with twenty-four-hour ATMs, or GE Capital in insurance.

Economic transformation was the backdrop to the more comprehensive breakup of the old regime. The long-ruling Liberal Democratic Party split in July 1993, its thirty-eight year control of government giving way to a series of coalitions which over the next three years saw eleven different political parties sharing power and four individuals holding the office of prime minister. Among the new chief executives was Murayama Tomiichi, then leader of the conservatives' bête noire, the Japan Socialist Party. Political change was unmistakable.

The LDP was also mired in corruption scandals. These were hardly new to Japan or to the LDP, but the Recruit scandal (1988–89), which forced Prime Minister Takeshita to resign, made it unmistakable that massive amounts of money were suffusing electoral politics. The subsequent Sagawa Kyūbin case added to the perception. Longtime political godfather and LDP Deputy Prime Minister Kanemaru Shin was arrested on March 27, 1993, in conjunction with a payoff of ¥500 million from an up-and-coming trucking company seeking special treatment from transportation regulators. The Kanemaru scandal made particularly good television coverage when public prosecutors dragged some ¥3 billion in anonymous bond certificates, tens of millions of yen in banknotes, and some 100 kilograms in gold bullion from his various offices, town houses, and suites. The scandal also implicated several former civil servants in local governments, high-level officials from a series of construction companies, and a former minister of construction, Nakamura Kishirō, who became the first politician in twenty-seven years to be arrested while the parliament was in session.

In addition, media revelations streamed out about brokerage houses making payments to favored customers, thereby "guaranteeing" particular rates of return; massive donations by corporations at "encouragement parties" held by politicians; shady to undeniably illegal ties among brokerages, organized crime, and LDP politicians; massive local government expenditures for entertainment of national officials; bid rigging for public construction projects; and a host of other examples of "money politics."[9] While the net of inclusion of Japanese elites was somewhat less comprehensive than Italy's *Tangentopoli*, the unceasing Japanese scandals spread ever wider revealing a level of systematic corruption far deeper and more pervasive than any hinted at in earlier Japanese corruption cases.

Large-scale Japanese businesses were particularly upset by the extent of the corruption. The costly structure of doing business within the country—with its political bribes, high entertainment costs, and irrational and often whimsically interpreted regulations—led to demands for political reform. When it became clear in 1993 that the LDP, under Prime Minister Miyazawa, would not back the reforms demanded by business, the major business association Keidanren cut off automatic contributions to the party.

As the climate of criticism grew, a number of conservative politicians, but most notably Ozawa Ichirō (himself ironically a close ally of Kanemaru and a major recipient of monies from Sagawa), jumped on the "reform" bandwagon. The issues of corruption and astronomical electoral costs became fused with the call for what many conservative politicians had long hoped for: a replacement of Japan's multimember electoral system with some version of a single-member district system. The implicit, though unsupported and perhaps unsupportable, claim was that Japan's multimember district system inherently required vast sums of money which a single-member district system would reduce. A revised electoral system became equated with "political reform," and in 1994 a new system was enacted.[10]

The LDP was also mauled electorally. In the April 1995 Tokyo gubernatorial race seasoned ex-bureaucrat Ishihara Nobuo, despite the endorsement of every major noncommunist party, lost to a former actor by roughly a half-million votes. Simultaneously, in Osaka, another ex-bureaucrat fell to a former television comedian. Retired bureaucrats did poorly in the 1996 lower house elections as well. In the Upper House election of July 1998 the LDP was pummeled, winning less than 35 percent of the contested seats.

The previously cozy ties between cabinet and bureaucracy also were ruptured. Long tradition had kept promotions and retirements within the Japanese civil service relatively insulated from direct political interference. But on December 16, 1993, a member of Ozawa's Shinseitō, Kumagai Hiroshi, took over as MITI minister and, as one of his first acts, forced the retirement of the leading candidate for the highest nonpolitical position in the ministry, Naitō Masahisa. This explicitly partisan effort by the new, non-LDP government, shattered one of the key institutional arrangements of the previous conservative regime, namely, the "nonpartisan" treatment of all bureaucratic promotions.[11]

During the mid-1990s the national bureaucracy was mired in a series of gaffes and unparalleled ineptitudes that dramatically undermined its credibility as the stalwart guarantor of national success. Several of the more outrageous examples convey the general problem.

In January 1995 a massive earthquake struck the port city of Kobe and killed more than six thousand people. Lacking any emergency preparation or central control facilities, government officials took days to mobilize help. Meanwhile, national and international astonishment grew as bureaucratic agencies enforced seemingly absurd regulations that, among other things, prevented Swiss body-searching dogs from entering Kobe for rescue efforts without first undergoing six months of quarantine, denied an offer of free mobile telephones for use in rescue work because the phones lacked appropriate "certification labels" for the Kobe region, refused foreign blood and emergency supplies as "unnecessary" despite the apparent inability of the government to mobilize and deliver the proffered items, and kept emergency Self-Defense Force personnel out of the city because of real or imagined antimilitary sentiments by local politicians. Response to the Kobe earthquake showed the Japanese civil service at its "bureaucratic" worst.

Two months later, a different batch of agencies revealed their own ineptitude. On March 20, 1995, a group of religious zealots from the Aum Shinrikyō sect unleashed sarin gas at the Kasumigaseki subway stop in Tokyo, killing several and affecting over 5500 others. The attack was the culmination of a series of activities by the cult over several years that had included murders of its critics and those seeking to escape its network, the purchase of multimillion-dollar arsenals of weapons from the United States and Russia (including an MI-17 helicopter), a similar gas attack in the town of Matsumoto during June 1994 that killed seven and injured six hundred, and a series of thinly veiled warnings from a radio station the group had purchased in Vladivostok and was using openly to broadcast its apocalyptic intentions within Japan. Throughout that period neither the Japanese police, the Japanese Customs Office, nor various security agencies gave any hints of detecting anything to arouse their suspicions or help them prevent the subsequent attacks.

The Ministry of Health and Welfare had its own scandal as it was revealed to have colluded with commercial suppliers to allow HIV-contaminated blood to be donated to Japanese patients, primarily hemophiliacs. Both the ministry and the suppliers had ignored new and safer blood treatment procedures in an effort to avoid the costly destruction and replacement of the tainted blood. At the end of 1996, the ministry was again in the news as Administrative Vice Minister Okamitsu Nobuharu resigned amid charges that he had been given membership in a country club worth ¥16 million, along with other expensive favors, by the owner of a company that operated a string of old-age homes and had been seeking ministry subsidies of ¥9 billion to build new facilities. Okamitsu proved to be just the tip of an iceberg that eventually expanded to include seven additional agency officials. Ironically appointed to the ministry's top job in order to clean up the HIV mess, Okamitsu was eventually arrested in early December, the highest level civil servant to suffer such a fate in the postwar years.

The most spectacular of all of these mishaps was the ineptitude of the Ministry of Finance. The bursting of the economic bubble revealed that the Japanese financial sector had amassed a stunningly large collection of potentially unrecoverable loans. Officially acknowledged problem loans in November 1995 totaled ¥37.4 trillion, of which ¥18.3 was deemed unrecoverable. This meant an average of 6 percent of the loans outstanding by private-sector banks were in doubt.[12] By 1998 it became clear that bad bank loans totaled at least $600 billion, plus billions more off the balance sheets of government bodies and corporations, and further billions in underfunded pension programs.

The ministry first sought to cover up the extent of the problem only to find that the good faith and credit of all Japanese banks was subject to international punishments: Moody's, the international rating service, issued a report in June 1995 that downgraded the credit worthiness of Japanese banks to an average rating of D (uncertain), while international money markets imposed a so-called Japan Premium of several tenths of a percent on the cost of short-term funds to Japanese banks.[13] Furthermore, the Bank for International Settlements (BIS) required all banks to retain at least 8 percent of its total capital in hard assets, and Japanese banks consequently found themselves having to liquidate stock holdings or property, thereby further depressing domestic markets. Through it all, the Bank of Japan continued to keep the official discount rate at absurdly low levels (0.5 percent at some stages), transferring huge sums from Japanese savers to the financial bailout.

These transfers were explicit in the so-called *jūsen* problem. *Jūsen* are housing loan companies closely tied to the farming cooperatives and nominally under the regulatory control of the Ministry of Finance, with some responsibilities assigned to the Ministry of Agriculture. At the high point of the bubble economy, the *jūsen* had been aggressive lenders, allowing borrowers to use rapidly rising land and stock prices as collateral for loans. Not coincidentally, many of these borrowers proved to have close ties to organized crime as well as to elected officials. When land and stock prices collapsed, some $40 billion in loans became unrepayable. Several banks failed, for the first time since the 1920s, and the government eventually pushed through a program to use some $6.5 billion from the supporting banks and the Deposit Insurance Fund to liquidate seven failed *jūsen*.[14] The use of public money as part of the closure scheme attracted public outcry. It was widely seen as a means of covering up the greed or ineptitude of government bureaucrats, elected officials, mobsters, LDP-connected farming cooperatives and banking corporations.

The bureaucratic sleaze affected national and local officialdom as well. Officials in twenty of Japan's forty-seven prefectures were revealed to have squandered millions of dollars by wining and dining one another along with officials from Tokyo. Fabricated and padded expense accounts, bogus trips, and nonexistent staff were exposed as deeply entrenched "norms." At least three governors quit and some thirteen thousand officials were disciplined.[15] Numerous arrests were made of mid- to upper-level bureaucrats in several agencies, and in March 1998 the arrests reached the top echelons of the Ministry of Finance as Sakakibara Takashi, a deputy director in the Securities Bureau, became the first career MOF bureaucrat to be arrested since 1948.

Arrests were paralleled by a declining technical competence of public officials, most of whom had been trained as generalists and lacked the economic, computer, and technical skills to monitor effectively the increasingly complicated and fast-moving private-sector developments in derivatives trading, currency transactions, telecommunications, and the like. In the 1960s, bureaucratic and budgetary actions had targeted the most sophisticated segments of the Japanese economy; by the 1990s they were increasingly concerned with its least sophisticated—witness such costly public works as the virtually unused ¥45 billion Fukui Port, the ¥180 billion breakwater at almost empty Hitachi-Naka, or costly "agricultural" bridges such as the ¥20 billion bridge connecting the island town of Azumacho to the mainland to allow the island's 353 residents an "agricultural path" to easier markets.

All of this was in stark contrast to the civil service that had long burnished its reputation for consummate anticipatory skills and selfless dedication. A 1997 Mainichi poll showed that only 10 percent of respondents thought government officials were seeking to fulfill the public good.[16] Politicians had always been viewed as corrupt; that the bureaucracy was little better was new and shocking.

Japan also looked inept on the diplomatic front. No sequence of events dramatized this more fully than Japanese governmental reactions to Iraq's August 1990 invasion of Kuwait. Following the invasion, Japan spent four days doing what the United States did in ten hours—impose a trade ban on Iraq. Facing a choice between Iraq, the oil-producing country from which Japan got some 12 percent of its oil, and America, the country to which Japan sent some 27 percent of its exports and on whom it relied for its overall security, Japan really had no choice but to line up with the United States. But the government stumbled through a series of indecisive and contradictory moves around financial aid and the dispatch of personnel. Eventually Japan made a substantial economic contribution to the action, but the government's initial indecisiveness suggested an effort to buy off the United States rather than to pursue any systematic or considered strategy of foreign policy.

As the *Economist* noted at the time, "It is Japan's fluffing of its first—and maybe most telling—chance to show that in the new world order it will occupy something more than a narrow economic niche. Less abstractly, Japan's behavior has for now laid to rest the idea that it deserves the permanent seat on the UN Security Council it so covets."[17] At a minimum the Gulf crisis revealed a Japan whose foreign and security policies were far less safely ensconced in the clear network of relationships and priorities that had made it so easy to ignore China's testing of nuclear weapons in 1964. Instead, with the Gulf War, the ambiguities of Japan's international aspirations and abilities were laid bare.

Finally, in what is admittedly an artificial but symbolically important symmetry to the international successes of the mid-1960s, in 1996 Japan lost its bid to be the sole host of the World Cup and produced an Olympic embarrassment in the Nagano Winter games of 1998.

Japan had introduced a professional soccer league in May 1993. Within a few years, soccer jumped from being a poorly attended club sport to a well-funded and highly profitable professional association. Soccer matches in the newly formed J. League systematically drew more fans in both the stadiums and on television than did many baseball games[18] But for a last-minute draw won by the Iraqi team, Japan's national team would have made it to the 1994 World Cup, an unexpected and almost miraculous performance by a relative newcomer to international competition. The Japanese home television audience for the games from Qatar was well over 30 percent, and more than 50 percent of Tokyoites watched the final part of the last game. Clearly, soccer had added an entirely new internationalism to Japanese athletics.

This background set the stage for Japan's bid to host the World Cup in 2002. In the summer of 1994, a coalition of fifteen Japanese cities seemed absolutely assured of gaining the Federation of International Football Association (FIFA) bid to host the Cup. Each of the fifteen had either constructed or were prepared to construct new soccer stadiums for the expected games. Each had also put up ¥235 million for the lobbying effort being undertaken by Japan's national committee. Two years later, Japan found itself, for the first time in World Cup history, reduced to co-hosting the games with longtime national rival, South Korea.

Then on the Olympic front, Nagano had won the rights to the Winter Games for 1998, in large part because of the promise of massive financial support pledged by Japan's government during the height of the bubble. But unlike the 1964 Summer Games that had so highlighted Japan's growing prosperity, the 1998 Winter Games drew attention to the nation's economic problems. With the bursting of the bubble and the downturn in the economy, sponsorship fell off, construction fell behind schedule, and the International Olympic Committee issued sweeping criticisms of athletic housing, excessive regulation, bid rigging, and the character of competitive facilities. By the late 1990s Japan's overall stature in international athletics stood in dramatic contrast to what it had been at the height of the 1964 Olympics, reflecting the far broader decline in Japan's international and economic prestige.

Indicative of Japan's international standing was its failure to acquire a permanent seat on the UN Security Council. For decades, Japan had worked quietly behind the scenes to gain permanent membership. In the late 1980s, its chances appeared good, but by the mid-1990s the entire issue had been shelved, in large part because of Japan's fall from economic dominance, as well as its fumbling of the Gulf War situation.

The broad contrast is clear. The 1960s showed Japan making massive economic and foreign policy strides under a politically unified conservative party. A conservative regime that rested on a cohesive socioeconomic coalition, a particular mix of political and economic institutions, and a public policy profile of "embedded mercantilism" were all well entrenched and enjoyed great stability. That stability benefited from a positive cycle of politics, international relations, and economics. By the 1990s the cycle was spiraling downward.

The contrast between the late 1990s and the 1960s is clear in all three regime variables: the public policy profile of the country had changed, important economic and political institutions had been reconfigured, and the predominant socioeconomic base, as well as the main lines of socioeconomic cleavage, had shifted.

This is not to suggest that all residues of the earlier regime had somehow been swept into history's dustbin. Neither politics nor economics moves in straight lines. As noted earlier, changes in Japan—as anywhere—involve untidy blendings of old and new. As the next chapter will suggest, many of these changes have been evolutionary, with few visible cataclysms marking the shifts. In other instances, there have been short-term and radical alterations, but almost always the new and the old have been cobbled together. In short, change in Japan has been path dependent; the past has continually insinuated itself into the present. But the results have been to move the country's regime far away from its earlier moorings.

Public Policy Profile: Disembedding Mercantilism

In Chapter 2, I characterized the public policy profile of Japan's conservative regime as "embedded mercantilism." This broad-brush label covered several components of public policy including economic policy, social welfare policy, labor-management relations, and foreign policy. During the 1990s all four showed sharp breaks from past patterns.

Economic Policy

"Embedded mercantilism" involved macroeconomic policies that, for approximately the first twenty-five years after World War II (1945–71), rested on "developmentalist" catch-up. These policies included extensive economic planning; industrial reorganization; protection of domestic manufacturers, financial institutions, and agriculture; limits on foreign penetration of Japanese markets as well as on Japanese firms moving abroad; and strictly balanced budgets and fiscal tightness.

The policy tools serving these goals were many: high tariffs and restrictive quotas on most manufactured imports, tight controls over domestic consumption, restrictions on capital and technology flows into and out of Japan, a systematically undervalued yen that made Japanese exports cheap in world markets, a very restricted corporate bond market, policies to encourage high personal savings by citizens, and a strong reliance on foreign technology purchases. Furthermore, the government maintained a tight fiscal policy that kept taxes down, government small, and public expenditures low. In addition, deliberately low levels of defense spending freed up investment capital for use by domestic industries.

There was little dissent from this broad quilt of policies supporting embedded mercantilism. Political parties did not divide sharply on most of them. Although specific policies affected socioeconomic sectors differently, they provided generalized benefits to most groups. Most individual citizens enjoyed improving lifestyles while personal incomes remained relatively egalitarian in comparative terms. In short, Japan's 1960s mercantilism was indeed deeply embedded throughout the polity.

By the mid-1990s, many of these policy directions were dramatically different. Japan's capital markets and its currency had become deeply integrated into world markets. The Japanese yen, fixed at 360 to the U.S. dollar from 1947 until 1971, had more than quadrupled in value to about 80 at one point in 1995 and then, just as suddenly, had reversed course and fallen to 145 by mid-1998; MOF's ability to set exchange rates had become vastly superseded by international markets and currency speculators. Meanwhile, Japanese financial markets had been substantially liberalized, particularly with the revision of the Foreign Exchange and Control Law (1980) and the deregulation of the corporate bond market. Individual Japanese companies and financial institutions were, in the mid-1990s, free to issue bonds abroad in whatever was the most suitable currency and then swap the proceeds into yen. Japan had become the world market's major supplier of capital.[19] And indeed, individual Japanese corporations by the late 1990s were choosing to finance even domestic business deals denominated in dollars—further evidence of both their corporate autonomy and their independence from MOF oversight.

Even in the late 1970s, Japanese investors accounted for only 6 percent of direct investment outflows from the major industrial nations, 2 percent of equities outflows, 15 percent of bond outflows, and 12 percent of short-term bank outflows. By the late 1980s, these figures had swollen to 20 percent of international foreign direct investment, 25 percent of equities, 55 percent of bonds, and 50 percent of short-term bank loans.[20]

Individual Japanese firms were also far more heavily invested abroad. This in turn altered the export character of many Japanese manufacturers. From 1990 to the first quarter of 1996, exports from the Japanese islands grew by only 4 percent, the lowest rate in one fifteen-country OECD survey. (During this period, eight countries had export growth of 25 percent or more.)[21] Even more symbolically, in 1995, Japanese-owned firms manufactured more overseas (¥41.2 trillion) than they exported from the home islands (¥39.6 trillion).[22] Although Japanese-owned companies were often still international export powerhouses, their products were no longer manufactured exclusively—or in some cases predominantly—within Japan.

Formal trade barriers and limits on foreign direct investment had also been largely eliminated. Foreign brokerages, as was noted above, not only held seats on the Tokyo Stock Exchange but had acquired a total market share surpassing that of Japan's Big Four. A number of foreign banks were involved in government-bond underwriting while others had entered trust banking. Japanese imports, including imports of manufactured goods, increased substantially from the 1960s. Many Western firms had become $1 billion companies within the Japanese market, including IBM, Coca-Cola, Schick, Motorola, Texas Instruments, Nestle, Olivetti, Warner-Lambert, Mercedes Benz, and Amway. Coca-Cola in the 1990s, for example, drew a higher share of its world profit from Japan than from the United States, with "profit margins per gallon" at four times the U.S. rate. Also successful have been direct sellers to consumers such as Wella, Eddie Bauer, Compaq, Dell Computer, Proctor and Gamble, McDonalds, and Häagen Dazs. Large department stores stocking foreign products were more widespread. The service sector continued to show surplus sales for foreign firms. And by the late 1990s, the banking, insurance, and brokerage industries all had multimillion-dollar foreign participants. Clearly, the Japanese market had shed much of its earlier mercantilist character.

Japanese fiscal policy had also been transformed. During the 1960s government revenues had come largely from corporate and personal income taxes, while the Ministry of Finance pursued "overbalanced budgets" that kept down government expenditures, allowing conservative politicians to declare periodic and popular tax cuts. As a consequence, in 1964, the budget was balanced with only 1.35 percent of the general budget devoted to debt service. By 1995 nearly one-quarter of the government's revenues were derived from consumption taxes, over one-quarter of the budget was financed by borrowing, and debt service had risen to 18.6 percent.[23]

This latter figure put Japan ahead of the United States (13.9 percent), the United Kingdom (17.5 percent), Germany (10.7 percent) and France (17.9 percent).[24] Even more remarkably, Japan's cumulative public debt in 1997 had reached nearly 100 percent of GNP. Among the OECD countries only a few such as Belgium, Canada, and Italy confronted bigger gross debts.[25]

Monetary policies were also quite different. Trying to cover the fallout from the bubble, in 1992 the government had moved sharply away from previous monetary restraint, driving down official rates to 0.5 percent by the middle of the decade, the lowest levels in Japanese history. Moreover, the government launched a series of huge supplementary budgets between 1992 and 1995, which in total exceeded ¥70 trillion, while also dramatically expanding spending by the Fiscal Investment and Loan Program. Both monetary and fiscal policies had become far looser than ever before in postwar Japan.

On privatization and deregulation as well, Japanese policy had changed. In the 1990s once nationalized industries such the Japanese National Railways (JNR), Nippon Telephone and Telegraph (NTT), International Telegraph and Telephone (KDD), and the Tobacco and Salt Monopoly had been substantially privatized. Other industries such as the airlines, energy, the finance sector, and various pension systems had undergone varying degrees of deregulation.[26] Numerous areas of the once highly protected Japanese economy had thus become more open to influence by stockholders on the one hand and to foreign corporations and investors on the other.

Finally, whereas during the 1960s government effort and energy was focused largely on assisting Japan's high-value-added, technologically sophisticated firms to gain greater international competitiveness, by the end of the 1990s far more official effort was being directed toward Japan's declining industries. MITI was particularly active in supporting cartels in such industries as aluminum, cement, and petrochemicals,[27] while in other oligopolistic industries with high employment such as steel, shipping, and textiles, MITI policies encouraged economic adjustment but within a still protected domestic market.[28] MOF, in turn, was devoting its efforts in banking to protection of the inefficient rather than promotion of the competitive.

Perhaps the most striking difference from the 1960s was the lack of cohesiveness and singularity in economic policy, which was instead characterized by internal contradictions. The passage of the Fiscal Structural Reform Act in November 1997 aimed at reducing the issuance of deficit-covering bonds and capping major government spending. It was congruent with the rise in the consumption tax from 3 to 5 percent. Yet, almost immediately afterward, the government moved to create a completely contradictory fiscal policy involving ¥2 trillion in tax cuts and a massive expansion of public works spending. Exceptionally low interest rates allowed banks to borrow cheaply to work off their bad loans, but devastated the earnings of insurance companies. Government economic policies were no longer a cohesive strategy directed at national improvement, but rather an eclectic mixture of ad hoc efforts to plug holes in competing economic dikes.

Many of the newer policy directions in Japanese economic policy parallel those being undertaken in major Western European and North American countries. Among them: the reduction of barriers to inward and outward trade and capital flows, the coordinated floating of the national currency, the increase in outgoing foreign direct investment, the support for declining industries with political clout, and technological and investment arrangements transcending national boundaries. In all of these areas Japan's economic policies by the mid-1990s had moved considerably closer to those of the other industrialized democracies, thereby reducing some of Japan's erstwhile uniqueness. But the policy shifts hardly involved unidirectional convergence.

Despite the changes in economic policy, Japan in the late 1990s still differed from the other industrialized democracies in two important ways. First, Japanese markets for imports remained skewed against high-value-added manufacturing goods competitive with Japanese-made products. Japanese data show that manufactured goods in the late 1990s made up 21.7 percent of total imports, compared to only 5.4 percent in 1955. This seems a major change. Yet, much of the jump in imports is related to a relative decline in the import of oil and other raw materials, while another large portion is the result of intracompany trades from Japanese-owned multinationals manufacturing abroad, particularly in Southeast Asia.[29] In the mid-1990s, for example, nearly 40 percent of Japan's imports came from Japanese-owned subsidiaries abroad.[30]

The still rather closed character of the Japanese market is made even clearer by a second point, namely the limited amount of foreign direct investment in Japan. According to one comparative study, in 1986 only 1 percent of Japan's assets were owned by foreign-controlled firms, and just 0.4 percent of its workers were employed by them. In the United States, by way of contrast, foreign-controlled firms owned 9 percent of the assets, employed 4 percent of the workers, and accounted for one-tenth of all sales. And even the United States looked autarkic in comparison with the major European countries. In Britain foreign-controlled firms accounted for 14 percent of its assets, one-seventh of its workers, and one-fifth of the nation's sales. In West Germany foreign-owned companies held 17 percent of assets and accounted for 19 percent of sales, while in France foreign dominance was greater still.[31]

Even more striking, cross-national data for 1995 show that the United Kingdom had foreign direct investment averaging $3400 per capita; the figure for France was $2200; for the United States, $1700; for Germany, $1500. In contrast, foreign direct investment in Japan remained a lowly $135 per capita, or well below one-twelfth the average for the other four large economies.[32]

Thus even if the changes hammered out in Japan's macroeconomic policy portended a fundamentally more open economy, the old wine of mercantilism filled much of the new bottle of internationalism. Two facts do seem unassailable. First, although the Japanese government and Japanese firms had not fully abandoned their earlier mercantilist orientation, numerous components of the Japanese public policy profile were drastically less so than those of two decades earlier. Second, despite such changes, numerous remnants of Japan's earlier structures and orientations remained in evidence keeping Japan quite distinct from most other democracies.

Social Welfare Policy

The social welfare component of Japan's public policy matrix, like macroeconomic policy, showed continuities with the past. Social welfare continued to mark Japan as an outlier among industrialized democracies, although welfare rollbacks in other countries were bringing them closer to Japan's minimalism. In the 1960s the Japanese government had developed health insurance and public pension programs that were universal in coverage but low in payout levels. Long waits for pension eligibility and high co-payments for medical benefits restricted recipient benefits and minimized government costs. Thus, public spending on social policy left Japan unchallenged at the bottom of virtually all comparative statistical compilations of public spending for social welfare for the world's industrialized countries. As late as 1967–69, Japan's total public expenditure for social welfare as a percentage of GDP averaged only 19.2 percent, by far the lowest figure among the industrialized democracies; only Switzerland and Australia were spending less than 30 percent.[33]

Income maintenance expenditures were also low. Japan spent 2.1 percent of GDP for income maintenance programs in 1962 and 2.8 percent in 1972, both of which were only a third the OECD average.[34] Such minimalist governmental support for a variety of social welfare programs was very much in keeping with the broadly conservative character of Japan's government. By and large, conservatives treated social welfare as an unwarrantedly expensive frill likely to impede a fluid and inexpensive labor market, worker loyalty to firms, and overall economic growth. Meanwhile, workers in large firms drew their principal health and retirement benefits from the companies where they worked. Programs for such workers were relatively generous and were tied to the maintenance of a stable employment pool and a loyal company workforce.[35]

Social security policies in the 1990s had expanded in inclusiveness and total cost to the government. Moreover, extensive cross-subsidization had reduced the widespread differences in benefits under the more varied programs of the 1960s. But, on balance, little change had occurred in the policies' fundamental orientation. Corporate occupational welfare remained far more generous, comprehensive, and important than government programs. Japanese social welfare policies remained heavily residual, dualistic, and segmented by occupational status. Privileged "insiders" in large firms averaged benefits that were 30 percent higher than "outsiders" from smaller companies or workers with irregular employment contracts.[36] The retirement allowance for a male worker with thirty-five years seniority was three times higher if he worked for a large firm (1000 or more employees) than for a smaller firm (30–90 employees); and on average, university graduates received 20–25 percent more than those with only secondary diplomas.[37] Government employees were similarly privileged.

Meanwhile, welfare programs not directed toward the male breadwinner such as family benefits, child care, maternity leave, sickness, unemployment, and job promotion expanded only slightly from the 1960s, remaining modest in comparative terms and accounting for less than 2 percent of GNP, compared to 8 percent in the European Community and the other OECD countries.[38]

Overall, Japanese spending for social security at ¥455,000 per capita still left the country at the bottom of the OECD countries. Japanese government programs allocated only 11.9 percent of GNP for social welfare, well below Sweden (40 percent), Germany (27.6), France (30.9), the United States (21.3), Italy (25.8), and England (27.8).[39]

The appearance of simple continuity between 1964 and 1994 however must be qualified by three important caveats. First, by the 1990s Japan was facing tremendous underfunding of both its national life insurance and pension programs as well as numerous corporate pension plans. High levels of economic confidence during the years of the bubble economy had led to excessive public and corporate promises with regard to pensions without adequate reserves to meet them. Net Japanese pension liabilities had risen to over 100 percent in 1996, compared to 25 percent in the United States and less than 5 percent in the United Kingdom while assets in private pension schemes were underfunded by as much as 40 percent. Most such programs had been structured around expectations of between 5.0 and 5.5 percent rates of return, while in reality return rates on the government's long bond were much lower and the insurance companies which were the recipients of about one-third of these funds were reneging on promised payouts and offering returns of only 2.5 percent.[40] These serious problems in social welfare policy were new.

A second challenge to the notion of simple continuity is that during the 1970s and into the early 1980s Japanese social welfare policies made substantial breaks from the policies of the 1960s. New programs were introduced; different patterns of cross-subsidization were created; qualifications and co-payments were liberalized. All were part of what the government labeled a "Japanese-style welfare society." By the late 1980s, however, many of these efforts had been substantially rolled back as part of the administrative reform effort, leaving policy in the 1990s looking less like a thirty-year continuation and more like a return to an earlier pattern following a lurch away.

A third important qualification about the 1990s is that many government agencies were confronting Japan's "aging problem." Demographic data showed that Japan would undergo substantial demand for retirement and health benefits by the early decades of the twenty-first century. In the 1990s government agencies were scrambling to deal with the consequent welfare concerns. Overall, Japan continued to retain a broad governmental bias against the creation of a European-style social welfare system. At the same time, demanding simply that individual citizens or their families and companies provide for the massive numbers of new elderly was clearly no longer an option. The country was poised to consider substantial changes in past policies in recognition of future inevitabilities.

Having gone through a rollback of entitlement programs in the 1980s, Japan was in many ways less structurally committed to costly programs than were many other democracies. At the same time, given the incredible underfunding of its public and private pension programs and the expectation of vast jumps in the number of retirees and elderly, public policies designed to narrow the gap between promise and potential were almost certain to require a profound long-term increase in the tax burden.

Labor Policy

Labor-management policies were largely confrontational in the 1960s but cooperative in the 1990s. They had been especially vitriolic from the end of World War II well into the mid-1960s, when, under labor leaders such as Takano Minoru, Ōta Kaoru, and Iwai Akira, Japanese national union federations pursued either Marxian socialist or communist directions.[41] Japanese government and business, particularly Nikkeiren, had retaliated with a wide variety of union-busting and wage-reduction efforts. Well into the 1960s, Japanese politics at both the national political and the individual factory level were characterized by severe left-right, and business-labor confrontations.[42] The incidence of strikes was one of the few statistics where, in comparative terms, Japan was not a major outlier; here Japan looked like many other industrialized countries. Walter Korpi and Michael Shalev found that from 1946 to 1976 Japan ranked sixth of eighteen industrialized countries in strike involvement.[43]

Yet by the 1990s Japanese labor relations had become quiescent both at the level of the plant and in national politics. The ideological moderation of most unions and the broad inclusive character of the new labor federation, Rengō, led to far less confrontational labor policies. In the 1990s, as a result, Japan had one of the industrialized world's lowest strike rates, and a comparison of rates for the early 1990s with those for 1960–67 shows Japan had the second steepest decline (−240 percent) in the OECD. Only Austria, beginning from a much lower baseline, saw a sharper percentage drop. For the period after 1979 alone, strike participation fell by over 200 percent, by far the steepest decline among the major industrialized countries.[44] By the early 1990s, Japan's strike rates were as low as those of corporatist Sweden.

Most notably, Japan's once highly militant public-sector unions had pulled in their Marxian horns. As will be noted below, the vast majority of Japan's unions had become members of the moderate national federation, Rengō, and few sought to advance their aims through political confrontation. This moderation is particularly intriguing in comparative terms, since low strike rates have been most closely associated with national institutions of corporatist bargaining between business and labor such as are found in Austria, Norway, Sweden, or Germany. But at the national level no such institutions were present in Japan.[45] In fact, much of the locus of Japanese labor-management policy had devolved from the national level to the plant level, in the process fragmenting and deradicalizing the national Japanese labor movement even more than had been true in the 1960s.

Thus, even without such national corporatist institutions, both government and business policies toward labor had become far more cooperative and co-optive during the 1990s. Labor union representatives sat on various government advisory boards, and unions were involved in national- and plant-level consultation bodies. Personal contacts by union leaders with government officials and conservative party leaders were on the rise, as were measures of mutual trust and confidence.[46]

In addition, as the result of new legislation in the mid-1980s, the average number of hours worked by Japanese employees, which had been roughly four hundred hours per year higher than most other industrialized democracies (or ten extra weeks per year), fell to levels roughly comparable to those of the United States or the United Kingdom (although all three countries were still substantially higher than France, Germany, or most continental European countries).[47] Moreover, Japanese females had at least a nominal legislative equality in the workplace—which they had not enjoyed three decades earlier—even though males tended to do far better than females in wages and in positions of power.

In the general reduction of labor-management hostility, particularly in its reflection of the reduced bargaining power of labor, Japan does not look so unusual. In fact, it appears to be something of a leader for those countries attempting to enhance global competitiveness by reducing fixed labor costs and increasing labor productivity. This too was a much different profile from that of the 1960s.

Foreign Policies

Defense, security, and foreign policy have always been critical elements of Japan's political economy. This was true in the 1990s as it had been in the 1960s. The prevailing policy orientations in these areas remained similar in two important areas, different in three others, and mixed in yet another. But overall they pointed to a tentative move away from international passivity and toward greater international activism.

Most strikingly similar over the two periods is the continued reliance for military security on the United States. The U.S.-Japan Security Treaty provided the broad definitions of military and security ties between the two countries with few significant changes since its ratification in 1960. Close ties between the two countries were reflected in the continuation of U.S. bases on Japanese soil, institutional links between the two countries' militaries,[48] joint military exercises, technology-sharing and co-production agreements, extensive intelligence exchanges, and the like. Japan provided substantial cash support for the American military presence. By the early 1990s this involved about $45,000 per year per U.S. soldier, a figure higher than that of any other country where U.S. troops were stationed. Indeed, by paying 73 percent of the nonsalary costs of these forces, Tokyo made it cheaper for the United States to keep these troops in Japan than to bring them home. In 1996, despite serious anti-base protests on the most heavily militarized part of Japan, namely Okinawa, the United States and Japan reaffirmed the basic outlines of the alliance; and the alliance seemed unlikely to be seriously challenged politically in either country in the near future.

Also strikingly consistent was Japan's low level of military expenditures. A succession of governments, for the first thirty years following the end of World War II, held military expenditures to levels well below those of the other industrialized countries. The reasoning always hinged on attention to civilian industrial production, on deep levels of public pacifism, and, less frequently, on constitutional and legal limitations. Thus, the Japanese budget in 1964 provided less than 1 percent of GNP for military expenditures; that figure was almost identical in 1995.

Time and national economic growth meant, of course, a substantial jump in the absolute amounts spent, as well as in the sophistication and capabilities of the Japanese Self-Defense Forces.[49] While normally not thought of as a major military power, Japan by the mid-1990s deployed more tactical aircraft throughout Asia than did the United States, and it operated nearly twice as many destroyers. Such changes in mission and capability, however, involved no substantial reassessment of the basic principle of keeping a low military posture.[50]

Policies regarding indigenous production of military hardware by Japanese companies were more mixed. Japan's defense industry was gutted at the end of World War II, and well into the 1960s it was exceptionally limited in size, sophistication, and political influence.[51] Yet by the mid-1990s "technonationalism" and the "indigenization" of foreign technologies contributed to the greater sophistication of Japan's defense industry.[52] Domestic procurement of military equipment (*kokusanka*) as a proportion of total procurement was over 90 percent (versus about 75 percent in the early 1960s).[53] Nevertheless, Japanese defense industries remained far from autonomous, particularly in the production of sophisticated military equipment including fighter aircraft, Theater Missile Defense, antitank missiles and the like. Moreover, defense production remained a minuscule proportion of the total economy, accounting for well below 1 percent of Japan's total industrial output.[54]

Yet Japanese defense manufacturers had become important players in the overall development of sophisticated, high-value-added, "dual use" technologies. Japan's most advanced civilian electronics firms had, for example, "spun on" various applications to Japanese military products, just as defense production had often spun off technologies for commercial use.[55] The mixture of world-level sophistication in some areas of production and glaring gaps in others resulted by the 1990s in a series of joint-development projects by Japanese and American military producers.

Two things are important in this development: Japanese military production had become substantially more sophisticated, and production had moved away from pure "indigenization" toward greater collaboration with other (particularly U.S.) developers. A real shift occurred in the denationalization of much of Japan's defense industry. Even in the highly "nationalistic" area of weapons production, there was greater cross-national cooperation.[56]

Where Japanese policy change was unmistakable, even if somewhat low key, was in the greater willingness to take a more active leadership on a variety of international problems. For the most part, however, this leadership was exerted through economic rather than military or diplomatic efforts, and it typically involved not unilateral action but actions taken in collaboration with other countries or within international institutions. It consequently captured far fewer headlines or public attention.

In the 1960s Japan's unmistakably low posture in international relations grew out of efforts to regain world acceptance and to concentrate on domestic economic transformation. By the 1990s Japan had moved into notable roles in a number of regional organizations such as the Asia Development Bank, APEC, Pacific Economic Cooperation Council (PECC), the Pacific Basin Economic Council (PBEC), and the Pacific Trade and Development Conference (PAFTAD).

Furthermore, the country had taken leadership on Third World debt problems, as was the case, for example, with the Miyazawa Plan (subsequently the Brady Plan of 1989). This involved the development of a range of novel ways for major banks to deal with the exploding levels of Third World debt. Debt-equity swaps, exit bonds, and other techniques allowed the banks to reduce the debt service burdens of borrowers. The program also helped to restore greater financial confidence in the management, stability, and prospects of the borrowing countries. But, more important, the plan was critical in averting an international banking crisis in the 1980s.

Japanese diplomatic leadership was also demonstrated in its defusing of tensions surrounding North Korea's efforts to develop a nuclear weapons program. While the United States responded largely in military and strategic terms, Japan joined with South Korea and the United States to provide energy guarantees to the North in exchange for mutually satisfactory guarantees that any nuclear military potential the North had would be eliminated.

In the same vein, increased Japanese internationalism was also shown through overseas assistance. During the 1960s Japan had no significant foreign aid program. What existed was niggardly in size, almost exclusively bilateral, and tied to the subsequent purchase of Japanese goods or services. By the early 1990s all that had changed. Japan's share of official development aid made it the largest or the second largest contributor worldwide. In the 1990s, an increasing portion of Japanese aid was given via international financial institutions such as World Bank and Asia Development Bank. Moreover, by 1989 only 17 percent of Japan's bilateral aid was fully or partially tied, in contrast to the OECD group average of 39 percent and the United States average of 58 percent.[57] (At the same time, Japanese companies continued to do well as a result of governmental aid projects; in the year ending March 1992, for example, Japanese firms won 31 percent of the contracts financed by Japanese assistance. This figure probably understates the linkage since it does not include joint-venture partners of Japanese firms or infrastructural projects that subsequently benefit Japanese companies.)[58]

Moreover, Japanese aid had become more "international" in its targets. In the 1960s virtually all Japanese aid went to Asia; by 1993 less than 60 percent did. Moreover, four of Japan's largest ten recipients were non–Asian countries (Egypt, Jordan, Peru, and Turkey), and two others (India and Sri Lanka) are in South Asia and not within Japan's traditional definition of Asia. In short, foreign aid offered some important hints of a greater internationalism in Japanese foreign policy.

Far and away the most dramatic shift came with Japan's willingness to allow its troops to be used overseas. This change followed internal debates about Japan's possible dispatch of troops for the Gulf War of 1990. Under previous official interpretations of Article 9 of the Constitution, such actions would have been violations.

Following a wrenching domestic debate, Japan in 1991 passed legislation (the United Nations Peacekeeping Operations Cooperation Bill) allowing its troops to be used—under very constrained conditions—in UN-sponsored, noncombative peacekeeping activities abroad. As a result, Japanese minesweepers moved into the sea lanes in the Persian Gulf after the fighting between the United States and Iraq had ended. Japanese military personnel subsequently participated in UN peacekeeping operations in Cambodia, Mozambique, and the Golan Heights. Undertaken under United Nations' auspices, these actions were deemed constitutionally legitimate—certainly a dramatic reinterpretation of Article 9. They would have been politically impossible in the mid-1960s, given the strength of the left, its commitment to resisting any hint of "Japanese militarism," and the broad support such a commitment enjoyed among the general public. While Japanese troops were hardly in the midst of major combat, and indeed while military personnel worldwide were collectively amused at the timidity of Japanese actions, the parameters surrounding such activities had shifted dramatically.

Perhaps most important for understanding Japan's regime shift is the entire array of defense- and foreign-policy-related issues that, after polarizing Japan in the 1960s, had become largely nonissues by the mid-1990s. When JSP leader Murayama Tomiichi became prime minister, he renounced virtually every element of the long-standing JSP platform concerning defense, the Constitution, and the security arrangements with the United States. He accepted the constitutionality of the Self-Defense Forces; he agreed to the legitimacy of the U.S.-Japan Security Treaty and to the stationing of U.S. troops on Japanese soil; he accepted the conservative interpretations of Article 9. He oversaw the introduction of a host of patriotic measures, once opposed within Japan's schools. Essentially, Japanese foreign policies, once the most contentious item in Japanese party politics, while hardly consensual, no longer generated the kind of divisiveness among the leaders of Japan's major parties and interest groups that they had three decades earlier.

The composite public policy portrait that emerges from the above description suggests two major conclusions. On the one hand, there are clear breaks from earlier policies—especially in macroeconomics, the internationalization of the Japanese currency, industrial production, the loosening of fiscal policy, the underfunding of various pension funds, the more cooperative labor-management relations, and the shifts in foreign and defense policies. The policy nexus that prevailed under the conservative regime of the 1960s had undergone a substantial transformation. However one characterizes the current mix of policies, "embedded mercantilism" is surely inappropriate. On the other hand, important legacies from the past remain, most notably in the barriers to foreign direct investment, the retention of an occupationally based social welfare system, close ties to the United States, and in a generally low official commitment to using military means in advance of national goals.

This mixture of shifts and continuities has, however, not brought the country into close similarity with other industrialized democracies. Rather, they have left Japan's public policy with a highly individualistic profile, as an examination of the institutional components of the Japanese political economy in the mid-1990s will confirm.

Institutional Fragmentation at the Conservative Core

During the 1960s the centripetal bias of political and economic institutions contributed greatly to conservative stability. By the 1990s many of these institutions had lost their power to centralize and hold. Fragmentation, division, and differentiation were far more in evidence. Meanwhile the party system and the electoral system, which had been so sharply polarized and had worked so favorably for conservatives, no longer fragmented opponents of the conservatives or made it so difficult to mobilize voter opposition to the LDP.

Consider first the split in the LDP. Even though the party returned to government less than two years after its split, and even though it gained the largest number of seats in the lower house of parliament following the October 1996 election, the party no longer served as the single vehicle within which conservative politicians would contest national elections. The party's defeat in 1993 was less a defeat for "conservatives" and more a defeat for the party. By the mid-1990s the once vibrant political left had, in fact, surrendered to conservatives on most of the issues that had once divided the two camps, and conservatism as a broad philosophy had undeniably triumphed over socialism in a way that was unlikely to be reversed. Parties that espoused a left-of-center agenda had lost most of their appeal.

At the same time, the election of 1993 represented an institutional loss for the LDP, reflecting as it did the party's inability to retain the loyalty of its members and to be the single institutional beneficiary of the decline by the Japanese left. Except for the relatively minor split by the New Liberal Club in the summer of 1976 (involving only six parliamentarians), the LDP had consistently been the sole electoral vehicle for politicians identifying themselves as conservatives. The party consistently avoided situations under which conservative political entrepreneurs would bolt the party's ranks and strike out on their own—in new parties or altered alliances. That was no longer the case after 1993.

In the 1993 election three new conservative parties—the Japan New Party, the Japan Renewal Party, and the New Party Sakigake—all competed with the LDP for conservative votes.[59] Those who nominally "supported" the LDP in principle had consistently correlated with actual party voters at levels of between .859 and .884 in the elections held between 1980 and 1990. In the 1993 election, this correlation fell to .756; LDP supporters were clearly deserting the party.[60]

The continual recombination of political parties during the next few years witnessed further conservative fragmentation, entrepreneurship, and reorganization. The new electoral system contributed to this political fluidity and entrepreneurship. Replacing the multimember district system for the lower house was a system in which three hundred parliamentarians were selected from single-member districts and an additional two hundred were chosen from eleven regional districts on the basis of party lists and proportional representation. The roughly four-to-one rural bias of the old system was dramatically reduced, and within the single-member districts, at least, a premium on two-candidate competition had replaced the previous competition among five or more relatively viable candidates.

In the first election held under the new system, in 1996, six parties won ten or more seats; four of these drew the bulk of their members from the pre-split LDP. Although the LDP as a single organization did the best of all the parties, and indeed increased its postelection seat total by 28 despite a shrinkage in the total number of lower house seats by 11, it was by no means the cohesive electoral vehicle for conservatism that it had once been.

The LDP won nearly 48 percent of the seats, but other conservative parties drew 42 percent. And while the LDP won 53 percent of the seats contested in single-member districts, it won only 35 percent in the proportional representation districts. The other three conservative parties—including the Democratic Party, formed only weeks before the election—won a much more impressive 47.5 percent.[61]

In contrast, the old Socialist Party was cut in half (from 30 seats to 15), and several of the minor parties that had previously taken 7–10 percent of the vote merged into larger groupings. (The Japan Communist Party remained the only significant exception to this generalization, nearly doubling its numbers from 15 to 26.) More than anything else, the 1993 and 1996 elections showed the decimation of the parties of the left.

Three broadly conservative parties, the LDP (239 seats), the New Frontier Party (156), and the Democratic Party (52) had become the principal players. Overall, nearly 90 percent of the lower house could be categorized as conservative. The new government-opposition divide no longer fell along traditional left vs. right, business vs. labor lines, but instead was a division between conservative government and conservative opposition, with little issue clarity dividing the two.

Simultaneously, the former niche parties found it virtually impossible to win seats in the single-member districts. And even the proportional representation districts made smallness a disadvantage. The contesting parties hardly articulated clear-cut and distinctive policy positions, as many advocates of the new electoral system had predicted would be "inevitable." Rather, the conservative parties vaguely emulated one another's rhetorical positions on key issues. Consequently, even though the new single-member districts gave voters the chance to vote unmistakably for or against individual candidates, voter turnout was the lowest it had ever been in the postwar years, falling to below 60 percent.[62] In effect, electoral contests of the mid-1990s had lost the power to animate citizen involvement. A substantial party realignment was in process, but one that had crystallized more around personalities than around fundamental issue differences; and the key personalities generated little national voter appeal.

Voter support for the various political parties had also gone through a striking realignment. In the 1960s fewer than 10 percent of Japan's voters identified themselves as "independents." By the 1993 election that figure was up to 38 percent, and in January 1995 it was 50 percent.[63] Voters were available to be mobilized, but only if and when a particular political party or candidate could provide them with sufficient motivation. In the 1996 election, few found that motivation. But with roughly 40 percent thus "available," it seemed likely that parties would recombine in a continuing effort to reposition themselves to draw deeply from that pool.

Erstwhile conservative interest associations had also become more fragmented and less inherently loyal to the LDP. In 1960 the total number of interest associations in Japan was just over 10,000. By 1991 this had more than tripled to 36,000. Business associations also tripled from 4,600 to nearly 14,000. And meanwhile, political associations rose sevenfold from 169 to over 800.[64] Within this context, the agricultural cooperatives had stopped automatically supporting LDP candidates. Meanwhile, the major business federation, Keidanren, had grown increasingly divided internally and had ceased its automatic contributions to the LDP in 1993. Finally, there was a large increase in non-party-linked citizen groups, semipublic associations, and miscellaneous organizations. By 1986 this category had become the largest in Japan, moving ahead of the once predominant business-linked associations.[65] The cumulative effect was to make the process of political coordination—for both conservative political parties and bureaucratic agencies—far more complicated than it had been when there were fewer and generally more comprehensive organizations. Linkages among interest groups, parties, and bureaucratic agencies became far less automatic and predictably conservative than was true at the height of conservative power.

If conservative politicians were no longer united under a single electoral umbrella, and various interest associations had lost some of their earlier institutional unity, the national bureaucracy no longer stood together behind any hegemonic project in the way it had once united behind rapid economic growth. Japan's government agencies have long been noted for their reluctance to cooperate with one another.[66] Yet, rapid growth had induced considerable agency-to-agency cooperation in the 1960s; such cooperation around an overriding agenda had disappeared by the 1990s.[67]

By that time, several agencies (particularly the Ministries of Posts and Telecommunications, Agriculture, Transportation, Construction, and Home Affairs) had become heavily colonized by conservative politicians, in large measure through the LDP's Policy Affairs Bureau (Seimu chōsakai), the actions of so-called *zoku* politicians (politicians with special connections to the interest associations and government agency concerned with some particular functional area of policy), and most especially by the Tanaka-Takeshita political machine. Generally, agencies with the largest influence over highly lucrative sectors of the economy and those ripe for pork-barrel politics attracted the closest of these "iron triangle" links among politicians, interest associations, and government agencies.[68] Increasingly, their once general economic missions gave way to the particularistic ambition of generating benefits for conservative politicians and their allies.

Other agencies (International Trade and Industry, Finance, Foreign Affairs, and Education, to mention only the most prominent), while somewhat less prey to such political penetration and iron triangles, were caught up in the extensive competition over "turf." Numerous battles divided agencies over their respective responsibilities for emerging technologies such as biotechnology, development and regulation of high-definition TV, computer usage in schools, telecommunications, and the like.

Moreover, high-level bureaucrats began to show their political colors more clearly. Several former MOF officials, for example, resigned to run on the platform of Ozawa's Shinshintō in 1993, while the coalition government of 1993 attempted to purge certain senior bureaucrats deemed too close to the LDP. By the late 1990s, intra-conservative battles over deregulation and bureaucratic reorganization saw particular agencies linking their fortunes to one or another party presumed most likely to champion the agency's interests.

Not surprisingly, these shifts fed the overall demise of the bureaucracy's image as "above politics" and operating in the "national interest." The scandals noted in the first section of this chapter revealed that large numbers of high-ranking civil servants had been deeply enmeshed in extensive bribery schemes and closely tied to particular LDP leaders or interest groups. Meanwhile, many of the tools of bureaucratic power lost their earlier potency. This was particularly true of the power to control interest rates and to channel low-cost capital to targeted industries or firms. In addition, the mailed fist of arbitrary discretion, concealed inside the velvet glove of administrative guidance, was reduced by requirements for the publicized transparency of all government directives.

All of this contributed to the long-term demise of bureaucratic prestige. A very simple measure of this decline can be found in the competition rate for positions in the senior civil service. At the height of conservative dominance and high growth, as many as forty-three individuals competed for every one who was successful. By the early 1990s, this was down to fewer than fifteen candidates for each opening.[69] More and more of Japan's best and brightest were opting for jobs in other arenas.

While disintegration of conservative institutions was most institutionally transparent in the political sphere, there was also substantial disintegration within conservative economic institutions. Three warrant particular attention.

The most important single change was the greater internationalization of many Japanese firms. A major contributor to this trend was the rapid escalation in the value of the yen. *Endaka*, as the rising yen was called, made it economically suicidal for Japanese firms not to invest abroad. Continuing to manufacture at home became comparatively more costly in yen after the rest of the world's land prices, labor rates, and corporate evaluations had effectively been slashed by one-half or more. Business leaders were forced to ask themselves: how can we best take advantage?

Foreign direct investment by Japanese firms in the mid-1960s had been minuscule; by 1993 cumulative Japanese investment abroad totaled some $260 billion, making Japan the world's second largest overseas investor (behind the United States at $549 billion).[70] Once subject to heavy MITI and MOF directions designed to ensure conformity to various government industrial plans, firms became far freer to pursue their business strategies out from under the club of government capital controls. Technology transfer agreements leaped across national boundaries with nary a governmental signature. Profitable companies were free to finance activities through retained earnings. Others could raise capital through domestic equity markets, overseas warrants, international currency swaps, and domestic bond issues, leaving firms far freer to pursue strategies determined primarily by internal, company-specific needs rather than external government directives or national industrial policy proscriptions.

As larger numbers of Japanese firms, including many of their subcontractors, became more truly multinational, many also entered into strategic alliances with foreign-owned firms.[71] This marked a further fragmentation in the internal linkages among Japanese firms and *keiretsu*. At the core of the once privileged banking sector, Swiss Credit Bank forged an alliance with Japan's Long-Term Credit Bank involving an investment of one billion Swiss francs ($671 million), while Société Generale and Mitsui Trust teamed up, allowing Mitsui to market mutual funds from the French institution. Other tie-ups linked foreign and Japanese insurance firms and brokerages. Japan Air Lines joined an alliance with American Airlines while All Nippon Airways joined forces with Lufthansa and United. Meanwhile in manufacturing Toyota was teamed up with GM and Kia among others; in electronics, Fujitsu, NEC, Hitachi, and Toshiba all had alliances with American and European companies; NTT and KDD had done the same in telecommunications; Softbank and TV Asahi had various partners in software and commercial television; Mitsubishi Heavy Industries was in a venture with Daimler Benz, while Kawasaki Heavy Industries and Ishikawajima Harima Industries also teamed up with foreign partners in a variety of military production technologies. These were merely the tip of the international alliance iceberg. Indeed, Canon went so far as to adopt as its corporate slogan for the 1990s "Symbiosis with Global Partners."[72] The very nationality of many nominally Japanese firms came into question on both ownership and the place and nationality of the workforce.[73]

Though these changes were taking place in many segments of Japanese business, they were by no means universal. Many other firms in industries such as cement and construction were either unable to unwilling to invest abroad or to partner with foreign firms, enmeshed as many were in domestic public works projects pressed on their behalf by Japanese politicians. Similarly, while some of the subcontractors of Japan's larger manufacturers did follow them in setting up overseas operations, far more, particularly the smallest, remained in Japan only to watch their market shares dwindle. The number of manufacturing jobs in Japan fell by over one million in 1992–95 alone, catalyzing a national fear about the possible "hollowing out" of Japan.

Many of the most protected industries, including those within important service sectors such as insurance, brokering, and even commercial banking, remained unable or unmotivated to compete internationally. They remained locked into the domestic market, contributing heavily to the financial crisis of the 1990s.[74] The result of all of these shifts was to drive a series of wedges into a business community that had once been almost uniformly supportive of, and the automatic beneficiaries of, the politics of "embedded mercantilism."

Of particular importance to both the *keiretsu* and to various firms was the broadening of capital-raising options for nonfinancial firms. Deregulation of the corporate bond market was a key part of this process. As late as 1979 only two companies, Toyota Motors and Matsushita Electric, were qualified to issue unsecured convertible or straight bonds. A decade later some three hundred firms were able to issue straight or warrant-attached bonds, and five hundred could issue unsecured convertible bonds.[75] Deregulation also allowed many corporations to shift their sources of debt financing from the main banks to bonds. Thus bonds, including those issued abroad, gained an increased role. In 1965 Japanese industrial companies issued ¥391 billion worth of bonds, none overseas. In 1989 that figure was up to ¥9,284 billion domestically, while an even larger ¥11,129 billion was issued overseas.[76]

Hence, in the 1960s, most Japanese firms were raising the bulk of their needed capital through borrowing, primarily from their main banks, and the debt-to-equity ratio for Japanese firms in 1965 was nearly 90 percent for new inflows. By 1995 this ratio had fallen to 69.4 percent. Bank borrowings, which made up nearly 77 percent of total corporate finance in 1965–69, had dropped to 42.5 percent in 1990–91. Bond issues, which had been below 10 percent, jumped to 42.5 percent during the same period. Quite obviously, all of these changes reduced the dependency of manufacturing firms on the Japanese banking sector, but they also began to diminish the internal cohesion among the *keiretsu* as a whole.

Additionally, capital demands on both financial and nonfinancial companies, combined with the growing ability of individual firms to raise money abroad as well as the declining paper value of the stocks themselves, led to a substantial sell-off of once-sacrosanct cross-held shares, further eroding the internal cohesion of *keiretsu* and other corporate connections. As late as 1987, approximately 72 percent of the Tokyo Stock Exchange capitalization involved such relational cross holdings. By 1996 this proportion had fallen to 60 percent, and it was dropping at the rate of about 4 percent per year.

Meanwhile, in the financial crunch of the late 1990s, main banks cut off credit to over 12,000 firms. These changes also reduced the internal cohesion among the *keiretsu* while allowing individual firms, whether *keiretsu* members or not, far greater autonomy in their capital generation and business strategies.

By the 1990s, consequently, large numbers of Japanese-owned firms were no longer producing in and exporting from Japan; they had moved to international production and global investment and financing strategies. Japan had ceased to be an export platform. Individual firms and business groups had also gained considerable freedom from the capital controls they had experienced three decades earlier. While frequently of great benefit to individual firms, these moves contributed fundamentally to the conservative regime's fragmentation and loss of cohesion.

Not to be ignored in the focus on economic institutions is that labor had gained a degree of national unification. Japan's most radical unions had ceased to exist, and the once radical national labor federation, Sōhyō (Japan Confederation of Trade Unions), had been absorbed by the far more moderate Rengō, giving Japan the largest single labor federation in the world.[77] Yet labor cohesion was no longer inherently anti-conservative, and on many economic issues, individual unions were far more divided on a sector-by-sector basis than they were united with other unions.

The extent to which labor had made its peace with conservatives, bridging the once giant abyss between them, was perhaps never clearer than on May 1, 1996, when Prime Minister Hashimoto attended May Day celebrations, which during the 1950s and 1960s had been the single most antigovernment and anti-conservative occasion on the Japanese political calendar. At a similar level of symbolic significance on November 5, 1993, the president of Rengō, Yamagishi Akira, and the chairman of Nikkeiren, Nagano Shigeo, jointly visited Prime Minister Hosokawa to make a joint business-labor demand for a tax cut of ¥5 trillion designed to boost the Japanese economy.[78] Such business-labor cooperation on national economic policy had been unheard of in the 1960s.

Although Japan in the 1990s had traveled far from the 1960s, its institutional changes, like its policy changes, were mixed in that they moved Japan both toward and away from the other industrialized democracies. This same pattern is visible in the shifts in socioeconomic coalitions.

The New Socioeconomic Division

For most of its existence, the conservative political coalition did not have to make particularly hard choices among its potential supporters. Under the LDP the conservative camp from 1955 on was a socioeconomic coalition of big and small business, manufacturing and finance, diverse geographical areas, agriculture, and other socioeconomic support groups and organizations. Organized labor—and to a lesser extent intellectuals, urbanites, and students—constituted a competing, if flaccid, socioeconomic alliance. Despite the differing priorities of socioeconomic sectors at different times, the conservative regime's prevailing political institutions and policy profile made it by far the most attractive choice for a wide swath of Japanese society.

Moreover, when the conservative socioeconomic coalition did change, most shifts involved the adding of new support, not the jettisoning of old constituents. High levels of economic growth continued to generate expanding resources, making such additions comparatively easy from the 1960s into the late 1980s. The LDP became increasingly a "catch-all" party, while alternatives to conservative policies became decreasingly attractive to most groups.

By the early 1990s, consequently, the socioeconomic support base of the conservative regime had broadened substantially. Four changes are of particular note. First, as was noted earlier, organized labor—once the heart of the oppositional alliance—had abandoned its unmitigated hostility to the conservatives and no longer stood uniformly and automatically outside the regime. Second, agriculture and small businesses were providing substantially less support for, and less automatic identification with, the conservative camp. In many instances fragments of both sectors had actually broken ranks with the conservatives. Third, urbanites and white-collar workers had become significantly more important socioeconomically, although they were neither unambiguously pro- nor anti-conservative. Fourth, big business had become vastly more internally fragmented, dividing over the desirable character of post-1990s conservatism.

Organized labor had been the single most important socioeconomic sector hostile to the original conservative coalition. In the 1990s the new labor federation, Rengō, was a critical supporter of the anti-LDP coalition government of 1993; it helped to bring to power the first labor-backed government in Japan since the late 1940s.[79] At the same time, labor in the 1990s stood far closer to conservatives on numerous issues than it had three decades earlier. The radical left within the labor movement had become increasingly marginalized, and by the mid-1990s there was virtually no serious support for any dramatic moves away from private ownership; close security relations with the United States were accepted, albeit reluctantly; and business–labor divisions had given way to sectoral differences that pitted business and labor in single industries or firms against business and labor in others. In short, labor had long since surrendered its earlier anti-regime posture and become sufficiently moderate ideologically so that it could deal with virtually any plausible Japanese government.

Electoral support patterns by blue-collar workers reflected this narrowing gap between progressives and conservatives. Whereas in the 1960s conservative party support by union members was quite thin, by the 1990s significant proportions of labor were voting for the LDP.[80] In 1965, for example, 27 percent of industrial workers supported the LDP; by 1985 the number had risen to 49 percent, representing 12 percent of the total LDP support.[81]

Agriculture and small businesses also occupied different positions in the 1960s and the 1990s. Longtime electoral supporters of the LDP, farmers and small shopkeepers had enjoyed extensive protection through such measures as farm subsidies, import quotas on key agricultural goods (including a 100 percent ban on rice imports), low or no interest loans to small shopkeepers, and an "anti-supermarket law" that effectively gave local chambers of commerce veto power over any large stores proposed for an area.[82] In response to the liberalization of agricultural imports, farmers swung strongly against the LDP in the 1989 upper house election, with farm support for the party falling from 56 percent in the 1986 election to 41 percent in 1989.[83] This was the LDP's biggest loss from any socioeconomic group.

Although farmers and small businesses continued to be disproportionately strong supporters of conservative candidates electorally,[84] both groups had also shrunk in size, in economic significance, and in the electoral support they could provide for conservative politicians. In the 1955 election farmers made up 43 percent of the LDP's support; by 1965 the figure had dropped to 29 percent; by 1985, only 13 percent. Support from small businesses fell during the same period from 27 percent of the LDP's total to 19 percent,[85] shifts that made it clear that neither group could ensure the kind of conservative electoral hegemony that they had once delivered. Furthermore, their share in the nation's total economic activity had also dwindled. Consequently, both groups became less central to partisan (including conservative) electoral strategies and to national economic strategies, and both became far more vulnerable to economic changes from which the regime of embedded mercantilism had long protected them.

In 1960 just under sixty million Japanese lived in large cities; by 1990 this figure was up to ninety-five million, or over three-quarters of the total population.[86] Yet conservative electoral support in the large cities dropped precipitously between the 1960s and the 1990s.[87] It was their continued success in the less urbanized areas of the country that kept the LDP in power.

The loss of the electoral support from farmers and small businesses posed a serious threat to conservatives, and especially to specific conservative politicians in particular locales.[88] Because both groups had been such strong LDP supporters, it was by no means easy for the party or individual candidates to drop them in favor of some more numerous group, such as urban salaried workers. Hence, agriculture and small businesses retained disproportionate influence in specific electoral districts and with specific politicians, particularly through their links to personal support groups.

At the same time, the long-term trend was that of ever greater numbers of voters living within the metropolitan and suburban areas of the country. Although the LDP had made some electoral inroads into even the largest metropolitan areas, it was becoming increasingly clear that any candidate or party seeking to attract urban support was likely to lose support within the more traditional and rural sectors. Whereas the LDP had been able to expand its base throughout the 1980s, in the 1990s it could no longer do so. Economic policies that could keep all new add-ons happy without upsetting long-term supporters were no longer possible; trade-offs among potential constituencies were essential.

Trade-offs also divided the business sector. Business interests had cohesively supported embedded mercantilism during the 1960s. By the 1990s no such support existed. Numerous Japanese firms stood out as highly competitive by any international standard, particularly large manufacturers in areas such as electronics, machine tools, and automobiles. Yet the closed domestic economy had spared many other Japanese business sectors from ever confronting international competition. By the mid-1990s Japan's big business community had really become two different communities—one that was predominantly high-tech, internationally competitive, and highly profitable, relying on little or no direct governmental assistance, and another that was much less competitive and looked to the government for protection from foreign competition and guaranteed profitability within the domestic marketplace. Whereas high growth and protection had allowed the conservative regime to serve both constituencies effectively in the 1960s and 1970s, increased economic openness and slower growth made this problematic in the 1990s. Sharp internal cleavages arose within the Japanese business community over, among other things, deregulation, exchange rate policies, taxation, fiscal stimulation through government procurement, and overall protection and oligopolization of utilities, banks, the insurance industry, and holding companies.

The intra-conservative socioeconomic divisions of the early 1990s culminated in the actual split within the party in 1993. The LDP split reflected to some extent the urban-rural and competitive-uncompetitive divisions within conservatives. Even though many who split with the LDP, such as Ozawa, Hata, and Takemura were from rural areas, many of the younger dissidents who followed them were not. Moreover, the eventual anti-LDP coalition, with its inclusion of the Clean Government Party and Democratic Socialist Party had a distinctively more urban character. In the 1996 election, for example, the LDP won 51.7 percent of the single-member seats in towns and villages, compared to only 28.6 percent in cities of over 100,000 and 30.5 percent in the thirteen metropolitan areas. In contrast, the New Frontier Party (NFP) won only 17.8 percent of the rural seats, but 26.5 percent in the cities and 21.9 percent in the metropolitan areas. In the proportional representation districts the LDP did even worse in the cities and metropolitan areas, whereas the NFP did even better.[89]

The remnants of the LDP began to emerge as preponderantly rural and oriented toward pork-barrel politics, whereas the conservative opposition had become more urban, international, and antiregulatory. This division became even more apparent over the issue of deregulation. In August 1996 *Bungei Shunjū* published a poll of lower house parliamentarians. It showed a distinct gap in the orientations of the LDP and the NFP. Given a choice between "moving quickly toward socioeconomic regulation even though this will mean a coup de grace for the weaker elements in society" and "protecting the weaker members of society by taking a cautious approach to deregulation," 56 percent of the LDP members chose the more protectionist approach in contrast to only 23 percent of the NFP members and 24 percent of the Sakigake Party members. The overwhelming majority of the last two (76 percent of the NSP and 71 percent of Sakigake) preferred rapid deregulation despite its potential social costs.[90]

The same pattern emerged in the 1998 Upper House election when the LDP failed to win any seats in metropolitan districts such as Tokyo, Osaka, Kyoto, Aichi, Saitama, or Kanagawa. Its overt rural, pork-barrel focus meant the loss of urban support.

Japan's earlier webs of socioeconomic solidity were unraveling in another important way, namely, the growing income gap among Japanese citizens. In the mid-1960s Japanese income inequality was low; Japan was as economically egalitarian as many of the Scandinavian countries. In the mid-1990s, a widening gap opened between rich and poor. The Gini index, for example, crept steadily upward.[91] Unemployment rose steadily through the 1990s, with its strongest effects felt by new employees, older workers, and females. It became less obvious that all Japanese were riding in the same economic lifeboat. While Japan did not move as far toward class division as the United States or Britain, it was more economically divided in the 1990s than it had been three decades earlier.

In the 1990s, then, the conservative regime's once stolid socioeconomic base, previously held together through positive-sum politics and economics, had become zero sum: benefits to one socioeconomic sector increasingly meant the probable loss of benefits by another sector. Economic liberalization, currency shifts, overseas production, and market openings had driven wedges between agriculture, small business, and big business. The bursting of the bubble economy diminished the public treasury resources available to reward inefficient sectors. This in turn further exacerbated intra-conservative tensions over basic policy directions. During the 1990s a succession of conservative governments attempted without great success to accommodate the demands of their increasingly strange socioeconomic bedfellows in an ever shrinking futon.

Conclusion: Conservatism in the 1990s

The above analysis points to the numerous ways in which the once tightly integrated conservative regime had given way to far greater policy, institutional, and socioeconomic fragmentation. The previously vaunted Japanese economic growth machine had become mired in a bog of bad debt and collapsed consumer confidence; the once unbeatable conservative electoral machine was running out of fuel; and the once harmonious domestic and international linkages were acrimonious. Previous conservative institutions had lost their earlier fluidity and internal cohesion, leaving Japan in the midst of an unmistakable regime shift and struggling to find a new stability and equilibrium. What would replace the old regime was, as yet, unclear. Socioeconomic recombinations were still under way; so was the process of party system realignment and electoral recalibration. Institutional reorganization, particularly the reconfiguration and reregulation of the national bureaucracy and the financial sector, were principal items of debate. No public policy profile with anything like the clarity of embedded mercantilism and high economic growth had yet come into view. Japan in the late 1990s resembled in some respects the former communist regimes of the Soviet Union and Eastern Europe: that the old regime had been displaced was clear; that transition was under way was beyond question; but precisely how that transition would play out, and what new equilibrium would replace the old, was less evident. What was clear, however, was that, like Humpty Dumpty, the old regimes in Japan just as in the former communist countries could not be put back together again.

An observer of Japan in the late 1990s contemplating the next decade might reasonably assume that although the LDP may retain some measure of electoral success, the party will be very different from what it was in 1955, both in its support base and in its policy directions. Many Japanese industries will undoubtedly continue to be exceptionally competitive within world markets; indeed corporate profits and market shares of many major Japanese manufacturers rose substantially after the worst of the post-bubble economic debris was swept away. But the economy as a whole is unlikely to return soon to its previous growth rates, and any use of the label "Japan, Inc." is sure to be an even greater misnomer than it was when Japanese economic institutions were at their most harmonious. The Japanese bureaucracy is almost certain to retain powers that in comparative terms will be quite substantial, but it is unlikely that either government agencies or civil servants will command the control over business, let alone the social support, that they enjoyed in the 1960s. Japan will almost certainly continue to maintain close strategic, military, and economic ties with the United States, but the United States is unlikely to provide the same level of unmitigated support that it gave to Japan during the height of the cold war; nor is it likely that Japanese elites will expect it.

And yet, despite the changes, Japan in the late 1990s has remained an outlier among the industrialized democracies. Although the evolution of prevailing policies, socioeconomic support, and political and economic institutions has eroded some of Japan's earlier uniqueness, the country hardly seems to be converging with other industrialized democracies toward some powerful magnetic core. The increased fluidity of international capital undoubtedly challenges the ability of national governments and individual corporations in powerful ways. Yet, numerous other aspects of any country's political economy, from its foreign policy orientations to its socioeconomic composition to its political and business institutions, remain far more subject to national differentiation. Certainly public policies, institutions, and socioeconomic coalitions prevailing in Japan at the end of the century give every indication of remaining far from the laissez-faire pluralism of the Anglo-American democracies, the corporatist social welfare systems of continental Europe, and the "reformed" *partitocrazia* of Italy. Japan's most likely equilibrium will involve a political economy with its own distinct configuration, the main features of which are discussed in the concluding chapter.

The central question that this chapter raises is, How and why did the conservative regime of the 1960s deteriorate with such speed and completeness? What accounted for the shift? As we shall see in the next chapter, conservative leaders made highly successful adjustments to changing conditions and hence retained great power to shape the Japanese political economy during the 1970s and 1980s. But at the same time, many of those adjustments set in motion shifts and tensions within the regime that eventually led to its downfall.

CHAPTER SIX

Between Adjustment and Unraveling:
Protection and Erosion of the Old Regime

In the last chapter I contrasted Japan during the late 1990s with Japan in the mid-1960s. Despite the headline-grabbing drama of the 1990s and some sharp breaks with the past, political and economic transformations neither happened overnight nor as the evolutionary conclusion of some tidily linear progression. Rather, the new political economy of the 1990s emerged from a jumble of successful adaptations and regime unravelings. In this chapter I examine these transformations with two separate purposes. First, I show how a series of adaptive changes kept the regime largely intact and in rough equilibrium for more than three decades—a story of successful conservative adaptation. Conservative control under the LDP was extended; the economy continued to advance exponentially; and security and defense policies remained largely unchallenged and insulated from debate. Second, I trace how several seemingly successful adaptations simultaneously exacerbated tensions that eventually opened the regime to splintering and failure. Adjustments that proved politically and economically positive in the short run contributed to harsh and abrupt alterations that eventually shattered the old regime. In this chapter I thus interweave two threads, regime adaptation and regime decomposition.

Neither process was inevitable. Adjustments that with hindsight seem to have been the result of brilliant prescience by conservative leaders could well have failed. Others that, in the disarray of the mid-1990s, appear to have foolishly positioned the conservative regime on a "slippery slope" downward could well have played out differently. In short, striking as certain linkages may appear in retrospect and internally reinforcing as many of the processes may have become, nothing in this analysis should be read as inherently deterministic.

I begin by examining three sets of challenges to the conservative regime that arose between the early 1970s and the late 1980s. One set came from outside Japan, the other two were endogenous. Together they exacerbated intraregime tensions, undermining its previous smoothness and fluidity. In the second section I analyze the most important first- and second-order adjustments that were made to meet these challenges. Most adjustments sought to continue rapid economic growth while also bolstering the regime's political base. These were largely successful, but they proved to have long-term consequences that led ultimately to the regime's unraveling by the late 1980s and early 1990s.

Challenges to Conservative Dominance

As we saw in Chapter 4, three central dilemmas continually confront any democratic regime. First, a socioeconomic dilemma: diverse socioeconomic supporters want different things, and their power and influence keeps shifting. Occasionally, some single course of action can meet these competing and fluid demands. More often, coalition maintenance requires ongoing compromises, trade-offs, and deferred gratifications; temporary gains and losses are continually offset and counterbalanced. Second, a democratic or electoral dilemma: good politics is often at odds with good policy, and actions designed to enhance electoral viability frequently clash with what might be desirable for a nation's economic well-being or security. Third, an international dilemma: what works domestically does not always work internationally and vice versa. In Chapter 4 we followed the interplay of these dilemmas in Sweden, the United States, Britain, and Italy between the late 1970s and the early 1990s.

Even at its smoothest in the mid-1960s, the conservative Japanese regime was hardly devoid of internal frictions. Nevertheless, the nation's main political fault lines were unmistakably between the conservatives and the political left rather than among regime supporters. With time that split was resolved in favor of the conservatives. Embedded mercantilism, high economic growth, and a limited military posture all redounded to conservative electoral success. Conservative supporters collectively benefited from peace and prosperity, either directly or through side payments. The international arena was broadly conducive to the policy directions, institutions, and coalitional makeup of Japan's conservative regime.

During the 1970s and 1980s the conservatives' response to the three dilemmas became increasingly labored. Economic success and transformation changed the relative strengths and incentives of many important socioeconomic groups; new political parties, independent movements, and changes in voting patterns challenged the conservative electoral hegemony; and the international arena became far less hospitable to Japanese domestic regime arrangements. Consequently, intra-conservative politics and economics began to supersede earlier left-right divisions, and the central concern within the conservative camp was preventing these changes from undermining the basic cohesion of the regime. Doing so, however, meant a continual balancing act between the increasingly conflictual goals of specific political actors and the broader goal of regime continuity.

Socioeconomic Challenges

Conservative dominance of the electoral process and governmental office generated public policies that strengthened the regime's socioeconomic base, discredited its political opponents, increased overall public support, minimized the need for compromises, and enhanced the conservatives' ability to control political offices. The result, as described in Chapter 1, was a "virtuous cycle" in which successes in economics and politics reinforced one another. Yet this same cycle brought socioeconomic changes that challenged the regime's equilibrium. Conservative economic policies transformed the nation's socioeconomic makeup, strengthening certain opponents and dramatically weakening many supporters.[1]

Four changes were especially important: a dramatic reduction in the proportion of the population dependent on farming and small business, an extension of the life span, a tightening of the labor supply, and an urbanization that turned the majority of Japan's citizens into what Murakami Yasusuke has called "Japan's new middle mass."[2]

In 1950 nearly half of Japan's workforce was economically dependent on agriculture and fishing; by 1970 this was about 17 percent; and by the mid-1990s, below 6 percent. Meanwhile, employment in manufacturing accounted for only 22 percent in 1950; by 1970 it had risen to 35 percent, where it remained into the 1990s. The tertiary sector meanwhile expanded steadily from 30 percent to 48 percent to 60 percent over the same period.[3]

In 1947 about 40 percent of Japanese worked in family businesses with another 20 percent self-employed. Only about 40 percent were employees of firms. By 1970 the figures were 16 percent, 18 percent, and 66 percent. Since 1985, firms have employed nearly 80 percent of Japanese workers.[4]

As larger and more technologically sophisticated industries and service sector firms gained increasing prominence in the national economy, the agricultural and small-business sectors—early cornerstones of the conservative regime's electoral coalition, as well as sources of cheap labor, distributors of mass produced consumer goods, and employers of last resort—shrank substantially in numbers and economic significance.

Simultaneously, improved health care and birth control reduced the size of the average family. Japan's once steep population pyramid flattened out. Immediately after the war, Japan had an unusually young population with only about 5 percent of the Japanese population aged sixty-five or older. Even in the 1970s the figure was only 7 percent, well below that for other industrialized countries. But by 1995 those over sixty-five had increased to more than 14 percent. This twenty-five-year doubling had taken 115 years to occur in France and sixty-six in the United States.[5] So rapid is the growth, furthermore, that the ratio of workers to retirees will increase from 7:1 in the 1970s to about 4:1 in the year 2000 and 3:1 in 2015.

Economic success and the changing age profile led to a tighter labor market. In the early postwar years, large numbers of returning war veterans and overseas repatriates—and, subsequently, baby boomers and an influx of rural residents—generated an expanding, low-cost, young, and highly skilled workforce for manufacturing and urban service work. This expansion did not last, however, and as the labor market tightened bargaining power shifted from managers to labor, starting as early as 1969.[6]

All these changes in demography, economic interests, preferences, and opportunities undercut many long-standing policies and institutional arrangements. It became more difficult for the original coalitional arrangements of the old regime to remain intact. Although these changes ultimately had important economic effects, they were played out even more tangibly in the electoral challenge they posed for the LDP.

The Electoral Challenge

As semiautomatic conservative voting blocs shrank in sheer numbers, the mobilizational capabilities of previously powerful village associations, farming cooperatives, youth and female groups, and local business associations also declined. More and more voters, particularly those in their twenties and thirties, women, and longtime city dwellers, identified themselves as party independents. By 1974 such independents outnumbered LDP supporters.[7]

As the character of the Japanese electorate changed, so did the electoral options. The first few elections following the 1955 consolidation of conservatives and socialists saw the two largest parties taking over 85 percent of the total vote between them. As late as the 1967 election the two largest parties still won 86 percent of the seats. But the formation of the Democratic Socialist Party (DSP), the Clean Government Party (CGP) and then in 1976 the formation of the New Liberal Club (NLC), as well as the transformation of the Japan Communist Party (JCP) into a "lovable" party, all meant increased electoral options.[8] An erosion of the dual monopoly of the LDP and the JSP followed. In 1972 the combined popular vote of the minor parties broke through the 25 percent barrier (giving them 21 percent of the seats).[9] No longer could the LDP attract support simply by presenting itself as the nonsocialist alternative (nor could the JSP present itself as the only alternative to the LDP).

The increased number of parties meant that the relative strength of the LDP actually increased vis-à-vis any individual party, but the cumulative impact of the new parties was to threaten conservative electoral hegemony.[10] Relative strength would count for naught if some combined opposition could forge a parliamentary majority.

As early as 1967 the LDP received less than a clear majority of the votes cast. Yet, gerrymandering and the biases in the electoral system awarded the LDP a sufficient bonus so that it still held 57 percent of the parliamentary seats.[11] Nevertheless, a secular decline in LDP support throughout the late 1960s and the decade of the 1970s was unmistakable (see Fig. 1). LDP electoral primacy at the national level dropped below the 50 percent margin in seats by the end of the 1970s,[12] leading to a period called *hakuchū jidai*, or relative equality between government and opposition.

Semiautomatic LDP dominance had long been a lubricant smoothing relations among conservative support groups. LDP dominance and opposition fragmenta-

Fig. 1. Electoral results of Lower House elections

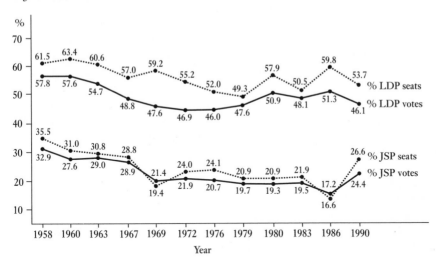

Source: Muramatsu Michio , Itō Mitsutoshi, and Tsujinaka Yutaka, *Nihon no Seiji* [Japanese politics] (Tokyo, Yūhikaku, 1992), pp. 122–23.

tion minimized the need for compromises with nonconservatives, further helping to wed conservative politicians to the LDP. Moreover, 10 or 11 percent annual growth greatly facilitated congenial coexistence among conservative backers: technologically sophisticated and more backward industries, importers and exporters, urban and rural interests, and otherwise fractious bureaucrats, business leaders, interest groups, and politicians. Conflicts that might have become zero sum under less advantageous economics were more readily reconcilable through side payments, compensation, and trade-offs.

Most supporters of the conservative regime agreed on the need to meet the electoral threat to the LDP. Should the LDP lose its parliamentary majority, defeated conservative parliamentarians would obviously lose their parliamentary salaries, perks, power, and prestige. But more threatening to the regime as a whole, any imaginable alternative government would be unlikely to continue the strongly pro-business climate for Japan's largest financial, brokerage, and insurance firms or to maintain policies so supportive of close security ties to the United States. Similarly, many senior-level bureaucrats—although their positions were nominally nonpolitical—would almost certainly find themselves out of favor, if not out of jobs, under a non-LDP government.[13] On only the rarest of occasions, and with minimal support, was any serious consideration given among conservative regime members to abandoning the LDP in favor of some other political party. The electoral threat to the LDP thus captured the undivided attention of conservatives of all stripes.

Yet how to attract new electoral support was by no means self-evident. Two possibilities were obvious. First, although hardly a natural target given the long-standing ideological chasm between the conservative and progressive camps, the conservatives could attempt to draw organized labor away from its traditional support for the DSP and the JSP. Second, and more plausibly, they could seek to attract Japan's "new middle mass," that is, relatively unorganized and undifferentiated white-collar urbanites with weak or nonexistent loyalty to any single political party.

LDP strength in the cities had been on a downturn as urban LDP voters fell from about 32 percent of the party's support in 1955 to 18 percent in 1975. Nonetheless, sheer numbers made urbanites a force that could not be ignored, particularly as the electoral evidence of the 1970s showed city dwellers were more likely not to vote than actively to support the opposition. Nonvoters in the cities rose from about 33 percent in 1955 to about 43 percent fifteen years later. As Ishikawa Masumi put it, "It is not that the progressives are strong in the big cities; ... more important, the conservatives are far too weak there. And they are weak because they have missed the chance to gain large numbers of potential supporters among the nonvoters."[14] Closely linked to these nonvoters were the nonpartisan voters. Less indifferent to politics and parties than nonvoters, the nonpartisans voted but rejected any permanent party affiliation. Combined, the two groups represented vast numbers of potential LDP supporters within the metropolitan areas and the large cities.

What the party should do to attract such potential supporters, however, was by no means uncontroversial. Many of the most obvious policy options that might have appealed to workers, urbanites, and the growing middle class challenged existing conservative supporters. The result was an ongoing dilemma for the party.

Diminishing margins between the government and the opposition also reduced the guarantee that parliament could automatically be counted on to ratify cabinet-initiated proposals. As noted in Chapter 2, from 1955 until 1970 over 90 percent of all successful legislation in Japan originated with the government; less than 20 percent went through any amendment process.[15] Government proposals rarely faced more than token resistance in the legislature. Intraparliamentary politics was predominantly symbolic, marked by boring ritual debates and languid approval punctuated by brief outbursts of anaerobic confrontation in the form of sit-downs, delayed balloting, seizures of the speaker's platform, battles between burly party staff members, and threatened resignations.

During the 1970s all this changed. Private member bills (the key vehicle for opposition-sponsored legislation) increased by nearly 20 percent between 1960–65 and 1975–80 while the success rate for government bills fell from 78 to 70 percent. Government legislation fell from nearly 170 laws per year to about seventy-five. Of those passed in 1975–80, over 21 percent were amended.[16] Parliament ceased to be the automatic ratifier of government proposals. Parliamentarians and party leaders were forced to cut deals not only within their own parties but across party lines.[17]

Adjustment bred compromise, and all opposition parties dramatically reduced their votes against government bills. Approval rates in 1979 compared with those in

1966 show the following jumps in support: for the DSP, from 80 to well over 90 percent; for the CGP, from 80 to about 85 percent; for the JSP, from 63 to 75 percent; and for the JCP, from 10 to over 60 percent.[18]

To the extent that the LDP held less sway in parliament, key aspects of the conservative agenda were held hostage. The distinction between the LDP and the opposition began to blur on many policy issues, reducing the ideological chasms across the party system as a whole.

LDP electoral hegemony was also being challenged locally. Coalition candidates from a variety of progressive parties were enjoying electoral successes in local assemblies, large prefectures and major cities.[19] Conservative candidates had won 83 percent of the prefectural governorships between 1964 and 1966 and 87.5 percent in the 1968–70 elections. By 1972–74 their success rate had fallen to 61.9 percent. Local-level shifts raised the possibility that opposition parties could build strong regional bases and gain governmental experience that would, as had happened in parts of Europe, enhance their ability to challenge national conservative continuity.[20]

Finally, conservative control was challenged by an outbreak of citizens' movements and student protests during the late 1960s and the early 1970s. Most took a nonparty approach to politics—demanding specific actions not linked to the policy programs of the established political parties.[21] These movements had two important consequences: they raised new and problematic issues not previously on the political agenda, and they mobilized people around issues and at times that had nothing to do with the electoral cycle. During elections, of course, opposition parties were highly critical of the conservative agenda; electoral campaigns frequently probed issues that the conservatives preferred to ignore. But once the votes had been counted, the conservatives could claim a mandate to move their agenda forward at least until the next election. Until then the LDP could effectively argue issues out in parliament, largely under its own timetable. As noted in Chapter 2, except during elections politicians rarely sought to mobilize citizens on any issue, and citizens' groups had limited powers to press most concerns. But protests by students and others ignored the electoral timetable and pressed numerous new issues, posing an undeniable threat to political predictability.

Thus the overriding conservative dominance of the electoral and legislative processes was challenged during the 1970s and 1980s. Meeting these changed circumstances presented an ongoing political problem for the LDP and its supporters during the 1970s; not until the elections of 1979–80 did the LDP appear to have dealt with them successfully.

International Challenges

From the end of the U.S. Occupation until the early 1970s international conditions were preponderantly benign for the conservative regime. From the "reverse course" onward, America's hegemony within the capitalist world had been unchallenged, and U.S. foreign policy toward Japan had been directed toward the creation and maintenance of a regime that would align itself with U.S. foreign policy goals and follow capitalist economic policies. America systematically promoted Japan as an anticommunist model of development while bolstering the country's prestige in Asia and the world at large.[22]

By the early 1970s the world had become much less hospitable to Japanese conservatives. External conditions challenged policies, threatened conservative socioeconomic support, and in several instances undermined existing institutions. Three such challenges were particularly critical. First, a mixture of challenges were posed to the existing insularity of Japanese exchange rate policies. Second, the international price of raw materials escalated, undercutting the profitability of Japanese mercantilism in energy-intensive manufactured goods. Third, recipients of Japanese exports, the United States in particular, began pressing for changes in various Japanese economic practices, and in defense and security policies as well.

Probably no short period in the postwar era presented more concentrated and fundamental challenges to Japan's conservative regime than the shocks associated with President Nixon's surprise visit to China, the breakdown of the Bretton Woods system of monetary exchange, the U.S. imposition of import tariffs—all in 1971—and the quadrupling of oil prices in 1973. These blows within a two-year period reverberated throughout Japan.

Nixon's July 1971 announcement about China struck Japan particularly hard. For the entire postwar period, Japan's conservatives had deferred to U.S. leadership on diplomatic matters. This had meant moving far more slowly than many Japanese conservatives had wished in improving economic ties with Beijing.

As late as 1968, Japan had supported a U.S. resolution allowing Taiwan to retain the "Chinese seat" in the United Nations. In the Sato-Nixon joint communiqué of November 1969, the two countries declared their common support for "maintenance and security in the Taiwan area." Twenty years of bilateral cooperation in support of Taiwan and isolation of the People's Republic of China were challenged when suddenly, only ten minutes before Nixon's television announcement, Prime Minister Sato was notified of a completely new American policy toward China. The wisdom of Japan's acquiescence to U.S. foreign policy leadership and the entire security strategy of the conservative regime was suddenly laid open to question.[23]

On August 15, 1971, President Nixon suspended dollar convertibility, leading to the breakdown of the Bretton Woods monetary system. The effect was profound throughout the industrialized world. In Japan, the breakdown had a massive impact on the standing exchange rate of 360 yen to the dollar. Within Japanese financial circles the number "360" had acquired talismanic (*seiiki*) status.[24] Originally justified on balance-of-payments grounds, the fixed exchange rate had gained additional potency by boosting Japan's exports, curtailing foreign entry into Japanese markets, and favoring Japanese manufacturers and producers over consumers.[25] Consequently, Japanese government officials initially sought to bolster the dollar and protect the exchange rate.[26] Government actions to protect a national currency from becoming stronger must be underscored as unusual. Governments often intervene to shore up currencies from weakening, largely in support of investors, importers, consumers, and national prestige. Keeping the national currency weak,

Fig. 2. Movements in the yen/dollar exchange rate, 1971–1998

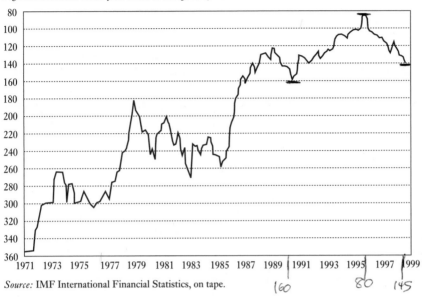

Source: IMF International Financial Statistics, on tape.

however, did benefit Japan's export industries, though at the expense of enhanced consumer purchasing power. Nonetheless, the futility of Japanese government efforts became apparent as the run on U.S. gold continued, the value of the dollar plummeted, and the drain of Japanese foreign reserves became a flood. Between August and December the Japanese economy lost some $2.5 billion.[27] When the yen was finally allowed to float, it appreciated by about one-third to a rate of roughly 240 yen by the mid-1970s.

Four major cycles of yen revaluation followed in the late 1970s, the mid-1980s, and the early and mid-1990s. As a result, the yen climbed from 290 to the dollar at the beginning of 1977 to 170 by October 1978—a 40 percent strengthening in less than two years—from there to between 110 and 120 yen as a result of the G-5 Plaza Accord of September 1985, and to just below 80 yen in 1995. The yen was by far the industrial world's most appreciated currency over the period from the Bretton Woods breakdown through the mid-1990s (see Fig. 2). Then between 1995 and 1998 it reversed direction to 145 yen to the dollar, making it one of the world's most rapidly depreciating currencies. No longer was it possible for Japanese conservatives to count on an undervalued currency to ward off foreign imports while simultaneously aiding Japanese exports. Equally important, the Japanese government's ability to control the value of the Japanese currency eroded, removing a major implement from its economic tool kit and making it tougher to use allocation of scarce foreign exchange as a way to shape business behavior.

If Bretton Woods was a hard body blow to the Japanese regime's midriff, the quadrupling of world oil prices in 1973 was an uppercut to the jaw. Japan's extreme dependence on imported oil left it far more vulnerable to such shifts than other industrialized countries.[28]

During the 1950s, the Japanese government, facing both the higher costs of domestic mining and the militancy of unionized coal miners, had opted for cheap world oil as a desirable energy substitute to fuel the nation's burgeoning industrial production.[29] Low and declining world transportation costs further enhanced oil's appeal. In a perverse way, Japan's ingrained dependency on imported raw materials had suddenly turned into an unexpected advantage. Instead of relying on domestic sources of raw materials, with their potentially escalating costs and negative political consequences, Japan's extensive network of trading companies could supply the needed energy at the best world prices from anyone willing to sell.

At the time of the oil shock, Japan relied on oil for 70 percent of its energy needs. Virtually all oil (99 percent) was imported, most of it (roughly 80 percent) from the Near and Middle East. Only Italy and Denmark came remotely close to such high dependency. Furthermore, because Japan had never supported Israel in the Arab-Israeli wars and major Japanese companies had deliberately stayed out of the Israeli market, its leaders were stunned when Arab countries announced a cut in oil supplies to Japan. Furthermore, Japan's oil supply was delivered largely through the major American and British oil companies, and Japanese government officials were convinced that their country was short-changed by these majors' favoring of home market customers.

The quadrupling of oil prices transferred some $14 billion from Japan to the oil producing countries in 1974 alone, a sum equal to about 3.1 percent of Japan's GNP. And the oil crisis came at the end of a rapid economic expansion in which domestic inflation was already running high. The escalation in energy prices reverberated throughout the Japanese economy. In February 1974 wholesale prices were up 37 percent over the preceding year; consumer prices jumped 25 percent between the spring and fall; consumers began a frenzied hoarding of staples such as kerosene, soap, and toilet paper.[30]

Beyond inflation, the oil shock threatened Japan's balance of payments, which had begun to turn positive for the first time in the postwar period. The dollar value of Japan's 1974 imports rose some 50 percent over the previous year.[31] Meanwhile, domestic productivity, especially in manufacturing, dropped sharply. By March 1975 Japanese manufacturing output was 20 percent below its peak, the sharpest drop among any of the major industrialized democracies. Declining productivity plus the rapid rise in domestic costs posed a critical threat to the continued success of Japanese exports; any serious rise in export prices threatened to erode the overseas market shares of all major exporters. Japan seemed destined for the same stagflation that was haunting most of the other industrialized democracies.

A second oil crisis in 1979–80 further increased world oil prices, this time about 2.8 times. Spread as it was over nearly two years, however, the shock was mitigated, and its inflationary impact was also less. Yet the continued threat to Japan's early presumptions of an infinite supply of cheap raw materials further drove home the impossibility of continuing past policies.

Finally, a third set of international challenges was presented by the increasing pressures from the United States and to a lesser extent Europe to reduce Japanese import penetration of their markets. America's early postwar foreign policy and anticommunism had privileged military and security considerations over commercial and economic concerns, even as priorities had been reversed in Japan. Nixon, although hardly rejecting the broad thrust of security-driven anticommunism, was the first U.S. president to challenge the bilateral basis of U.S.-Japan relations with any gusto. This was made evident in his textile negotiations with Japan and his imposition of a 10 percent surcharge on American imports in 1971. Nixon's successors, alert to political considerations of industries and labor at home, for the most part continued to press for revisions in Japanese export and investment policies well into the 1990s.

The United States focused first on reductions in Japanese tariffs, import quotas and various non-tariff barriers, very much in keeping with America's "internationalist" view: encourage Japan to conform to more generally accepted trade rules. A series of GATT rounds led over time to a rapid reduction in Japan's formal restrictions. Bilateral U.S.-Japan trade deficits continued to escalate, however, and U.S. pressures became increasingly bilateral and sector specific. For certain sectors, most notably steel, machine tools, televisions, automobiles, and later computer chips, the United States pressed for so-called voluntary export restraints (VERs).[32] Later, in response to a variety of domestic political interests, American policy shifted to measures designed to open the Japanese market, such as the MOSS (market oriented, sector specific) talks agreed to in January 1985,[33] the Structural Impediments Initiative (SII) of 1989, the 1994 Framework Talks (and the Yen-Dollar Working Group that preceded it), as well as explicit efforts at "managed trade as a second-best alternative," embodied in the bilateral Semiconductor Trade Agreement from 1986 to 1991.[34] The U.S. government also exerted direct pressure on behalf of a bevy of specific U.S. companies or regions that were attempting to enter Japanese markets, such as Motorola; tobacco, auto, and medical technology companies; the Florida citrus industry; Washington apple growers; and New York wine merchants, to name only a few. In all these ways, the United States, and to a lesser extent European governments, mounted steady pressures for substantial changes in vital aspects of Japan's economic policy profile and indirectly on the regime as a whole.[35]

Periodically, concerns over the apparent imbalance in the national economic successes of Japan and the United States spilled over from trade to defense. Thus, during the 1970s and 1980s, some U.S. officials began increasingly to contend that Japan was getting a "free ride" on defense. Maintaining U.S. troops in Japan was costly; so was America's so-called nuclear umbrella. Because the Japanese government allocated only 1 percent of GNP to military spending, many American politicians concluded that if Japan spent more money on defense, the country's civilian successes (and their own particular domestic political problems) would be diminished.

Western pressures typically ran counter to those of Japan's Asian neighbors, particularly South Korea and China, which demanded that Japan do *less* militarily.

Continually reminding Japanese conservatives of the horrific experiences of their countries with Japanese troops during the prewar period, the Asian attitude served as an international counterweight to U.S. pressures for a more active and powerful Japanese military.

Competing pressures ebbed and flowed, but they became particularly visible during the Gulf War of 1991. As noted in the previous chapter U.S. government officials pressed Japan to dispatch at least a nominal military force in support of U.S. troops. Some Japanese policy analysts argued that it would be rational and wise for Japan to send at least a small detachment of troops to the region, but they lost out in internal debates.[36] The government, citing the standard norms against the use of Japanese troops abroad and cognizant of strong public opposition to such actions, demurred.[37] Instead, Japan eventually contributed $13 billion. By the time the war had ended, however, debates within Japan made it clear that past policies of "separating politics from economics" and of keeping a "low posture" in security matters were no longer uniformly accepted within the conservative regime and would be difficult to sustain.

The equilibrium of the Japanese conservative regime was thus bombarded by external threats, challenges, and attacks. New economic and security conditions threatened the regime's policy profile and exacerbated tensions among its key socioeconomic supporters. These pressures induced waves of adjustments over twenty-odd years.

Not surprisingly, intra-conservative responses to these disparate challenges were far from consensual and unidirectional. Instead, competing elements within the conservative coalition sent policy and politics caroming first in one direction and then in another in divergent attempts to meet their competing demands. Many of these shifts were minor first-order changes; others, more sweeping and reverberating, were of the second order. But all kept the regime largely intact and equilibrated. Continued conservative rule and ongoing economic successes seemed to promise that the regime would retain its cohesion, control, and direction. There were no sweeping overhauls of policy profile, coalitional arrangements, or institutions. Yet, in the long run the adjustments proved insufficient to ward off far more fundamental changes. Instead, they increased existing rigidities within the regime, failed to resolve internal tensions, and led ultimately to a cataclysmic shattering of the regime. But before examining their consequences, let us examine the changes themselves.

First- and Second-Order Changes: Between Adjustment and Undermining

First-order changes, it will be recalled, are shifts that largely affect only one of the three regime component elements of a regime, whereas second-order changes affect at least two. Adjustments of both types during the 1970s and 1980s—an often inchoate sequence of alterations—kept the LDP in power, the economy expanding, and foreign allies relatively happy. Examples of first-order shifts in the regime's *policy profile* would include a movement away from U.S. policy on the Middle East toward a far more independent, pro-Arab position following the first oil shock; a variety of short-term shifts in monetary and fiscal policies; strict crackdowns on campus protests; and moderate adjustments that enhanced Japan's military roles. Another first-order response involved the blind eye the regime turned toward illegal immigrants working in the country's dirtier industries and tawdrier services. Despite the importance of many of these changes, few had major impacts on the regime's coalitional base or institutions.

Various attempts to bolster the regime's *socioeconomic support* also had limited repercussions. The introduction of the Small Stores Law in 1973 and its explicit strengthening in 1982 helped to protect Japan's smaller distributors from both domestic and foreign department stores and merchandise. Incentives for farmers to produce high-value-added crops or specific administrative changes to keep the medical profession profitable had similarly limited impacts. None represented a redirection in the national policy profile or entailed important institutional changes.

There were also several first-order *institutional changes:* the creation of the Environment Agency in 1971, the Natural Resources and Energy Agency in 1973, and the National Land Agency in 1974. Small additions were also made sequentially to the number of Diet seats in the lower house, thereby reducing the most egregious imbalances between urban and rural districts. Again, such changes had only limited impact on the regime's policy profile or its coalitional base. They merely tinkered with narrow and specific items—dispatching short-term problems, rewarding friends, punishing enemies—or made minimal shifts in the regime's internal cohesion and command of power. Since they did not seriously affect the regime's stability, I shall not deal discuss them further.

Much more important were the second-order shifts that substantially altered the regime's internal dynamics—much as the movement of one part of a mobile causes the others to swing. Here I will highlight the most important shifts and show how they both contributed to the regime's continuity in the short run and sowed the seeds of its longer-term demise.

Six changes are worth discussing. First, numerous components of the previous policy profile became less tightly linked to one another; policies became less collectively conducive of cumulative national growth and increasingly operated at cross-purposes. Second, Japan moved even more strongly toward firm-level cooperation between management and labor, thereby weakening the national labor movement and reducing the ideological gap between government and opposition. Third, the government initially embraced, and then withdrew from, substantial deficit finance, aimed heavily at political, rather than economic, targets. Fourth, and largely in response to expanding deficits, the conservatives went through a phase of fiscal austerity and privatization, marked most notably by "administrative reform" and the 1989 introduction of a consumption tax. Fifth, many powerful Japanese firms, particularly in manufacturing, moved away from their traditional domestic bases and became multinational producers and distributors. Finally, important changes occurred in defense and security policies.

This melange had no uniform directionality. Its zigzags reflected intra-conservative battles over how best to adjust to the regime's problems. Often one direction would be initiated only to be reversed or altered as circumstances changed. Yet over time these ongoing adjustments undercut the regime's entire delicate balance.

The Politicization of Economic Policies

Politics would not be politics without special favors. Candidates for office offer competing promises of how they will "do more" for their supporters. While many voters undoubtedly cast their ballots for largely selfless reasons, that is hardly the norm. Major interest associations, large socioeconomic blocs, and big donors typically expect some quid pro quo for their support. In the mid-1960s the policy profile of the ruling conservatives was predicated on providing generalized benefits for broad sectors of society and on overall economic catch-up and developmentalism. This changed significantly by the late 1960s and even more so into the 1970s and 1980s, largely in response to the changing demographics of Japan, the challenges to LDP hegemony, and the increasing influence within the conservative regime of career politicians, particularly those linked to Tanaka Kakuei. As a result many economic policies became more narrowly targeted and explicitly political.

One of the more important efforts to shore up the LDP through major policy shifts was MITI minister Tanaka Kakuei's Plan to Remodel the Archipelago.[38] Put forward in 1969, the proposal called for a major redirection of Japanese economic resources: the national priority of export success in high-value-added manufactured goods would give way to massive public infrastructural investment in virtually every region of the country. Japan had long led most other industrialized democracies in the amounts of money spent on pork barrel and infrastructure (see Table 2), and Tanaka's proposal promised to widen the gap further. The plan was to make national economic growth more reliant on bigger government budgets channeled to politically connected construction and real-estate sectors. Tanaka proposed to do for the nation what for decades he had done for his local Niigata constituency: deliver massive public works projects such as roads, tunnels, railways, senior citizens' centers, and the like—all of which would stimulate the local economy, create jobs, improve life styles, and, not at all incidentally, generate huge amounts of cash for the LDP and for individual conservative politicians from the beneficiaries who carried out the remodeling. Also rewarded would be the underdeveloped geographical regions that had long been electoral mainstays of the LDP.

Tanaka's plan never got off the ground. He took office as prime minister in August 1972, right in the middle of the "Nixon shocks" and just ahead of the oil shock. Consequently his proposal, in Gerald Curtis's words, "turned into a nightmare of inflation, land speculation, and ballooning government deficits."[39] His popularity fell faster than that of any other prime minister's—from a high of 62 percent when

Table 2. Infrastructure spending as a fraction of the GDP in major countries (%)

	Japan	United States	Britain	Germany	France
1970	4.5	2.6	4.7	4.4	3.6
1975	5.3	2.1	4.7	3.6	3.7
1980	6.1	1.7	2.4	3.4	3.1
1985	4.7	1.7	1.9	2.3	3.1
1990	5.1	1.7	2.3	2.2	3.3
1991	5.1	1.8	2.2	2.3	3.4
1992	5.7	1.8	2.1	2.3	3.5

Source: Japan Economic Institute, Report 4A, February 2, 1996, p. 3.

he took office to 27 percent only eight months later. And all before the 1973 oil shock, inflation, and subsequent revelations about Tanaka's shady business dealings particularly in conjunction with Lockheed.

The sudden change in world economic conditions and the slowdown in Japanese growth rates meant that Japan's governmental budget, which had previously generated automatic 10–15 percent increases annually, was forced into a holding pattern that made massive government expenditures far less electorally and economically feasible than they might have been five years earlier. Even so, over the next two decades the Tanaka faction continued to promote Tanaka's effort to link the construction industry, public works, the national treasury, and the LDP—albeit on a somewhat smaller scale.

Important to note in this regard is that although Japan spends a considerably higher proportion of its GNP on public construction than most other industrialized countries, the results have not necessarily created a deeper infrastructure. Construction in Japan is almost twice as expensive as in these other countries, due to high rates of collusive bidding (*dango*) among construction firms, bribes and kickbacks to politicians, regulatory burdens, and the like.

The explicit politicization of economic policy reflected the rising influence and orientation of "career politicians" within the LDP and the relative waning of the "ex-bureaucrats." In the Kishi, Ikeda, and Sato cabinets (1957–72), former bureaucrats typically held about 50 percent of the cabinet posts. In the first Tanaka cabinet in 1972 their numbers fell to 30 percent and remained low under the successor governments of Miki, Fukuda, and Suzuki. Moreover, many of the nominal ex-bureaucrats in the LDP began to enter politics not from the technical, economic, and administrative ministries such as Finance, International Trade and Industry, and Transportation, which had given early postwar conservative politics its technical-economic focus, but increasingly from the more "politicized" agencies such as Posts and Telecommunications, Labor, Police, Construction, and Agriculture.[40] In addition, these ex-bureaucrats of the 1970s and 1980s were more likely to have left the civil service in their late twenties or early thirties and to have taken up full-time political careers. In short, the character of the LDP's leadership began to reflect a strengthening of the career-track politicians whose primary concern was their local constituency and their own reelection rather than macroeconomic growth.

Correspondingly, the development and institutionalization of personal support groups within individual electoral districts gave individual conservative politicians considerably more independence from the party leadership than had been true in earlier times. Time and institutionalization made these personal support groups sufficiently cohesive that they could be passed on from father to son (or to nephew, personal secretary, son-in-law, and the like).[41] Between 1958 and 1990 the number of such seats rose from 34 to 105, or 36 percent of all LDP seats.[42] Political careers increasingly took on the characteristics of family businesses, with professional politicians becoming ever more autonomous from their party.

Since local network development cost money, it had to compete with the needs of the LDP as a party, the need of the national economy, and the needs of individual candidates. The rapidly rising costs of Japanese political life soon made Japanese electoral politics among the most expensive in the world. One 1993 study showed Japan spending over three times more per capita for politics than any other leading democracy.[43] Another showed that in 1992 a parliamentarian required ¥140 million ($1.4 million) annually for day-to-day activities even in nonelection years. Salary and party subsidies were perhaps $400,000 annually, leaving the parliamentarian about $1 million in the red.[44] Such costs, combined with the fact that most conservative parliamentarians faced their most serious electoral competition from other conservatives within the multimember electoral district system, raised the stakes for individual parliamentarians to generate ever more money. Faction leaders, responsible for helping their parliamentary supporters, faced even more enormous expenditures.

The obvious targets for fundraising were businesses and well-organized interests, not to mention the national treasury. But which groups would readily contribute and with what expectations in return? The major business federations and trade associations had long pooled monies collected from their members and made contributions to the LDP as a party. Yet as the costs of elections rose, many individual politicians began cultivating their own sources of money, and individual firms and sectors responded by parting with inordinately large amounts of cash in the expectation of special treatment beyond the generic benefits derived from a good macroeconomic climate.

This in turn greatly politicized the national bureaucracy and national economic policies. The budgetary process became increasingly subject to political interventions. Meanwhile Tanaka and his faction eventually succeeded in "colonizing" a number of government agencies, most notably the National Land Agency and the Ministries of Agriculture, Transportation, Posts and Telecommunications, and Construction, ensuring that top civil servants in those agencies would have close ties to, and a serious regard for the particularistic policy needs of, Tanaka and his faction. Other LDP parliamentarians developed parallel connections with individuals in specific agencies who were willing to provide them with otherwise confidential details of ministerial affairs.

The result was the rise of individual parliamentarians known as *zoku giin* (literally, "tribal parliamentarians"). These individuals became experts on specific policy areas, usually those that involved substantial amounts of discretionary public spending. Using this expertise, such politicians would broker deals between interest associations, industries, or firms, and the agencies with which they had to deal. Thus, there was a construction *zoku*, a defense *zoku*, a *zoku* linked to the National Land Agency, a labor *zoku*, a communications *zoku*, an agriculture *zoku*, and so forth.[45] The result was the enhanced sectionalization of politics and policy. "Iron triangles" emerged in which politicians provided special favors from the regulating bureaucratic agency and/or the national treasury to particular interest groups, sectors, or firms. In the process, monies and other favors were regularly exchanged. As Chalmers Johnson has phrased it: the politicians "did not displace the bureaucrats or seek to have regulations reduced or eliminated. Instead, they simply enriched themselves by seeking and accepting bribes from businesses that needed to get around the regulations."[46]

Politicians developed a host of other fund-raising techniques. Direct cash contributions under the table came to be supplemented by elaborate schemes involving rapid land and property transactions, direct rake-offs from public contracts, and somewhat bizarre techniques such as "ambulance stocks," in which a single publicly traded stock would be manipulated feverishly by contributing brokerage houses or firms, thereby guaranteeing suddenly cash-starved politicians the ability to buy low and sell high.

The cumulative result was an increased interweaving of the electoral needs of the LDP and powerful individual parliamentarians into the previously more nationally focused civil service, the increased politicization of the once unmediated relationships between agencies and interest groups that had prevailed in the 1960s, and the overt politicization of important aspects of economic policy. This process proved to be highly beneficial to the LDP and to individual conservative politicians in the short run. But ultimately these adjustments, like many others, came back to haunt the conservatives and to contribute to their toppling in the 1990s, largely as a result of corruption scandals and the increasing inefficiency of government economic policies.

Firm-Level Incomes Policy and the Moderation of Labor

Far less overtly political, at least in its initial formulation, was an attempt by government and business to head off the wage-price inflation generated by the rapid increase in the value of the yen in 1971 and the sudden rise in world oil prices in 1973. But the consequences for politics, as well as economics, ultimately proved to be profound.

As noted in Chapters 2 and 3, Japanese labor-management relations had been marked by high levels of conflict during the early postwar years, and during the late

1950s and early 1960s the conservative camp had successfully broken the backs of labor's most militant elements, at least within the private sector. Cumulatively, this led to a reduction in the power of the left and the simultaneous pacification of Japanese private-sector labor.[47] By the 1970s, private-sector unions increasingly identified less with working-class solidarity than with the bottom lines of individual company balance sheets. As the national labor supply began to shrink and manufacturing productivity soared, workers in private plants gained enhanced bargaining power and substantial wage hikes.

The externally induced inflation of 1973–74 might have given labor both the incentive and the power to demand large wage hikes to offset rapidly rising domestic costs. Doing so, however, would have seriously undermined the price competitiveness of Japanese manufacturing firms and exported goods, thereby threatening national economic growth. Quickly, a three-way "de facto incomes policy" was arranged. Private-sector labor agreed to moderate any wage demands in exchange for business guarantees of job security and retraining programs for union members, while the government guaranteed low taxes, anti-inflationary policies, and financial support for worker retraining and industrial reorganization.[48]

This arrangement quickly stemmed wage-price inflation and enabled Japan to become the first industrial country to snap back from the economic shocks of the early 1970s with only a minor hiatus in its growth. Government resources, managerial concessions, and labor linkages to firms proved to be key ingredients in warding off what might have been a severe challenge to national and company export competitiveness.

The agreement also strengthened ties between management and unionized blue-collar workers in the country's large private firms, which weakened latent appeals to class on the part of the union movement and the political left. It also diminished the interest of private-sector labor in national politics; labor's battleground increasingly centered on plant-level concerns. In contrast, many public-sector unions continued to stake out ideological positions on the far left, widening the wedge between private- and public-sector unions. Ultimately the private-sector unions won the internal battle, and as we noted in Chapter 4, the labor movement reorganized into Rengō, a single peak federation with a largely nonpolitical, economic agenda.[49] As economic interests shifted, so did electoral behavior, with significant numbers of blue-collar workers moving to support conservative candidates.[50]

Labor-management adjustments thus had sweeping impact on the regime. The bargain of the mid-1970s certainly solved the stagflation problem that was besetting the rest of the industrialized world; it also kept Japan's economic growth vibrant. But beyond economics, it profoundly fragmented the already disunited labor opposition, brought greater tranquility to labor-management relations, softened the ideological divisions within party politics, and garnered additional voter support for the LDP. The new support for the conservative's socioeconomic base entailed no loss of existing conservative supporters. Labor's increased conservatism came at no real expense to the conservative socioeconomic infrastructure, at least in the short-run.

Deficit Finance to Enhance Social Infrastructure

A different set of changes involved "quality of life" enhancements—efforts under-taken to enhance the conservatives' appeal to urbanites, to broaden the electoral base of the LDP, and to co-opt this potentially important issue from the political left. Two decades of rapid economic growth had generated major shifts in urban-ization, in environmental pollution and congestion, and in the age pyramid. Un-derlying all these was a broad public sentiment that Japan's growth should be re-flected in improvements in the lives of contemporary citizens, not simply those of unborn future generations.

Conservative economic policies had initially focused on economic growth and national catch-up. Social welfare problems related to sickness, unemployment, old age, disability, and the like were taken to be the responsibility not of the state but rather the family, the village, and, to some extent, the firm. Aside from family or village assistance, Japan's system of occupation-based welfare had historically been the principal source of most individuals' old age and medical help.

Moreover, rapid economic growth on Japan's crowded main islands had been driven by heavy industry, particularly chemicals, petrochemicals, steel, electric power plants, and closely configured industrial complexes, most of which were put in place with little regard for their environmental impact. Economic success and consumerism also generated increased automobile use with its consequent pollut-ing effects. Although Japanese conservatives were slow to take up these environ-mental questions, once they confronted the massive citizen movements noted above as well as court decisions favoring pollution victims, the government introduced strict emission standards. It also began underwriting part of the cost of manufac-turing and purchasing antipollution equipment and, as we shall see in more detail below, encouraged the overseas relocation of the worst polluting industries.[51]

Steps were also taken to revise national policies on social welfare. An important catalyst for this reassessment was the conservatives' desire to co-opt opposition is-sues and deflect the appeal of progressive local governments that were instituting widely popular social welfare and pollution control measures.[52] Even Japan's larger businesses, whose firm-level advantages would be partially undercut by any com-prehensive national program, urged government action to increase welfare as a way to ward off potential conservative electoral defeats.

Social welfare took top priority in the national budget in 1973, which the gov-ernment proclaimed "the first year of the welfare era." Free medical care for the el-derly, initially offered by progressive local governments, was introduced at the na-tional level. The proportion of total national medical expenses paid by the two public insurance programs was increased from 17.2 percent (1966–72) to 27.3 per-cent (1973–75). Payout levels in both the Employee Pension System and the Na-tional Pension System were also substantially enhanced.[53] The employee benefit was nearly doubled to about 45 percent of the average income; the national pension was increased proportionately. More important still, indexation to the cost of living was introduced into both systems.

These measures came, obviously, from a conservative government anxious to forestall electoral challenges rather than from a social democratic government desirous of institutionalizing egalitarian citizen rights. As such, they were more Bismarckian than Beveridgean. As a proportion of both the national budget and GNP, spending on social welfare increased steadily from 1973 until the early 1980s. Even so, as late as 1980, social security transfers in Japan remained low at 10.9 percent of GNP (compared to 22.9 percent in France, 15.3 percent in Germany, and 15.8 percent in Italy).[54] Modest as they were, they provided an important improvement for many citizens and generated a positive electoral response. They also began to account for a growing share of government expenditures.

If this "era of welfare" had lasted for a decade or so, Japan's welfare mix might have moved decisively toward a more "institutionalized" welfare state based on citizenship rights. Occupational welfare might have been reduced, which would in turn have weakened management's control over employee benefits and narrowed the differential access to social welfare. Welfare reforms, however, came face to face with a reassertion of fiscal austerity beginning in the mid-1980s. To appreciate the trade-off, it is necessary to examine the funding of social welfare—and that of pollution control and other urban and lifestyle improvements as well.

Policymakers initially expected Japan's twenty years of dramatic economic growth to continue, thereby providing the needed funding for new social programs (as well as Tanaka's remodeling plan). But the very first year of Japan's new "welfare era" coincided with the oil crisis, and prospects for Japanese growth dimmed quickly. Slower growth and lower government tax revenues, combined with the weakening political position of the LDP, meant that the new programs would have to be funded though higher taxes or deficit budgeting. The unpopularity of taxes made the political choice an easy one. In 1970 Japan's deficit dependency ratio had been just over 4 percent; in 1971–74 it rose rapidly to 11–16 percent, climbed to just below 30 percent in 1976 and 1977, hit 37 percent in 1978, and peaked near 40 percent the next year.[55]

Deficit financing had the obvious advantage of being far less visible to the general public than major hikes in taxes. But as public deficits mounted, the idea of emulating Western-style welfare programs came under withering attack, particularly from the business sector and the MOF. Furthermore, policy changes had preempted the opposition's ability to exploit pollution or welfare as issues to attack the conservatives. Indeed, in the 1979 lower house election the LDP finally stemmed its twenty-year decline in vote share. Then in the famous "double election" of 1980 its proportion of seats jumped from 49.3 to 57.9 percent and the opposition parties were effectively brushed to the sidelines. The electoral turnaround for the conservatives allowed a return from "lifestyle policies" to "fiscal restraint."

*Administrative Reform, "Japanese-Style Welfare,"
and Fiscal Restraint*

The conservatives' renewed electoral strength, the increased marginalization of the opposition parties, and a renewed close affinity between private-sector unions and management combined to leave the conservatives in a much stronger electoral position than they had been in the mid-1970s. As a result, conservative regime supporters who had initially opposed the radical departure from fiscal austerity to fund the new programs were poised to roll back the minimalist welfare and lifestyle programs that had barely been introduced.

Conservative intellectuals argued that excessive welfare services led to outbreaks of "advanced-country disease" or the "English disease." Expansion of public programs, it was contended, encouraged people to depend excessively upon the state, discouraged their desire to work, and weakened their incentives to invest and improve productivity. Furthermore, demographic models had already shown that Japan was destined to become an even bigger spender for health and retirement programs as the population continued to age. Such high long-term costs argued for a reversal of past trends.[56] Drawing on the theme that Japan was different from other advanced democracies and that welfare should be left primarily to the family and the firm, these conservatives advanced the notion of building a "welfare *society* with vitality" and creating a "Japanese-style welfare *society.*"

As early as the mid-1970s, LDP and government rhetoric adopted this new perspective. The Policy Affairs Council of the LDP released its "Lifetime Welfare Plan," which recommended that welfare be based on self-help and warned of the dangers of expanded public spending for welfare. The Economic Planning Agency issued a 1977 report which, for the first time, officially employed the catchphrase "Japanese-style welfare society."[57] Prime Minister Ōhira argued for just such a focus in his January 1979 policy speech to the Diet. With the publication of the government's New Economic and Social Seven-Year Plan in August of that year, the goal became official governmental policy.

Contending that free medical care for the elderly had turned hospitals into "old people's salons,"[58] the government passed an Old People's Health Bill in 1982 which introduced co-payments and pressured local governments to stem any initiatives to improve medical care for elderly patients. In 1985 the Employees Pension Plan was revised to slow down benefit increases, raise contributions, and reduce government subsidization. The pension system was made explicitly two-tiered, with a base pension for all citizens topped by a wage-linked pension tied to occupation.[59] Pensions for government employees were similarly slashed.

In all these ways, government costs were slowed or reduced, reversing the trend that had begun in the 1970s and reinstituting wide differentials in the retirement benefits provided by firms of different sizes in different sectors. But the changes also effectively capped the climbing expenditure on social security and medical care. Such spending plateaued at about 27 percent of the national budget during the 1980s, while spending for health and income security dropped slightly from 18 percent in 1982 to 16.3 percent in 1990.[60]

It was within this context that administrative reform began under the Suzuki cabinet in the early 1980s. Administrative reform was delegated to the Second Provisional Administrative Reform Commission (Rinchō), created in March 1981 by Nakasone Yasuhiro, then director-general of the Administrative Management Agency (and subsequently prime minister).[61] Picked to head Rinchō was Dokō Toshio, a business elder who had earlier served as chairman of the Keidanren. Dokō's austere personal lifestyle and reputation as a man of high moral character lent particular credibility to his role as national skinflint. His critics invariably looked selfish and devoid of concern for the national well-being. Staffing the commission were many close allies of Nakasone, giving it added political clout. Throughout the commission's deliberations, Nakasone and Dokō worked closely to promote its goals and deflect its opponents.

Administrative reform involved a fundamental intraregime shift to appease business and bureaucratic constituents who were upset with the radical jumps in government costs and with the potentially even greater deficits implied by automatic entitlement programs, who resented the government challenge to the ways in which firm-level benefits linked workers to their companies, and who feared that the "unique Japanese national character" would be undermined.

Rinchō was strict in its attacks on budget deficits and government entitlements. As noted in Chapter 2, Japanese government expenditures had been stable in the low 20 percent range of GNP until 1970; subsequently this figure had expanded to nearly 35 percent.[62] The bond-dependency ratio rose sharply as a result, and massive debt servicing costs became a built-in part of the annual budget. Debt servicing rose from 0.12 percent of GNP in 1966 to 0.39 percent in 1970 to 1.56 percent in 1978 and 2.94 percent in 1982.[63] To curtail this expansion, national budgets during 1982–84 were kept at zero, low, or negative rates of growth, thereby dramatically reducing program expansion and costs, as well as civil service growth.

The tightening was far from politically neutral. Individual agency requests were coordinated with LDP *zoku* members; MOF budget making was coordinated with the top three leaders in the LDP; and despite the overall cutbacks in the budget, subsidies for public works continued to increase.[64]

Beyond its budgetary focus, Rinchō also embarked on a substantial privatization of the railways, the telecommunications industry, the tobacco and salt monopolies, parts of Japan Airlines, and other public corporations, further reducing the size, scope, and cost of Japanese governmental activity. Not at all incidentally, privatization substantially undercut the political and economic power of many of the militant public-sector unions.[65]

Administrative reform, consequently, served multiple purposes. It met demands from the business community and the MOF for cutbacks in government expenditures; it returned the country to relatively strict macroeconomic fiscal policies; and simultaneously it hamstrung the public-sector union movement, one of Japan's last redoubts of Marxism, anti-American foreign policies, and the politics of confrontation. Ironically, despite its belt tightening, the administrative reform program also enhanced the conservative regime's popularity by creating a mood of national solidarity and demonstrating fiscal responsibility.

Congruent with Rinchō's fiscal tightening was the introduction in 1989 of a broad-based 3 percent consumption tax. In 1987 Japan along with the United States, remained the only OECD countries that did not have some form of national consumption tax. Japan's introduction of such a tax meant a major shift in the revenue stream for government budgets, giving the MOF a valuable weapon in its fight for fiscal tightness and allowing it to reduce the budgetary dependence on personal and business taxes. As commentators at the time pointed out, and as the subsequent hike of the tax rate to 5 percent in 1997 made clear, such a system allows for relatively easy expansion (although hardly without political cost) when government officials determine the need for greater revenue.[66]

Ironically the consumption tax had the effect—not immediately perceived—of reducing the tax burdens of urban salaried personnel and corporations while increasing those of farmers and small businesses. (In its initial implementation, however, the LDP allowed small businesses a massive loophole under which they could collect the tax but simply "estimate" their sales for purposes of payment to the government; the result was an extensive, if short-term, windfall for small businesses).[67] Few urbanites welcomed the tax shift, however, and ultimately it proved to be an electoral disaster for the LDP in the 1989 House of Councilors election, which took place only three months after its passage. That election, in turn, proved to be the beginning of the electoral split in the LDP.

In sum, once conservative electoral fortunes improved, largely as a result of quality-of-life programs funded through public deficits, Japan's conservatives returned to tighter fiscal policies. But a serious outgrowth of the changes was an exacerbation of intra-conservative tensions over the relative burdens and benefits of those shifts.

Overseas Investment

A weak position in foreign exchange during the 1940s and 1950s had led the Japanese government to institute strict measures discouraging direct overseas investments by Japanese companies except in ventures linked to the extraction of raw materials. From 1951 until 1971, consequently, Japanese direct foreign investment totaled just over $4 billion, with nearly 60 percent of that total coming in the years 1969–71.[68] Through fiscal 1972, nearly three-quarters of Japan's limited overseas investments were in nonmanufacturing ventures.

The rapid escalation in the value of the Japanese currency reconfigured government and business incentives regarding foreign investment. The stronger yen offered an automatic incentive for many firms to invest abroad; so did rising protectionist barriers against Japanese imports in the United States and Western Europe. Setting up production facilities in those potentially closed markets allowed Japanese-owned firms to bypass potential barricades against Japanese imports, while the rising value of the yen made it considerably cheaper to expand overseas. A tightening Japanese labor market further stimulated foreign direct investment, as did domestic demands for a cleaner environment. For many manufacturing firms producing for export, expansion of their overseas facilities became highly desirable.

For the government as well, liberalizing conditions for foreign direct investment allowed it to meet changing business demands and placate powerful foreign critics of Japanese trade policies in a manner that posed few threats to continued conservative dominance at home. The interests of the Japanese government and many private Japanese businesses thus resonated with the world's new monetary and trade conditions.

Large current account surpluses in 1971–72 had led the government to liberalize certain conditions for foreign direct investment by Japanese firms. As the yen appreciated, government constraints were softened further and Japanese firms responded with alacrity. A dramatic expansion in capital outflow and overseas investment ensued. Total investment for 1973–76 was nearly double that for the preceding twenty years.[69] This investment continued to escalate. Some $4.7 billion was invested in 1980, $12.2 billion in 1985, and $47 billion in 1988, ten times the figure of eight years earlier.[70]

Japanese investments occurred in virtually all sectors of manufacturing, not to mention massive equity, bond, and government note holdings in Europe and the United States. Japan's larger financial, commercial, and manufacturing institutions moved abroad; large numbers of subcontractors and other small firms followed. By the late 1980s, Japan was the world's largest creditor and its second largest overseas investor, behind only the United States.

The investment boom had wide consequences. Overseas operations (particularly in Asia) allowed Japanese-owned firms to reduce their labor costs while investment in North America and Europe enhanced their access to upscale markets. Overseas operations allowed many Japanese firms to come out from under governmental oversight. Within Japan, organized labor was further weakened. Meanwhile many secondary and tertiary subcontractors were left without markets for the components or services that they once supplied through vertical *keiretsu* contracts. In what was to prove an important development in the *keiretsu* as well, many manufacturers began to loosen their dependence on deficit financing and on their main banks.[71] In short, expanded overseas investment brought sweeping changes to Japanese economic structures, to links between government and business, and to the labor market within Japan.

Greater overseas investment by many sectors of the Japanese economy widened the gaps between segments of the Japanese economic community. Those that expanded overseas were forced to confront international market conditions far more directly than when they operated largely within Japan. Most underwent internal adjustments to enhance their competitiveness. Other sectors—those that continued to focus primarily on production and sales within Japan—could resist making such adjustments by relying on oligopolistic networks, extensive regulation, and government protection.

If conditions for the movement of Japanese-owned firms *out of* Japan were liberalized quickly, the movement of foreign products and companies *into* Japan was far slower to change. Foreign pressures for greater access to the Japanese market had led the government to reduce tariffs to an average of 2.5 percent. This meant, as the government was quick to report in virtually all its official publications, that formal tariff barriers in Japan were below the 2.7 percent level for the European Community, the 3.5 percent for the United States, and the 4.2 percent level for Canada.

Residual import restrictions were also reduced. In the 1960s Japan had restrictions on some 490 product categories. By February 1975 the number had dropped to 29 (7 in manufacturing and 22 in agriculture);[72] by 1992 agricultural restrictions were down to 13 and manufacturing restrictions down to 1, fewer than in other industrialized countries.[73]

Yet such reductions in formal barriers did not entail a wholesale rejection of embedded mercantilism, nor did Japanese business leaders or government officials suddenly embrace laissez-faire market philosophies and unfettered trade. Into the early 1990s, two major areas of import illiberality remained conspicuous: high-level manufactured goods and agriculture.

Imported manufactured goods expanded rapidly in the late 1980s but from such a low base that they continued to constitute an inordinately low ratio of Japan's total imports.[74] Rarely imported were products in categories where Japanese-owned firms were exporters; until the late 1980s imported manufactured goods rarely competed in the domestic market against Japanese exporters. Moreover, the rise in overseas investment by Japanese manufacturers, as well as the development of regionally integrated production facilities in Asia with Japanese firms at their core, meant that much of the rise in Japanese manufactured imports was simply the result of Japanese-owned plants overseas involved in intracompany transfers or sales back to facilities or markets in the home country. True foreign penetration was a much smaller part of the changing import picture.

As noted in Chapter 4, changes in the Foreign Exchange and Control Law in 1980 had allowed foreign firms to invest directly in Japan. Long-term Japanese giants like IBM-Japan, Coca-Cola and Nestlé were joined by Western brokerage houses, banks, catalogue sales operations, food franchises, and firms selling a variety of consumer nondurables. Many achieved high levels of profitability by the early 1990s. So did a number of high-prestige brand-name goods from Royal Dalton to Mercedes-Benz. But important pockets of protection remained, including insurance, construction, energy, air transport, and telecommunications. As with manufactured imports, widespread foreign penetration remained the exception. Even into the late 1990s, the Japanese economy remained, on a per capita basis, much less penetrated by foreign investment than any other industrialized nation.

In agriculture as well, Japan hardly embraced free trade. Japan is one of the industrial world's largest importers of many agricultural products. Food and agricultural goods make up some 15 percent of total Japanese imports. Japan is by far the best market for U.S. agricultural exports, buying more than America's second, third, and fourth largest markets combined. Moreover, in the late 1980s Japan liberalized once highly sensitive items including beef, citrus fruits, processed cheese, canned pineapple, and orange juice.[75] All required politically painful concessions to Western pressure at the expense of the conservative regime's own rural supporters. Rice, however, remained a noteworthy exception. Japan remained steadfastly opposed to any liberalization of imported rice until the end of the Uruguay Round, insisting on a policy of "not one single grain of imported rice." Following Uruguay, Japan began moving toward the eventual tariffication of rice, and even the sacrosanct rice market began to open slowly.

Changes in overseas investment and trade opened chinks in the armor of embedded mercantilism. Many government-to-firm and bank-to-firm connections were weakened, and some economically less competitive sectors of the economy—many of them normally supportive of conservatives—faced serious economic threats. Nonetheless Japan remained one of the countries in the industrialized world most closed to foreign direct investment—proof of embedded mercantilism's pervasive stickiness. But the overall expansion in overseas investment, combined with even the modest openings of the home market, began to undermine the socioeconomic support base of the LDP and to loosen the once rigid bonds holding the conservative regime together.

Defense and Security

From the 1970s and into the late 1990s Japan's conservative regime continued its commitment to low military spending, its minimalist security posture, and its reliance on the U.S. Security Treaty, the American nuclear umbrella, and the Seventh Fleet. Except for the radical left, fewer and fewer Japanese challenged this continued commitment. Overall support for these policies grew among the public. Indeed, several decisions during the 1970s and the early 1980s reaffirmed the longstanding Yoshida line: the Three Non-nuclear Principles, limits on arms exports, the continued commitment to spending no more than 1 percent of GNP on defense, and the Nuclear Nonproliferation Treaty. Prime Minister Nakasone in the 1983 Williamsburg economic summit went so far as to declare that "the security of our countries is indivisible." And in 1996 President Clinton and Prime Minister Hashimoto reaffirmed their two countries' commitment to the Security Treaty, with a revised set of defense guidelines being promulgated in September 1997.

Yet several shifts occurred that both kept the regime largely on course and sowed seeds for change. Prime Minister Nakasone sought to move Japan toward a more active military role in world affairs; the Japanese Self-Defense Forces expanded slightly their military mission; in 1988 Japan and the United States entered into an agreement to share military technologies; many government and business officials emerged to champion enhanced domestic production of arms equipment. Overall, however, the adjustments that Japan's conservatives made in defense and security remained within the broad framework that had prevailed since the 1950s.

One noteworthy deviation came with the adoption of a policy of "comprehensive security." Responding to the oil and energy crises, as well as to U.S. pressures for an increase in Japan's defense spending, "comprehensive security" moved the discussion of defense beyond matters of guns and alliances into the arenas of energy, food security, and foreign assistance. The policy crystallized in 1980 when, under Prime

Minister Ōhira's initiative, a study group put forward the *Report on Comprehensive Security*.[76] Claiming that American military supremacy had ended and that the United States could no longer guarantee support for all its allies, the report went on to argue that Japan's security depended on more than military prowess and included economic well-being and access to natural resources. It argued that Japanese defense policy be conducted at three levels: overall efforts to create a positive climate in world affairs, self-reliant efforts to cope with external threats, and a reliance on closer ties with those countries that shared Japan's ideals and interests.[77]

The result was a new perspective on national security, weaving together foreign aid, energy and raw materials, food, sea transportation, science and technology, economic planning, military affairs, and diplomacy and placing them all under the nominal umbrella of security. The policy underscored the official commitment to advancing foreign policy through nonmilitary means. At the same time, it provided a justification allowing numerous Japanese government agencies to tie their missions to "security." Simultaneously, Japanese officials could deflect attention away from the country's low commitment to military security and point instead to Japan's larger "burden sharing." In particular, the policy deflected American criticisms of Japan's "free ride on defense," since Japanese foreign aid was increasingly directed toward political goals congruent with U.S. foreign policy.

Since "comprehensive security" resonated less with the rhetoric of the 1930s and 1940s than did "alliances," "defense," or "military spending," the policy also defused some of the pacifist appeals of the traditional left. By including enhanced foreign aid as an important component of Japanese security, Asian criticisms of an alleged "Japanese militarism" were also mitigated. One further consequence was also important: by connecting Japanese economic and security interests so closely, the policy tightened some hitherto loose connections among various conservative groups, even though it involved only minimal deviations from past policies and institutions.

In short, then, adjustments and shifts occurred in various aspects of the conservative regime's policy profile, coalitional arrangements, and institutional base during the 1970s and 1980s. These both ensured the continued political and economic success of the regime and undermined many aspects that had held it together during the 1960s. Before examining the conservative regime's collapse, we need to highlight how it appears to have successfully adapted by the late 1980s.

Intimations of "Successful" Adjustment

During the late 1980s Japanese conservatism appeared to have made the kinds of adjustments that would ensure continuity and success for the prevailing regime. This was especially true at the electoral level. The LDP attracted substantial new socioeconomic support—from white-collar voters, urbanites, and segments of organized labor—that did not dramatically undercut core conservative support in the well-organized sectors of agriculture and small business. Not until the very late 1980s did the government begin taking policy actions that began to hurt these former core supporters. The public increasingly perceived the LDP as the only party capable of maintaining macroeconomic success; good economic performance over the years reinforced the party's political hold.

In the 1979 and 1980 elections the LDP reversed its twenty years of linear decline, and the 1980s became a decade of unchallenged LDP dominance. The JSP drew less than 20 percent of the total vote and none of the other minor parties were able to win over 10 percent in two consecutive elections. In the 1986 lower house election, for example, the LDP drew 51.3 percent of the vote and won 59.8 percent of the seats.

Equally notable was the apparently successful economic adjustment. The oil shocks and the labor shortages had been dealt with far more successfully than in other countries. Major manufacturing firms had emerged far stronger. The rapid rise in the yen had encouraged many of them to shift their focus from "exporter" to "investor." Consequently, numerous Japanese firms prospered despite the oil shocks, the stunning escalation in the yen, and the rise in overseas protectionism. Asset holders were particular beneficiaries. Between 1986 and 1990, land prices and Tokyo stock exchange values soared. Japanese tourists, toting wads of the ever more valuable yen, roamed the world filling Louis Vitton suitcases with foreign goods. Glitzy Ginza tea shops catered to the nouveaux riches by offering chocolates sprinkled with shards of real gold. Japanese journalists delighted in noting that the book value of the five-kilometer circle of land that housed the Japanese Imperial Palace had a value greater than the entire state of California. A wave of worldwide trophy purchases came under Japanese ownership. Real growth rates averaged 4.5 percent per year from 1985 to 1989, a full percentage point or more ahead of any other industrialized democracy. Trade boomed, current accounts ballooned, foreign reserves expanded geometrically. Nine of the world's ten largest banks were Japanese. Flush with capital, Japan became the world's largest creditor nation. The economy seemed to defy comparative economic experiences and business cycles. Triumphalism swept the nation.

The combination of LDP electoral victories and the continued success of the Japanese economy, particularly its phenomenal performance in the last half of the 1980s, suggested that the reconfigured and suitably adjusted conservative regime would remain in power, that foreign policy problems would be minuscule, that Japan's economic performance would continue to outstrip that of all other major democracies, and that the LDP would continue its dominance without interruption. But these appearances proved deceiving. As we saw in the preceding chapter, the 1990s were marked by the bursting of the economic bubble and a seemingly endless cycle of debt, deflation, declining demand, and deindustrialization. Politically, the fragmentation of the LDP and the party's replacement by a coalition of "everyone but the LDP" made it unmistakably clear that the old regime had ended. But the question remains why the collapse was so stark and sudden after what would have appeared to have been a decade of successful adaptation.

The LDP Split and the Bursting
of the Bubble: Regime Collapse

The bursting of the economic bubble and the split within the LDP shattered the long-standing equilibrium of Japan's conservative regime. Underlying both events were two central tensions that regime adjustment and recalibration had exacerbated rather than eliminated: a widening division within the regime's socioeconomic support base and an increased institutional fragmentation.

On the first point, as noted above, conservative electoral adjustments during the 1970s and 1980s attracted new supporters without alienating old ones; the socio-economic base of "conservatism" was continually expanded but never realigned. Moreover, as the ideological division between government and opposition narrowed, more and more voters ceased to identify firmly with one or another party or bloc. The result was the rapid growth in the number of nonaligned voters.

During the 1980s the LDP had been able to attract significant segments of these new constituencies, but it had been unable to provide an institutional framework or consistent economic policy profile that would enmesh them in regular and continuing support for the party. By the end of the decade, therefore, LDP support was broad but shallow. So long as hard policy choices could be skirted, and so long as the economy performed well, the shallowness was unproblematic. But as economic problems deepened and hard choices became unavoidable, winners and losers under alternative scenarios became much more apparent.

Consider five such trade-offs. As noted above, the electoral system for the lower house discriminated severely against urban areas.[78] Any reconfiguration of the electoral system to provide greater weight to urban areas was deeply opposed by incumbent conservative (and opposition) politicians. The promise of lower prices—of great appeal to urban voters and organized labor—posed the threat of reduced protection for domestically produced agricultural and food products, a significant deregulation of cartelized industries, and a reduction in the import and investment barriers against foreign consumer goods. Such moves were directly counter to the interests of core conservative supporters such as the farmers' cooperatives, many major businesses, utilities companies, many small businesses, and those conservative politicians whose specific electoral prospects depended on strong organizational ties to such organizations. Furthermore, any such policy shifts posed a direct threat to those government agencies whose power rested on the organization and implementation of protectionist policies.

Tax reform was similarly divisive. Japan's tax system was widely criticized as being a 9–6–4 system: wage and salary earners paid about 90 percent of the taxes they owed, small businesses only 60 percent, and agricultural households a mere 40 percent.[79] (Cynics often referred to the system as 9–6–4–1, with the final 10 percent figure being the rate presumably paid by politicians.) Any tax reform favoring salaried employees would obviously increase the burden on core conservative support groups. And the imposition of any new taxes such as the 1989 value-added tax, regardless of its redistributive effects, was inherently unpopular.

Expansion of public welfare benefits also divided conservative supporters. The expansion of so-called "social wages" has historically been an appealing substitute for direct improvements in income or reductions in prices.[80] While certain government agencies, such as the Ministry of Health and Welfare, obviously favored such measures, governmental largesse had led to substantial deficit financing and was resisted by Finance Ministry bureaucrats, by the private financial and corporate sector, and by farm groups and small-business organizations whose members would be least likely to benefit from such programs.

Even cleaning up the environment and providing healthier, cleaner surroundings had been problematic, despite its electoral desirability. While no political actors overtly favored "pollution," most divided widely over how to target specific toxins and wastes, which by-products were truly noxious, how to pay for cleanups, and the like. Dirty manufacturing industries viewed the issue quite differently from small, clean businesses. Labor too was divided: workers in jobs and industries targeted by antipollution measures were far more concerned about their jobs and their companies' profits than about carbon in the air or mercury in the water.[81] Nor was it inherently clear just which specific locations should be the sites of nuclear plants, toxic waste dumps, garbage processing facilities, airports, highways, or railways. In Japan, as elsewhere, a strong NIMBY ("not in my backyard") mentality generated numerous protests by those opposed to "best interest" solutions.[82]

Equally important in undermining the old regime was the way individual LDP parliamentarians strengthened their district-level support bases (*kōenkai*) by buffering them against voter shifts that might affect the LDP as a whole. These individual power bases often worked against the collective interests of the party, increasingly decoupling the electoral fortunes of individual LDP backbenchers from those of the party and its leadership.

Just as the electoral problems of the LDP opened up a variety of intra-conservative tensions, so did the international economic and security challenges. The decline in currency autonomy, rising oil prices, and U.S. pressures against Japanese exports challenged the regime's commitment to embedded mercantilism as they exposed the conflicting economic interests of its members. For example, the rising yen meant a relative drop in the costs of imported raw materials, including oil. Correspondingly however, the cost of Japanese manufactured products around the world increased. The rising yen thus threatened earlier business harmony as it divided exporters from importers and high energy users from others. Furthermore, combined with Western protectionism the rising yen enhanced the incentives for many Japanese firms, particularly in manufacturing, to expand abroad: by producing overseas, firms could lower their labor costs, get closer to end markets, and skirt potential trade barriers. Other firms with far less flexible production capabilities, such as construction, utilities, and aluminum, lacked that option. Meanwhile investments abroad often led to job losses and fewer business opportunities at home.

Many U.S. demands for opening the economy might have been strategically wise for the national economy, and many would have been economically beneficial to large numbers of urban consumers and hence been electorally advantageous as well.

But any substantial liberalization of the Japanese home market would have had un-even consequences for the business community. Internationally competitive indus-tries such as automobiles, electronics, fiber optics, and semiconductors were far better positioned to undergo liberalization than were less competitive sectors such as textiles, aluminum, most of the distribution sector, agriculture, construction and cement, and the financial sector.

Divisions within the business community also emerged over the relative merits of continued government economic regulation. Generically, such controls were often used to impede foreign imports, but as such they hurt not only foreign firms but also those Japanese industries that might have benefited from cheaper imported components. Moreover, those businesses that had become competitive domestically and internationally increasingly chafed under existing regulatory policies.

As just one example, yen revaluation posed a serious regulatory problem since banks, trading companies, and major manufacturers confronted vastly greater for-eign exchange vulnerabilities under a floating yen. Many were anxious to eliminate government restrictions that would prevent them from utilizing internationally ac-cepted hedging strategies to minimize those risks. Many new firms not directly as-sociated with Japan's corporatist *keirestu* structures, including major manufacturers such as Sony, Canon, or Honda, also opposed government controls, as did discount retailers like Aoki International and Aoyama Trading, private brand retailers like Daiei, and a number of upstart cosmetics firms.[83]

Just as many other industries, however, were quick to embrace government over-sight. Firms and sectors that had never enjoyed international competitiveness, or had lost it, welcomed government-approved protection cartels. Government re-striction of corporate freedom was more than offset by the benefits such cartels provided for long-term market shares and overall profitability.[84] Many firms and sectors desired regulation and foreign exchange controls in order to protect their market shares and profitability.

Even such seemingly unexceptional goals as fiscal austerity became controver-sial. Appealing as austerity was to MOF bureaucrats, it threatened such politically popular measures as across-the-board tax cuts, program expansions, subsidies for important constituent groups or regions, public research and development and sup-port for high-tech and public works.

Consequently, the relative harmony that had prevailed within most segments of the conservative regime during the 1950s and the 1960s increasingly gave way to di-verse sectoral and firm specific pressures during the 1970s and 1980s. The conser-vative regime was rife with often conflicting views over how to meet the challenges it faced. Devising economic policies that could satisfy all segments of the conser-vative support base became increasingly difficult as groups pulled in opposite di-rections—more protection versus less protection, more pork-barrel politics versus tighter fiscal restraints, high yen versus low yen, and so on.

Linked to these socioeconomic divisions was a second important problem, namely, the splintering in the once airtight institutional cohesion of the old regime. Econom-ically, the fiscal health of many Japanese blue-chip firms, overseas investment, fiscal deregulation, the decline in the role of the main banks, the growing role of equity markets, and a host of other changes had undermined connections within business and between business and the government. Numerous Japanese firms began to operate in accord with individually determined business plans, which meant the pursuit of increasingly competitive strategies not always in accord with government policies or the needs of other businesses or sectors. As ideological lines blurred between government and opposition, the LDP thus lost much of its cohesiveness. Ideological and policy differences between it and the other parties became blurred; socioeconomic support groups divided sharply over goals and strategies; and individual LDP parliamentarians with strong local support and independent funding grew less dependent on the party for their electoral success.

The unraveling of the conservative regime ultimately came down to three simple propositions: (1) the economic bubble proved unsustainable, (2) corruption and economic failure threatened the LDP as a party, and (3) many individual LDP members, fearful of going down with a sinking ship, opted to break ranks and reorganize conservatism on a different socioeconomic basis with new policy goals.

The economic bubble and its end is a complex but increasingly well told story.[85] It started with the massive run-up in the value of the yen after the Plaza Accord of 1985 and the consequent shifts in Japanese exchange rate and monetary policy. These overlapped with a number of peculiar characteristics of Japanese banking.

As we saw in Chapter 4, the Reagan Administration had pursued a policy of increased government spending, particularly for the military, combined with sweeping tax cuts. When those tax cuts failed to increase government revenues as had been promised by monetarists, America's expanding budget deficit had to be funded. Japanese institutions including insurance companies, trust banks, casualty companies, and regional banks all stepped in, investing vast sums in U.S. treasuries. This investment was made possible by expanding national surpluses that rose with Japanese export success. By recycling dollars received for Japanese exports into a funding of the U.S. debt, the Japanese government partially defused American vehemence over the bilateral trade imbalance and also helped to keep down U.S. interest rates. But ultimately, as the yen strengthened geometrically, dollar-denominated holdings actually decreased in value for Japanese holders.

Fearful of the effects of a strong yen on the profitability to both U.S. debt holders and Japanese exporters, and simultaneously anxious to maintain the politically positive aura of an expanding consumer economy, the MOF opted for an exceptionally loose monetary policy designed, among other things, to drive down the value of the yen. Finance "ordered the Bank of Japan to open the monetary floodgates while the ministry injected massive amounts of fresh spending into the economy via a series of fiscal packages and the expanded investment of postal savings funds."[86]

With the official discount rate at a postwar low of 2.5 percent, asset markets predictably skyrocketed. Commercial property values soared. The Nikkei Dow tripled in value between 1985 and 1989, turning the stock market into an endlessly spewing cash machine. Securities firms were feverish in their churning of stocks, in some cases promising their favored clients (often bigwigs in politics and organized crime) that the brokerage house would guarantee them against any losses. Individual companies flush with cash engaged in complex financial schemes known as *zaiteku* (financial high tech). Some, such as Toyota, began reaping more of their profits through *zaiteku* than through manufacturing. "Free money" could be made by issuing Eurobonds with warrants on rising stocks and by swapping the dollar exposure back into yen.

Banks, meanwhile, having lost many of their normal blue-chip borrowers due to financial liberalization and the opportunities that major firms had for raising monies on either domestic or foreign equities markets, began lending to increasingly less well established clients. With the government exerting little control over interest rates, banks and businesses borrowed and lent heavily, collateralizing their loans with rising land and stock values. Vast sums were poured into increasingly dubious ventures, often linked to politicians, the agricultural cooperatives, land speculators, construction firms, and organized crime.

The belief was widespread that cheap money could indefinitely continue to support the white-hot economy. A popular slogan said that if everyone crosses the street against the light, then no one can get hurt. As with many aphorisms, the grain of truth was lost in oversimplification, but the slogan reflected the extent to which national hubris had translated Japanese "uniqueness" into "invulnerability."

Only after five years of unprecedented prosperity did the Bank of Japan, in May 1989, finally tighten credit. By August 1990 rates had been raised from 2.5 to 6 percent (a 140 percent jump).[87] The upward economic spiral quickly turned down. Firms cut back on their capital expenditures; land prices collapsed quickly; the stock market fell from ¥38,915 at its height on the last day of 1989 to ¥14,820 by 1992. Meanwhile, as a result of the recently installed minimum capital requirements of the Bank for International Settlements (BIS), Japanese banks were increasingly forced to liquidate assets, usually at sharply deflated prices. The spiral continued; numerous property companies and several major banks failed; a massive government liquidation was required for the *jūsen;* major securities firms underwent sweeping purges of top management; international rating agencies such as Moody's and Standard and Poor's downgraded the creditworthiness of Japanese banks; international markets placed a "Japanese premium" on borrowing by the country's institutions; foreign mutual funds dumped Japanese securities; and so it went. As of mid-1998, no significant letup was in sight at least for the financial sector.

As the bubble burst, the underlying corruption that accompanied it became increasingly apparent, thereby undermining the once unquestioning public and business trust in the ability of the Japanese bureaucracy and the LDP to govern the economy. Nor did it help that the bubble had such wide effects across Japanese society: land owners and stockholders had seen their net assets blossom; others, lacking such assets, fell immediately into arrears. Not surprisingly, the bubble reversed Japan's once highly egalitarian Gini index, revealing growing disparities in Japanese income levels. And when land and stock prices fell, those who lost their newfound money looked to extract political retribution. The consumption tax meanwhile had made conservative politicians particularly unpopular.

Corruption had always been a problem for conservative politicians. But the bubble burst and the consumption tax came at a time when several scandals were gaining high visibility. The Recruit and Sagawa Kyūbin scandals proved undeniably that politicians and senior bureaucrats had systematically accepted bribes in exchange for making exceptions to Japan's nominally rigid regulatory rules. Coming in the midst of economic chaos, these scandals could no longer be shrugged off by the suggestion that corruption was but a small price to pay for policies beneficial to the nation as a whole. While "cleaning up" Japanese politics had surfaced with predictable regularity every decade or so, it had previously disappeared with equal speed. This time demands for structural overhauls to clean out the Augean stables of Japanese politics gained stridency and persistence.

Both the bubble and corruption worsened the underlying tensions among conservative support groups. The LDP had long deflected the problem of how to restructure its electoral and socioeconomic base; electoral successes and the party's expanding base during the 1980s deferred the need to make hard choices. A catch-all approach seemed ideal. Increasingly competitive international economic conditions and the economic decline brought the issue to a head, however. Liberalization would benefit consumers, labor, and urbanites; protection was essential for agriculture, utilities, many troubled industries, small businesses, and oligopolies. Conservatives could no longer promote both. Should the party leave farmers, small business people, and declining industries to the mercy of international competition while siding with urbanites and blue- and white-collar workers? Or should it resist foreign pressures and perhaps take the consequences in the form of retaliation against their exported manufactured goods? Who should pay to bail out the banks and the *jūsen?* Could pork-barrel politics continue unabated during a long recession? How should corruption be dealt with—through structural changes or smoke and mirrors?

Continued economic success had long been a safety valve that reduced the pressure on conservatives to force adjustments within Japan's less competitive sectors. Some measures to liberalize these segments of the economy had been introduced, albeit reluctantly. As one of the major targets of U.S. pressures under the Structural Impediments Initiative in 1990, the so-called Large Scale Retail Store Law had been revised, despite strong opposition from owners of small businesses. Larger supermarkets, chain stores, discount outlets, mail order shops, and large leisure centers all flourished. While some small shopkeepers adjusted to the new system, far more did not. But overall, numerous pockets of protected industrial inefficiency remained throughout the economy.

Meanwhile, farmers confronted even more drastic changes. The food control system had been restructured, rice subsidies had been reduced drastically, imports of meat and citrus fruits had been liberalized, and an active land diversification program sought to move farmers off the land or into non-rice crops.[88] While Japan in the Uruguay Round sought to protect its agricultural sector to the very end, the groundwork was laid for the eventual tariffication of rice that would undercut the well-protected heart of Japan's farm population.

Agricultural coops urged their members to break with conservative candidates in the 1989 election as a means of protest. Subsequently, proposals surfaced for an all-farmer Agricultural Party. Farm votes were the largest bloc to shift in the 1989 election. Coming as this did with more widespread reactions to the consumption tax and to the growing corruption scandals, the result was a disastrous loss of the LDP's majority in the upper house.[89]

Within the party, the upper house defeat dissipated any lingering convictions among individual politicians that the party was invulnerable and that unswerving loyalty would somehow assure them a lifetime career. A Darwinian struggle for individual survival broke out. For many, the multimember district system was presumed to be the source of corruption because of the vast amounts of money poured into intra-conservative battles within the same district. Its replacement became tantamount to reform. For others, electoral reform offered a way to revise the support base of the party. Still others, more idealistic, sought a sweeping weakening of the links among money, politics, and policy.

The Japanese Supreme Court had declared the existing electoral system to be unconstitutional because of the vast overrepresentation of Japan's rural electoral voters, which had reached 4:1 proportions in the worst instances. The court, however, did not call for any specific new system, so the decision fell to politicians. The LDP leadership had long preferred an electoral system with single-member districts, which most projections indicated would be highly favorable to the party.[90] The smaller opposition parties, realizing that their survival depended on some form of proportional representation, were opposed. No politician from any party wanted reforms that would cost him his career. Consequently, conspicuous movement on electoral reform was difficult to generate. Prime Ministers Kaifu and Miyazawa foundered on the issue. After promising electoral reform, neither was able to deliver a reform bill that could pass parliament.

It was in this context that the LDP split widened. As noted, the 1989 election had convinced many individual LDP politicians that sticking with the party was no longer a guarantee of permanent political employment. The result was an explosion of political entrepreneurship by clusters of conservative politicians. In their efforts they found ready allies in groups such as Rengō, the labor federation that earlier conservative-led changes had empowered. If corruption was unpopular, these entrepreneurs would embrace "reform." If government economic policies were unpopular among core constituents in their home districts, then they would oppose them. If the bureaucracy appeared inept, they would come out for administrative reorganization. Widespread party system dealignment was the consequence.

Three separate groups left the LDP initially. Hosokawa Morihiro and those who won seats as members of the Japan New Party were largely idealistic reformers. Primarily urban and genuinely disturbed by the deep-seated corruption, they sought a more responsible party politics, a more deregulated economy, and a more internationalized Japan. A second orientation existed among the thirteen to fifteen relatively young Diet members who split to form Sakigake (Harbinger Party). All had rather secure "second-generation" seats and strong *kōenkai* that essentially ensured their reelection; all were committed to sweeping reforms, particularly to ending the spread of corruption at the core of the civil service. They favored the creation of a single-member district system in the somewhat naive belief that this would reduce the need for large campaign funds. They split from the party primarily when their demands for cleanup were ignored by most senior party leaders (with the exception of a small number including Gotoda Masahara and Itō Masayoshi). Finally, a third group was headed by Ozawa Ichirō and Hata Tsutomu. Ozawa, it was argued, was one of the rare politicians in the LDP concerned with the long-term prospects of the nation.[91] As such he stated his opposition to the extensive use of the spoils system, economic protectionism, and a low international posture. Instead, he sought, in the phrase widely associated with him, to make Japan into "a normal country." The Ozawa group generally favored a single-member district system. But Ozawa was also a classical "money" politician. He had learned his politics from men like Takeshita and Kanemaru, both of whom were deeply involved in the emerging scandals. A Japanese Machiavelli, he had been LDP secretary-general and a major fund-raiser, and his policy positions were closely tied to his desire to gain national control. Party realignment seemed to offer him that opportunity.

The splits by these groups proved to be only the first wave of defections, and the LDP fragmented further in subsequent months. It was Hosokawa, in a pivotal position, who was chosen to head Japan's first non-LDP government since 1955. Despite strong support from the general public and the widespread sense that the time was ripe for change, however, Hosokawa's reign proved to be short lived. In April 1994, unable to pass a series of electoral reform proposals and simultaneously plagued by allegations of financial improprieties analogous to those of the LDP members from whom he had sought to distance himself, Hosokawa was replaced by a member of his own cabinet, Hata Tsutomu of the Renewal Party (Shinseitō). Then, after only two months in office, Hata's coalition split as its largest single member, the Social Democratic Party of Japan (SDPJ, or Shakaitō), bolted from the anti-LDP coalition and leaped across the ideological spectrum to form a hitherto imponderable coalition with the remnants of their long-standing nemesis, the LDP. The resulting new government, an ideological idiosyncrasy united more by its fear of losing power than by any coherent program or direction, held together into 1996.

Japan's seventh prime minister in five years, Murayama Tomiichi, was a socialist, the first prime minister from his party since 1947; after completely gutting the JSP program, he resigned and was replaced by the LDP's new head, Hashimoto Ryūtarō. Eventually, in the October 1996 lower house election, Hashimoto engineered a return to single-party government under the LDP (even though the party lacked a parliamentary majority in both houses of parliament).[92] The chance for radical political overhaul seemed to have passed with the end of the reform governments, the splintering of the opposition, and the return of the LDP. But the underlying structural pressures for change continued, albeit far less dramatically.

Japan's new electoral system, only the second since 1928,[93] passed the legislature in late January 1994. Elections for the House of Representatives combined two systems. Three hundred representatives are selected from single-seat, first-past-the-post districts; another two hundred are chosen from party-selected slates according to proportional representation in eleven regional districts. Citizens have two ballots, allowing them to split their votes in ways that will protect smaller parties. In its first use during the October 1996 election, at least four parties competed as "conservatives." The LDP won a plurality, and most other conservative groups retained roughly the same number of seats with which they entered the election. The biggest loser was the SDPJ, the former JSP. However, while the LDP was back in government by the mid-1990s, its hold was far from secure; party realignment threatened to continue, and the party system had been undeniably transformed.

The uncertainty of the LDP's electoral hold was underscored by its stunning 17-seat loss in the Upper House election of July 12, 1998. Nearly 60 percent of the eligible voters turned out, and the LDP won only 44 of 126 contested seats—well short of its target of 61–65. This loss led to the resignation of Prime Minister Hashimoto and the likelihood of further intra-party defections.

As of mid-1998, the Japanese political economy was in a state of flux. While there is obvious risk in making short-term prognostications during periods of high political mutability, it seems clear that the era of one-party LDP dominance has ended and that the Japanese economy will not return soon to any unparalleled string of successes. To that extent, the previous regime has ended.

The shape of any new regime will depend on the new alliances that socioeconomic groups form, on the new institutional arrangements they develop to hold themselves together, and on the particular mixture of public policies that they devise. The major possibilities for these changes will be broached in the concluding chapter. But for the present, the process of change and reform is under way on fundamental, rather than superficial, grounds. As Herman Schwartz has phrased it in a different context, "reorganizers are engaged in a strategic politics that attempts to change the rules of the game rather than just seeking their preferred outcome in the context of extant rules."[94]

Far more fragmentation, realignment, and false starts are likely before any new equilibrated regime can be identified. Indeed, there is no guarantee that such clarity will emerge for some time. More like Sweden and Italy than Britain or the United States, Japan has no new and stable regime yet in place. Two things seem eminently clear, however: no political party is likely in the near future to regain the kind of unbridled hegemony that the LDP enjoyed over the preceding four decades, and the national economy will not return easily to the unmitigated successes it enjoyed at the height of "embedded mercantilism." To that extent the ancien régime has definitely passed.

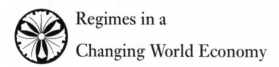

Regimes in a
Changing World Economy

In late 1997 stock markets, banks, real estate prices, and national currencies collapsed throughout Thailand. Within weeks that country's problems were echoed in Malaysia, Indonesia, Singapore, and the Philippines. Prime Minister Mohamad Mahatir of Malaysia was outspoken in his condemnation of various dark and conspiratorial "outside forces" whom he alleged were responsible for his country's troubles. But his efforts to shore up the Malaysian currency and stock market soon proved futile before international investors.

Shortly thereafter, stock prices fell dramatically throughout Japan, Europe, and North America, just as they had during the Mexican currency crisis several years before. To many, this string of events, devastating to numerous asset holders in many parts of the world, simply confirmed a growing conviction that international markets had become ever more tightly fused. As a consequence, the powers of economic globalization would continue their leveling effects, making it harder for any single nation or government to set an autonomous agenda.

This book has centered on national differences rather than convergences. Partly this is a result of the time periods considered: Part I emphasized the years immediately following World War II. Part II focused on shifts in regimes since the late 1970s. Although my concern was with national differences rather than common adaptations, Part II could well be read by globalists as reflecting the increasing power of international economic forces over domestic institutions and coalitions.

I conclude this book with an eye to its implications, particularly for the tradeoffs between national and global forces. To do so, I concentrate on three problems: first, the general applicability of the notion of regimes for comparative study; second, the probable evolution of the Japanese political economy; and third, the possible links between my findings and the issues of globalization and internationalization. I show that despite global pressures, national differences among regimes, including Japan's, are likely to continue.

"Regime" as a Conceptual Tool of Analysis

Dichotomies dominate the study of contemporary political economy: state versus society, domestic versus international, elective versus nonelective, change versus continuity, state versus market. I have downplayed such polarities, focusing instead on how specific regimes fuse and integrate these apparently dichotomous forces.

How states and markets interact, and how states either dominate societies or are permeated by them, may well be important characteristics of particular regimes. But it is the mutually contingent character of state structures, markets, and societal organization that is central to understanding regimes. Similarly, regime analysis reflects the interweaving of domestic and international factors in single countries rather than how one trumps the other across time and place. Throughout this book the stress has been on the ways in which such linkages have been mutually reinforcing, recursive, and equilibrating within industrial democracies. The character of any particular regime is marked less by "either-or" and more by "both-and."

Examining regimes as whole systems allows for broad-brush comparisons of the deep-seated biases and axes of power in the political economies of nation-states. Individual regimes are distinctively constructed, but the forces that shape them and the outcomes that emerge are often so similar that different political economies resemble one another for long periods. This was certainly the case with the corporatist systems that emerged in many small states of Europe in the 1930s, as with the press toward fascism in others.[1]

Corporatist Sweden, collectivist Britain, the pluralist United States, and party-dominated Italy all established distinct postwar political economies. Each regime had its own long-standing socioeconomic divisions, distinct mixture of political and economic institutions, and a particular public policy profile. The result was a consistent and predictable political economy in each of these nation-states over one or more generations.

In Sweden, from the mid-1930s into the mid-1980s a specific socioeconomic alliance—first the Red-Green alliance between organized labor and agriculture, and subsequently the Red-White alliance between blue-collar workers and white-collar wage earners—held electoral predominance. Corporatist bargaining mechanisms facilitated a positive-sum game of economic bargaining between peak associations of labor and business that was highly conducive to the improved productivity and enhanced competitiveness of Swedish business while at the same time allowing for the creation of an extensive program of state-operated social welfare programs. Meanwhile, Sweden's policy profile and formal institutions enhanced the political and economic power of the social democratic left and the union movement, even while retaining broad legitimacy within Swedish business and capital. There really was a basis for talking about what Marcus Childs has called Sweden's "middle way."[2]

British collectivism also involved a degree of business–labor cooperation and the diminution of preexisting left–right political gaps, but the British mixture proved to be shorter lived and far less conducive to national economic dynamism in manufacturing than was the Swedish pattern. Labor unions and the Labour Party were central to the evolution of British collectivism, but British labor structures were never as comprehensive and corporatist as their Swedish counterparts, and they had fewer structural incentives to link union goals to enhanced business productivity. Nor was the Labour Party ever able to generate a policy profile so deeply committed to de-commodified social welfare benefits as was developed under Swedish social democracy. Meanwhile British capital was far more internally cohesive than British labor, and also far more directed by finance than by manufacturing. Finally, the alternating parliamentary governments that emerged from Britain's essentially two-party competition meant that despite a relatively encompassing agreement between both parties, policies frequently reflected the zigs and zags of specific Labour or Conservative governments.[3] By the end of the 1970s, few British manufacturing firms retained more than minimal international competitiveness, the national economy was lagging behind most of the other OECD countries, and Britain became widely scorned as "the sick man of Europe." While the symptoms of Britain's alleged illness were primarily economic, the system as a whole was perceived by politicians and pundits to be in mortal danger and in need of comprehensive surgery.

America's exceptional institutional pluralism and its complex mix of economic and cultural identities made for a highly stable, if particularistic and decentralized, public policy profile for most of the period from the 1940s through the 1970s. At the congressional level, the Democratic and Republican Parties enjoyed little of the national cohesion of Britain's two parties. Still, the complex New Deal coalition initially woven together by Roosevelt remained sufficiently intact to allow the Democrats to set most of the policy agenda, even while special interest groups, bureaucratic agencies, and congressional committees forged their own bipartisan iron triangles. For nearly three decades after World War II, American manufacturers and financiers stood head and shoulders over their foreign competitors, providing strong productivity and employment growth at home. Unions in large manufacturing sectors benefited from lucrative business–union accords, even though union membership levels and state-provided welfare programs remained among the lowest in the industrialized world. As a result the national power of labor was geographically uneven and quite industry specific. Through it all, the United States played an exceptionally active role in developing and maintaining the international monetary and trade systems and the pro-Western alliance structure. The many critical components of the U.S. regime, far more numerous than in many other political economies, interacted like the parts of a complex mobile.

Postwar Italy developed a regime which provided social benefits almost as extensive as those of Sweden, despite the limited power of the Italian left. But these benefits were delivered through paternalism and patronage led by the Christian Democrats, not by a politically neutral state system as in Britain or Sweden. In Italy, unlike Sweden or Britain, the left was fragmented, and the right was far more cohesive. As in the United States, issues of foreign policy, religion, and culture were superimposed on economic divisions. Geographically Italy was really two nations, a high-productivity center of small and medium-sized manufacturing in the north and a primarily stagnant agricultural zone in the south, dependent on clientelistic largesse from Rome.[4] It truly was a regime without governance.

Political and economic actors within all four of these regimes either accepted, or were powerless to reconfigure, the predominant coalitional arrangements, institutions, and public policy profile. As a result, all four demonstrated stability during the first thirty or more years after World War II. Although they differed from one another in important ways, none was unique. Sweden looked quite similar to Norway, Denmark, and Austria.[5] British collectivism bore considerable similarity to regimes in New Zealand and, to some extent, Canada and Australia. For most of the postwar period, the Italian regime resembled that of the French Third Republic and Weimar Germany; with respect to the central role of party politics, anticommunism, and religion, it even bore certain similarities to the United States.

It was really the United States that was the most idiosyncratic. As both strategic and economic hegemon, and as the country with the largest GNP and the most heterogeneous population, the United States had no real peers. At the same time, its two-party politics likened it to most of the Anglo-Saxon countries; with its powerful agribusiness sector it resembled Canada and Australia; its cultural complexity had certain parallels in Canada, Switzerland, and even France and England. American open trade and investment policies were replicated throughout much of the industrial world.

By far the most truly distinctive regime of those examined here was Japan's. Only in the Japanese regime—from the mid-1950s into the late 1980s—was organized labor isolated from significant governmental participation while a countercoalition of big and small business and organized agriculture dominated the political economy. National bureaucratic agencies, but particularly MITI and MOF, exerted a strong regulatory control over national economic development, particularly in the early postwar years, while numerous manufacturing and financial firms, both large and small, linked their economic fortunes to one another through extensive *keiretsu* networks. A policy profile of "embedded mercantilism" kept the domestic economy sealed off from significant foreign penetration, while numerous manufacturing firms parlayed strong domestic market positions into ever larger international market shares through aggressive exporting. More so than in the United States, social welfare in Japan was residual, means tested, and occupation dependent. The country enjoyed exceptionally rapid economic growth but in ways that, despite the absence of left-of-center governments, proved to be highly egalitarian—a result primarily of public works programs and subsidies to slow-growing regions of the country, to agriculture and small businesses, and to decreasingly competitive industrial sectors. As in all regimes, the specific pieces that constituted Japan's regime were mutually reinforcing, but their particular combination gave the Japanese political economy distinct biases and political axes.

Any social equilibrium is usually transient, particularly when politico-economic arrangements are complex. As I have made clear, the seemingly paradoxical antinomies of continuity and change are interwoven in any regime. Changes in external conditions alter the preferences of key political and economic actors; so do the continually changing situations and relative power balances among them. None of the arrangements put into place in these four countries in the years following World War II held through to the late 1990s. Rather, all five regimes underwent fundamental shifts away from their previously established equilibrium points.

All were subject to the disequilibration of rapidly changing international economic forces, as globalists are quick to stress. For example, both the Italian and Swedish regimes were shaken by the perceived need to meet the Maastricht Treaty's criteria for the European Currency Union. Still, international pressures were hardly the sole source of the regime shifts I examined: specific internal tensions also contributed to the breakdown of preexisting arrangements. Thus it is hard to imagine Italy's *partitocrazia* collapsing so rapidly and completely without the corruption scandals associated with *Tangentopoli*, just as it is impossible to conceive of Sweden's changes without understanding the tensions between public- and private-sector unions. And while the United States is perhaps the easiest case to link to financial globalization, few of the political changes that catapulted the Republicans to power are understandable without taking into account the cultural hostility toward civil rights actions, the women's movement, and antiwar protests—and subsequently the antiabortion and "family values" issues pressed onto the national agenda by Christian fundamentalists.

Just as the specific catalysts of change often differed, so did the mechanisms by which the regimes came apart. New electoral coalitions were far more important catalysts to the regime shifts of Britain and the United States than to those of Italy or Sweden. In Japan party fragmentation, most notably within the LDP, and the internal collapse of the asset bubble were most critical.

Thus, a host of common international economic pressures impinged on the once stable regimes of the various industrialized democracies and nudged them out of their stable orbits. But these pressures were neither uniformly felt nor uniformly filtered through domestic institutions and political arrangements. Moreover, discrete and idiosyncratic domestic changes contributed mightily to the ultimate shifts. By the turn of the century, there was no denying that whatever commonalities might be identified among the five regimes, each retained a high degree of individuality and domestic distinctiveness.

Although Britain and the United States clearly established new equilibrium points by the late 1990s, Italy, Sweden, and Japan were still wobbling through uncertain transitions toward new patterns of stability. But there is little to suggest that, once they have reached new equilibriums, these three regimes will be similar. This is certainly true when one considers the most likely prospects for Japan.

Prospects for Japan's New Regime

Japan's regime in the late 1990s differed conspicuously from what it had been two or three decades earlier. The economy and economic policies had been transformed, and the national budget was deeply in the red; the official discount rate was at its lowest in fifty years; the value of the yen was fluctuating wildly; national debt had reached a higher percentage of GNP than in almost any other industrialized country; official unemployment was rising faster than at any other time in the previous thirty years; manufacturing productivity had been stagnant for seven years; the national treasury was facing demands for gargantuan payouts to offset bad loans throughout the financial sector; underfunded pension funds were under renewed threat; public-sector interest payments were mounting; and electorally fearful politicians were insatiable in their demand for patronage projects. Even though national economic performance had deteriorated substantially from 1990 to 1997, there was little suggestion that government officials had agreed on a common set of policies designed to reverse the debacle. Instead, an ongoing struggle left policy oscillating between efforts at austerity in one quarter and fiscal stimulation in the next and between deregulatory promises and reregulatory realities.

Although Japan's stalled economy attracted the biggest headlines, by the end of the 1990s many other noteworthy changes had taken place in Japan's conservative regime: a new electoral system, a reconfigured but highly fluid party system, and a massive dealignment of voters; a weakening of both the vertical and horizontal linkages connecting Japan's most powerful *keiretsu* and an increased presence of foreign-owned firms; a substantial reduction in the number and power of the policy tools available to economic bureaucrats; the pacification and emasculation of radical labor and leftist organizations; the economic and, to a lesser extent, political marginalization of organized agriculture; a substantial increase in the average age of the Japanese population; and a steady erosion of voter loyalty to parties.

By the late 1980s the classic divisions between business and labor and between conservatives and socialists had been historically settled. Ideology had hardly become irrelevant, and history had hardly ended, but the classic battles of the past were largely resolved and had lost their power to animate important political activity. Similarly resolved and off the political table were most of the broad questions surrounding security relations with the United States and those of nationalism and pacifism. Fifty years of economic transformation and the end of the cold war had made most of them moot, while the meltdown of the Japan Socialist Party emasculated the most forceful historical articulator of opposition to conservatism. This is not to say that future political battles in Japan will never be fought over issues of economic distribution or over the constitution, military spending, U.S. troops, or the symbols of Japanese nationalism. Almost certainly they will. But the articulation of any such issues in the next ten to fifteen years will almost certainly bear little resemblance to the forms in which they arose over the last 40–50 years.

In short, the socioeconomic, institutional, and policy underpinnings of the old regime have shifted, and the change seems irreversible. Although political actors battle over the extent and direction of desirable changes, no clear agenda commands comprehensive support. Any newly equilibrated Japanese regime will result from new socioeconomic cleavages, the institutions through which these gain expression, and the public policy profile constructed to ensure their smooth resolution and interaction. Let us examine each of these before venturing predictions about a future regime.

The most central socioeconomic cleavage confronting Japan at the end of the century is that between its internationally competitive and its noncompetitive sectors, firms, and groups. At one extreme stands a Japan composed of the nation's international success stories: world-spanning, technologically sophisticated, high-value-added firms using skilled workforces to produce internationally competitive products, high profits, and expanding market shares. At this same pole are found the nation's cosmopolitans—citizens with quality education, highly marketable skills, good incomes, and an abiding attraction for the consumerist lifestyle—and various business associations, private-sector unions, and a small number of government and quasi-governmental organizations. For all of them, greater internationalization, economic openness, and deregulation are far more appealing than ominous.

At the other extreme lie Japan's more protected, less sophisticated firms with mixtures of low-skilled, undertrained, or inefficient workforces, firms whose profitability has become a function more of political protection and governmental subsidization than international market competitiveness. Individuals at this pole are less educated, possess fewer cutting-edge skills, have lower incomes, and are anxious about the risks of rapid economic change. The most easily identified sectors are construction, cement, pharmaceuticals, agriculture, large numbers of distributors, many rural residents and semiskilled workers, the insurance, brokerage and banking sectors, and many others. They are joined in their concerns by most government regulatory agencies, numerous entrenched interest associations, and even many groups nominally favoring "consumers."

Such a division is classic. It suggests that the future of Japan's political economy will be a zero-sum struggle between these two competing forces. Reduced to its journalistic expression, the future thus boils down to whether Japan will deregulate its economy or not, whether trade and investment will become substantially more open or not, and ultimately whether Japan will recapture its position at the cutting edge of world economic developments or remain mired in regulatory red tape, protectionism, and the exploitation of consumers. From this one-dimensional perspective, the prospects for any new regime are dualistic: to move forward or backward, to remain regulated or not, to be open or closed.

Yet, this socioeconomic cleavage is by no means the only important one. Japan is also split over whether it should keep its predominantly pacifist role in foreign affairs or become more "normal." In addition, a strong bloc of citizens is anxious to see an end to endemic corruption. Issues related to pension funding, the environment, freedom of information, immigration, energy, and local autonomy further

complicate the national public policy agenda. Many such issues were of high electoral salience during the mid- to late 1990s; others have catalyzed voter interest at
various times and promise to do so in the future.

Of course, socioeconomic forces do not operate in an institutional or policy vacuum. For such splits to acquire political salience, they require institutional voices
capable of providing alternative policy choices. To date, neither the institutions nor
the clear policy choices are in evidence with enough clarity to give tangible expression to the division between protectionists and internationalists. Certainly no important Japanese bureaucratic agency has emerged as the institutional advocate for
a deregulatory and internationalist coalition. To be sure, the Ministry of Foreign
Affairs, the Japan Fair Trade Commission, and the Japan Management and Coordination Agency have long advocated policies broadly favored by Japan's internationalists. But all are relatively weak players in the political game. Most other ministries—Education, Construction, Home Affairs, Transportation, and Agriculture,
Forestry, and Fisheries—focus inward and are constituency oriented. None are
strong advocates of any deregulatory or internationalist mix of policies and bureaucratic structures.[6] MITI has been somewhat more mixed, as has MOF. Yet both
agencies, and MOF in particular, have favored the protection of traditional constituents as well as their own regulatory frameworks. This was particularly true of
MOF in its reluctance to expose the nation's relatively noncompetitive financial,
insurance, and brokerage sectors to the challenge of international competition.

Any potential institutional backing for a more economically internationalist
regime is unlikely to come, therefore, from Japan's bureaucratic world. Instead, as
Vogel has put it, the most distinctive feature of bureaucratic regulatory proposals in
the 1980s and 1990s could be characterized as "the ministries' effort to turn liberalization into a protracted process in which their ability to determine the timing
and conditions of new market entry generates a powerful new source of leverage
over industry."[7] Hence few Japanese ministries have consistently advocated massive
deregulation or wide-open markets, particularly when these would reduce the regulatory powers of the agencies themselves. Similarly, few senior bureaucrats are
eager to threaten the public corporations (or their budgets) that typically offer these
officials their postbureaucratic careers.

Some "deregulators" and "internationalists" have appeared within the political
sphere, however. Party reorganization in 1993 presented an opportunity to advocate
dismantling the old system and replacing it with a more open, less regulated
regime. Although only a few members of Prime Minister Hosokawa's inchoate
coalition government strongly advocated sweeping reform, the coalition as a whole
was committed to some such agenda, however vague. The coalition began to put
forward proposals that could have led to significant new institutions, but Hosokawa
and his movement proved exceptionally short lived.

Subsequently Prime Minister Hashimoto and the Administrative Reform Council called for deregulation in six broad arenas: bureaucratic restructuring, budgeting, economic structure, finance, education, and social welfare. The most trum-
peted proposals called for the privatization of the postal savings system, the division

of functions once the sole responsibility of the Ministry of Finance, a reduction in the number of public corporations, and a substantial slimming of government agencies.[8] Meanwhile a proposed "Big Bang" was to deregulate the banking, securities, and insurance sectors.[9]

Although many of these proposals and promises sounded appealing, they had at best weak institutional support, and after months of debate and political airing, most ran into political pullback. No political party, notably, has solidly favored such proposals. The two major parties at the time, the LDP and the NFP, did diverge by 1997 on the desirability of extensive institutional and policy reforms, but neither party clearly advocated one or the other side.[10] By 1998 the more pro-internationalist NFP had fragmented, and its various successors were desperately in search of a more internationalist policy agenda that might give them some institutional cohesion. At the end of the 1990s, thus, Japan's internationalists lacked a powerful electoral vehicle to advance their interests.

Such a vehicle may well develop. Party realignment seems likely to continue, and given the vast number of businesses, citizens, and geographical constituencies that would benefit from less regulation and more openness, it is plausible to expect new political entrepreneurs to advance deregulatory and internationalist interests through a new party, new policy proposals, or electoral competition.

The 1994 electoral system for the House of Representatives, which favors greater bipolarity than the earlier system, makes the rise of political entrepreneurs advocating an internationalist agenda and deregulatory institutional changes somewhat more likely. Certainly, it is well established that single-seat competition favors issue polarization. But there is little reason to expect that any such polarization *within individual electoral districts* will take the form of internationalism versus protectionism. Indeed, the new single-member districts, considerably smaller and more compact than those they replaced, are almost certain to provide an even greater spur to electoral and economic parochialism.

Throughout the postwar period, Japan's most powerful individual politicians have had strong local constituencies and well-established personal support groups, neither of which is likely to disappear in the near future. The new, smaller districts should, consequently, retain or expand their strongly local character. Two or more candidates competing in any single district will more likely attempt to outdo one another in local pork-barrel promises and concessions to local economic wishes— whether protectionist or internationalist—than to articulate a broad vision for the national economy. Thus, in some districts electoral competition will probably pit two or more candidates advocating local protection against one another, while elsewhere competitors will seek to outdo one another in their demands for deregulation and more open markets. Any political party that gains a parliamentary majority on the basis of single-member districts is therefore likely to be a complex amalgam of advocates of both protection and openness.

The proportional representation segment of the electoral system offers greater incentives for sharp policy divisions between parties. But even here, if parties use proportional representation victories to seat parliamentary candidates who failed to win single-member seats, as happened in the 1996 election, the likelihood of party differences on national economic policy will be limited.[11]

Still, the old electoral system had an antiurban bias: four times more votes were needed to win a metropolitan seat that to capture one in the hinterlands. The new system is more favorable to urban areas, with the worst overrepresentation of rural areas being little more than two to one. Urban consumers therefore have the potential to gain greater electoral voice. But as I have stressed throughout, it will take the creation of a significant political party to crystallize urban and internationalist aspirations. Without a party whose agenda articulates the preferences of Japan's potential internationalists, changes in that direction are unlikely. As V. O. Key noted years ago, "The voice of the people is but an echo. The output of an echo chamber bears an inevitable and invariable relation to the input. . . . [T]he people's verdict can be no more than a selective reflection from among the alternatives and outlooks presented to them. . . . If the people can choose only from among rascals, they are certain to choose a rascal."[12] Much the same can be said of protectionists: if Japanese voters are offered choices only among protectionist candidates, they are sure to opt for protection. Absent a political party favoring an urban, internationalist, and deregulatory agenda, those policies are unlikely to emerge, no matter how strong the social support for such policies.

Clearly, an essential element in the eventual balance between internationalist and protectionist forces, and hence in the eventual configuration of any new regime, will be Japanese business. In the increasingly tedious academic debates about whether Japanese bureaucrats or politicians are the more powerful, business has remained an all but ignored element. Yet, an extensive literature on comparative capitalism has established the political importance of meeting the economic demands of business and retaining "business confidence." Furthermore, the previous chapters make clear the power of big business in Japan, whether one focuses on the contribution of business to the formation of the LDP in 1955 or on the success of the major banks and *jūsen* in extracting public financing to cover the costs of their poor lending policies in the 1990s.

Japan's businesses are generally united behind a broad agenda of small government, deregulation, and tax reform; but they are divided on specifics. The country's most internationally successful business firms have strong incentives to support a political regime and elected politicians likely to deregulate electric utilities, transportation, telecommunications, finance, and the like. Conversely, many businesses in sectors such as cement, construction, finance, insurance, and retailing would be highly threatened by substantial deregulation and economic openness of the domestic market in their industries. Tax reform translates into less pork for some companies, more pork for others. Consequently, the major business organization, Keidanren, while nominally supportive of the principles of deregulation, has been internally divided on most specifics. In this regard, the organization reflects the much deeper divisions within its membership.

Particularly during the 1960s and well into the early 1980s, Japanese politics and economics were linked in a positive upward spiral. Politics enhanced Japanese economic transformation and corporate profitability. This is no longer the case. By the end of the 1980s Japanese politics was a mixture of corruption, protection, and pork that benefited limited business sectors only; the true engines of national economic growth were operating independently of politicians and bureaucrats. By the late 1990s numerous firms were feeling the results of the economy's structural flaws in diminished profits and declining competitiveness. The frustrations of big business with the political world was most notable in Keidanren's 1993 decision to cease automatic contributions to the LDP.

Future political actions by Japan's business leaders will certainly be driven by the performance of Japan's economy generally and by that of their own firms and sectors more specifically. If Japan and its most successful firms are able to regain comparatively high growth, the pressures from business for massive and rapid political reform are likely to be muted. Conversely, a continuation of the slow growth and declining competitiveness that characterized Japan's financial and service sector throughout the 1990s is almost certain to invigorate business pressures for political changes, whether through the autonomous promotion of policy alternatives, lobbying, or even reshaping the party system.

One thing is certain: it is difficult to imagine a new policy profile that will satisfy the competing constituencies of contemporary Japanese conservatism the way high growth did from the 1960s through the 1980s. The economic policy choices confronting Japan in the late 1990s have become more zero-sum.

Nevertheless, the central question for any future Japanese regime is the extent to which an underlying socioeconomic bifurcation—between deregulation and internationalism, on the one hand, and regulation and nationalism on the other—is played out politically. The first tendency still has at best a limited voice within the upper echelons of government and no clear electoral champion. The deregulatory voices may be stronger within the top ranks of business, but, thus far, most businesses favoring such policies have done little to advance the political institutionalization of their views.

The right combination of entrepreneurship, opportunity, and luck could well change the party system and provide voters with clear choices between the two economic agendas. A political party could emerge that would appeal to Japan's substantial constituency for deregulation and openness and win power through the electoral process. Certainly this was what happened in large part during the party system dealignment of the early 1990s, although the policy proposals and the lineups of politicians were by no means so clearly bifurcated. With such a realignment, if it could hold power long enough, a coalition favoring deregulation might well transform Japan's economy. Clearly, however, institutional forces are currently far better mobilized to impede such actions than to advance them, and it is unlikely that a deregulatory coalition could defy them. Indeed, there are almost sure to be strong political, bureaucratic, and business voices for continuing protectionism. Yet protectionist voices are unlikely to retain political hegemony. Too many voters and important businesses would be seriously disadvantaged.

Thus a most probable *first scenario* for Japan's new regime centers on some electoral and party-driven mixture of continued regulation, nationalism, and mercantilism tempered by deregulation, internationalism, and economic openness. Some future party realignment could generate one (or more) parties taking positions favorable to Japan's international businesses, to unions employed in export industries, and to others who would benefit from a more open Japanese market (such as urban consumers). Gravitating toward an opposing pole would be one (or more) parties more narrowly nationalistic and representative of Japan's small shopkeepers, farmers, declining or less competitive industries, and other elements less favorable to foreign direct investment and foreign imports.

Some hint of this polarity within the party system was reflected in the somewhat disproportionate "internationalist" orientation of many NFP members and the conversely more "protectionist" biases and constituencies of the LDP. With the fracturing of the NFP, the Democratic Party has sought to capture the mantle of a consumerist/internationalist party. To date it has remained small. But even if some major nationalist-internationalist realignment occurs, any large party or coalition is almost certain to contain mixtures of both nationalism and internationalism.

The relative balance between any such parties and their agendas would hinge on changes within the party system and the outcome of elections. But if two or three parties provided clear-cut alternatives for continuity or change, Japan's political economy would probably go through a series of ad hoc episodes favoring one group or the other. In this scenario, even a government nominally committed to more deregulation and internationalization would be hard pressed to continue some form of social safety net as well as side-payments to those most injured by any newly deregulated system. Such provisions would be costly under the moderate-to-slow growth that Japan is almost certain to face, but they would be almost politically impossible to avoid. Moreover, such a regime would also confront the massive demands for payouts to rectify the financial debacle and to ensure a well-funded pension system, slowing economic growth even further and resulting in more difficult and painful political choices.

After some period, the major parties would be likely to gravitate toward some relatively common middle ground. Any Reaganesque-Thatcherite pressure for the unmitigated embrace of "market principles" seems politically implausible, flying as it would in the face of the entrenched institutional power of those who would suffer under such Eastern European–style "shock therapy."

At least as probable, however, is a *second scenario,* a muddied mix of politicians and parties resembling Italy in the 1970s or 1980s. Rather than providing broad promises of alternative economic agendas, parties would remain highly fragmented and inchoate in their economic positions. Individual politicians and bureaucratic agencies would continue to protect their respective constituencies through collective public pilferage. Protection would continue relatively unabated for the country's farmers, small businesses, marginalized regions, noncompetitive sectors, and troubled industries. Voters and businesses thus benefiting would provide electoral backing for their political protectors, while voters unhappy with the limited choices they were offered at the polls would simply stay home, as happened in Japan's 1996 elections.

Meanwhile, foreign firms would gain major shares of Japan's capital market and forge alliances with individual Japanese firms. The two worlds of economics and politics would be far less tightly coupled than in the past. Internationally successful firms and multinationals would go about their business without excessively frustrating interference from, or inordinate dependence on, politics and bureaucratic regulation. Raising money in international markets, and partnered with other global firms, they would be largely decoupled from the worst consequences of increased public expenditures in Japan, so long as creative international accounting allowed them to avoid major tax bites. Periodically, one or another deregulatory measure would occur, but always with caution and with serious side-payments to those negatively affected. Change would proceed but at a slow pace. The national economy would continue to be bifurcated. Some firms and sectors would fare exceptionally well, but most others would be reduced to slow growth; the macroeconomy would face rapidly escalating government spending and public deficits. International borrowing costs would be high for the Japanese government; the yen would lose value; long-term debts would mount; many frustrated Japanese citizens might well emigrate. But so long as the system did not penalize Japan's best economic performers excessively and so long as international pressures for an opening of Japanese markets remained diffuse and product specific, such a situation might well last a long time. It would certainly not generate the exceptional economic transformations and high growth of two decades earlier, but it could muddle along without serious challenge, as it did in Italy for perhaps thirty years.

Finally, a *third scenario* must be considered. Its key lies in the rise of social movements outside the existing party system. In effect, if economic conditions become bad enough, if reforms to the fiscal system and the pension system continue to be persistently avoided, if overseas expansion and individual firm reorganizations generate substantial increases in unemployment, and if politicians and civil servants cannot erase their image as self-serving pigs at the public trough, then public discontent might well be manifested in the kind of nonparty politics that characterized the Poujadist or Le Pen movements in France, the skinhead movement in Britain, the Christian Right in the United States, or, within Japan, the labor radicalism of the immediate postwar years, the environmental and student movements of the late 1960s, or the nationalist movements of the 1930s. Certainly such a scenario seems unlikely to become permanently entrenched in Japan, but it might well emerge as a historical prelude to a more permanent re-equilibrating of the Japanese regime.

Regimes in a Globalizing Political Economy

International finance and manufacturing have unquestionably become increasingly global. Numerous multinational corporations have globalized their production, service, and sales operations. More than $1.2 trillion in foreign currency moves across national borders daily. Strong and consistent pressures consequently impinge on all industrialized democracies—pressures to reduce their regulatory barriers to such operations, pressures to attract capital and job-creating industries, pressures to limit the ability of organized labor and social welfare systems to extract benefits from the ever more mobile and return-sensitive capital.

At the same time, official discount rates have not become universal, or even particularly convergent, across national borders. Multinational manufacturing firms do not automatically gravitate to the cheapest sources of labor; if they did, job creation would be far greater in Bangladesh than in Boston or Bristol, whereas the reverse is true. Numerous multinational corporations remain stubbornly monocultural within their top ranks. Thus, the proportion of foreign-born board members of America's top five hundred corporations in 1991 was only 2.1 percent, the same as ten years earlier. In France, half the heads of the top two hundred companies were educated in the same six *grandes écoles*.[13] Some geographical areas enjoy vastly greater dominance of specific industries than do others: Hollywood in filmmaking, Silicon Valley in computing and networking, Prato and Paris in fashion and design, New York and London in finance and insurance.

Such national and geographical differences are hardly likely to disappear in the near future, regardless of the pervasiveness of global forces. Indeed, they will continue to function as highly critical filters for such forces. Some countries, particularly those with smaller domestic markets and open economies, will be forced to adjust more quickly and adroitly. Larger countries are almost certain to enjoy the luxury of slower response times. But even the most rapidly adjusting countries have continually adapted in accord with established domestic political and economic arrangements. Austria adjusts quite differently than Switzerland.[14] Certainly any stable regime in Britain will continue to differ from one that emerges in Italy, while Japan will remain distinct from Sweden.

International forces will therefore continue to influence particular national regimes. Stable regimes within industrialized democracies will have to accommodate international pressures far more consciously than they did in the 1950s or 1970s. The challenges of internationalism and globalism are real. But challenges will simultaneously be posed by domestic changes, only some of which will be linked to activities that begin outside the national borders. In their continual reassessment of their opportunities and challenges, political actors must look in two directions simultaneously. They must be sensitive to both the national and international arenas as they calculate their political and economic strategies. But ultimately their competing perspectives will be articulated within political economies that remain preponderantly shaped by national events and choices. Institutions, coalitions, and policy profiles will continue to take shape primarily within national borders, and individual regimes will continue to reflect their particular strengths and weaknesses. The study of different regimes will remain critically important for understanding not only comparative political economy but our world as a whole.

NOTES

Introduction: Long Continuities, Radical Shifts

1. On Japanese conservative dominance in comparative perspective, see T. J. Pempel, ed., *Uncommon Democracies: The One-Party Dominant Regimes* (Ithaca, Cornell University Press, 1990). In Japanese see *Ittō yūisei no hōkai* [The collapse of one-party dominance], *Leviathan* (special issue 1994).

2. Douglass C. North, *Institutions, Institutional Change and Economic Performance* (Cambridge, Cambridge University Press, 1990), p. 6.

3. Among the many studies on this problem see Michel Albert, *Capitalism vs. Capitalism* (New York, Four Wall Eight Windows, 1993); Peter Gourevitch, *Politics in Hard Times: Comparative Responses to International Economic Crises* (Ithaca, Cornell University Press, 1986); J. Rogers Hollingsworth, Philippe C. Schmitter, and Wolfgang Streeck, eds., *Governing Capitalist Economies: Performance and Control of Economic Sectors* (New York, Oxford University Press, 1994); Peter J. Katzenstein, ed., *Between Power and Plenty* (Madison, University of Wisconsin Press, 1978); Gregory Luebbert, *Liberalism, Fascism, or Social Democracy: Social Classes and the Political Origins of Regimes in Interwar Europe* (New York, Oxford University Press, 1991); Herman M. Schwartz, *States versus Markets: History, Geography, and the Development of the International Economy* (New York, St. Martin's, 1994).

4. See, e.g., Charles Kindleberger, *American Business Abroad* (New Haven, Yale University Press, 1969); Clark Kerr et al., *The Future of Industrial Societies* (Cambridge, Harvard University Press, 1960); Daniel Bell, *The Coming of Post-Industrial Society* (New York, Basic Books, 1973). See also Suzanne Berger and Ronald Dore, eds., *National Diversity and Global Capitalism* (Ithaca, Cornell University Press, 1996); Colin Crouch and Wolfgang Streeck, eds., *Political Economy of Modern Capitalism: Mapping Convergence and Diversity* (London, Sage, 1997); Hollingsworth, Schmitter, and Streeck, *Governing Capitalist Economies*.

5. The obvious exception to this proves the point. Not surprisingly, most of the numerous comparisons of Japan and the United States have concluded that the differences are far more striking than the similarities. More nuanced studies in the late 1980s and early 1990s compared Japan to one or more similar capitalist democracies, particularly to Germany, but it was still far more common for Japan to emerge as the "exception."

6. Kobayashi Yoshiaki, *Sengo Nihon no senkyō* [Elections in postwar Japan] (Tokyo, Tokyo Daigaku Shuppan, 1991), as cited in Muramatsu Michio, Itō Mitsutoshi, and Tsujinaka Yutaka, *Nihon no seiji* [Japanese politics] (Tokyo, Yūhikaku, 1992), p. 126.

7. For a useful and detailed examination of Japanese public support for parties, see Miyake Ichirō, *Seitō shiji no bunseki* [An analysis of political party support] (Tokyo, Sōbunsha, 1985).

8. Based on data presented in Yamakawa Katsumi, Mada Hiroshi, and Moriwaki Toshimasa, *Seijigaku deeta bukku* [Handbook of political science data] (Kyoto, Sorinsha, 1981), pp. 144–45.

9. Ibid., p. 124.

10. Deane E. Neubauer, "Some Conditions of Democracy," *American Political Science Review* 61, 4 (1967): 1007.

11. This is not a self-evident point. Sweden, after all, saw the Social Democrats in power from 1932 until 1976 (forty-four years); the Christian Democrats held the Italian prime ministership from 1945 until 1980 (thirty-five years); in Belgium, the PSC was out of power for only four years between 1947 and 1987; the KVP was in all governments in the Netherlands between 1946 and 1977. See Kaare Strom, *Minority Government and Majority Rule* (Cambridge, Cambridge University Press, 1990), app. A. But all of these parties ruled at least part of the time in coalition, whereas the LDP had clear parliamentary majorities and held virtually all cabinet posts throughout this entire period, with the minor exception of the New Liberal Club, a minuscule LDP offshoot, from 1983 until 1986. On this general point see Pempel, *Uncommon Democracies.*

12. OECD Report, *Public Management Development: Annex II* (Paris, OECD, 1991), p. 74. These data show that in 1980 government employees formed only 8.8 percent of Japan's workforce, and by 1990 the figure had shrunk to 7.9 percent, compared to figures of between 15 and 32 percent for the other advanced democracies.

13. Takashi Inoguchi, "The Political Economy of Conservative Resurgence under Recession: Public Policies and Political Support in Japan, 1977–1983," in Pempel, *Uncommon Democracies*, pp. 189–225.

14. Various efforts have been made to unravel this puzzle. See Gourevitch, *Politics in Hard Times;* David Cameron, "Social Democracy, Corporatism, Labor Quiescence, and the Representation of Economic Interest in Advanced Capitalist Countries," in John H. Goldthorpe, ed., *Order and Conflict in Contemporary Capitalism* (Cambridge, Cambridge University Press, 1984); Katzenstein, *Between Power and Plenty.*

15. See Masahiko Aoki, *Information, Incentives and Bargaining in the Japanese Economy* (Cambridge, Cambridge University Press, 1988); "The Japanese Firm in Transition," in Kozo Yamamura and Yasukichi Yasuba, eds., *The Political Economy of Japan* (Stanford, Stanford University Press, 1987), 1:263–88; Ronald P. Dore, *Flexible Rigidities* (Stanford, Stanford University Press, 1986); Murakami Yasusuke, *Han-koten no seiji keizaigaku* [An anticlassical analysis of political economy] (Tokyo, Chūō Kōronsha, 1992). On the general question of multiple capitalisms, see Colin Crouch and Wolfgang Streeck, eds., *Modern Capitalism or Modern Capitalisms?* (London, Francis Pinter, 1995).

16. Michael Shalev, "The Social Democratic Model and Beyond: Two Generations of Comparative Research on the Welfare State," *Comparative Social Research* 6 (1983): 315–51; David Cameron, "Expansion of the Public Economy: A Comparative Analysis," *American Political Science Review* 72, 4 (1978): 1243–61; Adam Przeworski and Michael Wallerstein, "The Structure of Class Conflict in Democratic Societies," *American Political Science Review* 76, 2 (1982): 215–38.

17. Goran Therborn, *Why Some Peoples are More Unemployed Than Others* (London, Verso, 1986).

18. The question of whether all of these workers were truly "productive" or not has been opened with vigor in the harsher economic times of the early 1990s. On the links between Ministry of Labor policies and the character of Japanese employment and unemployment, see Ikuo Kume, "Institutionalizing the Active Labor Market Policy in Japan: A Comparative View," in Hyung-ki Kim, Michio Muramatsu, T. J. Pempel, and Kozo Yamamura, eds., *The*

Japanese Civil Service and Economic Development: Catalysts of Development (Oxford, Oxford University Press, 1995), pp. 311–36.

19. Evidence indicates that this equality began to diminish during the land price "bubble" of the late 1980s, when a gap emerged between owners of land, whose wealth rose dramatically, and those who lacked land and homes.

20. Malcolm Sawyer, *Income Distribution in OECD Countries* (Paris, OECD, 1976).

21. David R. Cameron, "Politics, Public Policy, and Distributional Inequality: A Comparative Analysis," in Ian Shapiro and Grant Becher, eds., *Power, Inequality and Democratic Politics* (Boulder, Westview, 1988), pp. 223, 232.

22. Imada Takatoshi, *Shakai Kaisō to Seiji* [Social stratification and politics] (Tokyo, Tokyo Daigaku Shuppankai, 1990), p. 123.

23. Martin Bronfenbrenner and Yasukichi Yasuba, "Economic Welfare," in Yamamura and Yasuba, *Political Economy of Japan*, vol. 1; Sidney Verba et al., *Elites and the Idea of Equality* (Cambridge, Harvard University Press, 1987); Yutaka Kosai and Yoshitaro Ogino, *The Contemporary Japanese Economy* (Armonk, N.Y., M. E. Sharpe, 1984). It is possible that there was some reversal of the tendency toward greater equality between 1975 and 1985. See *Gendai Nihon no kaisō-kōzō* [Stratification in contemporary Japan], vols. 1–4 (Tokyo, Tokyo Daigaku Shuppankai, 1990); see also Kenji Kosaka, ed., *Social Stratification in Contemporary Japan* (London, Kegan Paul International, 1994), pp. 35–36. John R. Freeman, *Democracy and Markets: The Politics of Mixed Economies* (Ithaca, Cornell University Press, 1989), pp. 140–46; see especially fig. 6 (p. 141) for an indication of how radically unusual Japan's position appears in comparative perspective when growth is graphed against income equality.

24. Yasusuke Murakami, "Toward a Socioinstitutional Explanation of Japan's Economic Performance," in Kozo Yamamura, ed., *Policy and Trade Issues of the Japanese Economy: American and Japanese Perspectives* (Seattle, University of Washington Press, 1982), p. 28.

25. Yasusuke Murakami, "The Age of New Middle Mass Politics: The Case of Japan," *Journal of Japanese Studies* 8, 1 (1982). On the other hand, Japan does have numerous important social divisions along class lines, and social mobility is affected by father's occupation and one's own schooling. See Imada, *Shakai kaisō to seiji*, esp. pp. 102–16; also Hiroshi Ishida, *Social Mobility in Contemporary Japan* (Stanford, Stanford University Press, 1993).

26. Accuracy demands that one recognize that Japan is relatively egalitarian in incomes but less so in wealth. Moreover, even income equality diminished during the late 1980s.

27. Walter Korpi and Michael Shalev, "Strikes, Power, and Politics in the Western Nations: 1900–1976," in Maurice Zeitlin, *Political Power and Social Theory* (Greenwich, Conn., JAI, 1980), 1:301–34.

28. Jelle Visser, "The Strength of Union Movements in Advanced Capitalist Democracies," in Marino Regini, ed., *The Future of Labor Movements* (London, Sage, 1992), p. 13; Michael Shalev, "The Resurgence of Labor Quiescence," in ibid., pp. 102–32.

29. On this see Joel Krieger, *Reagan, Thatcher and the Politics of Decline* (New York, Oxford University Press, 1986). For a comparative examination of the conservative politics of the 1980s in Japan, England, and the United States, see Ōtake Hideo, *Jiyūshugiteki Kaikaku no Jidai* [The period of liberal reforms] (Tokyo, Chūō Kōronsha, 1994).

30. Among the easier areas to criticize are gender discrimination, an educational system structured against individuality, limited housing, parks, and recreational facilities, a well-entrenched class of organized criminals, an economy biased to favor producers over consumers, and few state programs that "decomodify" benefits.

31. See Freeman, *Democracy and Markets*, p. 137 n. 1: "Data on the Japanese case are included here, but only for purposes of exposition. I will make no effort to demonstrate the applicability of the theory in an Asian setting."

32. T. J. Pempel, *Policy and Politics in Japan: Creative Conservatism* (Philadelphia, Temple University Press, 1982). Also, "Japan's Creative Conservatism: Continuity under Challenge,"

in Francis G. Castles, ed., *The Comparative History of Public Policy* (Oxford, Polity, 1989), pp. 149–91.

33. Chalmers Johnson, *MITI and the Japanese Miracle: The Growth of Industrial Policy, 1925–1975* (Stanford, Stanford University Press, 1982); Karel van Wolferen, *The Enigma of Japanese Power* (New York, Knopf, 1989); Michio Muramatsu and Ellis Krauss, "The Conservative Party Line and the Development of Patterned Pluralism," in Yamamura and Yasuba, *Political Economy of Japan*, 1:516–54; Inoguchi Takashi, *Nihon seiji keizai no kōzu* [The structure of the political economy of contemporary Japan] (Tokyo, Tōyō Keizai Shimbunsha, 1983); Richard J. Samuels, *The Business of the Japanese State: Energy Markets in Comparative and Historical Perspective* (Ithaca, Cornell University Press, 1987); Kent Calder, *Crisis and Compensation: Public Policy and Political Stability in Japan, 1949–1986* (Princeton, Princeton University Press, 1988).

34. Thus, a sequence of polls in 1995 taken in both countries showed that each had come to view the other more as an "adversary and competitor" than as an "ally and partner" (76 percent versus 19 percent for the United States; 50 percent versus 40 percent for Japan). Original polls by *Wall Street Journal* and *Nihon Keizai Shimbun*, March 1995, as reported in Everett Carll Ladd and Karlyn H. Bowman, *Public Opinion in America and Japan: How We See Each Other* (Washington, D.C., American Enterprise Institute, 1996), p. 29.

35. For a popular rendition of such views, see "The Compass Swings," *Economist*, July 13, 1996.

1. Patterns of Political Economy: A Range of Regimes

1. Peter Calvert, ed., *The Process of Political Succession* (London, Macmillan, 1987); Stephanie Lawson, "Conceptual Issues on the Comparative Study of Regime Change and Democratization," *Comparative Politics* 25, 2 (January 1993): 185.

2. Cf. Calvert: "a regime is the name usually given to a government or sequence of governments in which power remains essentially in the hands of the same social group." *Process of Political Succession*, p. 18.

3. This point is excellently made in Gøsta Esping-Andersen, *Politics against Markets* (Princeton, Princeton University Press, 1985). Esping-Andersen demonstrates how single-party rule in Sweden allowed the SAP not only to universalize benefits through its social welfare policies but also to forge a coalition between blue-collar and white-collar workers and thereby strengthen the party's electoral base.

4. Joel Kreiger, *Reagan, Thatcher and the Politics of Decline* (Oxford, Oxford University Press, 1986).

5. Peter J. Katzenstein, *Small States in World Markets: Industrial Policy in Europe* (Ithaca, Cornell University Press, 1985).

6. Goran Therborn, "'Pillarization' and 'Popular Movements': Two Variants of Welfare State Capitalism: The Netherlands and Sweden," in Francis G. Castles, ed., *Comparative History of Public Policy* (Oxford, Polity, 1989), pp. 192–241.

7. Fred Block, "Political Choice and the Multiple 'Logics' of Capital," *Theory and Society* 15 (1986): 182.

8. Francis G. Castles, *The Social Democratic Image of Society* (London, Routledge, 1978), pp. 118–31.

9. E. E. Schattschneider, *The Semi-Sovereign People: A Realist View of Democracy in America* (New York, Rhinehart and Winston, 1960).

10. Bob Jessop, "Regulation Theories in Retrospect and Prospect," *Economy and Society* 19, 2 (1990): 153–216.

11. Yamaguchi Yasushi, *Seiji taisei* [Political regimes] (Tokyo, Tokyo Daigaku Shuppankai, 1989).

12. Michael Shalev, *Labor and the Political Economy of Israel* (Oxford, Oxford University Press, 1992), p. 333.

13. Thomas S. Kuhn, *The Structure of Scientific Revolutions* (Chicago, University of Chicago Press, 1962, 1970). For similar usages see also Herbert Kitschelt, "Political Regime Change: Structure and Process-Driven Explanation?" *American Political Science Review* 86, 4 (1992): 1028–34; David Easton, *A Systems Analysis of Political Life* (New York, John Wiley, 1965), p. 193; Steven Elkin, "Pluralism in Its Place," in Roger Benjamin and Steven Elkin, *The Democratic State* (Lawrence, University Press of Kansas, 1985), p. 180.

The usage here also is congruent with that which prevails in the study of international relations. My concern is with continuities and discontinuities in the political, economic, and social biases within single countries; thus it is largely concerned with "domestic" or "comparative" politics. In international relations, by way of contrast, the notion of regime has been appropriated most recently to particular sets of formal agreements, norms, customs, institutions, and beliefs commonly accepted by a group of nation-states when dealing with specific problem areas such as trade, monetary regimes, the environment, security, and the like. Nonetheless, both usages of the term share an underlying assumption about the regularization and institutionalization of patterns of behavior and the expectation of consistency in conduct. A classic statement about the nature of regimes within international relations is that of Stephen D. Krasner, *International Regimes* (Ithaca, Cornell University Press, 1983). See also Oran R. Young, "International Regimes: Toward a New Theory of Institutions," *World Politics* 39, 1 (1986): 104–22.

14. The term "primordial" is that of Arendt Lijphart, "Religious vs. Linguistic vs. Class Voting: The 'Crucial Experiment' of Comparing Belgium, Canada, South Africa, and Switzerland," *American Political Science Review* 73, 2 (1979): 442–58. "Segmental cleavages" is from Scott C. Flannagan, "Models and Methods of Analysis," in Gabriel A. Almond et al., *Crisis, Choice and Change: Historical Studies of Political Development* (Boston, Little, Brown, 1973), pp. 43–102.

15. Gerschenkron, *Bread and Democracy in Germany* (Berkeley, University of California Press, 1943).

16. Barrington Moore, Jr., *Social Origins of Dictatorship and Democracy* (Boston, Beacon, 1966); Dietrich Rueschemeyer, Evelyne Huber Stephens, and John D. Stephens, *Capitalist Development and Democracy* (Chicago, University of Chicago Press, 1992).

17. Ronald Rogowski, *Commerce and Coalitions: How Trade Affects Domestic Political Alignments* (Princeton, Princeton University Press, 1989). See also his "Trade and the Variety of Democratic Institutions," *International Organization* 41, 2 (1986): 203–23; "Political Cleavages and Changing Exposure to Trade," *American Political Science Review* 81, 4 (1987): 1121–37.

18. Ruth Berins Collier and David Collier, *Shaping the Political Arena* (Princeton, Princeton University Press, 1991).

19. Gregory M. Luebbert, *Liberalism, Fascism, or Social Democracy* (New York, Oxford University Press, 1991); Luebbert, "Social Foundations of Political Order in Interwar Europe," *World Politics* 39, 4 (1987): 449–78.

20. Rogowski, *Commerce and Coalitions*, p. 99.

21. I am using the term "institutions" largely in the sense of formal organizations. In this regard it is analogous to the usage of most political scientists. It is also congruent with that of Oliver E. Williamson, *The Economic Institutions of Capitalism* (New York, Free Press, 1985). I do not use the term to mean broad social norms, as does Douglass C. North in *Institutions, Institutional Change and Economic Performance* (Cambridge, Cambridge University Press, 1990); my usage is closer to what North calls "organizations." My usage also differs from that of Roger Friedland and Robert R. Alford, who define institutions as "supraorganizational patterns of human activity by which individuals and organizations produce and reproduce their material subsistence and organize time and space" ("Bringing Society Back In: Symbols, Practices, and Institutional Contradictions," in Walter W. Powell and Paul J.

DiMaggio, eds., *The New Institutionalism in Organizational Analysis* [Chicago, University of Chicago Press, 1991], p. 232).

22. James G. March and Johan P. Olsen, "The New Institutionalism: Organizational Factors in Political Life," *American Political Science Review* 78, 3 (1984): 741.

23. See Peter Hall, *Governing the Economy: The Politics of State Intervention in Britain and France* (New York, Oxford University Press, 1986); James G. March and Johan P. Olsen, *Rediscovering Institutions* (New York, Free Press, 1989); Powell and DiMaggio, *New Institutionalism in Organizational Analysis;* and Sven Steinmo, Kathleen Thelen, and Frank Longstreth, eds., *Structuring Politics: Historical Institutionalism in Comparative Analysis* (Cambridge, Cambridge University Press, 1992). For a good review of some of the issues raised by these and other works see Thomas A. Koelble, "The New Institutionalism in Political Science and Sociology," *Comparative Politics* 27, 2 (1995): 231–43.

24. This distinction parallels to some extent that made between majoritarian and consensus systems in Arendt Lijphart, *Democracies: Patterns of Majoritarian and Consensus Government in Twenty-one Countries* (New Haven, Yale University Press, 1984).

25. K. J. Scott, *The New Zealand Constitution* (Oxford, Clarendon Press, 1962), p. 39.

26. Anthony King as quoted in Philip Norton, *The British Polity* (New York, Longman, 1994), p. 199.

27. See Michel Albert, *Capitalism vs. Capitalism* (New York, Four Walls Eight Windows, 1993); J. Rogers Hollingsworth, Philippe C. Schmitter, and Wolfgang Streeck, eds., *Governing Capitalist Economies: Performance and Control of Economic Sectors* (Oxford, Oxford University Press, 1994); Peter J. Katzenstein, ed., *Between Power and Plenty* (Madison, University of Wisconsin Press, 1978); and Katzenstein, *Small States in World Markets.*

28. Frans Stokman, N. Rolf Ziegler, and John Scott, eds., *Networks of Corporate Power: A Comparative Analysis of Ten Countries* (London, Polity Press, 1985), provides some sense of the range of variation just within Europe.

29. Based on data in "The Global 500 Ranked Within Countries," *Fortune,* August 5, 1996, pp. F 30–40.

30. See Charles S. Maier, *Changing Boundaries of the Political* (Cambridge, Cambridge University Press, 1987).

31. Philippe C. Schmitter, "Still the Century of Corporatism?" in Schmitter and Gerhard Lehmbruch, eds., *Trends toward Corporatist Intermediation* (Beverley Hills, Sage, 1979), pp. 15, 13. Schmitter's conceptualization of corporatism and pluralism is based fundamentally on the comprehensiveness and exclusivity of interest associations. In contrast, Peter Katzenstein builds from this perspective but stresses the importance for corporatism of an ideology of partnership between business and labor organizations, and among social groups more generally, a politics he labels "low voltage" (*Small States in World Markets,* p. 32).

32. In *Makt og Motiv: Et Festskrift til Jens Arup Seip* (Oslo, Glydendal Norsk Forlag, 1975), p. 217. My thanks to Christine Ingrebritsen for this reference.

33. Theda Skocpol, *Protecting Soldiers and Mothers* (Cambridge, Harvard University Press, 1992).

34. Bo Rothstein, *The Social Democratic State: The Swedish Model and the Bureaucratic Problem of Social Reforms* (Pittsburgh, University of Pittsburgh Press, 1996).

35. Esping-Andersen, *Politics against Markets.*

36. Castles, *Social Democratic Image of Society.*

37. This is not the place to debate the independent role of ideas and ideologies. See, for example, Kathryn Sikkink, *Ideas and Institutions: Developmentalism in Brazil and Argentina* (Ithaca, Cornell University Press, 1991); Judith Goldstein, *Ideas, Interests, and American Trade Policy* (Ithaca, Cornell University Press, 1993); Judith Goldstein and Robert Keohane, eds., *Ideas and Foreign Policy: Beliefs, Institutions and Political Change* (Ithaca, Cornell University Press, 1993). See also the work of Emanuel Adler on epistemic communities and the ongoing work of Peter J. Katzenstein on norms.

38. Weber, "Social Psychology of the World's Religions," in H. H. Gerth and C. Wright Mills, eds., *From Max Weber: Essays in Sociology* (New York, Oxford University Press, 1958), p. 280.

39. Peter A. Hall, "Policy Paradigms, Social Learning, and the State: The Case of Economic Policymaking in Britain," *Comparative Politics* 25, 3 (1993): 279.

40. Emile Durkheim, *The Rules of the Sociological Method,* tr. Sarah A. Solovay and John D. Mueller, ed. George E. G. Catlin (Chicago, University of Chicago Press, 1938), pp. 1061–62. See also Chantal Mouffe, "Hegemony and Ideology in Gramsci," in Tony Bennett et al., eds., *Culture, Ideology and Social Process* (London, Open University, 1987), p. 223.

41. Schattschneider, *Semi-Sovereign People,* p. 66.

42. Hall, *Governing the Economy,* p. 267.

43. In this regard such blocs differ from what Lijphart identifies as consociational systems, where the main socioeconomic divisions are along ethnic, religious, or linguistic lines. Arendt Lijphart, *The Politics of Accommodation* (Berkeley: University of California Press, 1968); "Consociational Democracy," *World Politics* 21 (October 1968). See also Kenneth D. McRae, ed., *Consociational Democracies: Political Accommodation in Segmented Societies* (Toronto, McClelland and Stewart, 1974).

44. Katzenstein, *Small States in World Markets;* Philippe C. Schmitter, "Still the Century of Corporatism?" and "Interest Intermediation and Regime Governability in Contemporary Western Europe and North America," in Schmitter and Lehmbruch, *Trends toward Corporatist Intermediation.*

45. Jonas Pontusson, "Comparative Political Economy of Advanced States: Sweden and France," *Kapitalistate* 10 (1983): 57.

46. Hugh Heclo and Henrik Madsen, *Policy and Politics in Sweden: Principled Pragmatism* (Philadelphia, Temple University Press, 1987), p. 11.

47. Gøsta Esping-Andersen, "Single-Party Dominance in Sweden: The Saga of Social Democracy," in T. J. Pempel, ed., *Uncommon Democracies: The One Party Dominant Regimes* (Ithaca, Cornell University Press, 1990), p. 41.

48. Esping-Andersen, "Single-Party Dominance in Sweden," pp. 33–57.

49. A contradictory focus on the role of capital in the establishment of these networks is found in Peter Swenson, "Bringing Capital Back In or Democracy Reconsidered," *World Politics* 43, 4 (1991): 513–32.

50. Jelle Visser, "The Strength of Union Movements in Advanced Capital Democracies: Social and Organizational Variations," in Marino Regini, ed., *The Future of Labor Movements* (London, Sage, 1992), p. 19.

51. Katzenstein, *Small States in World Markets,* pp. 113–15.

52. Joachim Israel, "Swedish Socialism and Big Business," *Acta Sociologica* 21, 4 (1978): 346. On the broader links between Swedish social democracy and business, see Swenson, "Bringing Capital Back In."

53. Andrew Martin has stated the problem succinctly: the "juxtaposition of a capitalist economy and a powerful labor movement renders the country especially vulnerable to distributive conflict between capital and labor. It places a high premium on managing that conflict so that foreign demand is not jeopardized" ("Wages, Profits, and Investment in Sweden," in Leon N. Lindberg and Charles S. Maier, eds., *The Politics of Inflation and Economic Stagnation* [Washington, Brookings, 1985], p. 403).

54. OECD, *Historical Statistics: 1960–1986* (Paris, OECD, 1988), p. 64.

55. See Goran Therborn, *Why Some Peoples Are More Unemployed Than Others* (London, Verso, 1986); David Cameron, "Social Democracy, Corporatism, Labor Quiescence and the Representation of Economic Interest in Advanced Capitalist Society," in John Goldthorpe, ed., *Order and Conflict in Contemporary Capitalism* (Cambridge, Cambridge University Press, 1984), pp. 143–78.

56. Peter Swenson, *Fair Shares: Unions, Pay, and Politics in Sweden and West Germany* (Ithaca, Cornell University Press, 1989).

57. Heclo and Madsen, *Policy and Politics in Sweden*, pp. 72–73.

58. See Robert H. Salisbury, "Why No Corporatism in America?" in Schmitter and Lehmbruch, *Trends toward Corporatist Intermediation*, pp. 213–30. Graham Wilson, "Why is There No Corporatism in the U.S.?" in Gerhard Lehmbruch and Philippe C. Schmitter, *Patterns of Corporatist Policy-Making* (Beverley Hills, Sage, 1982); Theodore Lowi, *The End of Liberalism* (New York, Norton, 1969).

59. Lowi, *End of Liberalism;* Grant McConnell, *Private Power and American Democracy* (New York, Knopf, 1966).

60. Paul R. Abramson, "Comparative Presidential Elections in the United States and Korea" (paper delivered at the seventeenth world congress of the International Political Science Association, Seoul, Korea, August 17–21, 1997), p. 7.

61. Robert R. Alford, *Party and Society* (Chicago, Rand-McNally, 1963).

62. Thomas Risse-Kapen, "Public Opinion, Domestic Structure, and Foreign Policy in Liberal Democracies," *World Politics* 43, 4 (1991): 490–91.

63. James Q. Wilson, *Bureaucracy: What Government Agencies Do and Why They Do It* (New York, Basic, 1989), pp. 197–98.

64. Hugh Heclo, *A Government of Strangers: Executive Politics in Washington* (Washington, D.C., Brookings, 1977).

65. Thomas Ferguson, "From Normalcy to New Deal: Industrial Structure, Party Competition, and American Public Policy in the Great Depression," *International Organization* 38, 1 (1984): 42.

66. Ibid., p. 46.

67. Peter Gourevitch, *Politics in Hard Times: Comparative Responses to International Economic Crises* (Ithaca, Cornell University Press, 1986), chap. 4.

68. Ferguson, "From Normalcy to New Deal," pp. 93–94.

69. The term is that of Samuel Bowles and Herbert Gintis, "The Crisis of Liberal Democratic Capitalism: The Case of the United States," *Politics and Society* 11, 1 (1982): 51–93.

70. Richard E. Neustadt, *Presidential* Power (New York, Wiley, 1960); Sven Steinmo, "Political Institutions and Tax Policy," *World Politics* 41, 4 (1989): 528.

71. Samuel Beer, *British Politics in the Collectivist Age,* 2d ed. (New York, Norton, 1982), p. 408.

72. Simon Mohun, "Continuity and Change in State Economic Intervention," in Allan Cochrane and James Anderson, eds., *Restructuring Britain: Politics in Transition* (London, Sage, 1989), p. 73.

73. I owe this phrase to P. A. Allum, *Italy—Republic without Government?* (New York, Norton, 1973).

74. Sidney Tarrow, "Maintaining Hegemony in Italy: The Softer They Rise the Slower They Fall," in Pempel, *Uncommon Democracies*, p. 330.

75. Gianfranco Pasquino, "Unregulated Regulators: Parties and Party Government," in Peter Lange and Marino Regini, eds., *State, Market, and Social Regulation: New Perspectives on Italy* (Cambridge, Cambridge University Press, 1989), p. 34; Richard S. Katz, "Party Government: A Rationalistic Conception," in Francis G. Castles and Rudolf Wildenmann, eds., *The Future of Party Government*, vol. 1, *Visions and Realities of Party Government* (Berlin, deGruyter, 1986), pp. 31–71.

76. Alan R. Posner, "Italy: Dependence and Political Fragmentation," in Katzenstein, *Power and Plenty*, p. 244.

77. Tarrow, "Maintaining Hegemony in Italy," p. 319.

78. Richard J. Samuels, "Great Forces and Great Choices: Italy and Japan in Comparative Perspective" (paper delivered at the annual meeting of the American Political Science Association, San Francisco, August 29–September 1, 1996).

79. Posner, "Italy: Dependence and Political Fragmentation," pp. 238–39.

80. Tarrow, "Maintaining Hegemony in Italy," p. 320.

81. Michael J. Piore and Charles F. Sabel, *The Second Industrial Divide: Possibilities for Prosperity* (New York, Basic, 1984), p. 177.

82. Richard Locke, "*Eppure Si Tocca: The Abolition of Scala Mobile*," in Carol Mershon and Gianfranco Pasquino, eds., *Italian Politics: Ending the First Republic* (Boulder, Westview, 1995), p. 187.

83. Richard Locke, *Remaking the Italian Economy* (Ithaca, Cornell University Press, 1995), p. 23.

84. Michael Shalev, "The Resurgence of Labor Quiescence," in Marino Regini, ed., *The Future of Labor Movements* (London, Sage, 1992), p. 105.

85. F. Roy Willis, *Italy Chooses Europe* (New York, Oxford University Press, 1971), p. 88.

86. Sabino Cassesse, "The Higher Civil Service in Italy," in Ezra Suleiman, ed., *Bureaucrats and Policymaking* (New York, Holmes and Meier, 1984), p. 45.

87. "A Survey of Italy," *Economist*, May 26, 1990, p. 12.

88. Michele Salvati, "The Crisis of Government in Italy," *New Left Review*, no. 213 (September/October 1995): 81.

2. Japan in the 1960s: Conservative Politics and Economic Growth

1. In one of the great ironies of the Olympics, the film as produced by Ichikawa was seen only once in its entirety—by the Olympic Organizing Committee, one of whose members, parliamentarian Kōno Ichirō, was severely disappointed with the film for being too artistic and insufficiently documentary. Beverley Bare Buehrer, *Japanese Films: A Filmography and Commentary, 1921–1989* (Jefferson, N.C., McFarland, 1990), pp. 185–87.

2. JNR President Sōgō Shinji announced the opening of the line, with its wide-gauge tracks, at the grave of Gotō Shimpei, former president of the Southern Manchurian Railroad. The location was all highly symbolic because Gotō and others had long advocated the use of narrow-gauge tracks for Japanese railroads as a means of preventing them from being taken over and used by any enemy forces, all of whom used wide tracks. Yutaka Kosai, *The Era of High-Speed Growth: Notes on the Postwar Japanese Economy* (Tokyo, University of Tokyo Press, 1986), p. 154.

3. Paul H. Noguchi, *Delayed Departures, Overdue Arrivals: Industrial Familism and the Japanese National Railroad* (Honolulu, University of Hawaii Press, 1990), p. 31.

4. Herman Kahn and Thomas Pepper, *The Japanese Challenge: The Success and Failure of Economic Success* (New York, Crowell, 1979), pp. 133–34.

5. This was a growth rate of 7.6 percent annually, in contrast to a 3.5 percent growth rate from 1870 to 1913 and only a 1.3 percent growth from 1913 to 1950. Angus Maddison, *Economic Growth in the West: Comparative Experience in Europe and North America* (New York, Twentieth Century Fund, 1964).

6. The shift was not unbroken. For two years during the late 1960s (1967 and 1968) and also for three years following the rapid jump in oil prices (1973, 1974, and 1975), Japan's export totals fell below that of its total imports. Nevertheless, the broad trend shifted from trade deficit to trade surplus in 1964.

7. Yoshikazu Miyazaki, "Excessive Competition and the Formation of *Keiretsu*," in Kazuo Sato, ed., *Industry and Business in Japan* (Armonk, N.Y., M. E. Sharpe, 1980), pp. 53–54.

8. *Nihon tōkei nenkan* [Japan statistical yearbook] (Tokyo, Prime Minister's Office, various years).

9. From *Automotive News*, various issues as cited in Herman Schwartz, *States versus Markets: History, Geography, and the Development of the International Political Economy* (New York, St. Martin's, 1994), p. 255. By 1980 the share had risen to 34 percent.

10. Nihon Kokusei Zue, *Suji de miru: Nihon no Hyakunen* [One hundred years of Japanese statistics] (Tokyo, Kokusei Zue, 1981), p. 167.

11. Kenneth Flamm, *Creating the Computer* (Washington, D.C., Brookings Institution, 1988), p. 187. See also Marie Anchordoguy, *Computers, Inc.: Japan's Challenge to IBM* (Cambridge, Harvard University Press, 1989). It is worth noting that despite the successes of several Japanese firms, in the same year, 1964, IBM still held a massive technological edge as it introduced its IBM 360 line using integrated circuitry.

12. Kosai, *Era of High Speed Growth*, p. 120.

13. Data based on Anchordoguy, *Computers, Inc.*, pp. 34–35.

14. In contrast see Scott Callon, *Divided Sun: MITI and the Breakdown of Japanese High-Tech Industrial Policy* (Stanford, Stanford University Press, 1995).

15. The law had first been introduced in the 43d Diet, which ran from late 1962 into the mid-1963, and was also introduced in the 44th Diet (October 23–December 23, 1963).

16. Chalmers Johnson, *MITI and the Japanese Miracle* (Stanford, Stanford University Press, 1982), pp. 255–67.

17. Hugh T. Patrick and Henry Rosovsky, eds., *Asia's New Giant: How the Japanese Economy Works* (Washington, Brookings Institution, 1976), p. 76.

18. Michael W. Donnelly, "Setting the Price of Rice," in T. J. Pempel, ed., *Policymaking in Contemporary Japan* (Ithaca, Cornell University Press, 1977), pp. 143–200.

19. Robert M. Uriu, *Troubled Industries: Confronting Economic Change in Japan* (Ithaca, Cornell University Press, 1996), p. 72.

20. Ibid., p. 71. See also H. Richard Friman, *Patchwork Protectionism: Textile Policy in the United States, Japan and West Germany* (Ithaca, Cornell University Press, 1988).

21. Richard Samuels, *The Business of the Japanese State: Energy Markets in Comparative and Historical Perspective* (Ithaca, Cornell University Press, 1987), pp. 68–134; Hayden S. Lesbirel, "Structural Adjustment in Japan: Terminating 'Old King Coal,'" *Asian Survey* 31, 11 (1991): 1079–94. Uriu, *Troubled Industries*, pp. 95–102.

22. See Uriu, *Troubled Industries;* Mark Tilton, *Restrained Trade: Cartels in Japan's Basic Materials Industry* (Ithaca, Cornell University Press, 1996).

23. Rōdōshō, *Tōkei Jōhōbū, Rōdō kumiai kihon chōsa* [Basic survey of trade unions] (Tokyo, Ōkurashō Insatsukyoku, annual).

24. On several of these indicators, various years before or after 1964 were slightly higher; but, overall, 1964 was perhaps the most tumultuous single year when all of the statistics are seen in conjunction. Regardless, the central point is that the year was one in which labor-management relations were at a low ebb.

25. Nevertheless, it was not until the 1976 election that the combined seat total of the LDP and the JSP in the lower house fell below 75 percent.

26. Yamaguchi Yasushi, "Sengo Nihon no seiji taisei to seiji katei" [The political system and the political processes of postwar Japan], in Miyake Ichiro et al., *Nihon seiji no zahyō* [The coordinates of Japanese politics] (Tokyo, Yūhikaku, 1985), p. 97.

27. Beverley Smith, "Democracy Derailed: Citizens' Movements in Historical Perspective," in Gavan McCormack and Yoshio Sugimoto, eds., *Democracy in Contemporary Japan* (Armonk, N.Y., M. E. Sharpe, 1986), p. 164.

28. Muramatsu Michio, Itō Mitsutoshi, and Tsujinaka Yutaka, Nihon no Seiji [Japanese politics] (Tokyo, Yūhikaku, 1992), pp. 122–23. The 1972 election for the lower house was the only possibly noteworthy reversal during this period, when the JSP vote total rose from 19.4 to 21.9 percent; in 1983 it also rose (from 20.9 to 21.9 percent), but overall the trend was clearly down, dropping from 29.0 percent of the vote (and 30.8 percent of the seats) in 1963 to 17.2 percent of the vote and 16.8 percent of the seats in 1986. Only in 1990 did a real reversal take place, with a jump to 24.4 percent of the vote and 26.6 percent of the seats.

29. Seizaburo Satō and Tetsuhisa Matsuzaki, *Jimintō seiken* [The LDP regime] (Tokyo, Chūō Kōronsha, 1986), p. 360.

30. *Journal of the Social and Political Ideas of Japan*, 3, 2 (1965): 52, as cited in Kenneth Pyle, *The Japan Question* (Washington, AEI, 1992), p. 28.

31. Walter LaFeber, "Decline of Relations during the Vietnam War," in Akira Iriye and Warren I. Cohen, eds., *The U.S. and Japan in the Postwar World* (Lexington, University of Kentucky Press, 1989), p. 97.

32. Richard J. Samuels, *"Rich Nation, Strong Army: National Security and the Technological Transformation of Japan"* (Ithaca, Cornell University Press, 1994); Michael Green, *Rearming Japan* (New York, Columbia University Press, 1996). Both authors deal with Japan's long-standing efforts to develop and to indigenize international technologies.

33. Ōtake Hideo, "Hatoyama-Kishi Jidai ni okeru 'Chiisai Seifu' Ron" [An essay on 'small government' during the Hatoyama-Kishi period], in Nihon Seiji Gakkai, ed., *Sengo kokka no keisei to keizai hatten: Senryō igo* [Postwar state structure and economic development: From the occupation onward] (Tokyo, Iwanami Shoten, 1992), pp. 165–85.

34. David S. Landes, "Japan and Europe: Contrasts in Industrialization," in William W. Lockwood, ed., *The State and Economic Enterprise in Japan* (Princeton, Princeton University Press, 1965), p. 153.

35. James Horne, *Japan's Financial Markets: Conflict and Consensus in Policymaking* (Sydney, George Allen and Unwin, 1985), p. 144.

36. Dennis Encarnation, *Rivals beyond Trade: America versus Japan in Global Competition* (Ithaca, Cornell University Press, 1992), pp. 49–50.

37. Lawrence B. Krause, "Evolution of Foreign Direct Investment: The United States and Japan," in Jerome Cohen, ed., *Pacific Partnership: United States–Japan Trade—Prospects and Recommendations for the Seventies* (New York, Japan Society and Lexington Books, 1972), p. 164.

38. The exceptions most worth noting were the yen-based companies that invested early even though profits could not be repatriated to the home country.

39. Mark Mason, *American Multinationals and Japan: The Political Economy of Japanese Capital Controls, 1899–1980* (Cambridge, Harvard University Press, 1992), pp. 193, 197.

40. Itō Motoshige, *Sangyōseisaku no keizai bunseki* [An economic analysis of industrial policy] (Tokyo, University of Tokyo Press, 1991), p. 22.

41. See *Kokusei Zue* annual for specific figures. While most of the major industrial countries had imports made up of approximately 50–65 percent manufactured goods, Japan in the mid-1970s had only 30 percent. Meanwhile, no other country came close to Japan's 95 percent manufacturing exports.

42. This point was particularly interesting in the case of Texas Instruments, which concluded an agreement on licensing technology for semiconductors that prevented any single Japanese firm from monopolizing the technology. See "TI Gives in to Tokyo," *Business Week*, January 27, 1968, p. 132.

43. Slightly different figures and calculations, but with the same thrust are given in Krause, "Evolution of Foreign Direct Investment," pp. 166–68.

44. This process worked through the Foreign Investment and Loan Program (FILP). Yukio Noguchi, "The Role of the Fiscal Investment and Loan Program in Postwar Japanese Economic Growth," in Hyung-ki Kim, Michio Muramatsu, T. J. Pempel, and Kozo Yamamura, eds., *The Japanese Civil Service and Economic Development: Catalysts of Change* (Oxford, Oxford University Press, 1995), pp. 261–87; Kent E. Calder, "Linking Welfare and the Developmental State: Postal Savings in Japan," *Journal of Japanese Studies* 16, 1 (1990): 31–60; Hiromitsu Ishi, "The Fiscal investment and Loan Program and Public Enterprise," in Tokue Shibata, ed., *Japan's Public Sector: How the Government Is Financed* (Tokyo, University of Tokyo Press, 1993), pp. 82–102.

45. One survey of top Japanese business leaders in the mid-1960s showed this homogeneity and the congruity with national bureaucrats; 90 percent were university graduates, and of these fully eighty-five percent graduated from just six universities; most had served with their companies for virtually their entire occupational lives. Yoshimatsu Aonuma,

"Business Leadership in Japan," *Bessatsu Chūō Kōron,* spring 1963, pp. 298–307, as translated in *Journal of Social and Political Ideas in Japan* 3, 3 (1965): 54–60. On the broader point of economic nationalism, see Noguchi Yuichiro, *Nihon no keizai nashonarizumu* [Japanese economic nationalism] (Tokyo, Diyamondosha, 1976), esp. chap. 1.

46. Charles P. Kindleberger, *Power and Money* (New York, Basic Books, 1970), p. 120.

47. The distinction is spelled out in great detail by John Zysman in *Governments, Markets, and Growth: Financial Systems and the Politics of Industrial Change* (Ithaca, Cornell University Press, 1983), pp. 35–42; see also John Zysman and Stephen Cohen, "Double or Nothing: Open Trade and Competitive Industry," *Foreign Affairs,* summer 1983, pp. 1113–39.

48. Kōsei Torihiki Iinkai, *Kōsei torihiki iinkai nenji hōkoku* [Annual report of the Japan Fair Trade Commission] (Tokyo, Ōkurasho Insatsukyoku, 1975), p. 177.

49. Nihon Kokusei Zue, 1976, pp. 414, 416.

50. Japan Steel (Nippon Seitetsu) was a single firm that under the U.S. occupation had been broken up into Yawata and Fuji. Hence the postwar merger was in fact a reconsolidation.

51. Samuels, *Business of the Japanese State,* esp. chap. 1.

52. Koichi Hamada and Akiyoshi Horiuchi, "The Political Economy of the Financial Market," in Kozo Yamamura and Yasukichi Yasuba, eds., *The Political Economy of Japan,* vol. 1 (Stanford, Stanford University Press, 1987), p. 233.

53. Imamura Shigekazu, *Gyōseihō Nyūmon: Shimpan* [Introduction to administrative law: Revised edition] (Tokyo, Yūhikaku, 1975); Frank K. Upham, *Law and Social Change in Postwar Japan* (Cambridge, Harvard University Press, 1987), chap. 5.

54. A useful discussion of these linkage effects is George C. Eads and Kozo Yamamura, "The Future of Industrial Policy," in Yamamura and Yasuba, *Political Economy of Japan,* 1:424–29.

55. T. J. Pempel, "Japanese Foreign Economic Policy: The Domestic Bases for International Behavior," in Peter J. Katzenstein, ed., *Between Power and Plenty* (Madison, University of Wisconsin Press, 1978), pp. 139–90.

56. See Samuels, "Rich Nation, Strong Army," pp. 324–26.

57. Richard Rosecrance, *The Rise of the Trading State: Commerce and Conquest in the Modern World* (New York, Basic Books, 1986).

58. Nihon Kokusei Zue, *Suji De Miru,* pp. 344–45, 350–51.

59. Initially, the figure was 50 percent; in 1967 it was raised to 80 percent of income derived from exports.

60. Yoichi Okita, "Japan's Fiscal Incentives for Exports," in Isiah Frank, ed., *The Japanese Economy in International Perspective* (Baltimore, Johns Hopkins University Press, 1975), p. 226.

61. Ogawa Kunihiko, *Kuroi keizai kyōryoku* [Dirty economic aid] (Tokyo, Shimpō Shinsho, 1974), elaborates on some of the more sordid arrangements worked out in conjunction with reparations.

62. The classic study on the budget in English is John Creighton Campbell, *Contemporary Japanese Budget Politics* (Berkeley, University of California Press, 1977).

63. The 1 percent of GNP figure is based on official Japanese calculations, which differ from, and are biased toward lower percentages than, calculations done by NATO. Nonetheless, even by the NATO calculations, Japanese figures are still only about 1.5 percent of GNP.

64. Hugh Patrick and Henry Rosovsky, "Japan's Economic Performance: An Overview," in Patrick and Rosovsky, *Asia's New Giant,* pp. 44–45. Robert Dekle, on the other hand, contends that average growth would have dropped only from 9.29 percent to 8.76 percent, or less that one-half of one percent per year for the period 1961–71. Robert Dekle, "The Relationship between Defense Spending and Economic Performance in Japan," in John H. Makin and Donald C. Hellmann, eds., *Sharing World Leadership? A New Era for America and Japan* (Washington, American Enterprise Institute, 1989), pp. 127–49. A different and much more conservative set of calculations for the period 1970–85 suggests that capital stock

would have decreased by about 17 percent at the end of the period had Japan devoted 3 percent of its GNP to defense, leaving total GNP down about 3 percent after the fifteen-year period. Kar-yiu Wong, "National Defense and Foreign Trade," in Makin and Hellmann, *Sharing World Leadership?* pp. 108–9.

65. The contrast here is most explicitly with the Scandinavian concept of complete citizen entitlement to a variety of social programs. See Gøsta Esping-Andersen, *The Three Worlds of Welfare Capitalism* (Cambridge, Polity Press, 1990). See also Kuniaki Tanabe, "Social Policy in Japan: Building a Welfare State in a Conservative One Dominant Party State," in Michio Muramatsu and Frieder Naschold, eds., *State and Administration in Japan and Germany* (Berlin, DeGruyter, 1997), pp. 107–31.

66. OECD, *Public Expenditure on Income Maintenance Programmes* (Paris, OECD, 1976), pp. 25, 36.

67. John C. Campbell, *How Policies Change: The Japanese Government and the Aging Society* (Princeton, Princeton University Press, 1992), pp. 139–41.

68. Ikuo Kume, "Institutionalizing the Active Labor Market Policy in Japan: A Comparative View," in Kim et al., *Japanese Civil Service,* pp. 312–13.

69. Based on data in *Suji de miru: Nihon no hyakunen* [One hundred years of Japan as seen through statistics] (Tokyo, Kokuseisha, 1991), p. 183.

70. Based on figures in Kazushi Ohkawa and Henry Rosovsky, *Japanese Economic Growth: Trend Acceleration in the Twentieth Century* (Stanford, Stanford University Press, 1973), p. 285.

71. Ibid., pp. 310–11; K. Bieda, *The Structure and Operation of the Japanese Economy* (New York, John Wiley, 1970), p. 259.

72. As a result, the total Japanese farming population dwindled from 14.5 million to slightly less than 6.9 million between 1960 and 1972. By 1970 fewer than 16 percent of the employed population was in farming; by 1980 the figure was just under 10 percent and by 1990 it was 6.3 percent. In addition, from the 1960s onward there was a sharp increase in the proportion of part-time rather than full-time farmers. Kokuseisha, *Nihon Kokusei Zue,* 1993, p. 90.

73. Bieda, *Structure and Operation of the Japanese Economy,* p. 263.

74. Donnelly, "Setting the Price of Rice," p. 148.

75. Michael W. Donnelly, "Conflict over Government Authority and Markets: Japan's Rice Economy," in Ellis S. Krauss, Thomas P. Rohlen, and Patricia G. Steinhoff, eds., *Conflict in Japan* (Honolulu, University of Hawaii Press, 1984), p. 336.

76. Hugh T. Patrick and Thomas P. Rohlen, "Small-Scale Family Enterprises," in Yamamura and Yasuba, *Political Economy of Japan,* 1:332.

77. Tatsurō Uchino, *Japan's Postwar Economy: An Insider's View of Its History and Its Future* (Tokyo, Kodansha, 1978), p. 137.

78. Kobayashi Naoki, "Chūshō kigyō dantai soshikihō no rippō katei" [The policymaking process of the small and medium-sized enterprise law], *Tokyo Daigaku kyōyō gakubu shakaigagu kiyō* [Social Science Bulletin, University of Tokyo] 7 (1958): 1–104.

79. Patrick and Rohlen, "Small-Scale Family Enterprises," p. 367.

80. John Gerard Ruggie, "International Regimes, Transactions, and Change: Embedded Liberalism in the Postwar Economic Order," in Stephen D. Krasner, ed., *International Regimes* (Ithaca, Cornell University Press, 1983), pp. 195–232. See also Ronald Rogowski, *Commerce and Coalitions: How Trade Affects Domestic Political Alignments* (Princeton, Princeton University Press, 1989).

81. Dekle, "Defense Spending and Economic Performance," p. 139.

82. Patrick and Rohlen, for example, suggest an implicit political exchange between the LDP and the small family enterprises: "support us and we won't tax you" ("Small-Scale Family Enterprises," p. 367). At the same time, it is useful to recognize that small firms became even more central targets of governmental policies in the early to mid-1970s, with numerous expansions in subsidies, loan guarantees and the like. Kent Calder, *Crisis and Compensation:*

Public Policy and Political Stability in Japan, 1949–1986 (Princeton, Princeton University Press, 1988), chap. 7.

83. Calder, *Crisis and Compensation*, pp. 234–35.

84. Donnelly, "Conflict over Government Authority and Markets," p. 336.

85. On the development of the Japanese civil service, see Bernard Silberman, *Cages of Reason* (Chicago, University of Chicago Press, 1993); Tsuji Kiyoaki, *Nihon kanryōsei no kenkyū* [A study of the Japanese bureaucratic system] (Tokyo, Tokyo University Press, 1969); Itō Daiichi, *Gendai Nihon kanryōsei no bunseki* [An analysis of the contemporary Japanese bureaucratic system] (Tokyo, Tokyo Daigaku Shuppankai, 1980); Muramatsu Michio, *Sengo Nihon no Kanryōsei* [The postwar Japanese bureaucratic system] (Tokyo, Tōyō Keizai, 1981); Kim et al., *Japanese Civil Service*.

86. This level of competition continued to grow from 11.1 persons per position in 1964 to a high of 42.7 in 1978. Japan, National Personnel Authority, *Annual Report* (Tokyo, NPA, annual).

87. Steven K. Vogel, *Freer Markets, More Rules: Regulatory Reform in Advanced Industrial Countries* (Ithaca, Cornell University Press, 1996), p. 202.

88. This statement is based on the restrictions surrounding the creation of various kōekihōjin in Japan, most of which involve either explicit governmental legislation, funding, or permission to develop. On the broader powers endemic to bureaucratic licensing in Japan, see Yul Sohn, "Institutionalizing Japanese-Style Regulation: The Rise and Development of the Licensing System," in Lonny E. Carlile and Mark Tilton, eds., *Regulation and Regulatory Reform in Japan: Are Things Changing?* (Washington, D.C., Brookings Institution, 1998).

89. Thomas F. Cargill and Shoichi Royama, "The Evolution of Japanese Banking and Finance," in George G. Kaufman, ed., *Banking Structures in Major Countries* (Boston, Kluwer Academic, 1992), p. 345.

90. "Reforming Japan's Finance Ministry, Or Not, as the Case May Be," *Economist*, August 10–16, 1996, p. 58.

91. Yukio Noguchi, "The Role of the Fiscal Investment and Loan Program in Postwar Japanese Economic Growth," in Kim et al., *Japanese Civil Service*, p. 269.

92. Abe Hitoshi, Shindo Muneyuki and Kawato Tadafumi, *Gendai Nihon no Seiji* [Contemporary Japanese politics] (Tokyo, Tokyo Daigaku Shuppankai, 1992), pp. 49–50.

93. Gyōsei Kanri Kenkyū Sentaa, *Gyōsei kanri yōran 1980* [Outline of administration and management, 1980] (Tokyo, Gyōsei Kanri Kenkyū Sentaa, 1980), pp. 26–27. On these public policy companies, see also Chalmers Johnson, *Japan's Public Policy Companies* (Washington, AEI, 1977).

94. See Leonard H. Lynn and Timothy J. McKeown, *Organizing Business: Trade Associations in America and Japan* (Washington, AEI, 1988), p. 92.

95. An excellent study of the ways in which the diverse specialties, resources, and interests of MITI and MOF were blended for coherent national purposes is Masaru Mabuchi, "Financing Japanese Industry: The Interplay between the Financial and Industrial Bureaucracies," in Kim et al., *Japanese Civil Service*, pp. 288–310.

96. Chūshō Kigyōshō, *Chūshō kigyōshō hakusho 1969* [White paper on small and medium-sized industry 1969] (Tokyo, Okurasho Insatsukyoku, 1969), chap. 1; note also that a large proportion of the smaller firms have no regular employees, being run by self-employed persons carrying out their businesses with unsalaried family help, if at all.

97. Koike Kazuo, "Josetsu: Howaitokara-ka kumiai moderu" [Introduction: A model of the white-collarized union], in Nihon Rōdōkyōkai, ed., *Hachijūnendai no rōshi kankei* [Labor relations in the 1980s] (Tokyo, Nihon Rōdōkyōkai, 1983); see also his *Nihon no jukuren* [Skill formation in Japan] (Tokyo, Yūhikaku, 1981).

98. Robert C. Wood, "Japan's Multitier Wage System," *Forbes*, August 18, 1980, pp. 53–58.

99. Ibid., pp. 58.

100. Nihon Seisansei Hombu, *Sanka jidai no rōshi kankei: Rōshi kankei seido jittai chōsa hōkoku* [Industrial relations in the age of participation: A report on practices within the industrial relations system] (Tokyo, Nihon Seisansei Hombu, 1973), p. 43.

101. K. Bieda (*Structure and Operation of the Japanese Economy*, p. 203) notes only the United Africa and Swiss Trading Corporations, both based in South Africa, and the Société Générale in Belgium.

102. On the trading companies, see M. Y. Yoshino and Thomas B. Lifson, *The Invisible Link: Japan's Sogo Shosha and the Organization of Trade* (Cambridge, MIT Press, 1986); also Alexander Young, *The Sogo Shosha: Japan's Multinational Trading Companies* (Boulder, Westview, 1978).

103. Hamada and Horiuchi, "The Political Economy of the Financial Market," p. 233.

104. For a diversity of such schemes see Rodney Clark, *The Japanese Company* (New Haven, Yale University Press, 1971), pp. 73–87; Eleanor Hadley, *Antitrust in Japan* (Princeton, Princeton University Press, 1970), pp. 301–15; and Michael Gerlach, *Alliance Capitalism: The Social Organization of Japanese Business* (Berkeley, University of California Press, 1992), p. 67.

105. On the Japanese main bank system see Masahiko Aoki and Hugh Patrick, eds., *The Japanese Main Bank System: Its Relevance for Developing and Transforming Economies* (Oxford, Oxford University Press, 1995).

106. The latter figure is from *Fortune*, July 15, 1991, p. 76.

107. R. Taggart Murphey, "Power without Purpose: The Crisis of Japan's Global Finance Dominance," *Harvard Business Review*, March–April 1989, p. 72.

108. This distinction follows that of Gerlach, *Alliance Capitalism*, pp. 68–69.

109. Daniel Okimoto and Thomas P. Rohlen, *Inside the Japanese System: Readings on Contemporary Society and Political Economy* (Stanford, Stanford University Press, 1988), pp. 83–84.

110. Based on Bolitho, *Japan: An Economic Survey, 1953–1973* (London, Oxford University Press, 1975), pp. 27, 28.

111. Ronald Dore, *Flexible Rigidities: Industrial Policy and Structural Adjustment in the Japanese Economy, 1970–80* (Stanford, Stanford University Press, 1986), pp. 72–85.

112. Michael J. Piore and Charles F. Sabel, *The Second Industrial Divide* (New York, Basic Books, 1984), p. 225.

113. Data from Yutaka Tsujinaka, "Interest Group Basis of Japanese Global Leadership" (paper presented at the conference of SSRC/JSPS Global Leadership Sharing Project, Kapalua, Maui, Hawaii, January 4–6, 1996).

114. See Lynn and McKeown, *Organizing Business*, esp. chaps. 2, 4, 5.

115. On FEO, see Sumitani Mikio, "Keidanren," in Asahi Jaanaru, ed., *Nihon no kyōdai soshiki* [Japan's large organizations] (Tokyo, Keisōsha, 1966), pp. 70–89; Akimoto Hideo, *Keidanren* [The Federation of Economic Organizations] (Tokyo, Setsugesho, 1968); Yomiuri Shimbun, *Zaikai* [The financial world] (Tokyo, Yomiuri Shimbunsha, 1972), esp. pp. 9–93.

116. It is useful to note that segments of organized agriculture also provide regular support for various opposition parties, most notably Zennichinō for the JSP and Zennō for the DSP. For the most part, however, these are relatively small bodies compared to Nōkyō.

117. Donnelly, "Conflict over Government Authority and Markets," p. 343.

118. Ibid., p. 343. The laws under which these links are maintained include the Basic Law on Agriculture, the Basic Law concerning the Central Bank for Agriculture and Forestry, the Livestock Price Stabilization Law, the Law for the Stabilization of Stockfeed Demand and Supply, and the Law for the Promotion of Dairy Farming. On these see Aurelia George, "Japanese Interest Group Behavior," in J. A. A. Stockwin et al., eds., *Dynamic and Immobilist Politics in Japan* (Honolulu, University of Hawaii Press, 1988), p. 136.

119. On the organization and lobbying efforts of various types of groups see Muramatsu Michio, Itō Mitsutoshi, and Tsujinaka Yutaka, *Sengo Nihon no atsuryoku dantai* [Postwar Japanese interest groups] (Tokyo, Tōyō Keizai Shimbunsha, 1986), esp. chaps. 4–5.

120. Much of this line of thinking traces back to the prewar efforts by political parties in Japan to gain a foothold in policy formation that had been dominated by the combination of oligarchs and bureaucrats and remains central to the thinking behind the "principal-agent" approaches to Japanese politics. On this latter see J. Mark Ramseyer and Frances Rosenbluth, *Japan's Political Marketplace* (Cambridge, Harvard University Press, 1993), chap. 6; also Mathew D. McCubbins and Gregory W. Noble, "The Appearance of Power: Legislators, Bureaucrats, and the Budget Process in the United States and Japan," in Peter F. Cowhey and Mathew D. McCubbins, eds., *Structure and Policy in Japan and the United States* (Cambridge, Cambridge University Press, 1995), pp. 56–80.

121. In this regard I find myself in agreement with Ramseyer and Rosenbluth, *Japan's Political Marketplace,* chap. 6. They argue that "if bureaucrats flout legislative preferences, legislators may reverse those bureaucratic decisions and cut the bureaucrats' discretion and perquisites. . . . Bureaucrats will do what legislators want, but only because legislators will punish them if they do anything else. . . . But bureaucrats know that if they deviate too far from legislative preferences, disgruntled legislators will intervene" (pp. 102–3). At the same time, their analysis treats bureaucrats simply as agents of the LDP. I believe the data and historical experience show that civil servants have considerably more flexibility than is implied in such a treatment.

122. John C. Campbell provides examples in Contemporary Japanese Budget Politics (Berkeley, University of California Press, 1977).

123. One could cite the sustained efforts of the Ministry of Finance to introduce a consumption tax as one such example. Similarly, the overall success of bureaucratic agencies in resisting the "administrative reform" efforts of the early 1960s would also fit. On the former, see Junko Kato, *The Problem of Bureaucratic Rationality* (Princeton, Princeton University Press, 1994); on the latter, see Ōta Kaoru, *Yakunin o kiru* [Cut down the bureaucrats!] (Tokyo, Tōyō Keizai Shimpōsha, 1973).

124. Joel D. Aberbach, Robert D. Putnam, and Bert A. Rockman, *Bureaucrats and Politicians in Western Democracies* (Cambridge, Harvard University Press, 1981). For a Japanese extension of their argument, see Kubota Akira and Tomita Noboru, "Nihon seifu kōkan no ishiki kōzō" [The structure of consciousness of high government officials in Japan], *Chūō Kōron* 1079 (February 1977): 190–96.

125. As compiled from *Asahi Nenkan,* various years; see also T. J. Pempel, "Uneasy toward Autonomy: Parliament and Parliamentarians in Japan," in Ezra Suleiman, ed., *Parliaments and Parliamentarians in Democratic Politics* (New York, Holmes and Meier, 1986), p. 143, for a complete tabulation through 1983.

126. In addition, one half of Japan's prefectural governors have usually had careers in either the national or the local civil service (my calculations from *Asahi Nenkan* annual).

127. See Takenori Inoki, "Japanese Bureaucrats at Retirement: The Mobility of Human Resources from Central Government to Public Corporations," in Kim et al., *Japanese Civil Service,* pp. 216–17; see also Kent E. Calder, "Elites in an Equalizing Role: Ex-Bureaucrats as Coordinators and Intermediaries in the Japanese Government-Business Relationship," *Comparative Politics* 21, 4 (1989): 379–403.

128. John Owen Haley, *Authority without Power* (New York, Oxford University Press, 1991), p. 160.

129. Fritz W. Scharpf, Crisis and Choice in European Social Democracy (Ithaca, Cornell University Press, 1991), p. 17.

130. Moreover, the members of the LDP's PARC, particularly during the 1960s and into the early 1970s, were disproportionately drawn from the former bureaucratic members of the LDP. See Yamamoto Masao, ed., *Keizai kanryō no jittai: Seisaku kettei no mekanizumu*

[The realities of the economic bureaucracy: The mechanics of policy formation] (Tokyo, Mainichi Shimbunsha, 1972), p. 115.

131. A good example of this concerned the problem of value-added networks in telecommunications. See Chalmers Johnson, "MITI, MPT, and the Telecom Wars: How Japan Makes Policy for High Technology," in Chalmers Johnson, Laura D'Andrea Tyson, and John Zysman, eds., *Policy and Productivity: How Japan's Development Strategy Works* (New York, Harper Business, 1989), pp. 177–244.

132. Particularly perplexing are suggestions that any identification of bureaucratic power in Japan implies that legislative officials have thereby "abdicated" power. This not only misses the reality of the close bureaucratic-political interactions in Japan but also creates a straw man that ignores the powers of the Japanese bureaucracy in comparison either to the Japanese parliament or to bureaucracies in other countries. See Matthew D. McCubbins and Gregory W. Noble, "The Appearance of Power: Legislators, Bureaucrats, and the Budget Process in the United States and Japan," in Cowhey and McCubbins, *Structure and Policy*, pp. 56–80.

133. Muramatsu, Itō, and Tsujinaka, *Sengo Nihon no atsuryoku dantai*, p. 180. See also Tsujinaka Yutaka, *Rieki shūdan* [Interest groups] (Tokyo, Tokyo Daigaku Shuppankai, 1988), p. 127. Tsujinaka shows that except for labor and citizen groups, the major interest associations have the bulk of their party linkages to the LDP (peace and student groups were not included).

134. See Tsujinaka, *Rieki shūdan*, pp. 143–44.

135. On amakudari see Takenori Inoki, "Japanese Bureaucrats at Retirement: The Mobility of Human Resources from Central Government to Public Corporations," in Kim et al., *Japanese Civil Service*, pp. 213–34; Muramatsu, *Sengo Nihon no kanryōsei*, pp. 79–80; Calder, "Elites in an Equalizing Role," pp. 379–403.

136. I owe this formulation to Ellis Krauss, based largely on "Changing Television News" (paper presented to the Association for Asian Studies, Chicago, March 13–16, 1997).

137. Wakata Kyoji calculates that for the lower house in 1974, 43 percent of the DSP members, 62 percent of the JSP members, and 25 percent of the JCP members were drawn from the ranks of labor unions. Wakata, *Gendai Nihon no seiji to fūdo* [The politics and climate of contemporary Japan] (Tokyo, Mineruba Shobō, 1981), p. 46. Aurelia George identifies ninety-two parliamentarians as members of one or another trade union federation during the early 1980s; she does not calculate percentages by party. George, "Japanese Interest Group Behavior: An Institutional Approach," in Stockwin, *Dynamic and Immobilist Politics in Japan*, pp. 110–11.

138. Hideo Otake, "Defense Controversies and One Party Dominance: The Opposition in West Germany and Japan," in T. J. Pempel, ed., *Uncommon Democracies: The One-Party Dominant Regimes* (Ithaca, Cornell University Press, 1989).

139. Ronald Dore, *British Factory—Japanese Factory: The Origins of National Diversity in Industrial Relations* (Berkeley, University of California Press, 1973), p. 173.

140. The opposition faced a perennial dilemma: on issues where they confronted proposals they considered unacceptable, they could seek to mobilize public opposition. By doing so, however, they ran the constant risk of overplaying their hand and "crying wolf" too often. Conversely, they could bargain behind the scenes and work for detailed compromises. Here the risk was that any contributions they made would redound to the credit, not of the opposition groups or individuals who made them, but rather to the conservatives. T. J. Pempel, "The Dilemma of the Parliamentary Opposition in Japan," *Polity* 8, 1 (1975).

3. From Chaos to Cohesion: Formation of the Conservative Regime

1. On the political-business cycle, see D. Chappell and D. A. Peel, "On the Political Theory of the Business Cycle," *Economics Letters* 2 (1979): 327–32; Victor Ginsberg and

Philippe Michel, "Random Timing of Elections and the Political Business Cycle," *Public Choice* 40 (1983): 155–64. On the application to the Japanese case, see Thomas Cargill and Michael Hutchinson, "Political Business Cycles in a Parliamentary Setting: The Case of Japan," Working Paper 88–08 (San Francisco: Federal Reserve Bank of San Francisco, 1990); Takatoshi Ito, "The Timing of Elections and Political Business Cycles in Japan," *Journal of Asian Economics* 1 (1990): 135–56.

2. Kozo Yamamura, "The Cost of Rapid Growth and Capitalist Democracy in Japan," in Leon Lindberg and Charles Maier, eds., *The Politics of Inflation and Economic Stagnation* (Washington, D.C., Brookings Institution, 1985), p. 468. Yamamura's phrase seems to have been anticipated by Kosaka Masataka, "Tsūshō kokka Nihon no unmei" [The fate of the Japanese trading state], *Chūō Kōron*, November 1975, where he declares that "the international environment of the 1960s looked as though Heaven had created it for Japan's growth"; cited in Kenneth Pyle, *The Japanese Question: Power and Purpose in a New Era* (Washington, D.C., American Enterprise Institute, 1992), p. 44.

3. This method of reexamining the historical record with an eye toward nonobvious alternatives is congruent with that of Charles Tilly, "Reflections on the History of European State-Making," in Charles Tilly, ed., *The Formation of National States in Western Europe* (Princeton, Princeton University Press, 1975).

4. This picture is congruent with, although hardly a mirror image of, the arguments found in such works as Barrington Moore, *Social Origins of Dictatorship and Democracy* (Boston, Beacon, 1966); Tilly, "Reflections on the History of European State-Making"; Charles Maier, *Recasting Bourgeois Europe* (Princeton, Princeton University Press, 1975); Dietrich Reuschemeyer, Evelyn Huber Stephens, and John D. Stephens, *Capitalist Development and Democracy* (Chicago, University of Chicago Press, 1992).

5. Arendt Lijphart, *Democracies: Patterns of Majoritarian and Consensus Government in Twenty-One Countries* (New Haven, Yale University Press, 1984), pp. 201–6, examines the use of referenda in various industrialized democracies. Japan emerges as one of only nine industrialized democracies to lack any experience with referenda between 1945 and 1980.

6. On the importance of transforming the Home Ministry and increasing local autonomy, see Amakawa Akira, "Seiji seido no minshūka—chihō seido no minshuka to naimushō no kaitai" [The democratization of the political system—democratization of the system of local government and the dissolution of the Ministry of Home Affairs], in Takemae Eiji and Amakawa Akira, *Nihon senryō hishi* [A secret history of the occupation] (Tokyo, Asahi Shimbunsha, 1977), 1:277–314.

7. Chalmers Johnson, *MITI and the Japanese Miracle* (Stanford, Stanford University Press, 1982), pp. 41–42, argues that only forty-two higher officials were purged from MITI's predecessor, the Ministry of Commerce and Industry, and only nine from the Ministry of Finance.

8. For more details, see T. J. Pempel, "The Tar Baby Target: 'Reform' of the Japanese Bureaucracy," in Robert E. Ward and Yoshikazu Sakamoto, eds., *Democratizing Japan: The American Occupation* (Honolulu, University of Hawaii Press, 1987), pp. 157–87; "Organizing for Efficiency: The Higher Civil Service in Japan," in Ezra Suleiman, ed., *Bureaucrats and Policymaking* (New York, Holmes and Meier, 1984), pp. 72–106.

9. Henry Emerson Wildes, *Typhoon in Tokyo: The Occupation and Its Aftermath* (New York, Macmillan, 1954), p. 92, as cited in Johnson, *MITI and the Japanese Miracle*, p. 44.

10. Herbert P. Bix, "Inventing the 'Symbol Monarchy' in Japan, 1945–52," *Journal of Japanese Studies* 21, 2 (1995): 319–64.

11. On this point see Peter J. Katzenstein and Nobuo Okawara, *Japan's National Security: Structures, Norms and Policy Responses in a Changing World* (Ithaca, Cornell University East Asia Program, 1993), esp. chap. 3, stressing civilian control. It is an interesting irony of the postwar Constitution that while Article 9 explicitly bans the maintenance of any military force, Article 66 redundantly states that all cabinet members "must be civilians."

12. This view was at odds with the fact that, within Japan, the same *zaibatsu* had been vilified by the military and the ultranationalists as excessively pacifist, liberal, and pro-American. Masumi Junnosuke, *Postwar Politics in Japan, 1945–1955*, trans. Lonnie E. Carlile (Berkeley, Univerity of California Press, 1995), p. 240.

13. As quoted in Laura Hein, *Fueling Growth: The Energy Revolution and Economic Policy in Postwar Japan* (Cambridge, Harvard University Press, 1990), pp. 56–57.

14. U.S. Department of State, *Foreign Relations of the United States, 1945: The Far East* (Washington, D.C., Government Printing Office, 1945), pp. 825–27.

15. Various figures are given by different authors. Hans Baerwald, *The Purge of Japanese Leaders under the Occupation* (Berkeley, University of California Press, 1959), pp. 80–82, uses the number 1898. Masumi Junnosuke, *Sengo Seiji, 1945–1955* [Postwar politics] (Tokyo, Tokyo Daigaku Shuppankai, 1983), 1:239, suggests the number 3080.

16. John Dower, *Empire and Aftermath: Yoshida Shigeru and the Japanese Experience, 1878–1954* (Cambridge, Harvard University Press, 1979), p. 309.

17. Ishikawa Masumi, *Sengo seiji kōzōshi* [A structural history of postwar politics] (Tokyo, Nihon Hyōronsha, 1978), p. 4.

18. On this election and its consequences, see Ishikawa, *Sengo seiji kozoshi*, pp. 5–12. Also Suzuki Masashi, *Sengo Nihon no Shiteki Bunseki* [A historical analysis of postwar Japan] (Tokyo Aoki Shoten, 1969), pp. 55–58; Fujii Shoichi and Oe Shinobu, *Sengo Nihon no rekishi, jo* [A history of postwar Japan, vol. 1] (Tokyo, Aoki Shoten, 1970), pp. 48–50.

19. SCAP, *Political Reorientation of Japan* (Washington, D.C., Government Printing Office, 1949), p. 741.

20. Hein, *Fueling the Growth*, p. 60.

21. The two major federations were the All Japan General Confederation of Trade Unions (Zen-Nihon Rōdō Kumiai Sōdōmei), usually known as Sōdōmei, which was controlled by the Japan Socialist Party, and the National Congress of Industrial Unions (Zenkoku Sangyō-betsu Rōdō Kumiai Kaigi), known as Sanbetsu. Sanbetsu denied links to the Japan Communist Party, but several of its leaders, including Kikunami Katsumi and Dobashi Kazuyoshi eventually made public their membership in the JCP. Rodger Swearington and Paul Langer, *Red Flag Over Japan: International Communism in Action* (Westport. Conn., Greenwood, 1952), p. 147.

22. In the fall of 1945, telephone operators at Sendai carried out a "strike" in which they remained at their switchboards but greeted callers with "Moshi moshi. We are on strike! Long live democracy! Number, please?" Miriam Farley, *Aspects of Japan's Labor Problems* (New York, John Day, 1950), pp. 88–89. At Mitsui's Bibai coal mine in Hokkaido, workers increased production from 250 to over 650 tons per day, while cutting the workday from twelve to eight hours. Beatrice G. Reubens, "'Production Control' in Japan," *Far Eastern Survey*, 15, 22 (1946): 344–47.

23. Surely MacArthur had not sought politically oriented unions. Members of the Labor Section of SCAP, including Labor Division Chief Theodore Cohen, however, were clearly far more sympathetic. Indeed, Cohen was instrumental in helping the JCP-oriented Sanbetsu in its establishment and in a variety of its political activities.

24. Hideo Ōtake, "The *Zaikai* under the Occupation: The Formation and Transformation of Managerial Councils," in Ward and Sakamoto, *Democratizing Japan*, pp. 366–91.

25. Actually the Union did not hold its first official Congress until February 1946, but members were recruited before that inauguration. See Andrew J. Grad, *Land and Peasant in Japan: An Introductory Survey* (New York, Institute of Pacific Relations, 1952), pp. 135–41. Ronald Dore, *Land Reform in Japan* (New York, Oxford University Press, 1959), p. 168.

26. Asahi Shimbunsha, ed., *Nihon no seiji ishiki* [Japanese political attitudes] (Tokyo, Asahi Shimbunsha, 1976).

27. Allan B. Cole, George C. Totten, and Cecil H. Uyehara, *Socialist Parties in Postwar Japan* (New Haven, Yale University Press, 1966), p. 386.

28. Kent Calder, *Crisis and Compensation: Public Policy and Political Stability in Japan, 1949–1986* (Princeton, Princeton University Press, 1988), p. 254.

29. Yamakawa Katsumi, Yoda Hiroshi, and Moriwaki Toshimasa, *Seijigaku deeta bukku* [Political science databook] (Tokyo, Sorinsha, 1981), pp. 122–23; Ishikawa, *Sengo seiji kōzōshi*, p. 43.

30. See Iizuka Shigetarō, Uji Toshihiko, and Habara Kiyomasa, *Kettō Yonjūnen—Nihon Shakaitō* [The fortieth anniversary of the party—the Japan Socialist Party] (Tokyo, Gyōsei Mondai Kenkyūjo, 1985), pp. 66–68.

31. It is thus interesting to note that most official histories of the Japan Socialist Party either do not mention or else give minimal attention to the creation and early actions of the Japan Farmers' Union. See, for example, Kettō Nijūnen Kinen Shuppan, ed., *Nihon Shakaitō Nijūnen no Kiroku* [A record of the twenty-year history of the Japan Socialist Party] (Tokyo, Nihon Shakaitō, 1965).

32. Hugh T. Patrick and Thomas P. Rohlen, "Small-Scale Family Enterprises," in Yamamura and Yasuba, eds., *Political Economy of Japan* (Stanford, Stanford University Press, 1987), pp. 1:335–36.

33. Ryutaro Komiya, *The Japanese Economy: Trade, Industry, and Government* (Tokyo, University of Tokyo Press, 1990), p. 139.

34. Indeed, the sector with the highest unionization rates is the public sector. See data in Jelle Visser, "The Strength of Union Movements in Advanced Capital Democracies," in Marino Regini, ed., *The Future of Labor Movements* (London, Sage, 1992), p. 27. On the difficulties of organizing labor in smaller firms, see Michael Goldfield, "Worker Insurgency, Radical Organization, and New Deal Labor," *American Political Science Review* 83, 4 (1989): 1257.

35. Generally speaking Italy, France and Australia had the highest strike rates during this time period. Walter Korpi and Michael Shalev ranked Japanese strike rates as "medium" along with New Zealand, Finland, the United States, Canada, Ireland, and the United Kingdom. Korpi and Shalev, "Strikes, Industrial Relations and Class Conflict in Capitalist Societies," *British Journal of Sociology* 30, 2 (1979): 178–79. The years covered, however, were 1946–76, and in the later period, Japan experienced a decline in participation rates and duration of strikes. In a seven-country comparison, Kazuo Kōike finds Japan as the third-highest country for 1955–59, behind Italy and the United States but ahead of France, the United Kingdom, Sweden, and Germany. Kōike, "Internal Labor Markets: Workers in Large Firms," in Taishirō Shirai, ed., *Contemporary Industrial Relations in Japan* (Madison, University of Wisconsin Press, 1983), p. 37.

36. As quoted in Dower, *Empire and Aftermath*, p. 311.

37. William Chapman, *Inventing Japan: An Unconventional Account of the Postwar Years* (New York, Prentice-Hall, 1991), p. 22.

38. John Owen Haley, *Authority without Power: Law and the Japanese Paradox* (Oxford, Oxford University Press, 1991), p. 151.

39. Ibid., p. 152.

40. As Takemae Eiji and others have noted, with the 1948 presidential election looming ahead, the last thing MacArthur wanted was to be seen as having allowed a left-wing revolution to take place in the Japan he ruled. This too surely played a part in his actions. Takemae, "Rōdōnō Minshuka" [The democratization of labor], in Takemae and Amakawa, *Nihon Senryō Hishi*, p. 94.

41. Satō Tatsuo, "Kokka Komuinhō Seiritsu no Keitei" [Establishment of the National Public Service Law], *Referensu* 138 (July 1962): 1–15; 139 (August): 11–31.

42. Takemae, "Rōdōno Minshuka," p. 94.

43. Sheldon Garon, *The State and Labor in Modern Japan* (Princeton, Princeton University Press, 1987), p. 239.

44. As quoted in Farley, *Aspects of Japan's Labor Problems*, pp. 148–49.

45. Hirosuke Kawanishi, *Enterprise Unionism in Japan* (London and New York, Kegan Paul, 1992), pp. 293–304.

46. Chitoshi Yanaga, *Big Business in Japanese Politics* (New Haven, Yale University Press, 1968), pp. 41–42.

47. The Basic Law on Small and Medium Enterprises defines small businesses as those transportation, mining, or manufacturing companies having ¥100 million or less in capital *or* fewer than 300 employees; those wholesale companies having ¥30 million or less in capital *or* fewer than 100 employees; and those retail or service industry companies having ¥10 million or less in capital *or* less than 50 employees.

48. OECD, *The Industrial Policy of Japan* (Paris, OECD, 1972), p. 186.

49. *Sandee Mainichi*, November 24, 1957, as cited in Naoki Kobayashi, "Interest Groups in the Legislative Process," in Hiroshi Itoh, trans. and ed., *Japanese Politics—An Inside View* (Ithaca, Cornell University Press, 1973), p. 74.

50. Sheldon Garon and Mike Mochizuki, "Negotiating Social Contracts: State and Society in Postwar Japan," in Andrew Gordon, ed., *Postwar Japan as History* (Berkeley, University of California Press, 1993), p. 149.

51. Naoki Kobayashi, "The Small and Medium-Sized Enterprises Organization Law," in Itoh, *Japanese Politics*, p. 51.

52. Kobayashi, "Interest Groups in the Legislative Process," pp. 70–73.

53. As Tsujinaka Yutaka points out, later laws further strengthened the sector, including the Law for Leagues of Environmental Sanitation (Kankyō Eisei Kumiai Hō) and the Law on Promotional Associations for Shopping Areas (Shotengai Shinkyokai Ho) (1962). Tsujinaka, *Rieki Shūdan* (Tokyo, Tokyo Daigaku Shuppankai, 1988), p. 57.

54. Garon and Mochizuki, "Negotiating Social Contracts," p. 149.

55. Kazushi Ohkawa and Henry Rosovsky, *Japanese Economic Growth: Trend Acceleration in the Twentieth Century* (Stanford, Stanford University Press, 1973), p. 283.

56. Arisawa Hiromi and Inaba Shūzō, eds., *Shiryō: Sengo nijūnenshi: 2 keizai* [Source materials: Twenty years of postwar history, vol. 2, Economics] (Tokyo, Nihon Hyōronsha, 1967), p. 129.

57. Kajinishi Mitsuhaya et al., *Nihon shihonshugi no botsuraku* [The collapse of Japanese capitalism] (Tokyo, Tokyo Daigaku Shuppankai, 1974), p. 1381.

58. Michael W. Donnelly, "Setting the Price of Rice: A Study in Political Decisionmaking," in T. J. Pempel, ed., *Policymaking in Contemporary Japan* (Ithaca, Cornell University Press, 1977), p. 153.

59. Robert A. Scalapino and Junnosuke Masumi, *Parties and Politics in Postwar Japan* (Berkeley, University of California Press, 1962), p. 90.

60. Another 9.2 percent dated back to the prewar period; the remaining 42.1 percent were formed after 1956. Muramatsu Michio, Itō Mitsutoshi, and Tsujinaka Yutaka, *Sengo Nihon no atsuryoku dantai* [Pressure groups in postwar Japan] (Tokyo, Tōyō Keizai, 1986), as reported by Muramatsu in Miyake Ichiro et al., *Nihon seiji no zahyō* [A diagnosis of Japanese politics] (Tokyo, Yūhikaku, 1985), p. 218.

61. Tsukjinaka Yutaka, *Rieki shūdan* [Interest groups] (Tokyo, Tokyo Daigaku Shuppankai, 1988), p. 18–19.

62. T. J. Pempel, "Uneasy toward Autonomy: Parliament and Parliamentarians in Japan," in Ezra Suleiman, ed., *Parliaments and Parliamentarians in Democratic Politics* (New York, Holmes and Meier, 1986), p. 117.

63. Michael Shaller, *The American Occupation of Japan: The Origins of the Cold War* (New York, Oxford University Press, 1985), p. 47.

64. Masumi Junnosuke, *Nihon seijishi 4: Senryōkaikaku jimintōshihai* [Political history of Japan, vol. 4, Occupational reform; LDP control] (Tokyo, Tokyo Daigaku Shuppankai, 1988), p. 72.

65. A SCAP memorandum of March 17, 1947, "The Merits of the Electoral System Proposed by Mr. Yoshida," concluded that "while there is nothing undemocratic about the proposed system it is, *in comparison to the existing system*, definitely advantageous to the parties now in power, and unfavorable to minority representation and to women." Box 2032, RG 331, National Archives, Suitland, Md., as cited in Dower, *Empire and Its Aftermath*, p. 549.

66. T. A. Bisson, *Democracy in Japan* (New York, Macmillan, 1949), p. 59.

67. My calculations from Yamakawa, Yoda, and Moriwaki, *Seijigaku deeta bukku*, p. 123.

68. Ibid., pp. 122–23.

69. This trend was reversed in the 1990 lower house elections when the JSP went from its historical low of 16.6 percent of the seats to 26.6 percent. At the same time, that 1990 figure represented only a return to a proportion of seats slightly lower than the JSP had held following the 1967 election. See Muramatsu Michio, Itō Mitsutoshi and Tsujinaka Yutaka, *Nihon no seiji* [Japanese politics] (Tokyo,Yūhikaku, 1992), pp. 122–23.

70. This point is elaborated at greater length in Pempel, "Uneasy toward Autonomy," pp. 141–48. It is worth noting that the proportion of ex-bureaucrats rose to about 55 percent in the second Ikeda cabinet (1960) and the third Sato cabinet (1972).

71. Masumi, *Postwar Politics in Japan*, pp. 276–77.

72. *Asahi Shimbun*, January 15, 1955, as quoted in Masumi, *Contemporary Politics in Japan*, p. 218.

73. Mike Mochizuki, *Conservative Hegemony: Party Strategies and Social Coalitions in Japan* (Ph.D. diss., Harvard University, 1991) , p. 1.

74. Joji Watanuki, "Social Structure and Voting Behavior," in Scott C. Flanagan et al., eds., *The Japanese Voter* (New Haven, Yale University Press, 1991), pp. 50–51.

75. Ishida Hirohide, "Hoshu seitō no bijon" [A vision of the Conservative Party], *Chūō Kōron* 78, 1 (1963): 88–97.

76. Hata Ikuhito, "Nihon senryō to kokusai kankyō [The Japanese occupation and the international environment], in Takemae and Amakawa, *Nihon senryō hishi*, 2:108–55. On the broader problem of Japanese defense and security see also Ōtake Hideo, *Nihon no bōei to kokunai seiji* [Japanese defense and domestic politics] (Tokyo, Sanichi Shobō, 1983).

77. Laura Hein, "In Search of Peace and Democracy: Japanese Economic Debate in Political Context," *Journal of Asian Studies* 53, 3 (1994): 758.

78. *Asahi Shimbun*, September 1, 1950.

79. Kaizai Kikakuchō Sengokeizaishi Hensanshitsu, ed., *Sengo keizaishi: Sōkanhen* [Postwar economic history: First edition] (Tokyo, Ōkurashō Insatsukyoku, 1957), pp. 296–309.

80. Wage restrictions for public servants were fixed in July 1947 and were set on the basis of food consumption levels of 1,550 calories per day.

81. Shigeto Tsuru, *Japan's Capitalism: Creative Defeat and Beyond* (Berkeley, University of California Press, 1993), p. 49.

82. Allan B. Cole, George O. Totten, and Cecil H. Uyehara, *Socialist Parties in Postwar Japan* (New Haven, Yale University Press, 1966), p. 61.

83. One of the best analyses of the process behind the Police Duties Bill is Hatakeyama Hirobumi, "Keishokuhō kakusei to seijiteki riidaashippu" [Reform of the Police Duties Bill and political leadership], in Ōtake Hideo, *Nihon seiji no sōten* [Issues in Japanese politics] (Tokyo, Sanichi Shobō, 1984), pp. 71–126.

84. Miriam A. Golden, *Heroic Defeats: The Politics of Job Loss* (Cambridge, Cambridge University Press, 1997), pp. 104–8.

85. Cole, Totten, and Uyehara, *Socialist Parties in Postwar Japan*, p. 79.

86. On these internal divisions within the LDP see Watanabe Tsuneo, *Habatsu—hōshuto no kaibō* [Factions—a dissection of the Conservative Party] (Tokyo, Kōbundo, 1958); Watanabe Tsuneo, *Habatsu—Nihon hoshutō no bunseki* [Factions—analysis of the Japanese Conservative Party] (Tokyo, Kōbundo, 1962), esp. chap. 1; Asahi Shimbunsha, *Seitō to habatsu* [Parties and factions] (Tokyo, Asahi Shimbunsha, 1968), pp. 10–14.

87. See Ōtake Hideo, *Sengo Nihon no ideorogii tairitsu* [Ideological conflict in postwar Japan] (Tokyo, Sanichi Shobō, 1996), pp. 110–46.

88. Itō Takashi, "Sengo seitō no keisei katei" [The origins of the postwar parties], in Itō Takashi, ed., *Shōwaki no seiji* [Politics in the Showa era] (Tokyo, Yamakawa Shuppan, 1983).

89. Ōtake Hideo, *Adenaua to Yoshida Shigeru* [Adenauer and Yoshida Shigeru] (Tokyo, Chūō Kōronsha, 1986), chaps. 4–5. Kume Ikuo, "Sengo rōdōshi wakai taisei no keisei" [Institutionalizing labor accommodation in postwar Japan], in Nihon Seiji Gakkai, ed., *Sengo kokka no keisei to keizai hatten* [Establishment of the postwar state and economic development] (Tokyo, Iwanami Shoten, 1992), pp. 187–209.

90. *Asahi Shimbun*, March 3, 1950.

91. The "politics of productivity" is a term used by Charles S. Maier, "The Politics of Productivity: Foundations of American International Economic Policy after World War II," in Peter J. Katzenstein, ed., *Between Power and Plenty: Foreign Economic Policies of Advanced Industrial States* (Madison, University of Wisconsin Press, 1978), pp. 23–49.

92. Meredith Woo-Cumings, "East Asia's American Problem," in Meredith Woo-Cumings and Michael Loriaux, eds., *Past as Prelude: History in the Making of a New World Order* (Boulder, Westview, 1993), p. 144.

93. Ōtake, *Sengo Nihon no ideorogii tairitsu*, pp. 110–12.

94. Ito Daiichi, "The Bureaucracy: Its Attitudes and Behavior," *Developing Economies* 4, 4 (1968): 451.

95. Kayano Mitsuo, "Keizai-ha kanryō wa kapposuru" [The bureaucrats in the economic faction are swaggering], *Chūō Kōron*, November 1961, pp. 260–68.

96. Ikuo Kume, "Party Politics and Industrial Policy: A Case of Japan" (paper delivered to the International Conference on Government-Industry Relations, Exeter, May 20–22, 1992).

97. Ekonomisuto Henshūbu, *Shogen kōdō seicho no Nihon, jō* [Testimony: Japan in the era of high economic growth, vol. 1] (Tokyo, Mainichi Shimbunsha, 1984), pp. 42, 66; as cited in Ikuo Kume, "Disparaged Success: Labor Politics in Postwar Japan" (Ph.D. diss., Cornell University, 1995), chap. 4, pp. 28–29.

98. Kume, "Party Politics and Industrial Policy." On the period see also Kōnō Yasuko, "Yoshida gaiko to kokunai seiji" [The Yoshida foreign policy and domestic politics], in Nihon Seijigakkai, ed., *Sengo kokka no keisei to keizai hatten* [Structure and economic development of the postwar state], *Nenpō Seijigaku* [Annals of the Japan Political Science Association] (Tokyo, Nihon Seijigakkai, 1991), pp. 29–52.

99. Indeed Kōnō Yasuko notes how the creation of MITI out of the planning-oriented Ministry of Commerce and Industry and the export-oriented Agency of Trade also worked to aid Yoshida's export-oriented version of planning. Kōnō, "Yoshida gaiko to kokunai seiji," pp. 29–52.

100. Okita Saburo, *Nihon no Keizai Seisaku* [Japanese economic policy] (Tokyo, Yuki Shobo, 1961), pp. 120–21.

101. Ōtake, *Adenaua to Yoshida*, p. 264.

102. At the same time, the labor unions and the Japan Socialist Party collectively denounced the plan, not as "income doubling" but as "price doubling." The JSP also charged that the plan would widen the gap in incomes between larger corporations on the one hand and farming villages and smaller firms on the other. See Masumi Junnosuke, *Nihon seiji shi* [Japanese political history] (Tokyo, Tokyo Daigaku Shuppankai, 1988), 4:284.

4. Transition and Breakdown: An Era of Reconfigurations

1. Herbert Kitschelt, *The Logics of Party Formation: Ecological Politics in Belgium and West Germany* (Ithaca, Cornell University Press, 1989), p. 3.

2. The classic study is Walter Dean Burnham, *Critical Elections and the Mainsprings of American Politics* (New York, Norton, 1970).

3. An important example of how such business power is often overlooked is Peter Swenson, "Bringing Capital Back In, or Social Democracy Reconsidered: Employer Power,

Cross-Class Alliances, and Centralization of Industrial Relations in Denmark and Sweden," *World Politics* 43, 4 (1991): 513–44. See also Jeffrey Winters, *Power in Motion* (Ithaca, Cornell University Press, 1996), chap. 1.

4. The dilemma this poses for socialist parties can be acute and has been interestingly addressed in Adam Przeworski and John Sprague, *Paper Stones: A History of Electoral Socialism* (Chicago, University of Chicago Press, 1986); Adam Przeworski and Michael Wallerstein, "The Structure of Class Conflict in Democratic Capitalist Societies," *American Political Science Review*, 76 (1982): 215–38. An interesting empirical examination of the problem in Sweden is Sven Steinmo, "Social Democracy vs. Socialism: Goal Adaptation in Social Democratic Sweden," *Politics and Society* 16, 4 (1988): 403–46.

5. As cited in Christopher Hitchens, "Pulp Politics," *New York Review of Books*, February 29, 1996, p. 25.

6. In this context, consider the comments of James Carvell, electoral advisor to President Clinton. Following Clinton's election, Carvell announced that in his next incarnation he wanted to come back as "the bond market," because then he'd *really* have power over politicians. In a similar vein see R. Taggart Murphy, *The Weight of the Yen* (New York, Norton, 1996) on the power of currency rates in Japan and the United States.

7. Robert D. Putnam, "Diplomacy and Domestic Policies: The Logic of Two-Level Games," *International Organization* 42, 3 (1988): 427–60.

8. Sidney Tarrow, *Power in Movement: Social Protest, Reform, and Revolution* (Cambridge, Cambridge University Press, 1993).

9. The classic statement of this position is found in Robert Keohane and Joseph Nye, *Power and Interdependence* (Boston, Little, Brown, 1977).

10. I have tried in a preliminary way to explore this situation for the cross-national coalitions that have formed in Japan. These have involved various multinational banks and corporations, the U.S. military, various departments of foreign governments, and the like. See T. J. Pempel, "The Unbundling of 'Japan, Inc.': Changes in Japanese Policymaking," *Journal of Japanese Studies* 13, 2 (1987): 271–306.

11. A parallel formulation is that of David Lake, who speaks of within-structure changes and changes in the structures themselves. David S. Lake, *Power, Protection, and Free Trade: International Sources of U.S. Commercial Strategy, 1887–1939* (Ithaca, Cornell University Press, 1988), p. 49.

12. Jonas Pontusson, *The Limits of Social Democracy* (Ithaca, Cornell University Press, 1992).

13. Jonas Pontusson and Peter Swenson, "Labor Markets, Production Strategies, and Wage Bargaining Institutions," *Comparative Political Studies* 29, 2 (1996): 229.

14. Jonas Pontusson, "Between Neo-Liberalism and the German Model: Swedish Capitalism in Transition," in Colin Crouch and Wolfgang Streeck, eds., *Political Economy of Modern Capitalism: Mapping Convergence and Diversity* (London, Sage, 1997), p. 58.

15. Jonas Pontusson and Peter Swenson, "Labor Markets, Production Strategies, and Wage Bargaining Institutions: The Swedish Employer Offensive in Comparative Perspective," *Comparative Political Studies*, 29, 2 (1996): 223–50.

16. Pontusson, "Between Neoliberalism and the German Model," pp. 5–8.

17. David Cameron, "Social Democracy, Corporatism, Labor Quiescence, and the Representation of Economic Interest in Advanced Capitalist Countries," in John H. Goldthorpe, ed., *Order and Conflict in Contemporary Capitalism* (Cambridge, Cambridge University Press, 1984), p. 144; "Economic Indicators," *Economist*, September 27–October 3, 1997, p. 114.

18. Thus, the New Politics movement succeeded in 1968 in changing the rules for the Democratic Party convention to "encourage" states to select delegates through primaries and open caucuses, which would ensure that future conventions be made up of blacks, women, and youth in a "reasonable relationship to their presence in the population of the State." See Austin Ranney, *Curing the Mischief of Faction: Party Reform in America* (Berkeley, University of California Press, 1975); Martin Shefter, "Party, Bureaucracy, and Political

Change in the United States," in Louis Maisel and Joseph Cooper, eds., *Political Parties: Development and Decay* (Beverly Hills, Sage, 1978), pp. 246–47.

19. David Mayhew, *Party Loyalty among Congressmen* (New Haven, Yale University Press, 1966).

20. Michael Goldfield, "Worker Insurgency, Radical Organization, and New Deal Labor," *American Political Science Review* 83, 4 (1989): 1257–66.

21. Sven Steinmo, "Political Institutions and Tax Policy in the United States, Sweden, and Britain," *World Politics* 41, 4 (1989): 512.

22. Indeed, Lyndon Johnson, in signing the Civil Rights Act of 1964, indicated that doing so would mean the end of the once solid South and the probable demise of the Democratic Party, a prediction that began to be borne out almost immediately with Richard Nixon's "southern strategy."

23. Godfrey Hodgson, *The World Turned Right Side Up: A History of the Conservative Ascendancy in America* (New York, Houghton Mifflin, 1996). See also Kevin Philipps, *The Emerging Republican Majority* (New York, Arlington House, 1969).

24. This proposal came from its major shareholder, Carl C. Icahn, in an apparent effort to force the company to "take bolder initiatives to increase the value of the stock." "Ichan's USX Plan May Be Gaining Support," *New York Times*, March 19, 1990, pp. D1–D2.

25. Alessandro Pizzorno, "Interests and Parties in Pluralism," in Suzanne Berger, ed., *Organizing Interests in Western Europe* (Cambridge, Cambridge University Press, 1981), p. 279.

26. See Joel Krieger, *Reagan, Thatcher and the Politics of Decline* (Oxford, Oxford University Press, 1986) for a particularly persuasive comparison.

27. Krieger, *Reagan, Thatcher*, p. 74.

28. David Butler and Dennis Kavanagh, *The British General Election of 1979* (London, Macmillan, 1980), pp. 53–54.

29. Krieger, *Reagan, Thatcher*, pp. 76–77.

30. Peter Hall, *Governing the Economy: The Politics of State Intervention in Britain and France* (Oxford, Oxford University Press, 1986), p. 108.

31. Ibid., p. 115.

32. Ibid., p. 124.

33. "Britain in 1997: Rich Nation, Poor Nation, and a Little in Between," *New York Times*, April 29, 1997, p. D4.

34. Peter Jenkins, "Thatcher's Britain," *Geopolitique* 31 (autumn 1990), pp. 14–15.

35. *New York Times*, April 24, 1997.

36. Steinmo, "Political Institutions and Tax Policy," pp. 533–34.

37. Michele Salvati, "May 1968 and the Hot Autumn of 1969: The Responses of Two Ruling Classes," in Berger, *Organizing Interests in Western Europe*, pp. 331–65.

38. Richard M. Locke, *Remaking the Italian Economy* (Ithaca, Cornell University Press, 1995), p. 2.

39. Gianfranco Pasquino, "Programmatic Renewal, and Much More: From the PCI to the PDS," *West European Politics* 16, 1 (1993), pp. 156–73.

40. "A Survey of Italy," *Economist*, June 26, 1993, p. 19.

41. Michele Salvati, "The Crisis of Government in Italy," *New Left Review* 213 (September/October 1995): 81–82.

42. On this division, see Sidney Tarrow, *Peasant Communism in Southern Italy* (New Haven, Yale University Press, 1979); Robert D. Putnam, *Making Democracy Work: Civic Traditions in Modern Italy* (Princeton, Princeton University Press, 1993).

43. On the referenda and the electoral shifts, see Simon Parker, "Electoral Reform and Political Change in Italy, 1991–1994," in Stephen Gundle and Simon Parker, eds., *The New Italian Republic: From the Fall of the Berlin Wall to Berlusconi* (London, Routledge, 1996), pp. 40–59.

44. Carol Mershon and Gianfranco Pasquino, "Introduction," in *Italian Politics: Ending the First Republic* (Boulder, Westview, 1995), p. 41.

45. Ibid., p. 42.

46. Michele Salvati and Stefano Passigli, "Roots of the Olive Tree," *New Statesman and Society* 9, 401 (1996), p. 22.

47. "Burning While Rome Fiddles," *Economist*, April 5, 1997, pp. 46–47.

48. Richard Locke, "*Eppure Si Tocca:* The Abolition of *Scala Mobile*," in Mershon and Pasquino, *Italian Politics*, p. 185.

49. Salvati, "Crisis of Government in Italy," p. 85.

5. Japan in the 1990s: Fragmented Politics and Economic Chaos

1. On the collapse see Noguchi Yukio, *Baburu no keizaigaku* [The economics of the bubble economy] (Tokyo, Tōyō Keizai Shimbunsha, 1992), p. 25.

2. Peter J. Katzenstein and Nobuo Okawara, *Japan's National Security: Structures, Norms and Policy Responses in a Changing World* (Ithaca, Cornell East Asia Series, 1993); Sato Hideo, *Taigai seisaku* (Tokyo, Tokyo Daigaku Shuppankai, 1989).

3. Vogel, *Freer Markets, More Rules* (Ithaca, Cornell University Press, 1996).

4. See the preceding chapter. Also J. Rogers Hollingsworth, Philippe C. Schmitter, and Wolfgang Streeck, eds., *Governing Capitalist Economies: Performance and Control of Economic Sectors* (New York, Oxford University Press, 1994); Yasusuke Murakami, *An Anticlassical Political-Economic Analysis* (Stanford, Stanford University Press, 1996); Michel Albert, *Capitalism vs. Capitalism* (New York, Four Walls Eight Windows, 1993); Suzanne Berger and Ronald Dore, eds., *National Diversity and Global Capitalism* (Ithaca, Cornell University Press, 1996).

5. Based on NEEDS (Nikkei Economic Electronic Databank System), as reported in *Nikkei Weekly*, September 22, 1997.

6. As reported in *Nikkei Weekly*, July 7, 1997.

7. *Far Eastern Economic Review*, July 30, 1994, p. 47; *Economist*, February 21, 1998, p. 108.

8. "Payoff Scandal Threatens Reign of Big Four," *Nikkei Weekly*, September 22, 1997, p. 11.

9. Chalmers Johnson, *Japan, Who Governs?* (New York, Norton, 1995), p. 224.

10. On the LDP split, see Ōtake Hideo, "Jimintō wakate kaikakuha to Ozawa guruupu—'seiji kaikaku' o mezashita futatsu no seiji seiryoku" [The LDP's young reformers and the Ozawa Group—two strands of political power focusing on reform], *Leviathan* 17 (1995): 7–29.

11. In addition, several former Ministry of Finance bureaucrats resigned and ran for office under the banner of the Shinshintō, breaking the long-standing lock between the ministry and the LDP.

12. David Asher, "What Became of the Japanese Miracle?" *Orbis*, spring 1996, p. 10.

13. Ibid., p. 11.

14. Various monies from the agricultural cooperative banks were to be included, but it is not clear that these monies will in fact be paid.

15. Yomiuri Shimbun as cited in *Washington Post National Weekly Edition*, January 13, 1997, p. 17.

16. Ibid.

17. "How Japan Missed the Boat," *Economist*, September 22, 1990, p. 35.

18. Tetsuya Tōmiya and Kōichi Hazama, "The Dramatic Debut of Professional Soccer," *Japan Echo* 20, 4 (1993): 86–88.

19. Japan was the world's largest creditor nation in 1996 with 16.7 percent of its GDP or $742 billion in net foreign assets. "Financial Indicators," *Economist*, November 9, 1996, p. 123.

20. Jeffry A. Frieden, "Domestic Politics and Regional Cooperation: The United States, Japan, and Pacific Money and Finance," in Jeffrey A. Frankel and Miles Kahler, eds., *Re-

gionalism and Rivalry: Japan and the United States in Pacific Asia (Chicago, University of Chicago Press, 1993), p. 434.

21. "Financial Indicators," *Economist*, November 23, 1996, p. 119.

22. Sumie Kawakami, "Exporting a Surplus," *Far Eastern Economic Review*, July 4, 1996, p. 45.

23. My calculations from Nihon Kokusei Zue, *Suji de miru Nihon no hyakunen*, p. 392 (for data on 1964); *Nihon kokusei zue 96/97*, p. 414 (for data on 1995).

24. Keizai Kōhō Center, *Japan, 1996*, p. 91.

25. "The Japanese Numbers Game," Economist, March 2, 1996, p. 71; "The New Twist in Japan," *Economist*, October 26, 1996, p. 18. It should be noted that Japanese government authorities argue that this figure leaves out the assets of Japan's postal savings system and public-sector pension funds. Yet even this net figure has grown dramatically.

26. Ōtake Hideo, *Jiyūshugiteki kaikaku no jidai* [The era of liberal reforms] (Tokyo, Chūō Kōronsha, 1994), pt. 2, chaps. 2, 3, 4, 5, 6, pp. 78–161. At the same time, as Steven Vogel argues, in many instances the processes involved "more rules" (*Freer Markets, More Rules*).

27. Mark Tilton, *Restrained Trade: Cartels in Japan's Basic Materials Industries* (Ithaca, Cornell University Press, 1996).

28. Robert M. Uriu, *Troubled Industries: Confronting Economic Change in Japan* (Ithaca, Cornell University Press, 1996).

29. See Walter Hatch and Kozo Yamamura, *Asia in Japan's Embrace: Building a Regional Production Alliance* (Cambridge, Cambridge University Press, 1996); Peter J. Katzenstein and Takashi Shiraishi, *Network Capitalism: Japan in Asia* (Ithaca, Cornell University Press, 1997); Peter A. Petri, "Market Structure, Comparative Advantage, and Japanese Trade Under a Strong Yen," in Paul Krugman, ed., *Trade with Japan: Has the Door Opened Wider?* rev. ed. (Chicago, University of Chicago Press, 1995), pp. 51–84.

30. My thanks to Ron Bevacqua for passing this data on to me after calculations from data he had collected from MITI, *Kaigai jigyō katsudō* [Overseas enterprise activities] (Tokyo, MITI, 1996). These figures are congruent with those for a slightly earlier period as reported in Yung Chul Park and Won-am Park, "Changing Japanese Trade Patterns and the East Asian NICs," in Krugman, *Trade with Japan*, pp. 98–99, 105–8.

31. DeAnne Julius, *Global Companies and Public Policy* (RIIA/Pinter, n.d.) as cited in "The Myth of Economic Sovereignty," *Economist*, June 23, 1990, p. 67.

32. These are my calculations based on data for both total foreign direct investment and population in *Nihon kokusei zue 1996/97*.

33. Francis G. Castles, ed., *The Impact of Parties: Politics and Policies in Democratic Capitalist States* (London, Sage, 1982), p. 49.

34. OECD, *Public Expenditure on Income Maintenance Programmes* (Paris, OECD, 1976), p. 36.

35. See Toshimitsu Shinkawa and T. J. Pempel, "Occupational Welfare and the Japanese Experience," in Michael Shalev, ed., *Occupational Welfare and the Welfare State in Comparative Perspective* (London, Macmillan, 1996); see also Shinkawa Toshimitsu, *Nihongata fukushi no seijikeizaigaku* [The political economy of Japanese-style welfare] (Tokyo, San'ichi Shobō, 1993).

36. R. Goodman and I. Peng, "The East Asian Welfare States," in Gosta Esping-Andersen, ed., *Welfare States in Transition: National Adaptations in Global Economics* (London, Sage, 1996).

37. Japan Institute of Labor, *Japanese Work Life Profile* (Tokyo, JIL, 1990), table 74, as cited in Gøsta Esping-Andersen, "The Distinctiveness of the Japanese Welfare State," introduction to Japanese edition of *Three Worlds of Welfare Capitalism* (in press).

38. OECD, *New Directions in Social Policy* (Paris, OECD, 1994).

39. All data compiled from *Nihon kokusei zue 96/97*, p. 500. Data are for 1993.

40. Smithers and Co., Ltd. "Financing Japan's Ageing Society," Report No. 103, April 24, 1997, pp. 5–7.

41. In *The Evolution of Labor Relations in Japan: Heavy Industry, 1853–1955* (Cambridge, Harvard University Press, 1985) Andrew Gordon points out that there were indeed significant strikes in certain advanced manufacturing sectors particularly during the 1920s. Sheldon Garon, in *The State and Labor in Modern Japan* (Princeton, Princeton University Press, 1987), provides a comparable argument. Both agree on the strong antiunion regulations imposed by the government initially at the turn of the century, again in 1925, and during the 1930s.

42. On comparative strike rates during this period see Walter Korpi and Michael Shalev, "Strikes, Power and Politics in Western Nations, 1900–1976," in Maurice Zeitlin, ed., *Political Power and Social Theory* (Greenwich, Conn., JAI, 1980), 1:301–34; Douglas A. Hibbs, Jr., "On the Political Economy of Long-Run Trends in Strike Activity," *British Journal of Political Science* 8, 2 (1978): 153–75.

43. Korpi and Shalev, "Strikes, Power and Politics in the Western Nations, 1900–1976," in Zeitlin, *Political Power and Social Theory*, 1:313.

44. Michael Shalev, "The Resurgence of Labor Quiescence," in Marino Regini, ed., *The Future of Labor Movements* (London, Sage, 1992), p. 105.

45. David Cameron, "Social Democracy, Corporatism, Labor Quiescence, and the Representation of Economic Interest in Advanced Capitalist Society," in John H. Goldthorpe, ed., *Order and Conflict in Contemporary Capitalism* (Cambridge, Cambridge University Press, 1984).

46. Ikuo Kume, "Disparaged Success: Labor Politics in Postwar Japan" (Ph.D. diss., Cornell University, 1995), chap. 7.

47. The 1993 figures show Japan with 1966 hours per year; the U.S. with 1976 and the U.K. with 1902. French workers averaged 1678 hours per year and German workers 1529. *Asahi Shimbun Japan Almanac 1996*, p. 99.

48. For an outline of some of the most important see Peter J. Katzenstein, *Cultural Norms and National Security: Policy and Military in Postwar Japan* (Ithaca, Cornell University Press, 1996), pp. 100–102.

49. John D. Rockefeller IV, "The Nakasone Legacy—Japan's Increase Commitment to Security," a speech delivered in the U.S. Senate, December 17, 1987, as reprinted in Jon K. T. Choy, ed., *Japan Exploring New Paths* (Washington, D.C., Japan Economic Institute, 1988), p. 134. Expansion of missions continued into the 1990s. See Michael J. Green, *Arming Japan: Defense Production, Alliance Politics, and the Postwar Search for Autonomy* (New York, Columbia University Press, 1996).

50. Prime Minister Nakasone did make an effort to expand Japan's military budget. Moreover, during the early to mid-1980s, the share of Japan's budget allocated to defense was one of only three areas exempted from the zero-growth freeze imposed on other budget categories (the other two being foreign aid and technology).

51. Richard J. Samuels, *"Rich Nation, Strong Army": National Security and the Technological Transformation of Japan* (Ithaca, Cornell University Press, 1994), chap. 5; Reinhard Drifte, *Arms Production in Japan: The Military Application of Civilian Technology* (Boulder, Westview, 1986).

52. Samuels, "Rich Nation, Strong Army"; Green, *Arming Japan*.

53. Green, *Arming Japan*, p. 15.

54. Ibid., p. 18.

55. On these differences see Samuels, *"Rich Nation, Strong Army,"* pp. 18–32.

56. T. J. Pempel, "From Trade to Technology: Japan's Reassessment of Military Policies," *Jerusalem Journal of International Relations* 12, 4 (1990): 1–28.

57. At the same time in a discussion I had with a Bangladeshi financial official in March 1994, he indicated that though formally untied, most Japanese aid to Bangladesh is at least implicitly expected to be used for purchases from Japanese companies, often at inflated prices guaranteed to give them a substantial profit.

58. "Japan Ties Up the Asian Market," *Economist,* April 24, 1993, pp. 33–34.

59. On this election see *Leviathan* 15 (1994).

60. Kabashima Ikuo, "Shintō no Tōjō to Jimintō Ittō Yūitaisei no Hōkei" [The rise of new parties and the end to the Liberal Democratic Party's single-party dominance], *Leviathan* 15 (1994): 19.

61. Akarui Senkyō Saishinkyōkai, *Dai41kai Shūgiin sōsenkyō no jittai* [Realities of the 41st general election for the Lower House] (Tokyo, ASSK, 1996), p. 38.

62. It should be noted however that the LDP allowed many of its contestants in single-member districts to take spots on the proportional representation lists, in effect guaranteeing those who lost in the first arena that they would still retain their seats. As might be imagined, this was one of the features of the new system that came in for explicit voter criticism as its results became clear.

63. Aiji Tanaka and Herbert Weisberg, "Political Independence in Japan in the 1990s: Multidimensional Party Identification during a Dealignment" (paper presented at the annual meeting of the American Political Science Association, San Francisco, August 29–September 1, 1996), p. 1. See also Aiji Tanaka and Yoshitaka Nishizawa, "Critical Elections of Japan in the 1990s: Does the LDP's Comeback in 1996 Mean Voter Realignment or Dealignment?" (paper delivered at the world congress of the International Political Science Association, August 17–21, 1997), p. 5; fig. 2.

64. Yutaka Tsujinaka, "Interest Group Basis of Japanese Global Leadership: An Examination of International/Transnational and Domestic NGOs and Interest Group Arrangement" (paper presented to the conference of SSRC/JSPS Global Leadership Sharing Project, Maui, Hawaii, January 4–6, 1996).

65. Yutaka Tsujinaka, "Interest Group Basis of Japan's Democratic Regime Changes in the 1990s" (paper presented at the seventeenth world congress of the International Political Science Association, Seoul, Korea, August 17–21, 1997), fig. 4.

66. One of the classic statements on this is Tsuji Kiyoaki, *Nihon no kanryōsei no kenkyū* [A study of the Japanese bureaucratic system] (Tokyo, Tokyo University Press, 1969). See also Muramatsu Michio, *Sengo Nihon no kanryōsei* [The postwar Japanese bureaucratic system] (Tokyo, Tōyō Keizai, 1981).

67. An excellent example of this kind of cooperation was that between the Ministry of Finance and the Ministry of International Trade and Industry on many projects where the expertise of each was needed by the other in order to carry out their respective missions. See Masaru Mabuchi, "Financing Japanese Industry: The Interplay between the Financial and Industrial Bureaucracies," in Hyung-ki Kim, Michio Muramatsu, T. J. Pempel, and Kozo Yamamura, eds., *The Japanese Civil Service and Economic Development: Catalysts of Change* (Oxford, Oxford University Press, 1995), pp. 288–310.

68. Inoguchi Takashi and Iwai Tomoaki, *"Zoku-giin" no kenkyū* [A study of the "Diet-tribesmen"] (Tokyo, Nihon Keizaishimbunsha, 1987); Iwai Tomoaki, *"Seijishikin" no kenkyū* [A study of "political contributions"] (Tokyo, Nihon Keizai Shimbunsha, 1990).

69. Japan, National Personnel Authority, annual reports; the data are also compiled on an annual basis in T. J. Pempel and Michio Muramatsu, "Structuring a Proactive Civil Service," in Kim et al., *Japanese Civil Service,* p. 46.

70. Jetro, *White Paper on Foreign Direct Investment* (Tokyo, Jetro, 1995).

71. On the general subject see Michael E. Porter, "Towards a Dynamic Theory of Strategy," Strategic Management Journal 12 (winter 1991): 95–117. On such alliances by Japanese electronic companies, see Fred Burton and Freddy Saelens, "International Alliances as a Strategic Took of Japanese Electronic Companies," in Nigel Campbell and Fred Burton, eds., *Japanese Multinationals: Strategies and Management in the Global Kaisha* (London, Routledge, 1994), pp. 58–70.

72. As cited in Yoshiya Teramoto et al., "Global Strategy in the Japanese Semiconductor Industry," in Campbell and Burton, *Japanese Multinationals,* p. 82.

73. At the same time, there were important differences between Japanese multinationals and those of the United States and Germany, as Louis W. Pauley and Simon Reich point out, "Enduring MNC Differences despite Globalization," *International Organization* 51, 1 (1997): 1–30.

74. Noguchi, *Baburu no keizaigaku;* David Asher, "What Became of the Japanese Miracle?" *Orbis*, spring 1996, pp. 1–21.

75. John Y. Campbell and Yasushi Hamao, "Changing Patterns of Corporate Financing and the Main Bank System in Japan," in Masahiko Aoki and Hugh Patrick, eds., *The Japanese Main Bank System: Its Relevance for Developing and Transforming Economies* (Oxford, Oxford University Press, 1995), p. 330.

76. J. Mark Ramseyer, "Explicit Reasons for Implicit Contracts: The Legal Logic to the Japanese Main Bank System," in Aoki and Patrick, *Japanese Main Bank System,* p. 240.

77. On such developments see Tsujinaka Yutaka, "Rōdōkai no saihen to hachijūroku nen taisei no imi" [The significance of the reorganization of labor relations and the 1986 system], *Leviathan* 1 (1987).

78. Kume, "Disparaged Success," chap 7.

79. On Rengō's early activities, see Tsujinaka, "Rōdōkai no saihen," pp. 47–72. For its later activities see Oumi Naoto, "Gendai Nihon no makuro-kooporatizumu" [Contemporary Japanese macrocorporatism], in Oumi Naoto et al., *Neo-kooporatizumu no kokusai hikaku* [An international comparison of neocorporatism] (Tokyo, Nihon Rōdō Kenkyū Kikō, 1994), pp. 278–339.

80. Satō Seizaburo and Matsuzaki Tetsuhisa, *Jimintō-seiken* [LDP power] (Tokyo, Chūō Kōronsha, 1986); Miyake Ichiro, ed., *Seitō shiji no bunseki* (Tokyo, Sokobunsha, 1985) points out some of the early shifts in party support. For the comparisons across time see Miyake Ichiro, *Tōhyō kōdō* [Voting behavior] (Tokyo, Tokyo Daigaku Shuppankai, 1989), p. 88.

81. Miyake, *Tōhyō kōdō*, p. 88.

82. This last law is quite similar to the Royer Law in France in the early 1960s. See Suzanne D. Berger, "Regime and Interest Representation: The French Traditional Middle Classes," in Berger, ed., *Organizing Interests in Western Europe* (Cambridge, Cambridge University Press, 1981), p. 94.

83. Miyake Ichiro, "Hachijūkyūnen sangiin senkyō to 'seitō saihensei'" [The 1989 upper house election and "party realignment"], *Leviathan* 10 (1992): 36.

84. Thus in the 1990 lower house election 54.5 percent of the farm vote and 42.2 percent of the self-employed vote went to the LDP. Kobayashi Yoshiaki, *Gendai Nihon no senkyō* [Elections in contemporary Japan] (Tokyo, Tokyo Daigaku Shuppankai, 1991), p. 130.

85. Miyake, *Tōhyō kōdō*, p. 58.

86. Nihon Kokusei Zue, ed., *Suji de miru Nihon no hyakunen* (Tokyo, Nihon Kokusei Zue, 1991), p. 68.

87. Ishikawa Masumi and Hirose Michisada, *Jimintō: chōki shiji no kōzō* [The Liberal Democratic Party: Structure of its long-term support] (Tokyo, Iwanami Shoten, 1989), pp. 73–85.

88. In the 1989 upper house election many farm groups voted against LDP candidates in protest against increased liberalization of agricultural imports and declines in price supports. See, e.g., Miyake, "Hachijūkyū-nen Sangiin Senkyō," pp. 32–61.

89. Asarui Senkyō Saishinkyōkai, *Dai47kai Shūgiin sōsenkyō*, pp. 61–62.

90. Uchida Kenzō, Kunemasa Takeshige, and Sone Yasunori, "Nihon no kiro o tō" [Japan at the crossroads], *Bungei Shunjū*, August 1996, pp. 96–99.

91. Sōmucho, *Zenkoku shoho jittai hōkoku* [Report on the outlines of national conditions] (Tokyo, PMO, annual).

6. Between Adjustment and Unraveling: Protection and Erosion of the Old Regime

1. This line of thinking builds on Robert Bates, *Beyond the Miracle of the Market: The Political Economy of Agrarian Reform in Kenya* (Cambridge, Cambridge University Press, 1989), and Peter Evans, *Embedded Autonomy: States and Industrial Transformation* (Princeton, Princeton University Press, 1995). But ultimately, it reflects Karl Marx's notion that the bourgeoisie will call forth its own gravedigger in the form of the proletariat.

2. Murakami Yasusuke, *Shinchūkan taishū no jidai* [The age of new middle mass] (Tokyo, Chūō Kōronsha, 1984).

3. Bank of Japan, *Comparative International Statistics,* various years.

4. Calculated from *Suji de miru Nihon no hyakunen* [One hundred years of Japanese statistics] (Tokyo, Kokuseisha, 1991), p. 78.

5. Akiko Hashimoto, *Gift of Generations: Japanese and American Perspectives on Aging and the Social Contract* (Cambridge, Cambridge University Press, 1996). See also Keizai Koho Center, *Japan, 1992* (Tokyo, 1992), p. 9.

6. Based on data from Rōdōshō, *Rōdō hakusho* [White paper on labor] (Tokyo, Ōkurasho Insatsukyoku, annual).

7. Miyake Ichirō, *Nihon no seiji to senkyō* (Tokyo, Tokyo Daigaku Shuppankai, 1995); *Tōhyō kōdō* [Voting behavior] (Tokyo, Tokyo Daigaku Shuppankai, 1989); Muramatsu Michio et al., *Nihon no seiji* (Tokyo, Yūhikaku, 1992), p. 126; Kobayashi Yoshiake, *Gendai Nihon no senkyō* (Tokyo, Tokyo Daigaku Shuppan, 1991) pp. 52–59. Gerald Curtis, *The Japanese Way of Politics* (New York, Columbia University Press, 1988), chaps. 1, 6.

8. Masumi Junnosuke, *Gendai seiji* [Contemporary politics] (Tokyo, Tokyo Daigaku Shuppankai, 1985), 2:540–41, 650–53; Kamishima Jirō, *Gendai Nihon no seiji kōzō* [The political structures of contemporary Japan] (Tokyo, Hōritsu Bunka, 1985), pp. 178–79.

9. Richard J. Samuels, *The Politics of Regional Policy in Japan* (Princeton, Princeton University Press, 1983), p. 215.

10. Kamishima, *Gendai Nihon no seiji kōzō,* pp. 170–78.

11. Based on data in Muramatsu et al., *Nihon no seiji,* pp. 122–23.

12. Ishikawa Masumi, *Sengo seiji kōzōshi* (Tokyo, Nihon Hyoronsha, 1978), p. 148; also Yamakawa Katsumi, Yoda Hiroshi, and Moriwaki Toshimasa, *Seijigaku deeta bukku* [Political science data book] (Tokyo, Sorinsha, 1981), p. 122.

13. This point was brought home to senior bureaucrats once the LDP had splintered in 1993. MITI minister Kumagai Hiroshi, himself a former MITI bureaucrat, forced the resignation of Naitō Masahisa, the MITI bureau chief heading the Industrial Policy Bureau. Kumagai, who was a member of Shinseitō and an ally of Ozawa Ichirō, considered Naitō too closely affiliated with the formerly dominant LDP. See Kaga Kōei, "Kumagai Tsūsanshō yo, hinsei geretsu wa anata no hō da," [MITI minister Kumagai: You are a man without character], *Shūkan Bunshun,* February 24, 1994, pp. 182–85.

14. Ishikawa, *Sengo seiji kōzōshi,* pp. 116–18.

15. See, for example, Nakamura Akira and Takeshita Yuzuru, *Nihon no seisaku katei* [The policymaking process in Japan] (Chiba-ken, Azusa Shuppansha, 1984), p. 32.

16. T. J. Pempel, "Uneasy toward Autonomy: Parliament and Parliamentarians in Japan," in Ezra Suleiman, ed., *Parliaments and Parliamentarians in Democratic Politics* (New York: Holmes and Meier, 1986), pp. 118–37; Kishimoto Koicho, *Nihon no gikai seiji* [Parliamentary politics in Japan] (Tokyo, Gyōsei Mondai Kenkyūjo, 1976).

17. On the mechanisms of such cooperation, see Ellis S. Krauss, "Conflict in the Diet: Toward Conflict Management in Parliamentary Politics," in Ellis S. Krauss, Thomas P. Rohlen, and Patricia G. Steinhoff, eds., *Conflict in Japan* (Honolulu, University of Hawaii Press, 1984), pp. 243–93.

18. Nakamura and Takeshita, *Nihon no seisaku katei,* p. 73. Iwai Tomoaki, *Rippō katei* [The legislative process] (Tokyo, Tokyo Daigaku Shuppankai, 1988). Muramatsu et al., *Nihon no seiji,* p. 174.

19. Miyake Ichirō et al., *Nihon seiji no zahyō* [Diagnosis of Japanese politics] (Tokyo, Yūhikaku, 1985), pp. 135–42.

20. On the French and Italian cases, see Sidney Tarrow, *Between Center and Periphery: Grassroots Politicians in Italy and France* (New Haven, Yale University Press, 1977).

21. For example, Yokohama Shimin Undō Rengō, ed., *Shimin undō tanjō* [The birth of a citizens' movement] (Tokyo, Rōdō Junpōsha, 1969); Ōhashi Hisatoshi, *Shiryō: Daigaku no jichi* [Source materials: University autonomy] (Tokyo, San'ichi Shobō, 1970), p. 265.

22. The literature on this is immense; for a broad overview with a sustained argument see Meredith Woo-Cumings, "East Asia's American Problem," in Meredith Woo-Cumings and Michael Loriaux, eds., *Past as Prelude: History in the Making of a New World Order* (Boulder, Westview, 1993), pp. 137–58. It is worth noting that in addition to the broad policy support given by the American government, the Central Intelligence Agency was apparently an important donor of monies to the Liberal Democratic Party.

23. See Haruhiro Fukui, "Tanaka Goes to Peking: A Case Study in Foreign Policymaking," in T. J. Pempel, ed., *Policymaking in Contemporary Japan* (Ithaca, Cornell University Press, 1977), pp. 60–102.

24. See Andō H., *Sekinin to genkai: Akaji zaisei no kiseki* [Responsibility and limits: An analysis of deficit finance] (Tokyo, Kinyū Zaisei Jijo Kenkyūkai, 1987), 1:205.

25. See, e.g., Richard J. Samuels, "Consuming for Production: Japan," *International Organization* 43, 4 (1989): 625–46.

26. Within the Ministry of Finance a so-called Alpha Plan for a series of yen revaluations through a crawling peg had been circulating. Authored by Hayashi Taizo of the Ministerial Secretariat, the plan presupposed drastic changes in the Japanese economy and predicted long-term growth in its balance of payments surplus. Many critics within the ministry believed that the recent gains were merely cyclical and hence argued strongly against any revaluation. See Hayashi, "'Arufuu—yen kiriage—sagyō' shimatsuki, 1–2" [Behind the scenes in the Alpha Plan to float the yen], *Kinyū zaisei jijō*, June 24, 1974, pp. 14–17; July 1, 1974, pp. 14–17.

27. Toshio Shishido, "The Framework of Decision-Making in Japanese Economic Policies," in Allen Taylor, ed., *Perspectives on U.S.-Japan Economic Relations* (Cambridge, Ballinger, 1973), p. 205.

28. Kusano Atsushi, "Kokusai seijikeizai to Nihon" [The international political economy and Japan], in Watanabe Akio, ed., *Sengo Nihon no taigai seisaku* [The foreign policies of postwar Japan] (Tokyo, Yuhikaku, 1985), pp. 265–67.

29. On this shift, see Kanamori Hisao, *Seminaa: Nihon keizai no joshiki* [Seminar: Making sense of the Japanese economy] (Tokyo, Nihon Hyōronsha, 1976), pp. 16–18; Hayashi Shintaro and Watanabe Fukutarō, *Kokusai keizai kyoshitsu* [A primer on international economics] (Tokyo, Yuhikaku, 1973); Noguchi Ichiro, *Nihon no keizai nashonarizumu* [Japanese economic nationalism] (Tokyo, Daiyamondosha, 1976).

30. Ryutaro Komiya, *The Japanese Economy: Trade, Industry, and Government* (Tokyo, University of Tokyo Press, 1990), pp. 319–20.

31. Ibid., p. 319.

32. European countries followed the U.S. lead on voluntary export agreements, with France being particularly successful in gaining Japanese consent to restrict exports in color televisions, TV tubes, cars, light commercial vehicles, forklift trucks, motorcycles, quartz watches, and audio devices. David Yoffie, "Protecting World Markets," in Thomas K. McCraw, ed., *America versus Japan* (Boston, Harvard Business School Press, 1986), p. 66.

33. Four industries were chosen for market opening measures—forest products, medical equipment and pharmaceuticals, electronic products, and telecommunications equipment and services. On the negotiations and their outcome, see Edward J. Lincoln, *Japan's Unequal Trade* (Washington, Brookings, 1990), pp. 148–51.

34. The phrase is from Laura D'Andrea Tyson, *Who's Bashing Whom? Trade Conflict in High-Technology Industries* (Washington, Institute for International Economics, 1992),

pp. 133–36, in reference to the perceived successes of the U.S.-Japan agreement on semiconductors that provided a de facto 20 percent market share to U.S. companies.

35. Watanabe, *Sengo Nihon no taigai seisaku*, p. 258. Kusano Atsushi, *Nichi-Bei: Massatsu no kōzō* [Japan-U.S.: The structure of friction] (Tokyo: PHP, 1984).

36. Thomas U. Berger, "Norms, Identity, and National Security in Germany and Japan," in Peter J. Katzenstein, ed., *The Culture of National Security: Norms and Identity in World Politics* (New York, Columbia University Press, 1996), p. 322.

37. Only 10 percent of the Japanese population supported unlimited use of SDF troops; even LDP supporters opposed such use by 3:1 margins. *Nikkei Shimbun*, October 15, 1990.

38. Tanaka Kakuei, *Building a New Japan: A Plan for Remodeling the Japanese Archipelago* (Tokyo, Simul, 1969).

39. Curtis, *Japanese Way of Politics*, p. 65.

40. Pempel, "Uneasy toward Autonomy," pp. 142–44, provides details of some of these shifts.

41. Ichikawa Taichi, '*Seshū' daigishi no kenkyū* [A study of 'hereditary' parliamentarians] (Tokyo, Nihon Keizai Shimbunsha, 1990).

42. Kitamura Shinichi, *Jimintō: Seikentō no sanjūhachinen* [The LDP: Thirty-eight years as the party in power] (Tokyo, Yomiuri Shimbunsha, 1995), p. 137.

43. As cited in Chalmers Johnson, "Puppets and Puppeteers: Japanese Political Reform," in Johnson, ed., *Japan: Who Governs? The Rise of the Developmental State* (New York, Norton, 1995), p. 215. The figures he offers are ¥1698 for Japan, ¥506 for Germany, ¥403 for the United States, and ¥94 for the United Kingdom.

44. Iwai Tomoaki, *"Seiji shikin" no kenkyū* [A study of "political money"] (Tokyo, Tōyō Keizai, 1990), chap. 5.

45. Inoguchi Takashi and Iwai Tomoaki, *"Zoku-giin" no kenkyū* [A study of the "Diet-tribesmen"] (Tokyo, Nihon Keizaishimbunsha, 1987), p. 150.

46. Johnson, "Puppets and Puppeteers," p. 214.

47. Public-sector labor, particularly in transportation, teaching, communications, and white-collar work, tended to be a mainstay of labor militancy even into the mid-1980s.

48. Shinkawa Toshimitsu, "Senkyūhyaku nanajūgonen shuntōto keizai kiki kanri" [The 1975 Shunto and the management of economic crisis], in Ōtake Hideo, ed., *Nihon seiji no shoten* [Problems in Japanese politics] (Tokyo, Sanichi Shobō, 1984); Ikuo Kume, *Disparaged Success* (Ithaca, Cornell University Press, 1998).

49. Tsujinaka Yutaka, "Rodokai no saihen to hachijurokunen taisei no imi" [The significance of the reorganization of labor relations and the 1986 system], *Leviathan* 1 (1987), pp. 47–72.

50. Satō Seizaburō and Matsuzaki Tetsuhisa, *Jimintō-seiken* [LDP power] (Tokyo, Chūō Kōronsha, 1986); Miyake Ichiro, ed., *Seitō shiji no bunseki* [An analysis of political support] (Tokyo, Shokubunsha, 1985).

51. T. J. Pempel, "Environmental Pollution: Turning Adversity to Advantage," in *Policy and Politics in Japan: Creative Conservatism* (Philadelphia, Temple University Press, 1982), pp. 218–54, deals with this entire process.

52. Toshimitsu Shinkawa, *Nihonteki fukushi no seiji keizaigaku* [The political economy of Japanese-style welfare] (Tokyo, Sanichi Shobō, 1993).

53. Fujita Sei, *Fukushi seisaku to zaisei* [Welfare policies and public finance] (Tokyo, Nihon Keizai Shimbunsha, 1984), p. 30.

54. Noguchi Yukio, "Public Finance," in Kozo Yamamura and Yasukichi Yasuba, eds., *The Political Economy of Japan* (Stanford, Stanford University Press, 1987), p. 188.

55. Kozo Yamamura, "The Cost of Rapid Growth and Capitalist Democracy in Japan," in Leon N. Lindberg and Charles S. Maier, eds., *The Politics of Inflation and Economic Stagnation* (Washington, Brookings, 1985), pp. 497–98.

56. Koyama Kenichi, *Eikokubyō nokyōkun* [Lessons from the English disease] (Kyoto: PHP, 1978); Kanbara Masaru, *Tenkanki no seiji katei* [Politics at the turning point] (Tokyo, Sōgō Rodō Kenkyūjo, 1986), pp. 118–43.

57. Although the EPA originally opposed enterprise welfare, it changed its view in a subsequent report by stating that the company connection was more important than ties of kinship and neighborhood.

58. *Asahi Nenkan*, 1983, p. 440.

59. Kato Junko, "Seisaku kettei katei kenkyū no riron to jisshō: Kōteki nenkin seido kaikaku to iryō hōken seido kaikaku no kesu wo megutte" [A theoretical and empirical study of the policymaking process: Analysis of the reform processes of the public pension and health insurance systems], *Leviathan* 8 (1991): 165–84.

60. Keizai Kōhō Center, *Japan, 1992*, p. 80.

61. On administrative reform, see Noguchi Yukio, *Gyōzaisei kaikaku* [Administrative and financial reform] (Tokyo, PHP, 1981); Gyōsei Kanri Kenkyū Center, *Gyōsei kaikaku no bijon* [A vision of administrative reform], 3 vols. (Tokyo, Gyōkankyū Center, 1979).

62. Provisional Commission on Administrative Reform, *The Fifth Report on Administrative Reform—The Final Report* (Tokyo, Institute of Administrative Management, March 1984), p. 1.

63. Economic Planning Agency, *Yearbook of National Account Statistics* (Tokyo, Government Printing Office, annual), as cited in Noguchi, "Public Finance," p. 202.

64. Shindo Muneyuki, *Zaisei hatan to zeisei kaikaku* [Financial collapse and tax reform] (Tokyo, Iwanami Shoten, 1989), pp. 55–57.

65. See Ōtake Hideo, *Jiyūshugiteki kaikaku no jidai* [The period of liberal reforms] (Tokyo, Chūō Kōronsha, 1994), chaps. 2–5.

66. Shindō, *Zaisei hatan to zeisei kaikaku*, pp. 207–36.

67. On the politics of the tax see Junko Kato, *The Problem of Bureaucratic Rationality: Tax Politics in Japan* (Princeton, Princeton University Press, 1994).

68. Slightly different figures and calculations, but with the same thrust, are given in Lawrence B. Krause, "Evolution of Foreign Direct Investment: The United States and Japan," in Jerome Cohen, ed., *Pacific Partnership; United States-Japan Trade—Prospects and Recommendations for the Seventies* (New York, Japan Society and Lexington Books, 1972), pp. 166–68.

69. Keizai Kōhō Center, *Japan 1987: An International Comparison* (Tokyo, Japan Institute for Social and Economic Affairs, 1987), p. 56.

70. Ministry of Finance figures as presented in *Japan, 1990: An International Comparison* (Tokyo, Japan Institute for Social and Economic Affairs, 1990), p. 56. The jump would be less monumental but still impressive if denominated in yen.

71. Nakatani Iwao, *Nihon keizai no rekishiteki tenkan* [Historical change in the Japanese economy] (Tokyo, Tōyō Keizai Shimbunsha, 1996), chap. 5.

72. Economic Affairs Bureau, Ministry of Foreign Affairs, *Statistical Survey of Japan's Economy, 1975* (Tokyo, Ministry of Foreign Affairs, 1975), p. 53.

73. These figures are from GATT and JETRO as presented in *Japan, 1990*, p. 44. Alternative figures presenting somewhat the same picture are in Watanabe, *Sengo Nihon no taigai seisaku* (Tokyo, Yūhikaku, 1985), p. 258. Watanabe cites Japan as maintaining twenty-seven categories, including five in manufacturing. This latter figure accords also with Leon Hollerman, *Japan, Disincorporated: The Economic Liberalization Process* (Stanford, Hoover Institution, 1988), p. 44.

74. Edward Lincoln, *Japan's Unequal Trade* (Washington, D.C., Brookings Institution, 1990, pp. 18–25.

75. Kusano, *Nichi-Bei: Massatsu no kōzō*.

76. The report traces to a Nomura Research Institute report of 1977.

77. As reported in Comprehensive National Security Study Group, *Report on Comprehensive National Security* (Tokyo, Foreign Affairs translation typescript, 1980).

78. In effect, the electoral system's bias meant that an urban vote was worth only 60 percent of a rural vote. Ishikawa Masumi and Hirose Michisada, *Jimintō—shōki shihai no kōzō* [The LDP—structures of long-term support] (Tokyo, Iwanami Shoten, 1989), p. 85.

79. One Ministry of Finance survey in 1985 showed that 86 percent of all wage earners paid taxes, compared to only 40 percent of the self-employed and only 20 percent of farmers.

80. This point was widely made in Sweden under the Social Democratic government as a means to reduce wage pressures by unions. It was also made in Japan during efforts to reduce labor demands for wage hikes in the mid-1970s.

81. This point was made clear in the case of Chisso (Shin Nihon Chisso Hiryō) in Minamata, Kumamoto Prefecture. When Chisso was accused by local residents of dumping methyl mercury in the local bay and thereby poisoning fish and ultimately causing massive human injury and suffering, the Chisso workers, some of whose members were actually afflicted with the disease, cooperated with management in attacking and criticizing the protesting residents. See Honda Junsuke and Kataoka Noboru, *Kōgai to rōdōsha* [Pollution and workers] (Kyoto, Hōritsu Bunkasha, 1971).

82. Hayden Lesbirel, *NIMBY Politics in Japan* (Ithaca, Cornell University Press, 1998).

83. On some of these, see Charles Smith, "Opening Time," *Far Eastern Economic Review*, May 5, 1994, pp. 62–70.

84. See, for example, Richard J. Samuels, *The Business of the Japanese State: Energy Markets in Comparative and Historical Perspective* (Ithaca, Cornell University Press, 1987); Mark Tilton, *Restrained Trade: Cartels in Japan's Basic Materials Industry* (Ithaca, Cornell University Press, 1996); Robert Uriu, *Troubled Industries* (Ithaca, Cornell University Press, 1996).

85. Noguchi Yukio, *Babaru no keizagaku* [The economics of the bubble] (Tokyo, Nihon Keizaishimbunsha, 1992); Christopher Wood, *The Bubble Economy* (New York, Atlantic Monthly Press, 1992); R. Taggert Murphy, *The Weight of the Yen* (New York, Norton, 1996).

86. David Asher, "What Became of the Japanese Miracle?" *Orbis*, spring 1996, p. 2.

87. Ibid., p. 4.

88. This problem is analyzed further in T. J. Pempel, "The Unbundling of 'Japan, Inc.': The Changing Dynamics of Japanese Policy Formation," *Journal of Japanese Studies* 13, 2 (1987), pp. 287–88. See also Michael Donnelly, "Conflict over Government Authority and Markets: Japan's Rice Economy," in Ellis Krauss et al., eds., *Conflict in Japan* (Honolulu, University of Hawaii Press, 1984).

89. On that election, see the special issue of *Leviathan* 10 (1992).

90. In 1956 Prime Minister Hatoyama had proposed the introduction of a single-member district, winner-take-all system. This was designed to generate a two-thirds vote for the LDP to allow them to revise the so-called MacArthur constitution. Similarly, in 1973 Prime Minister Tanaka made a proposal that would have introduced single-member districts, with 40 percent of the Diet representatives being chosen by proportional representation.

91. Ōtake Hideo, "Jimintō wakate kaikakuha to Ozawa guruupu" [The young reformers in the LDP and the Ozawa Group], *Leviathan* 17 (1995): 17.

92. Yamaguchi Jirō, *Nihon seiji no kadai: Shinseiji kaikakuron* [Current issues in Japanese politics: A new approach to political reform] (Tokyo, Iwanami Shinsho, 1997).

93. Soma Masao, *Nihon senkyō seidoshi* [A history of the Japanese electoral system] (Fukuoka, Kyūshū Daigaku Shuppankai, 1986).

94. Herman Schwartz, "Small States in Big Trouble: State Reorganization in Australia, Denmark, New Zealand, and Sweden in the 1980s," *World Politics* 46, 4 (1994): 529.

Conclusion: Regimes in a Changing World Economy

1. See Gregory Luebbert, *Liberalism, Fascism, or Social Democracy* (New York, Oxford University Press, 1991).

2. Marquis Childs, *Sweden: The Middle Way on Trial* (New Haven, Yale University Press, 1980).

3. See Sven Steinmo, "Political Institutions and Tax Policy," *World Politics* 41, 4 (1989): 500–536.

4. In addition to their economic differences the two regions had different civic cultures. See Robert D. Putnam with Robert Leonardi and Raffaella Y. Nanetti, *Making Democracy Work: Civic Traditions in Modern Italy* (Princeton, Princeton University Press, 1993), for an argument about the ways in which these evolved.

5. See Peter J. Katzenstein, *Small States in World Markets: Industrial Policy in Europe* (Ithaca, Cornell University Press, 1985); also Gerhard Lehmbruch, "Concertation and the Structure of Corporatist Networks," and David Cameron, "Social Democracy, Corporatism, Labor Quiescence, and the Representation of Economic Interest in Advanced Capitalist Countries," in John H. Goldthorpe, ed., *Order and Conflict in Contemporary Capitalism* (Cambridge, Cambridge University Press, 1984).

6. Muramatsu Michio, Itō Mitsutoshi, and Tsujinaka Yūtaka, *Sengo Nihon no atsuryoku dantai* [Interest groups in postwar Japan] (Tokyo, Tōyō Keizai Shimposha, 1986), esp. chaps. 4, 5. Proposed bureaucratic reorganization would merge several of the more protectionist agencies (such as MAFF, Construction, and Transport) into a single Ministry of Land Development, making for an even larger bastion of regulatory control.

7. Steven Vogel, *Freer Markets, More Rules: Regulatory Reform in Advanced Industrial Countries* (Ithaca, Cornell University Press, 1996), p. 257.

8. "Reform Proposals Get Mixed Start," *Nikkei Weekly,* August 25, 1997.

9. "'Big Bang' Program Taking Clearer Shape," *Nikkei Weekly,* June 16, 1997.

10. Uchida Kenzō, Kunemasa Takeshige, and Sone Yasunori, "Nihon no kiro o tō" [Japan at the crossroads], *Bungei Shunjū,* August 1996, pp. 96–99. LDP "conservatism" was also evidence in its 1996 budget, which was heavily laden with public spending programs.

11. Parties were able to do this by co-ranking multiple candidates and then choosing after the election, on the basis of single-seat competition results, which of the co-ranked candidates to actually seat. See Margaret McKean and Ethan Scheiner, "Can Japanese Voters Ever Throw the Rascals Out? Electoral Reform Enhances Permanent Employment for Politicians" (paper presented at the Conference on Democratic Institutions in East Asia, Duke University, November 8–9, 1996).

12. V. O. Key, *The Responsible Electorate: Rationality in Presidential Voting: 1936–1960* (New York, Vintage, 1966), pp. 2–3.

13. "Big Is Back: A Survey of Multinationals," *Economist,* June 24, 1995, p. 14.

14. Peter J. Katzenstein, *Corporatism and Change* (Ithaca, Cornell University Press, 1985).

INDEX

257